BRINGING READING RESEARCH TO LIFE

BRINGING READING RESEARCH TO LIFE

Edited by
MARGARET G. McKEOWN
LINDA KUCAN

THE GUILFORD PRESS
New York   London

© 2010 The Guilford Press
A Division of Guilford Publications, Inc.
72 Spring Street, New York, NY 10012
www.guilford.com

Printed in the United States of America

This book is printed on acid-free paper.

Last digit is print number: 9   8   7   6   5   4   3   2   1

Library of Congress Cataloging-in-Publication Data

Bringing reading research to life / edited by Margaret G. McKeown, Linda Kucan.
  p. cm.
 Includes bibliographical references and index.
 ISBN 978-1-60623-474-7 (hardcover : alk. paper)
1. Reading—Research.   2. Reading comprehension.   3. Reading—Phonetic
method.   4. Vocabulary.   5. Beck, Isabel L.   I. McKeown, Margaret G.
II. Kucan, Linda.
 LB1050.6.B75 2010
 428.407′2—dc22

                                                    2009021917

For Isabel L. Beck,

in honor of her ongoing contributions to improving literacy instruction

ABOUT THE EDITORS

Margaret G. McKeown, PhD, is Clinical Professor of Education and Senior Scientist at the Learning Research and Development Center, University of Pittsburgh. Her work covers the areas of learning, instruction, and teacher professional development in reading comprehension and vocabulary.

Linda Kucan, PhD, is Assistant Professor of Reading Education in the Department of Instruction and Learning at the University of Pittsburgh. Her interests include teacher education, classroom discourse about text, the design of meaningful and motivating tasks to support comprehension of text, and vocabulary instruction.

CONTRIBUTORS

Richard C. Anderson, EdD, Department of Educational Psychology and Bureau of Educational Research, University of Illinois at Urbana–Champaign, Champaign, Illinois

Anthi Archodidou, MA, Center for the Study of Reading, University of Illinois at Urbana–Champaign, Champaign, Illinois

Elizabeth Beck, PhD, School of Social Work, Georgia State University, Atlanta, Georgia

Mark Beck, LLD, School of Education, University of Pittsburgh, Pittsburgh, Pennsylvania

Jason Braasch, MA, Department of Psychology, University of Illinois at Chicago, Chicago, Illinois

Suzanne H. Broughton, PhD, Department of Psychology, Arizona State University, Tempe, Arizona

Mary E. Curtis, PhD, Center for Special Education, School of Education, Lesley University, Cambridge, Massachusetts

Janice A. Dole, PhD, Department of Educational Psychology, College of Education, University of Utah, Salt Lake City, Utah

Susan R. Goldman, PhD, Departments of Psychology and Curriculum and Instruction, Learning Sciences Research Institute, University of Illinois at Chicago, Chicago, Illinois

Kimberly W. Gomez, PhD, Department of Instruction and Learning, School of Education, University of Pittsburgh, Pittsburgh, Pennsylvania

Kay Grabow, MS, Urbana School District, Urbana, Illinois

Art Graesser, PhD, Department of Psychology, University of Memphis, Memphis, Tennessee

Elfrieda H. Hiebert, PhD, Graduate School of Education, University of California, Berkeley, Berkeley, California

May Jadallah, PhD, Center for the Study of Reading, University of Illinois at Urbana–Champaign, Champaign, Illinois

Connie Juel, PhD, School of Education, Stanford University, Stanford, California

Walter Kintsch, PhD, Department of Psychology, University of Colorado at Boulder, Boulder, Colorado

Kimberly A. Lawless, PhD, Department of Educational Psychology, University of Illinois at Chicago, Chicago, Illinois

Shaunna MacLeod, BA, Learning Sciences Research Institute, University of Illinois at Chicago, Chicago, Illinois

Flori Manning, MEd, Department of Educational Psychology, University of Illinois at Chicago, Chicago, Illinois

Brian Miller, MS, Bureau of Educational Research, University of Illinois at Urbana–Champaign, Champaign, Illinois

P. Karen Murphy, PhD, Department of Educational Psychology, College of Education, Pennsylvania State University, University Park, Pennsylvania

William E. Nagy, PhD, School of Education, Seattle Pacific University, Seattle, Washington

Kim Nguyen-Jahiel, EdM, Bureau of Educational Research and Department of Educational Psychology, College of Education, University of Illinois at Urbana–Champaign, Champaign, Illinois

Jean Osborn, MEd, Bureau of Educational Research, University of Illinois at Urbana–Champaign, Champaign, Illinois

Yasuhiro Ozuru, PhD, Learning Sciences Research Institute, University of Illinois at Chicago, Chicago, Illinois

Charles Perfetti, PhD, Learning Research and Development Center, University of Pittsburgh, Pittsburgh, Pennsylvania

Leona Schauble, PhD, Department of Teaching and Learning, Peabody College of Education and Human Development, Vanderbilt University, Nashville, Tennessee

Gale M. Sinatra, PhD, Department of Educational Psychology, University of Nevada, Las Vegas, Las Vegas, Nevada

Anna O. Soter, PhD, School of Teaching and Learning, College of Education and Human Ecology, Ohio State University, Columbus, Ohio

Marcy Stein, PhD, Education Program, University of Washington, Tacoma, Tacoma, Washington

Jeremiah Sullins, MS, Department of Psychology, University of Memphis, Memphis, Tennessee

Sharon Vaughn, PhD, Department of Special Education, College of Education, University of Texas at Austin, Austin, Texas

Ian A. G. Wilkinson, PhD, School of Teaching and Learning, College of Education and Human Ecology, Ohio State University, Columbus, Ohio

Jie Zhang, PhD, Department of Educational Psychology, College of Education, University of Illinois at Urbana–Champaign, Champaign, Illinois

PREFACE

The chapters in this book are derived from presentations at a conference held in honor of Isabel L. Beck's retirement from the University of Pittsburgh. The title of this volume reflects the structure of the conference presentations. We requested that the presenters not only describe their research, but also include some personal history about what motivated the direction of their work. We found the results so interesting that we wanted that material included in this volume as well. The pieces of personal history that contributors relay are sometimes surprising, often amusing, and truly revealing of how early experiences shape interests. The contributions of the conference participants also provide insight into where the reading field has been and illustrate, in powerful ways, the field's advancement.

Chapter 1, by Jean Osborn and Marcy Stein, offers a tribute to Isabel and her work. The authors bring a light-hearted touch to some of the thorny issues that the reading field has faced and that have marked Isabel's career. In the second chapter, Connie Juel begins with questions she had about her students' reading when she taught elementary school. She then takes us through a research agenda, highlighting how taking account of all the dimensions of reading and a rich variety of research methodologies enabled her to put together various facets of the reading puzzle.

In Chapter 3, Sharon Vaughn provides a fascinating account of how early experiences led to professional choices—beginning with a playground at a mental institution! The heart of Vaughn's chapter details her research around the response-to-intervention framework and how this is leading her and her colleagues to help more students to become able readers.

Janice A. Dole's chapter reports what she describes as a "professional journey." Her rich description offers powerful insights into school reform in reading, what works, obstacles that stand in the way, and, painfully, factors that seem to cancel out gains. In Chapter 5, William E. Nagy plays word games in his discussion of vocabulary and its stubborn nature as a field of research. That stubbornness arises from the tricky relationships between vocabulary learning and context, and between vocabulary knowledge and comprehension. Nagy shows that although these two relationships at first might seem quite obvious, they are fraught with troublesome questions and competing perspectives.

Chapter 6, by Mary E. Curtis, also focuses on the vocabulary domain. Curtis describes how puzzlement over lack of reading comprehension in college students led her to research tracking down how reading develops and why it sometimes does not develop successfully. The chapter describes Curtis's investigations and discoveries from lower-level processes in reading to vocabulary's role, and working with adolescents and adults who struggle with reading.

Art Graesser, Yasuhiro Ozuru, and Jeremiah Sullins turn their attention to what makes a good question in Chapter 7. An interest in questions grew from Graesser's observation that even highly qualified students asked very few questions. From there, the authors take us through a landscape of questions, including categorical models of questions and the development of a computer tutor to promote productive question asking.

In Chapter 8, Ian A. G. Wilkinson, Anna O. Soter, and P. Karen Murphy explore the realm of classroom talk. Starting with the question of how language mediates learning, the authors describe their research and synthesis of approaches to classroom text-based discourse. They then introduce a model of effective talk that grew from their investigation.

Chapter 9, by May Jadallah, Brian Miller, Richard C. Anderson, and colleagues, focuses on collaborative reasoning. Collaborative reasoning is an instructional approach designed to engage students in deliberations about important questions related to ethical dilemmas. The goal of the approach is to socially construct reasoned arguments about issues raised in texts. The chapter that follows is by Walter Kintsch, who describes another instructional approach to support student thinking about text information. Kintsch and his colleagues have developed a computer program called *Summary Street* that allows individual students to generate summaries and then receive feedback about the quality of their writing.

In Chapter 11, Elfrieda H. Hiebert considers how students are challenged to understand text and how teacher support can mediate that challenge if students' attention is directed to an analysis of the words the text includes. Specifically, she describes a model called Text Elements by Task (TExT), which analyzes the number of new, unique words; the frequency of the words; and how the words are spelled with reference to common or less common vowel patterns.

Chapter 12, by Suzanne H. Broughton and Gale M. Sinatra, provides an analysis of other text challenges, specifically the challenges presented by science texts. To address the impact of misconceptions on comprehension of science text, Broughton and Sinatra suggest the use of refutational texts. Refutational texts specifically foreground common misconceptions, then provide a refutation and a scientific explanation. Such texts have been shown to scaffold conceptual change in students.

While refutational texts provide a juxtaposition of conflicting information in a single text, in Chapter 13, Susan R. Goldman and her colleagues focus on the impact on comprehension of the use of multiple texts—in both traditional and digital formats—to conduct inquiry in history. These researchers are collecting information from middle school students about how they used specific sources and how they evaluated the importance and utility of those sources in completing an inquiry-based project.

The last three chapters relate to Isabel in very specific and personal ways. In Chapter 14, Leona Schauble describes Isabel's career in terms of how research can influence instruction if the researcher is willing to take on the "nitty-gritty" work of figuring out the details of implementation that will make a difference to teachers and students—which Isabel does. And that work, as Charles Perfetti describes it in Chapter 15, addresses what he calls the "golden triangle of reading skill"—decoding, vocabulary, and comprehension. Perfetti celebrates Isabel's work in all three areas through her programs of systematic, research-based interventions, including word building, robust vocabulary instruction, and Questioning the Author. Finally, in Chapter 16, Isabel's children, Elizabeth and Mark, provide a personal context for considering Isabel as a mother who also happened to be involved in educational research.

Isabel's work provided a perfect opportunity to bring together scholars from across the spectrum of reading research and practice to launch a conference whose theme was "threads of coherence in reading research." That is because Isabel's interests and expertise have focused on the earliest stages of reading development, through advanced levels of comprehension and learning from text, and basic research, to applied work and full-fledged development of instructional approaches.

And what has been the character of that work? That might best be described by a colleague, who in reacting to the description of a study that Isabel and her research group were recently involved in, noted that getting the results out to the field would be "paddling upstream." That is a profoundly apt description—Isabel's career is a story of paddling upstream. She has championed phonics in a time of whole language, promoted vocabulary teaching in a time of context clues, and emphasized engagement with text ideas for comprehension instruction in a time of strategies.

One might ask, why does she make it so hard on herself? One response is because she has cultivated a deep understanding of the reading process, delving into theory and research, always drawing insights from observing what learners do, and she has followed the evidence, all the while keeping her eye on two questions: Why does it happen that way? and How can this help students learn?

In Isabel's early teaching experience with first-graders and then with, interestingly enough, army sergeants, she noticed some things that unsettled her. Many of her young and older students did not seem to thrive on the kind of instruction she'd learned about in her education courses. So she began to, as she describes, "break the rules" and help students sound out words. And she noticed it seemed to help them remember the words.

Subsequently, Isabel was able to match up the observations she'd made with research about reading as a complex process. These kinds of experiences prompted her to develop deep, multifaceted understandings of what learning to read was like for learners, especially those who struggled. And from those understandings grew effective new approaches to instruction.

Work in vocabulary sprang from a kernel of an idea: What if you taught kids a word a day? Thinking about how this might work combined with understanding of the instructional scene and perspectives on semantic processing led to a full and principled approach to vocabulary instruction—and insights into what it took to affect comprehension by teaching vocabulary.

In comprehension, a question that led Isabel's thinking was: What if you just ask kids to think aloud about what they are reading? And from this grew an approach framed around a cognitive processing view of the reading process called Questioning the Author.

In her uphill battle, Isabel has been in good company—fellow travelers, if you will, who have pondered and investigated how processes work and what that means for learners and teachers. Over the years, these comrades have sometimes challenged each other's ideas, sometimes bolstered them—but always enriched them. And those are the researchers represented in this book, which celebrates work done in reading that has moved those understandings forward. Isabel and her work have been at the center of that.

As her former students and current colleagues, we are honored to be able to present this book to those who pursue Isabel's deepest commitment—to provide the best reading instruction for students and the best support for their teachers.

MARGARET G. MCKEOWN, PHD
LINDA KUCAN, PHD

CONTENTS

1

A Tribute to the Diva of Scientifically Based Instruction

Jean Osborn *and* Marcy Stein

Isabel Beck is both a practitioner and a researcher. Practice has always informed her research as research has visibly informed her practice. Throughout her career, Isabel's work in classrooms has shaped the ways in which she and her colleagues have developed, tested, and disseminated instruction that helps teachers promote vocabulary development, foster reading comprehension, and enable their students to read the words on the page accurately and fluently. We value her outstanding contributions to these three critically important aspects of teaching children to read. We admire her long-standing dedication to *scientifically based* reading instruction, a term and even a concept that has gained importance only in the past decade. We particularly admire her continuing focus on the instructional needs of those students whose success in school depends on effective instruction.

We first became aware of the work of Isabel Beck more than 25 years ago, when someone handed us a 126-page report from the Learning Research and Development Center (LRDC) at the University of Pittsburgh. This report had a stiff black cover, a number of dense tables, many appendices that included specific examples of beginning reading instruction, and a long list of references. Its authors were Isabel Beck and Ellen S. McCaslin. The report's publication date was 1978. Its rather daunting title was very attractive to us: *An Analysis of Dimensions That Affect the Development of Code-Breaking Ability in Eight Beginning Read-*

ing Programs. We immediately set to work plowing through this report. Why did we spend the time so avidly reading the report? We read it because we had never before encountered anything like it in the reading research literature and because its content was so relevant to the classrooms of teachers and children that we knew.

As staff members of one of the instructional models taking part in the U.S. Department of Education's Follow Through program, we had spent a number of years working in kindergarten through third-grade classrooms in schools throughout the United States. We had worked in crowded inner-city schools, in small-town schools, on remote Indian reservations, and in isolated rural schools. Our job was to help teachers provide effective instruction in language, reading, and arithmetic for the students in their classrooms. The goal of the model was for all of the children to be performing at grade level or above in reading and arithmetic when they entered fourth grade.

We provided teachers with carefully designed curricula and well-thought-out teaching strategies developed to meet the considerable instructional needs of the at-risk children participating in the program. But sometimes we met with resistance. For example, we heard comments such as the following: "Written English is too irregular to teach systematically"; "Teaching phonics is boring for the children and tedious for the teachers"; "Children should read children's books of literary value rather than waste their time on simple-minded books."

We did our best to respond to these objections. We agreed that children should read books of literary value. But we pointed out that children benefit from being taught *how* to read before being asked to read the oftentimes complex texts of authentic children's literature. We turned to professional journals, hoping to find research that would help us respond to these protests. At that time, we did not find many studies that were of significant help to us. In fact, we came to the conclusion that most reading researchers had never entered the kinds of classrooms with which we had become so well acquainted. But the Beck and McCaslin report was different in that it was immediately relevant to the work we were doing with children who were at risk for reading failure.

THE BECK AND McCASLIN REPORT

What did Beck and McCaslin write about that was so relevant to the children and teachers in our classrooms?

Let's begin with what the authors said they were going to do in their report:

1. Attempt to discriminate among the instructional elements in eight published reading programs in terms of their potential effectiveness and efficiency for beginning decoding skills.
2. Determine how much is taught in these programs during the first two grades and the sequencing of instruction in those grades.
3. Examine the kind of pedagogy employed by the programs to teach word-attack strategies (Beck & McCaslin, 1978, p. 5).

Beck and McCaslin (1978) examined real programs that were being used in the classrooms of American elementary schools. That is, they actually sat down and analyzed eight different programs developed by commercial publishing companies. They examined the recommended instruction in the teacher's manuals and the stories in the student textbooks.

They provided us with a short history of reading instruction in American schools and clearly described the two most popular but very different approaches to teaching reading—code emphasis and meaning emphasis.

They synthesized the findings of theoretical researchers to help formulate their own view of beginning reading instruction. They wrote, "We believe that the primary objective of beginning reading is the acquisition of word-attack skills and word-recognition abilities" (1978, p. 5).

We read every page of the report. We resonated with the level of detail that Beck and McCaslin brought to their task. For example, in the section on letter–sound correspondences, they included well-reasoned answers to questions regarding how and what to teach in a word-attack program. Having neither the time nor the space to describe each one of their recommendations, we list a few:

- What letter–sound correspondences should be taught? (Consider ease of learning the correspondences and the utility of the correspondences.)
- What about teaching single consonants versus consonant clusters? (Emphasize single consonants.)
- How should letters that look alike best be addressed? (Teach confusable letters at a wide distance from each other.)
- What about letters that have more than one sound? (Take the middle ground—not too far apart, but not too close together.)

We also liked the 1978 report's careful consideration of essential instructional strategies. For example, their examination of eight programs found only a few that included blending instruction and only one that included blending instruction that they thought would be effective.

They highlighted the importance of auditory tasks that do not include print stimuli. Only in the past decade have commercial reading program developers incorporated such tasks, now labeled as "phonemic awareness activities," into their programs.

Beck and McCaslin (1978) were severe in their criticism of instruction that attempts to teach children to follow such bewildering directions as "When the vowel letter is between two consonants, the corresponding vowel sound is usually unglided." They pointed out the confusion that can result from teaching cumbersome rules and concepts, including vocabulary such as *long vowels* and *short vowels.*

Significantly, in their report, Beck and McCaslin were among the first to highlight the importance of having students read practice stories that contain words composed of the letter–sound correspondences they were learning. In analyzing the eight programs, they found only a few examples of programs that featured this kind of text. They would no doubt find more today. Currently, most commercially developed reading programs provide "decodable text" in their beginning reading programs.

In this well-respected classic example of the application of research to practice, Beck and McCaslin were clearly ahead of their time.

THE READING WARS

Although our enthusiasm for the Beck and McCaslin report grew during the period following its publication, we soon came to realize that other forces were at work in the arena of beginning reading instruction. The well-reasoned recommendations of that report became lost in what have often been described as the "Reading Wars." In the 1980s a new and very popular approach to reading instruction, called *whole language,* swept through the country. More a philosophy than a method, the whole-language approach advocated that children should learn to read "holistically" by immersion in literature. Phonics were not to be ignored but were to be considered as only one of many beginning reading strategies. Certainly, the approach to reading instruction that the

Beck and McCaslin report advocated was not embraced by the whole-language movement.

The Reading Wars engaged the attention of many reading teachers, curriculum directors, professors of education, and authors of textbooks about the teaching of reading. The journals of reading education and reading research featured articles on whole language. The panel discussions, workshop sessions, and keynote addresses of local, state, and national reading conferences promoted the whole-language view of reading instruction. In some of these journals and meetings, the attacks on those who proposed the importance of phonics instruction became extreme. For reasons we have never been able to figure out, the teaching of reading became politicized. Advocates of phonics instruction were sometimes accused of belonging to the political right wing. On the other hand, supporters of whole language were accused of being "liberals."

Whole language became the underlying philosophy of many "how to teach" reading textbooks that were used in undergraduate and graduate university courses. Many of these books offered suggestions for the whole-language teacher to present as alternatives to systematic phonics instruction. Here are some of those suggestions:

- Skip the difficult word.
- Read on to the end of the sentence or paragraph. Go back to the beginning of the sentence and try again.
- Substitute a word that makes sense.
- Read the word using only the beginning and ending sounds.
- Read the word without the vowels.
- Look for picture cues.
- Predict and anticipate what could come next.

Phonics programs were not completely abandoned. In fact, various new phonics programs were created by newcomers to the game. The developers of some of these programs had a tendency to become fanciful. One program furnished a list of foods that could be used to help children learn letter–sound correspondences—for example, "Feed the children applesauce or animal crackers for *Aa*"; "a bite of banana or bubble gum for *Bb*"; "some candy or carrots for *Cc*"; "give them donuts for *Dd*"; ... and on to "pass out zingers for *Zz*."

Another program provided a kit containing objects the children feel to learn the beginning sounds of words. The first consonants presented included *basket* for *b*, *dinosaur* for *d*, *mouse* for *m*; the vowels included *apple* for *a*, *iguana* for *i*, and *umbrella* for *u*.

There were also less fanciful phonics programs that were developed and advertised widely to parents and teachers. These "phonics-with-a-vengeance" programs often required the students to learn lots of letter–sound relationships, followed by reading long lists of words, most of which were not in the vocabulary of young children. Back then, there were no connected texts or stories in sight.

We know that Beck and McCaslin worried about many aspects of such programs, not the least of which was the requirement that the children read lists of words whose meanings they didn't know.

More than a decade later, we find that the Beck and McCaslin work of 1978 is as relevant and important as ever. The major difference between then and now is the proliferation of evidence that supports their early work. In fact, Isabel's most recent work in the area of beginning reading, *Making Sense of Phonics: The Hows and Whys* (2006), is somewhat of a journey through the years from then until now. The chapters in the book start with a discussion of issues involved in learning to read words and then move to presenting detailed instructional procedures and numerous examples. "It is my experience that teachers appreciate examples," says Isabel. Furthermore, "it is my hope that the analyses and commentary on the examples will provide and enhance theoretical understanding as well."

We are confident that *Making Sense of Phonics* has enhanced the theoretical understandings and classroom practices of its readers. We also are sure that its readers have a good time reading the book. To our knowledge, there is no other book on reading written in two voices: a personal voice that describes the author's own experiences as a reading teacher and an analytical voice that connects those experiences to scientifically based reading research. *Making Sense of Phonics* is an important book that is a pleasure to read.

Now we turn to Isabel's work in two other arenas: vocabulary acquisition and reading comprehension.

VOCABULARY ACQUISITION AND COMPREHENSION INSTRUCTION

Two recent books exemplify Isabel's long-standing interest and significant contribution to the field in the areas of vocabulary acquisition and comprehension instruction. They also exemplify her insistence on the interconnections between research and practice. The first book, *Bringing Words to Life: Robust Vocabulary Instruction* (2002), was written by Isabel and her colleagues Margaret G. McKeown and Linda Kucan. Isabel and her colleagues began their work with vocabulary in the 1980s. This book is the result of those many years of work. It describes how teachers can most effectively work with their students to improve their vocabularies by using a variety of research-based activities. For example, teachers are advised how to select words for instruction, how to create useful explanations of new words, how to create meaningful learning activities, and how to get students involved in thinking about, using, and noticing new words. It is a marvelous book that should be in the hands of every teacher who says, "But they don't have the vocabulary to understand what they read."

The second book, Beck and McKeown's *Improving Comprehension with Questioning the Author,* was published in 2006. It, like Isabel's previous work, is the result of many years of research in the area of comprehension instruction. Beck and McKeown's approach to comprehension involves helping readers make sense of what they read *as* they read, rather than engaging in reading strategies that are to be used before or after reading. The Questioning the Author procedure involves teaching students to present "queries" to the author as they read through the text. The teacher guides students in discussing what the authors want their readers to know. As they engage in these discussions, students become stronger readers, better able to deal with the difficulties of more complex texts. Like *Bringing Words to Life,* this book is written so that teachers can apply its ideas and strategies in their classrooms. Examples and explanations abound. All are grounded in the authors' more than 15 years of classroom work; they estimate that they or their colleagues have been involved in training approximately 2,000 teachers to use Questioning the Author. It is another exceptional book that should be in the hands of all teachers concerned about their students' understanding of what they are reading.

EVIDENCE OF ISABEL'S INFLUENCE

The disarray in the field of reading exemplified by the Reading Wars prompted a renewed interest in research about reading instruction. In the past two decades, five major reports about reading instruction have appeared. Each of these reports was supported at least in part by the U.S. Department of Education. The work that Isabel has done in the area of beginning reading, vocabulary, and comprehension is reflected in each of these reports. The first of these reports and the one that started it all, *Becoming a Nation of Readers* (Anderson, Hiebert, Scott, & Wilkinson, 1985) was developed by the Commission on Reading, which had been appointed by the National Academy of Education.

Becoming a Nation of Readers

Isabel was a member of the Commission on Reading. The charge to this group was to do a careful and thorough synthesis of an extensive body of research on reading. Based on this synthesis, this group of experts was asked to comment on current knowledge of reading development and on the state of the art and practice in teaching reading. The report was to be written so as to be helpful to teachers.

Notably, 2 of its 17 recommendations reflect Isabel's interests in beginning reading instruction:

- Teachers of beginning reading should present well-designed phonics instruction.
- Reading primers should be interesting and comprehensible and should give children opportunities to apply phonics.

It should be noted that *Becoming a Nation of Readers* was one of the best-selling books ever published on the topic of reading. By the year 2000, 300,000 copies had been sold.

Four More Reports

Beginning to Read: Thinking and Learning about Print (1990) by Marilyn Adams is an extensive review and synthesis of research about the nature and development of reading proficiency drawn from the fields of cognitive psychology, developmental psychology, educational psychology, reading education, linguistics, computer science, and anthropology. In this book, Adams provides an integrated treatment of the knowledge and processes involved in skillful reading, discusses the issues surrounding their acquisition, and offers the implications for reading instruction. Among her conclusions are that "deep and thorough knowledge of letters, spelling patterns, and words, and of the phonological translations of all three, are of inescapable importance to both skillful reading and its acquisition."

Preventing Reading Difficulties in Young Children (Snow, Burns, & Griffin, 1998) identified and summarized research literature that was relevant to the acquisition of beginning reading skills. The report's recommendations include the provision of high-quality preschool and kindergarten so that children arrive in first grade motivated for literacy and possessing the necessary early literacy concepts and skills. Consistent with the previous reports, this report supports phonics instruction: "Getting started in alphabetic reading depends critically on mapping the letters and spellings of words onto the speech units that they represent; failure to master word recognition can impede text comprehension" (p. 416).

Teaching Children to Read: An Evidence-Based Assessment of the Scientific Research Literature on Reading and Its Implications for Reading Instruction (2000) is the report written by the National Reading Panel, a panel appointed by the director of the National Institute of Child Health and Human Development, in consultation with the Department of Education. Among their tasks, the panel was charged with assessing the status of research-based knowledge about reading and with evaluating the effectiveness of various approaches to teaching children to read. Consistent with previous reports, the panel found very strong support for the teaching of alphabetics—phonemic awareness and systematic phonics.

The Voice of Evidence in Reading Research (2004), the most recent of the comprehensive reports on reading, was edited by Peggy McCardle and Vinita Chhabra, literacy experts from the National Institute of Child Health and Development. This report extends previous work in the area by clarifying the importance of scientifically based research and how best to apply that research to teaching. The report also introduces updated additional findings to those of the National Reading Panel.

CONCLUSION

We believe that Isabel's steadfast commitment to instructional research that contributes to our understanding of "scientifically based instruction" has meant that *more* teachers are *more* successful with *more* students, particularly those students whose academic achievement depends on the quality of the instruction they receive.

Nothing is more gratifying to those of us in teacher education than to have teachers report that something we have done or said has caused them to change what they were doing in their classrooms and resulted in improving their students' achievement. Isabel and her colleagues are responsible for a lot of change—for changes in how beginning reading is taught in this country, for better designed vocabulary instruction, and for a different approach to comprehension instruction. We trust that Isabel is able to appreciate the importance of the changes she has inspired. We thank her for her lifetime of commitment to teachers and to students. She truly is the diva of scientifically based reading instruction.

REFERENCES

Adams, M. J. (1990). *Beginning to read: Thinking and learning about print.* Cambridge, MA: MIT Press.

Anderson, R. C., Hiebert, E. H., Scott, J. A., & Wilkinson, I. A. G. (1985). *Becoming a nation of readers: The report of the Commission on Reading.* Washington, DC: National Institute of Education. (Available from the University of Illinois, Becoming a Nation of Readers, P. O. Box 2774, Station A, Champaign, IL 61820-8774)

Beck, I. L. (2006). *Making sense of phonics: The hows and whys.* New York: Guilford Press.

Beck, I. L., & McCaslin, E. S. (1978). *An analysis of dimensions that affect the development of code-breaking ability in eight beginning reading programs* (LRDC Publication 1978/6). Pittsburgh, PA: University of Pittsburgh, Learning Research and Development Center.

Beck, I. L., & McKeown, M. G. (2006). *Improving comprehension with Questioning the Author: A fresh and expanded view of a powerful approach.* New York: Scholastic.

Beck, I. L., McKeown, M. G., & Kucan, L. (2002). *Bringing words to life: Robust vocabulary instruction.* New York: Guilford Press.

McCardle, P., & Chhabra, V. (Eds.). (2004). *The voice of evidence in reading research.* Baltimore: Brookes.

National Reading Panel. (2000). *Teaching children to read: An evidence-based assessment of the scientific research literature on reading and its implications for reading instruction.* Washington, DC: National Institute of Child Health and Human Development.

Snow, C. E., Burns, M. S., & Griffin, P. (Eds.). (1998). *Preventing reading difficulties in young children.* Washington, DC: National Academy Press.

2

TAKING A LONG VIEW
OF READING DEVELOPMENT

Connie Juel

INFLUENCES THAT MOTIVATED
THE DIRECTION OF MY WORK

Like Isabel Beck, my interest in reading research started in the elementary classroom. In the early 1970s I was a fourth-grade elementary school teacher. Two things puzzled me about my children's reading: (1) Why was there such a huge range in reading ability among these 9-year-olds? (2) Why were there a couple of children each year who were still learning to decode at a very basic level? I worked closely with my very poor readers and saw how hard they struggled to learn and how their poor reading was affecting almost all aspects of their schoolwork. I can still remember the face of a 9-year-old girl absolutely aglow when she sang during music time; yet that face turned downward and unsmiling as she stared at a printed page. This young girl determined my future.

After school one day I drove down to my alma mater and entered a building I had never been in as an undergraduate—the School of Education. I inquired in the dean's office about who could help me help children learn to read. There seemed some confusion and some asking around, which I thought was odd, as this seemed like a pretty reasonable question to pose in this building. Eventually I was directed to the office of Professor Robert Calfee. Fortunately, he was in, and even more fortunately, as I now know as a university professor myself, he was willing to invite this stranger in and to spend some time talking. I have to say that at the time I did not understand much of what he was saying, and as his doctoral student a couple of years later I would still struggle—but I came a lot closer. For he began by talking about design—specifically, fractional factorial research designs that could be used to carefully unpack the reading process. What I did understand at the time, though, was that to help my students with reading difficulties, I needed to understand the reading process—to *really* understand it, as he put it. A passion entered my mind; I wanted to do just that. So I would take a year off to study this process, get a master's degree, and head back to the classroom better equipped to help my students. But the passion turned into doing one of those fractional factorial studies on the reading process for my doctorate.

RESEARCH AGENDA

During the 1970s exploration into the reading process was dominated by psychology and cognitive information processing models (e.g., Gough, 1971). To start to test these types of models, factorial designs and analysis of variance worked well. For each hypothesized component process (what the boxes in the model represented), you needed to find some unique factors that influenced that process and that did not interact with other hypothesized component processes. You might hypothesize that decoding involved going through orthography and not subverting it by using top-down processing—that is, using knowledge of the topic you were reading rather than looking closely at letters in words as you read. You then needed to demonstrate that decoding was not affected by top-down factors but rather by factors unique to it (such as the regularity of a word's spelling patterns). This methodology would serve me well for several years as a researcher; I published several studies examining the reading process using factorial designs and this form of analysis.

Of course, boxes in a design of reading processes assume input by the reader. For each component process, you can consider how the learner's current ability, knowledge, and emotions affect that process. And, given that each individual is a unique constellation, there are likely different patterns for how the component processes might develop and interact and how the whole enterprise of reading development might be on different trajectories for every individual. There is likely, however, to be considerable overlap in the "component processes" developed on these trajectories. Stage models of reading, which I participated in, tried to capture those commonalities.

For those of us whose passion was education, the next step was to consider what and how school instruction contributes to the process of learning to read and write. Schools involve teachers, group settings, and textbooks, among other things. These various dimensions interact both with the component processes of reading and with the individual learner's contribution to those processes. Brian Byrne (2005) views what the schools need to do as a problem of subtraction: the components of reading processes minus what the learner contributes to each. Complexity, he would note, is added because every child does not bring the same ability to generalize and reason or the same knowledge to a component.

Consider that a component process of reading is word recognition (however you wish to subdivide it). Children bring to this process differential knowledge about letter sounds and words and differential skill in generalization and transfer. Clearly, teachers cannot teach every word that children will see in print or every spelling–sound mapping. Ability to generalize and transfer will vary between children, and teachers will need to teach accordingly (Byrne, 2005).

I think that the roles decodable text and phonics play, to a large extent, is to encourage children to generalize. Juel and Roper/Schneider (1985) found that children could induce untaught letter–sound correspondences better in decodable text than in less decodable text. The text itself seemed to foster generalizing, reasoning, and transfer.

In trying to understand reading—to *really* understand reading, as my advisor had put it—we must understand its component processes, what the individual contributes, and all that is involved in instruction. There are two other dimensions that I have been concerned with, one more than the other, in my own research. First, there is a social contribution to some, if not all, aspects of reading. There are home, community, and peer interactions and discourse in general that is permeated with social interactions that influence reading. Reading often seems to be a solitary activity, and I think that dimension should be valued, but, clearly, social constructivist thinking has highlighted the social aspects of learning and comprehending.

Second, a longitudinal view of learning has been a very important dimension of study for me. What contributes to learning to read in first grade, for example, may be something that was learned more in kindergarten than in first grade. Or knowledge that facilitates a process such as word recognition may change with age and exposure to text. It is the longitudinal aspect of my research work that I highlight in this chapter.

I have always been interested in how we change over time. Just as we aren't the same people today that we were as babies or teenagers or that we will be at the end of our lives, the reading process might change over time. From this perspective, I was interested in how classroom instruction affected the learning-to-read process and how the influence of this instruction would vary across time. If you were instructing a "baby" versus a "teenage" reader, how might instruction differentially affect the learner? And would instruction you received as a "baby" reader reach up to influence you as an older reader? Would, say, what you learned in kindergarten affect or even control what you learn in first grade?

My research agenda these past three decades has been to understand the reading process: the component processes of reading, the learner's contribution to these processes, and the instructional, social, and longitudinal contributions. My earliest work focused more, I initially thought, on the cognitive processes in reading than on instruction, but the outcome of that work would focus me squarely on instruction.

RELATIONSHIP OF RESEARCH TO INSTRUCTION

Early Research

Individual growth modeling (hierarchical linear modeling; HLM) was not available to reading researchers in the 1980s, or I would have been a quick convert. As it was, I began to use path analysis and regression to try to explore development of the reading process over time. The model I began with was heavily influenced by what would come to be known as the "simple view of reading" (Gough & Tunmer, 1986; Hoover & Gough, 1990). The simple view of reading is that reading comprehension is the product of two fundamental processes, word recognition and listening comprehension. If either process is missing, then no matter how good the other process, reading comprehension will be nonexistent. Assuming perfect word recognition, then, the reader comprehends written text as well as he or she would if the same text were spoken.

I also assumed a simple view of writing. This assumption led to the model in Figure 2.1. In a longitudinal study of first- and second-grade children, we tried to model development, particularly of word recognition skill (Juel, Griffith, & Gough, 1986). We thought that the foundational sources of knowledge that readers use to identify (or spell) words were cipher knowledge (i.e., the knowledge underlying spelling–sound patterns that enable pronunciation of pseudowords such as *buf* or *zlip*) and word-specific lexical knowledge (e.g., knowing that the "long" *e* in green is spelled *ee* rather than *ea* or *ene*). For accomplished readers, cipher knowledge may become a closed set, but we are always adding to our word-specific lexical knowledge. How, for example, do you spell *iridescence*—one or two r's? We thought word-specific lexical knowledge would come about largely through exposure to print, though for adults it may well be through writing.

Today it may be hard to think of a time when the term *phonemic awareness* was relatively unknown. It was not common to put phonemic awareness on the table in those days, but in this study we did. We thought it a prominent contributor, along with exposure to printed words, to a child's ability to create cipher knowledge. We also thought that whereas the first-grade child might be more dependent on cipher knowledge, the balance would shift in favor of lexical knowledge over time.

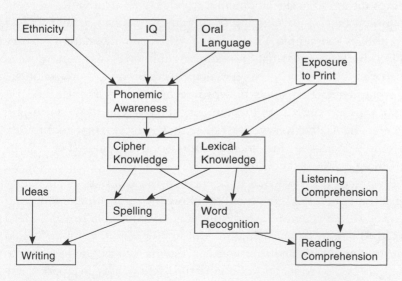

FIGURE 2.1. The simple model of literacy acquisition.

We were just starting to open the Pandora's box of phonemic awareness to look at what might predict it. We were studying children in Austin, Texas, who were about one-third Hispanic (I'm using labels from the locale and time period), one-third black, and one-third Anglo. We hypothesized that dialect and second language might influence development of phonemic awareness in English. Ethnicity did indeed influence phonemic awareness, but we could not verify our hypothesis in this study. Although we considered phonemic awareness as a precursor to developing cipher knowledge, I should have listened to my friend Isabel, who suggested that it developed in a reciprocal relation. That would be what other studies would find and what we would later jointly conclude (Beck & Juel, 1992). Like other researchers, we found generally low correlations among IQ, listening comprehension, and phonemic awareness. That is, phonemic awareness seemed to be a somewhat unique or modular understanding/skill in development: A child with either a high or a low IQ could have problems with phonemic awareness.

In terms of the simple view, we found that first-grade reading comprehension was largely determined by word recognition ability (defined, using a narrow view, as accurate pronunciation). Word recognition in first grade was largely determined by cipher knowledge in first grade, with a shift to lexical knowledge in second grade. These findings may hold as developmental trends. Two major views of word recognition that were emerging at this time, however, would indeed show this as too simple. First, Linnea Ehri's "amalgamation" theory and her studies suggest that these sources of knowledge are not so easily separated (Ehri, 1992; Ehri & Wilce, 1985). Second, "connectionist" computer-generated models of word recognition marked the beginning of research suggesting that almost every word is its own learning domain—that is, that it is words, rather than children, that go through, in a sense, "stages" of incremental knowledge additions (Plaut, 2005; Seidenberg & McClelland, 1989).

I wanted to know what happened to the children in our study after second grade, so I continued to follow their development through 2 more years, through fourth grade (Juel, 1988). I also learned that I wanted to talk to the participating children to see how things looked from their end. I wanted *their* words. This marked my departure into mixed methods. From here on, qualitative data would be a part of my quantitative studies. Even more, case studies became an interest. I took eight children from this study and did expanded case studies, with extensive interviews and reading and writing samples (Juel, 1994).

Probably the two most quoted findings from my research work over the years came from a longitudinal study (Juel, 1988). One finding was that the probability of a child still being a poor reader at the end of fourth grade, given that the child was a poor reader at the end of first grade, was .88. This probability was cited as though it were gospel; I always found this a bit strange, because it was a relatively small sample, because the children were all from one school, and because there was no intervention in place. Still other researchers, across curricula and languages, have found a similar statistic, though some have not. I think our current emphasis on early intervention has helped lessen the probability.

The interview data from this study revealed a very consistent and troubling pattern. Those children who, early on, struggled with reading began to hate reading. In this study I thought I was cleverly ascertaining motivation for reading by asking children such questions as, "Which would you rather do: clean your room or read a book?" This question did elicit the most quoted statement from this study. In response to this question, Javier volunteered, "I'd rather scrub the mold around the bathtub than read." The children who had struggled for 4 years with reading, however, were just as likely to respond to a direct question about their feelings toward reading with "I hate it."

Later Research

The finding of a .88 probability of not overcoming a poor start in reading, as well as children's subsequent development of hatred toward reading, had a big impact on me. In all my work after the 4-year longitudinal study I would engage in research with a direct focus on either intervention or classroom instruction.

I have been involved in several studies of different forms of early reading intervention that employ one-on-one tutoring. This form of tutoring builds on a common early method of learning: apprenticeship. Although tutoring is a common staple in upper-class families, it was not commonly available to the middle class until commercial enterprises such as Sylvan Learning made it financially possible. For lower-income families, however, it has remained out of reach unless the school system has made it available, as with Reading Recovery. It has not been financially possible, however, for school systems to provide enough one-on-one tutors for the number of children who could use a boost in developing reading and writing.

I had a unique opportunity when I was at the University of Texas at Austin to work with two ends of what Stanovich (1986) labeled the "Matthew effect"—adults who were poor readers and children on their way to becoming poor readers. Members of the men's athletic department were always concerned about students who were admitted to the university based on their athletic abilities rather than on their academic skills. Indeed, many star players, particularly in basketball, had come from some of our nation's poorest urban communities. In line with what we know about the relation between socioeconomic status (SES) and achievement, these now-adult students were often such poor readers and writers that college-level work proved extraordinarily difficult. The athletic department had tried to ameliorate this situation. They had required a year-long study-skills–reading–writing course for those students who scored poorly on entrance on reading and vocabulary assessments. The class was not very popular, however, so the department readily agreed to an experiment. Half their poor readers would enroll in the current year-long course; half would enroll in a new year-long course with me. In my group the students would tutor a first- or second-grade child twice a week for 45 minutes each time.

The tutored children attended an all-minority school (largely African American with a smaller Latino population) in one of the poorest areas in the city. In addition to tutoring, the university students attended a weekly night course for 2½ hours and did 4 hours of outside reading per week. They read in books selected by a committee of student athletes; these ranged from novels to books on sports to biographies of growing up poor and African American. We communicated about their reading in a written journal. Also, in class they shared their thoughts on the outside reading, we talked about tutoring, and we spent part of the class on our own version of "writing workshop." In the workshop the tutors wrote books for the children they tutored. These books often starred their children as the central characters and were very popular with the children. We "published" the books; hence the books needed to be edited before being bound, and this created a time to work on the mechanics of writing.

Embedded in the year-long course with tutoring were two experiments. First, pre–post comparisons were made in reading, vocabulary, and study skills between the university students in the tutoring course and those in the regular course; these comparisons showed significance in favor of the tutors in each area. Second, we compared the reading growth of tutored versus nontutored first- and second-grade children. Our nontutored children were not left without attention: Each had weekly visits from a student athlete who served as a mentor but who otherwise did not tutor the children. This "control" group did not perform as well in reading development as did those children who received tutoring.

This was an early attempt to develop a tutoring program, and I did not know what the most effective activities for the children would be. The tutors chose among seven tutoring activities for each 45-minute session: (1) reading children's literature; (2) hearing word sounds (phonemic awareness); (3) learning to write and recognize the alphabet; (4) working on phonics; (5) writing favorite words in a journal, then dictating sentences about the words to the tutor and drawing pictures about the words; (6) writing stories, postcards, and texts; and (7) making buildup readers. Buildup readers (Guszak, 1985) slowly introduce words from the basal readers used in the classrooms and words that exemplify taught phonics patterns. Five buildup readers were created, corresponding to the five levels of first-grade basal readers used in the classrooms. The length of the buildup readers ranged from 25 to 100 pages. On the first page of the first buildup reader, the word *run* appeared 30 times, with a few blanks to write in what was running. The child and tutor could jointly decide what to write in the blank—for example, what they wanted to have "run," be it a Ninja Turtle, themselves, or a pet. Buildup readers allow slow and repeated introduction to words throughout the levels of readers (though page 1 was by far the most dramatic, with only one word). Buildup readers formed a solid link to the words the children were expected to read in their classroom basal textbooks and in the tutoring sessions.

Although overall the tutored children outperformed the control group, there was considerable variation in effectiveness among tutoring dyads. So, in addition to the two central experiments, I examined the effectiveness of both time spent in the seven tutoring activities and the quality of those activities on child learning.

Time spent on the journal was one of the activities that were least predictive of reading growth. In fact, it had a negative correlation with growth, probably because tutoring time became drawing time. The most predictive activities were time spent on phonics and on the buildup readers. (In my current tutoring program at Stanford, the tutors use Beck, 2006, to guide the phonics portion of their lesson.) In the dyads that showed the most growth, tutors engaged in scaffolded instruction and modeling of what they were trying to teach much more than tutors in less successful dyads did.

In this study, there was no observed difference in the amount of bonding and affection shown between the most successful and least successful tutoring dyads. Simply put, they all exhibited these outcomes. There is no doubt a special circumstance involved in these dyads, with a largely African American group of males tutoring a largely African American group of children. Not only did almost all the tutors and children share a history of being financially poor, but also the tutors had all struggled with literacy, just as did those they tutored. The tutors frequently wrote in their journals about how they identified with the children and how motivated they were to help them. I believe these overlaps created an especially powerful bond between these adults and their tutees.

In the time since this initial tutoring study, however, I have been involved in other tutoring programs. I would say that, in general, tutors become quite attached and committed to the children being tutored— whether the tutors are community or university student volunteers or are tutoring as part of an official class. There is something special about the one-to-one experience itself that breeds a powerful bond.

Although tutoring is helpful, the heart of literacy instruction lies in the classroom. The two-pronged attempt to try to help children get off to a good start in reading led me from tutoring to studies of classroom instruction. I discuss two studies here because they build off each other. The first was a year-long study in which we closely examined four first-grade classrooms (Juel & Minden-Cupp, 2000). A central issue of this study was how to capture what was going on in classrooms in terms of word recognition instruction (e.g., phonics instruction done in small groups and focusing on phonograms). We were interested in delineating the instructional practices that seemed to best foster learning to read words for particular profiles of children (e.g., children with differential literacy skill). The second study was a larger longitudinal study of preschool through first grade, with 13 classrooms in kindergarten and 13 in first grade. This study built on the observational system developed in the first study.

A real obstacle, it seems to me, in doing research on classroom instruction is that we have no agreed-on observation instruments. This may be too much to ask, not only because every researcher wants to look at different things but also because we do not have agreed-on norms for what or how literacy instruction should go. So the first longitudinal study I describe was partly dedicated to developing a classroom observation system that I could use in the second study.

The grain size of the observation instrument, as well as the categories on it, determines what researchers find. In a large grain size, we might look at how often phonics is taught. In a smaller grain size, we might parse that out into types of phonics (e.g., onset–rime, letter-by-letter) and the instructional context (e.g., in small groups, using letter cards, reading decodable text, sounding out words as they are written), among other possibilities. A still finer grain analysis might capture what a specific child was told to do (e.g., "Sound it out, Nora") or whether a child was even directly spoken to during the instruction.

One problem with classroom research is deciding which grain size to capture. Sometimes you don't know where to aim. Because it is hard to recapture live instruction and because even video must be analyzed at some level, choosing what to look at is critical; the grain size of what is recorded will limit findings to that grain size. At first doing everything at a fine grain size might seem the most sure-footed, but such data can be unwieldy.

Another obstacle to classroom observation is that so much is going on at the same time in a classroom. Several reading groups or centers may be going at once; activities are frequently embedded in other activities (e.g., letter–sound instruction occurs in the context of writing a whole-class letter to another classroom). Of course, this is the reason that experimental work can be so helpful, as the researcher can control the factors of interest; but my interest lies in what goes on in real classrooms, and how to capture what goes on inside these rooms is very challenging.

We tried to create a flexible observation system that we could return to, as needed, to increase or decrease the grain size (Juel & Minden-Cupp, 2000). A classroom observer sat with a laptop creating a running narrative of everything possible, including children's names. We observed in each of four classrooms for a minimum of an hour every week throughout the school year—usually the entire 90-minute language arts block. These four classrooms each had three reading groups.

We observed each low group each week and the other two groups at least every 2 weeks. We also observed whole-class instruction when it occurred during language arts.

Two research assistants subsequently coded the laptop narratives until we achieved an interrater reliability over .95. We began by coding four things: (1) activities (e.g., a read-aloud by the teacher, phonics); (2) materials (e.g., trade books, picture sort); (3) strategies (e.g., analogy, sound and blend); and (4) units (e.g., phonogram, initial consonant, and word). We added distinctions under the headings as needed. We found that the focus of *activities* generally clumped into five major categories: reading, writing, oral language, letter sound, and whole word (Figure 2.2). We could move from these five broad-grained clumps (e.g., *writing*) to the finer grained analysis (e.g., the 37 listed categories, such as *morning message*), to an even finer grained analysis taken directly from the narratives (e.g., Nora was asked to write her cousin's name in the morning message).

In the four-classroom study we found the middle-grain analysis (i.e., the 37 categories) sufficient to characterize the four classrooms. In the next study I describe we had to go down to the fine-grained narrative analysis to understand what was happening. The point is that I don't think you always know ahead of time which grain size to use.

Let me start by discussing the first study of the four classrooms (Juel & Minden-Cupp, 2000). Here we examined the effects of different forms and contexts of classroom life on growth on various reading assessments given in September, December, and May. We also asked the children to read specific words introduced to their reading groups and to explain how they identified the words.

We found that instruction varied enormously in the four classrooms, even though they were within the same school. We also found a considerable interaction between the type of instruction and reading group. Children who entered first grade low in alphabet knowledge and were placed in the low reading group did exceedingly better if they were placed with the teacher who did the most phonics instruction. The phonics activities in this classroom were very hands-on, with 66% of them involving sorting word cards into categories based on orthographic patterns and 17% involving "writing for sound"—writing dictated words that contained target spelling patterns. After February, however, instruction in this classroom resembled that in the other two reading groups, with more of a focus on reading and little on phonics.

			Instructional Activities			
	Reading	Writing	Oral Language	Letter–Sound	Word	Other
1.	Reading text	Writing text	Discussion on topic	Oral phonemic awareness	Sight-reading words	Conference with teacher
2.	Choral reading	Individual writing	Meaning of story	Writing for sound	Spelling words	Peer coaching
3.	Round robin reading	Morning message	Read-aloud by teacher	Letter–sound/ decoding phonics	Word wall	Text structures
4.	Pair reading	Grammar or punctuation	Vocabulary	Letter identification	Cutting sentences up into words	Book/print awareness
5.	Individual reading	Handwriting		Word families	Concept of word	Nonliteracy activity
6.	Rereading	Language Experience Activity writing		Rhyming		
7.	Free choice/ reading	Copying		Matching letter cards to words		
8.	Expressive reading					
9.	Learning/ reciting memorized poem					

FIGURE 2.2. Overview of coding. After Juel and Minden-Cupp (2000).

This classroom had the most differentiated initial instruction overall and the highest overall mean passage-reading score at the end of first grade, a whopping mean level of late second grade.

In comparison, in another classroom there was little phonics instruction for anyone; rather, there was a considerable amount of reading in Little Books and trade books, a fair amount of journal writing, and some word wall use. The low-reading-group children fared exceptionally poorly in this classroom. The children did not learn to read the words they saw in the books, and they could not employ any useful strategies for decoding unknown words. On the other hand, those children who entered first grade at or above average in alphabet knowledge and letter–sound knowledge did exceptionally well in this classroom.

The need for differential instruction seemed clear. Yet the finding was based on only four classrooms. That led to the second study, following a larger group of children in different grades. I am just recently finishing the data analysis. True to form, it was a longitudinal study following the growth of literacy and language from the end of preschool through the end of first grade. In this study I wanted to examine the two main factors in determining children's reading achievement that have been investigated by researchers looking to improve children's long-term literacy outcomes: (1) the role of incoming characteristics and (2) the role of instruction. In particular, I was interested in how reading skill grew in response to different forms and amounts of instruction and different incoming literacy and language profiles of children.

Literacy and language profiles were created at three time points: preschool, kindergarten, and first grade. The idea behind these was that profiles of multiple skills and abilities would yield a richer glimpse of a child than would the typical research focus on one or two characteristics. The profiles were based on Konold, Juel, McKinnon, and Deffes (2003). I need to take a bit of time to discuss the development of these profiles.

Richard Woodcock graciously provided us with the cross-sectional norming sample data for the Woodcock Diagnostic Reading Battery (WDRB; Woodcock, 1997). These data came from 1,604 children ages 5–10 years. The WDRB includes six subtests of underlying types of knowledge thought to be involved in reading, as well as four subtests that assess reading achievement. The six underlying knowledge subtests include two measures of phonological skill: (1) Incomplete Words, in which a child hears a tape-recorded word that has one or more phonemes missing and has to identify the complete word; and (2) Sound Blending, in which an audiotape presents word parts (syllables and/or phonemes of words) and the child puts them together to form a word. Other underlying foundations for reading that are tested are: Oral Vocabulary, Listening Comprehension, Memory for Sentences, and Visual Matching. We used these six subtests to predict skill on the four reading achievement tests of Letter–Word Identification, Word Attack, Reading Vocabulary, and Passage Comprehension.

Cluster analysis yielded six profiles, three relatively flat: (1) 11% of 5- to 10-year-olds had flat profiles on all six subtest scores that hovered around a standard score of 80–85 with similarly below-average reading scores; (2) 25% of the children had flat profiles on all subtests, hovering in the mid- to low 90s, with slightly below-average reading scores; (3) 13% of children, with significantly more females, had subtest scores that were all high—above 110 and most about 120, with predictably high reading scores.

Three of the six profiles had distinctive spikes or dips in performance: (1) 17% of children had all standard scores around 100, except for a notable high Visual Matching score around 115; (2) 16% had all standard scores around 100, with particular strengths in phonological skills on Incomplete Words and Sound Blending; and (3) 15%, with a significantly larger number of boys, had average scores in Visual Matching and phonological skills but considerably higher scores in Memory for Sentences, Oral Vocabulary, and Listening Comprehension. It is perhaps telling that this last profile houses more males, for if an individual child had even more depressed scores in Visual Matching and in phonological skills, the profile would resemble those of children labeled dyslexic.

Not surprisingly, those children with flat profiles and high scores overall outperformed other clusters on all four reading measures, whereas children with flat but low scores scored below average on all four reading measures. The more interesting findings came by way of comparison between profiles defined by notable strengths. We found that at age 5 children with phonological strengths demonstrated statistically greater scores on Letter–Word Identification, Word Attack, and Reading Vocabulary than children with no secondary strengths or with secondary strengths in Visual Matching or Memory for Sentences. At age 6 children with both phonological processing strengths and visual matching strengths performed better on all four reading measures. Not until age 10 did those children with secondary strengths in Memory for Sentences, Oral Vocabulary, and Listening Comprehension show an advantage.

With that background, let me return to the second longitudinal study. We were interested in whether these clusters developed over time or in response to instruction. Our first mistake was to assume that we would find roughly these same percentages in the profiles in an overwhelmingly low-SES and minority population that did not equate to the population that formed the WDRB norming sample. We followed children from preschool age through the end of first grade. (That is, we followed about half the children from preschool because about half our sample did not attend preschool.)

There were six preschools that fed into three elementary schools—schools that were close to one another and that drew from a similar population. About half our sample attended preschool ($n = 64$). The largest public preschool, as well as the community Head Start preschools, were restricted to children from the lowest SES strata. About half our sample did not attend preschool ($n = 78$). On entry into kindergarten, we found that our preschool and nonpreschool samples (children who, whether because of parental choice or SES restrictions, did not attend preschool) did not differ in performance on the Wide Range Achievement Test (WRAT; Wilkinson, 1993). Both groups were still learning the letters of the alphabet on entrance to kindergarten.

There was some difference between those who were and those who were not in preschool in terms of the profiles on the WDRB in kindergarten. But for both groups, the majority of children were in the flat profile, with the lowest scores across the board. The actual statistics are really daunting: 62% of our preschoolers were in the lowest profile toward the end of preschool compared with 11% of the WDRB norming sample. That percentage decreased to 56% in kindergarten and to 31% by first grade. This is positive movement by first grade, but it occurs mainly because the children move to the slightly below-average flat profile at which 47% of them now reside. (Of our sample that did not go to preschool, 41% are in the lowest profile in kindergarten, decreasing to 21% in first grade, and again moving mainly to the second below-average flat profile, at which we find 39% of them.)

Despite this ominous standing in the profiles, the 142 children who were in our sample in kindergarten and first grade did, on average, learn to decode, and their word recognition on the WDRB and the WRAT were average by the end of first grade. But their oral vocabulary and listening comprehension skills remained in the lowest profile range, which clearly does not bode well for them as they advance through the grades. The three schools worked hard to bring children to grade level in reading. Overall they were successful in word recognition. The mean WDRB Letter–Word Identification score in first grade was a standard score of 103, which is impressive given the underlying profiles. Overall, a lot was done in kindergarten and first grade to promote word recognition, even though the amount of instruction varied considerably across classrooms. Oral Vocabulary, however, stayed at a standard score of 89 from preschool through first grade for those children who attended preschool ($n = 64$) and stayed at 91 from kindergarten through first grade for all others ($n = 78$). In other words, they needed attention to oral language, vocabulary, and knowledge along the lines identified by Beck, McKeown, and Kucan (2002).

Our second mistake was to assume that we would see profiles with secondary strengths emerge longitudinally and/or in response to specific instruction. We did see some growth in the profile with the rise in Visual Matching by first grade, approximating the population norm. The other secondary strength profiles failed to coalesce anywhere near the population norms. In other words, we found few children with a secondary strength in Memory for Sentences, Oral Vocabulary, and Listening Comprehension, nor children with secondary phonological strengths.

I want to go into more depth here describing the effects of instruction in kindergarten and first grade and why flexible grain size observation instruments are important. Again, we followed the kindergarten children through first grade, and they came from all the kindergarten and first-grade classrooms in three public elementary schools. The three schools drew from the same area of low-income and public housing projects, small duplexes, and apartments in a city in the Southeast. Of the 142 children, 68% qualified for free lunch, 2% for reduced fare; 68% were African American, 29% white, 51% male, and 49% female. Across the three schools there were 13 kindergarten and 13 first-grade classrooms. We administered the WDRB toward the end of kindergarten and first grade and the WRAT at the beginning and end of kindergarten and first grade.

We made observations in each of the 13 classrooms in kindergarten and first grade at least once a month, making sure that every child in the study was observed. Observers typed a running account of classroom instruction during language arts. These were later coded, with interrater reliability of .97, as per the method in Juel and Minden-Cupp (2000).

The most common instructional setting in kindergarten, used in eight classrooms, was to have the class divided into three heterogeneous groups for language arts. The same lessons, readings, and read-alouds were used for each group. The reasons given for having three groups were that kindergarten children attended better in small groups and that the teacher could be more aware of each child in the group. Children not in the group were usually in centers or at special programs in the school (e.g., music, physical education). Five classrooms largely used a whole-class structure for instruction.

In the heterogeneous small-grouped kindergarten classrooms, the time spent on various activities in the groups was virtually the same, although considerable variation existed among classrooms (as much within a school as between schools) as to the amount of the instruction devoted to particular activities. Following are some ranges in the proportion of the language arts period devoted to different activities in these heterogeneous groups between classrooms: a 12–42% range in language arts activities devoted to phonics, a 0–26% range in attention to isolated words (e.g., on a word wall or spelling), a 14–46% range in activities with potential to foster oral language (e.g., read-alouds by teacher, explicit vocabulary work), a range of 4–38% in reading (i.e., in which text reading involved the children in reading, such as in choral reading), and a range of 0–26% in writing activities (i.e., of text longer than a single word).

In the five kindergartens in which most instruction was done with the whole class, a similar diversity of activities existed, ranging, for example, from a high of 36% to a low of 14% in letter–sound activities. Two of these five classrooms occasionally broke down from the whole-class structure into small ability-group instruction with low, middle, and high groups. The instruction between these two classrooms, however, was quite different. The low group in one classroom received 75% letter–sound activities, whereas the low group in the other classroom received only 26%. But these low groups reflected the overall proclivity of the teachers. The middle and high groups in the 75% phonics classroom received, respectively, 65 and 52% phonics activities, whereas the middle and high groups in the other classroom received, respectively, 26 and 0% phonics activities. These two classrooms were in the same school.

We fully expected that these differences in kindergarten experiences, particularly with phonics, would make a big difference in children's growth on, say, the WRAT from the beginning to the end of kindergarten. This was our third mistake. (Well, not entirely.) Letter–sound instruction had a positive impact on those children who entered kindergarten with little letter recognition, but it actually seemed to have a negative impact on those children who entered with some degree of facility with letter sounds. Perhaps this should not have been such a surprise, as it echoes the finding of our previous work (Juel & Minden-Cupp, 2000). An HLM analysis in the current study showed that kindergarten letter–sound instruction had a positive reach into first grade for those with the humblest beginnings in alphabetic knowledge on entrance to kindergarten: The more letter–sound instruction these children had in kindergarten, the faster their growth in word recognition in first grade was. For the more advanced kindergarten children, however, more kindergarten letter–sound instruction was associated with slower growth in kindergarten (compared with their comparably endowed peers who received little such instruction but instead engaged in more reading and similar activities).

That is the conundrum for early literacy: how to balance phonics with other activities and especially how to manage differential instruction. Looking even more carefully at the observational data, we first wanted to understand why there was one particularly successful kindergarten for all the children. This was a kindergarten with the common three-heterogeneous-groups structure. In terms of sheer division of the group instruction, the class was low average in terms of percentage letter–sound instruction (22%), relatively high in word instruction (26%), and one of the highest in involving children in reading (33%). We never observed text writing in this class, and read-alouds and oral language were low average (17%). Perhaps this balance worked for these children in terms of their word recognition growth. On average, children who came in below the mean on the WRAT grew 22 points in their WRAT standard scores by the end of the year, whereas children who entered kindergarten with above-average letter–sound knowledge grew 5 points. We suspected that the division of activities was not the only positive driving force. And here we were glad that we had the small-grained level of the observation narratives to give us a hypothesis of what might be behind at least some of the success.

As we reread the classroom narratives of this front-runner kindergarten class, what stood out was the sheer number of times that *every* child was called on in each activity. In the course of direct group instruction, which lasted about 30 minutes, each child was called on an average of 10 times. We could tell this because we had recorded every child's name and response when he or she was called on. We then went back and recorded the number of times every child in the study was called on in language arts throughout kindergarten and first grade. It was clear that small-group instruction (whether heterogeneous or homogeneous in constituency) included calling both on more and on varied children than did whole-class instruction.

But how important was being called on? In a regression analysis predicting end-of-year kindergarten WRAT, two variables swamped the impact of all other skill and instructional variables ($R^2 = .71$): beta number of times called on = .542*** and beta raw score for WRAT at beginning of kindergarten = .976***.

We found a similar situation in first grade. Being called on mattered a lot, as did how the children entered first grade on the WRAT—this last one a predictable finding. In addition, development of Word Attack, as measured on the WDRB, and Sound Blending significantly influenced word growth. In two first-grade classrooms, the teacher had also been the children's kindergarten teacher. These two first grades demonstrated a high number of mean times called on, exceeding what the classrooms were like in kindergarten. Not surprisingly, these two classrooms, together with a first-grade class with a similarly high average number of "called on" children, topped the WRAT growth charts.

It is interesting that the teachers who remained with their students in first grade had not had distinctive classroom results in kindergarten nor more than average times-called-on scores. They distinguished themselves only in first grade. Certainly the two teachers knew the children well by first grade, and this may have contributed to the increased calling on *all* children. From the child's point of view, the consistency afforded by having the same adult as a teacher in two grades was no doubt important, too.

Overall, in 2 years of instruction—kindergarten through first grade—the factors that most predicted the WRAT at the end of first grade in regression ($R^2 = .71$) were raw score on WRAT at the beginning of kindergarten (beta = .31***), total times called on during the 2 years (beta = .21***), first-grade score on WDRB Word Attack (reading pseudowords; beta = .53***), and WDRB Sound Blending (beta = .17*).

I would be remiss and deny my roots if I didn't say that, at a macro level, in first grade the simple view of reading held sway. In a regression predicting the standard score on the Reading Comprehension cluster on the WDRB ($R^2 = .73$), WDRB letter–word recognition clocked in with significant beta at .76*** and the WDRB oral comprehension cluster at

.16**. However, at the top of my list of advice to teachers right now is simply to call on *every* child, and *often.*

CURRENT AND FUTURE DIRECTIONS

I doubt that the desire to follow people longitudinally will ever leave me, nor the tendency to collect almost too much data on them. (I am still analyzing data from the above-mentioned longitudinal study.) I am still passionate about observing interactions and learning in classrooms. I am still passionate about the promise of early intervention and tutoring and am currently conducting a study in that area. My new interest is a focus on teacher development. Together with my colleague Aki Murata I am studying teacher development from preservice to inservice years. We are involved in a longitudinal study, of course, comparing development in literacy and math. As I get older, there may not be any lengthy longitudinal studies ahead of me. But to *really* understand growth in reading skill, other researchers still have many more studies to do.

REFERENCES

Beck, I. L. (2006). *Making sense of phonics: The hows and whys.* New York: Guilford Press.

Beck, I., & Juel, C. (1992). The role of decoding in learning to read. In S. J. Samuels & A. E. Farstrup (Eds.), *What research has to say about reading instruction* (2nd ed., pp. 101–123). Newark, DE: International Reading Association.

Beck, I. L., McKeown, M. G., & Kucan, L. (2002). *Bringing words to life: Robust vocabulary instruction.* New York: Guilford Press.

Byrne, B. (2005). Theories of learning to read. In M. Snowling & C. Hulme (Eds.), *The science of reading: A handbook* (pp. 104–119). London: Blackwell.

Ehri, L. (1992). *Reconceptualizing the development of sight word reading and its relationship to recoding.* In P. Gough, L. Ehri, & R. Treiman (Eds.), *Reading acquisition* (pp. 107–143). Hillsdale, NJ: Erlbaum.

Ehri, L. & Wilce, L. S. (1985). Movement into reading: Is the first stage of printed word learning visual or phonetic? *Reading Research Quarterly, 20,* 163–179.

Gough, P. B. (1971). One second of reading. In J. Kavanaugh & I. Mattingly (Eds.), *Language by ear and by eye* (pp. 331–358). Cambridge, MA: MIT Press.

Gough, P. B., & Tunmer, W. E. (1986). Decoding, reading, and reading disability. *Remedial and Special Education, 7,* 6–10.

Guszak, F. J. (1985). *Diagnostic reading instruction in the elementary school* (3rd ed.). New York: Harper & Row.

Hoover, W. A., & Gough, P. B. (1990). The simple view of reading. *Reading and Writing, 2,* 127–160.

Juel, C. (1988). Learning to read and write: A longitudinal study of fifty-four children from first through fourth grades. *Journal of Educational Psychology, 80,* 437–447.

Juel, C. (1994). *Learning to read and write in one elementary school.* New York: Springer-Verlag.

Juel, C., Griffith, P. L., & Gough, P. B. (1986). Acquisition of literacy: A longitudinal study of children in first and second grade. *Journal of Educational Psychology, 78,* 243–255.

Juel, C., & Minden-Cupp, C. (2000). Learning to read words: Linguistic units and instructional strategies. *Reading Research Quarterly, 35,* 458–492.

Juel, C., & Roper/Schneider, D. (1985). The influence of basal readers on first grade reading. *Reading Research Quarterly, 20,* 134–152.

Konold, T. R., Juel, C., McKinnon, M., & Deffes, R. (2003). A multivariate model of early reading acquisition. *Applied Psycholinguistics, 24,* 89–112.

Plaut, D. (2005). Connectionist models. In M. Snowling & C. Hulme (Eds.), *The science of reading: A handbook* (pp. 24–38). London: Blackwell.

Seidenberg, M. S., & McClelland, J. L. (1989). A distributed developmental model of word recognition and naming. *Psychological Review, 96,* 523–568.

Stanovich, K. E. (1986). Matthew effects in reading: Some consequences of individual differences in the acquisition of reading. *Reading Research Quarterly, 21,* 360–407.

Wilkinson, G. S. (1993). *Wide Range Achievement Test—3.* San Antonio, TX: Harcourt.

Woodcock, R. W. (1997). *Woodcock Diagnostic Reading Battery.* Itasca, IL: Riverside.

3

RESEARCH ON STUDENTS WITH READING DISABILITIES

Sharon Vaughn

There are few professional things that are as worrisome to me as the thought that Isabel Beck is going to read what I am writing. This is the danger, of course, in contributing a chapter to a book in her honor. When I think of Isabel, I think of a woman who is relentless in her pursuit of understanding. Whether she is asking you questions about your latest research, totally invested in what you have to say and quick with the next question to be sure you don't get off on the wrong track, or whether she is telling you why commonly accepted reading practices are very unlikely to yield any decent outcomes for students, Isabel is sage. Her wisdom, insight, and right-minded research-to-instruction knowledge fills otherwise empty rooms with insights. With Isabel, you know that she will see through any lack of clarity or accuracy. In other words, you better speak and write with knowledge on your side.

INFLUENCES THAT HAVE
MOTIVATED MY WORK

From the time I was in first grade, I lived across the street from the Missouri State Psychiatric Hospital, since torn down. The hospital had acres of grounds that made an ideal playground for an inner-city youngster. In those days the place wasn't even gated, much less locked. Of course, I had to share my playground with the residents of the institution, many of whom were allowed to walk the grounds. Without revisiting the deinstitutionalization movement and my personal experience with it, I learned very early that I had an interest in and attraction to individuals with special needs. Twelve years later, when I started my undergraduate program at the University of Missouri, I decided to major in special education. At that time, the idea of learning disabilities was just being introduced, and I became fascinated with the idea of individuals who showed average or above-average performance in most areas but significant difficulties in one area—frequently, reading. That launched my interest, more than 30 years ago, in better understanding youngsters with learning and reading disabilities.

Early Work in Reading Disabilities

I recognized early that if I were going to understand and teach youngsters with significant reading disabilities, I would have to understand more than what was typically taught 30 years ago in classes for teachers preparing to instruct students with learning disabilities. Throughout the 1970s and even into the 1980s, many of the instructional practices focused on identifying underlying disorders, with limited attention to academic problems. There was a pervasive view that students with learning disabilities had processing disabilities (e.g., visual perception, auditory reception) that could be readily identified through assessments and that, once these disabilities were identified, treatment plans could be established and implemented to resolve these problems. Influencing this view of a processing model of identifying and remediating underlying deficits was the widespread use of tests such as the Illinois Test of Psycholinguistic Ability (ITPA) (Kirk, McCarthy, & Kirk, 1968; McCarthy & Kirk, 1968). According to Kirk and colleagues (Paraskevopoulos & Kirk, 1969, p. 26), "Each subtest was to measure one and only one discrete function. One process, at one level, via one channel, was to be measured by each subtest without contamination by requirements of another channel, process, or level." Unfortunately, the assessment and treatment of underlying processing deficits were not reliably identified, and corresponding treatments were not powerful enough to make discernable differences in academic learning (Hammill & Larsen, 1974; Larsen, Parker, & Hammill, 1982). As a result, focus on processing identification and treatment has been replaced with more academic assessments, progress monitoring using curriculum-based measures, and academic interventions. Much of this shift in how students with reading and learning disabilities are identified and treated is reflected in response to intervention (RTI) with the newly reauthorized Individuals with Disabilities Education Act (IDEA, 2004).

After graduating from the University of Missouri, I recognized that professionally I lacked two things: adequate knowledge about how to teach students with reading and learning disabilities and experience. Because I am chronically cold, I decided to apply for graduate work in the best institution with warm weather. At the time, Sam Kirk and Sydney Bijou had moved to the University of Arizona and, with other colleagues, were establishing the Institute on Learning Disabilities. I moved to Arizona, starting my master's degree program while I taught in the public schools. Teaching provided a startling introduction to just how little I knew about teaching children with reading problems. I enrolled in the master's degree program in reading so that I could learn the fundamental issues of teaching children to read and then subsequently the graduate degree program in learning disabilities so that I could learn more about teaching children with special needs.

Influencing my decisions professionally were a combination of whimsical choices based on personal interests (e.g., wanting to live in what appeared to be an exotic place—the desert) and professional goals, such as wanting to teach students with special needs (e.g., teaching in multiple grade levels, resource rooms, and special programs) and academic pursuits (e.g., recognizing that folks such as Sam Kirk and Sydney Bijou could teach me a great deal). My ultimate decisions seem much better planned now than they were at the time.

RESEARCH AGENDA

I have divided my research agenda into two sections. The first section addresses my early research, which I have deliberately made brief because it is of the least interest to me and probably to the reader. The second section addresses my current research.

Early Research Agenda

After teaching in such school districts as Flowing Wells in Tucson, Arizona, and the Hannibal public schools in Hannibal, Missouri, I decided that I was interested in pursuing a PhD. This much I knew for sure. When I decided to return to pursue a PhD, I had no idea what my research interests were. In fact, I was endlessly worried that I had no specific interests that I could hold onto. The most recent conversation in a doctoral seminar could send me off onto a new area of interest. Milling around in the "stacks" in the library could distract me for hours reading articles that were only loosely related to whatever paper I was trying to finish at the time. The only consistent focus I had was that I wanted to do intervention research so that I could have more confidence in what works for students with reading and learning disabilities. At the time that I was studying at the University of Arizona, scholars doing intervention research were in the Department of Child Development. I began taking classes in that department, teaching courses, and working as a graduate research assistant on intervention studies with young children with behavior problems. During these years, I wrote a preschool intervention for students with social and behavior problems, conducted several experimental studies evaluating its efficacy, and wrote these studies for publication. The work was not directly aligned with my academic interests, but it was exceedingly valuable to me then and now, as I learned how to write interventions, conduct experimental studies, and analyze and write up my findings. It was through my work in the Department of Child Development that I learned how to write papers for publication.

Current Research Agenda

As I reflect on my current research agenda, I'm reminded that my most consistent theme addresses improving understanding of effective practices for students who are typically provided the least effective instruction in schools. My current research agenda is organized around the framework of RTI, addressing three areas of current research: RTI with students in the younger grades, RTI with students in the older grades, and effective interventions for English language learners (ELLs).

Response to Intervention (RTI)

RTI is proposed as a framework for addressing the vexing problem that students may be identified for special education because they have not had adequate instruction to prevent reading difficulties. Essential to the effective implementation of RTI is universal screening; ongoing progress monitoring, particularly for students at risk; and layers of interventions provided in increasing intensity to support students in acquiring reading proficiency. The overall goals of RTI, then, are to identify students with reading difficulties early, so that appropriate interventions can be provided, and to ensure that students identified for and placed in special education are truly individuals with disabilities rather than instructional casualties (Fletcher, Coulter, Reschly, & Vaughn, 2004).

Fundamental to the acceptance of an RTI approach is the dismissal of the traditional IQ-discrepancy model as essential to determining the existence of a learning disability in reading. Within the past decade, significant syntheses have concluded that an IQ test is not necessary to the identification of a learning disability and is a costly process (e.g., Donovan & Cross, 2002; Fletcher et al., 1994; Francis, Shaywitz, Stuebing, Shaywitz, & Fletcher, 1996). The RTI framework, as applied to reading, is based on two key assumptions about reading and reading disabilities: (1) reading problems fall along a continuum from dyslexia or severe reading disabilities to superior reading, with biological, instructional, and environmental influences having some bearing on proficiency at all levels (Fletcher et al., 2002; Shaywitz, Fletcher, Holahan, & Shaywitz, 1992), and (2) there is a set of essential and well-integrated elements that requires systematic instruction for poor readers so they can develop a strong base in learning to read (Gresham, 2002; Jenkins & O'Connor, 2002; McMaster, Fuchs, Fuchs, & Compton, 2005).

The focus within an RTI approach is using a cut point to differentiate those who need instructional support from those who do not. This contrasts with approaches that impose a discrete set of individual criteria to determine whether students either have or do not have a reading disability. Applying the assumption of normal distribution of reading proficiency, poor readers would fall at the lower tail of the distribution. This tail would represent those students who read at substantially lower levels than would be expected given their reading instruction, age, and grade level. This view of reading disabilities uses a dimensional representation rather than a categorical one to operationalize the definition of struggling readers.

The dimensional view of reading disabilities aligns with an RTI framework because assessment and instruction are based directly on reading performance (Vaughn, Linan-Thompson, & Hickman, 2003; Vellutino et al., 1996). Essential to the implementation of RTI is the notion of ongoing screening, progress monitoring, and decision making about instruction. Interventions are not for an indeterminate period but are conceptualized as being for relatively brief periods, with exit from the intervention based on students' response to instruction. Typically, criterion-referenced assessments are used to determine who needs additional support in reading without consideration of the "cause" of the reading problem. Specifically, students who do not meet age- or grade-level performance in reading at specific times during the year are considered to be candidates for additional instructional support. Students who are provided additional instructional intervention and who fail to make adequate gains (thus the important role of ongoing progress monitoring) are determined to need ongoing intensive support and are candidates for referral for special services (e.g., special education) or to receive more intensive and individualized intervention. In summary, RTI frameworks seek first to prevent reading failure, and then, for those students who do not respond to intervention, assessment data linked to instruction are used to identify students who may require a more intensive intervention, perhaps through special education services. RTI is designed to prevent instructional casualties and to ensure that students who may be at risk are provided early interventions. RTI is conceived as a "safety net" to catch struggling readers before they fail in school. In some cases, RTI's implementation of early and ongoing appropriate research-based interventions makes the referral and identification of learning disabilities (LD) unnecessary.

Although RTI is recommended as part of the newly authorized law, IDEA (2004), there is inadequate research on RTI with older students (grades 4–12) in reading. There is also considerably less research in other academic areas (e.g., math, writing) than in reading. Fortunately for the sake of implementation, an RTI framework can take many forms and specific models based on the needs, resources, and preferences of particular schools or school districts (Batsche et al., 2005). Over the past 5 years, my colleagues and I have been funded by the Office of Special Education Programs within the U.S. Department of Education to conduct a longitudinal study examining the effectiveness of one of these frameworks, referred to as the three-tier reading framework. The three-tier reading framework has been implemented with students in grades K–3, in research settings (in which research staff delivers interventions and collects assessment data) as well as in practice (in which sites have implemented the model with their own personnel and resources).

OUR RTI STUDIES IN READING WITH YOUNG CHILDREN

An initial study of RTI used standardized multi-tiered protocols, which provided three increasingly intense intervention opportunities in 10-week time frames to second-grade students at risk for reading

problems (Vaughn et al., 2003). Students in this study received standard protocol instruction in fluency, phonological awareness, word
analysis, spelling, and instructional passage reading for 30 minutes
per day in 10-week increments. After each 10-week period, students
reaching criteria on reading fluency exited from the intervention. Of
the students who were given additional time in the standard intervention, many made progress and met exit criteria at both the 20-week and
30-week periods. But other students demonstrated insufficient response
throughout the 30 weeks and never exited from intervention. This
study provided valuable information about second-grade students'
RTI. We learned that (1) about 25% of the at-risk students made adequate progress within the initial 10 weeks of intervention, and most of
these students maintained their grade-level performances throughout
the year; (2) about 25% of the at-risk students made adequate progress
after the 100 sessions provided in 20 weeks, with the majority maintaining performance when no longer provided interventions, although
a number of these students "failed to thrive" with the instruction in
the general education classroom; (3) about 25% of the students needed
30 weeks, essentially a year-long intervention (150 daily sessions), and
reached benchmark for exiting from the intervention only at the end of
the school year; and (4) about 25% of the students did not meet criteria
for exit from the intervention even after 30 weeks. This study provided
us initial information about the variation in performance and the need
that some students would have for ongoing intervention to meet their
instructional needs.

In a series of subsequent studies conducted with young children
with reading difficulties (Vaughn, Linan-Thompson, & Elbaum, 2002;
Vaughn, Wanzek, & Fletcher, 2007; Vaughn, Wanzek, Linan-Thompson, & Murray, 2007), all first-grade students were screened, and those
meeting criteria for being at risk for reading problems in the fall of first
grade were randomly assigned to treatment and comparison groups,
with the treatment groups receiving intervention from the research
team and the students in the comparison group receiving typical school
services, which usually included additional interventions. At the end
of first grade, students were identified as either high or low responders to the intervention. Students who demonstrated adequate or better
performance (high responders) continued in the study, but only to be
tested, whereas students who scored below expectations (low responders) continued to receive intervention during the entire second grade.

Thus high responders received 1 year of intervention and low responders received 2 years of intervention.

The most important question about high responders was the extent to which their relatively positive response to intervention would prevent further difficulties and how their reading performance would compare with grade-level expectations at the end of second grade. We found that students who met criteria for exit from the interventions at the end of first grade after receiving either the research-based intervention or school services performed well within normative expectations on all critical elements of reading at the end of second grade. Their end-of-second-grade standard score means on the Woodcock Reading Mastery Test—Revised (WRMT-R; Woodcock, 1987) were at or above 100 for Word Identification, Word Attack, and Passage Comprehension. Additionally, the mean oral reading fluency scores for 1-minute cold reads on end-of-second-grade passages for students in the treatment condition were 82.65 (SD = 25.93) and 76.61 (SD = 18.48) for comparison students. Thus high-responding students from both groups performed within the average range on all critical indicators of reading success at the end of second grade.

As for students who were low responders at the end of first grade and who continued in intervention during second grade, we were most interested in whether the additional year-long intervention would assist them in compensating for their significant at-risk status and in closing the gap toward grade-level performance. The standard scores for students in the treatment group at the end of second grade were near average on the WRMT-R for Word Identification, Word Attack, and Passage Comprehension. The mean oral reading fluency scores for 1-minute cold reads on end-of-second-grade passages differed between treatment (46.57) and comparison (29.47) students. However, these fluency scores suggest that many students in both groups still showed labored and inefficient reading. These studies have taught us that the vast majority of early elementary students at risk for reading problems who are provided standardized interventions profit from these interventions. However, there is a small group of students (less than 5%) who continue to display significant reading difficulties even after intensive interventions (more than 2 years) have been provided. What we find noteworthy is that these students are likely to require specialized instruction for many years. Because these students did not respond to interventions that are typically effective, we apparently know the least about how to effectively teach these students to read.

OUR RTI STUDIES IN READING WITH OLDER READERS

The vast majority of research addressing RTI has been conducted in early reading. Recently, my colleagues and I (Vaughn et al., 2008) received funding from the National Institute of Child Health and Human Development (NICHD) to examine the effectiveness of an RTI approach with older readers with reading difficulties. There is currently little empirically based guidance for the applicability or effectiveness of RTI models for students in secondary school. In part, the reason is that the variation in reading-related difficulties is greater in older students. Some students require many of the elements related to reading difficulties in younger students, such as the alphabetic principle, word-reading strategies, and fluency. Other students may struggle with reading as a result of factors such as limited vocabulary and concept knowledge, lack of knowledge of comprehension strategies for reading diverse text types (particularly expository/informational texts), and low motivation for reading (Biancarosa & Snow, 2004).

Regardless of procedures used for implementing intervention with students with reading difficulties, essential to their effective implementation with older readers is confidence that the treatment protocols will be associated with positive student outcomes. Broadly speaking, there are two ways to conceptualize these treatment protocols or interventions: standardized or individualized. Researchers investigating effective reading interventions for younger students with reading difficulties typically use standard protocols of instruction (e.g., Lovett et al., 1994, 2000; Torgesen et al., 2001; Vellutino et al., 1996; Wise, Ring, & Olson, 1999). In standardized interventions, the critical elements of instruction are described conceptually, theoretically, and/or empirically and then linked to clearly identified instruction and practice routines. Although the materials and instruction are matched to the students' current level, the emphasis and procedures for implementing the instruction are similar for all students receiving the intervention.

Although many studies have reported improved outcomes for students following standard protocol interventions, individualized intervention is the hallmark of instruction for students with reading and learning disabilities (Cook & Schirmer, 2003). It is reasonable to think that individualized interventions may be of greater importance for older readers with reading difficulties, as they are likely to have previously participated in standardized interventions that were either insufficiently powerful or inadequate in other ways.

Individualized interventions are designed to provide differential instruction to meet the learning needs of students. The emphasis of instruction may change frequently throughout the intervention period to match changes in student's progress. Although individualized approaches have been used in practice (e.g., Ikeda, Tilly, Stumme, Volmer, & Allison, 1996; Marston, Muyskens, Lau, & Canter, 2003) and are referred to conceptually in the field of special education, limited data are available to document their effectiveness (Fuchs, Mock, Morgan, & Young, 2003; Wanzek & Vaughn, 2007).

Our goals for the 5 years of the NICHD project are to investigate through randomized control trials whether we can identify adolescents at risk for reading difficulties and successfully provide them with a standard protocol intervention. After conducting an initial study with middle school students, we intend to determine what proportion of these students with reading difficulties respond adequately to the standardized protocol after a 1-year secondary intervention. Our next series of experimental studies will address directly the effects of an individualized intervention compared with continuation in the standardized intervention. Through this work we will be able to descibe the RTI of subgroups of older students with reading difficulties and disabilities, including those who initially make adequate progress in intervention and then do not thrive over time and students who continue to make adequate progress in reading over time. We are currently conducting this series of experimental studies in seven middle schools in two sites in the southwestern United States.

EFFECTIVE INTERVENTIONS FOR ELLs

Research based on RTI with ELLs is less complete than that with monolingual students. To address this situation, my colleagues and I have conducted a series of studies with students who are bilingual (Spanish–English) and at risk for reading difficulties with the goal of determining the extent to which interventions are effective with these students and their overall RTI (e.g., Linan-Thompson, Vaughn, Prater, & Cirino, 2006; Vaughn, Cirino, et al., 2006; Vaughn, Linan-Thompson et al., 2006; Vaughn, Mathes, Linan-Thompson, & Francis, 2005; Vaughn, Mathes, et al., 2006). By conducting four large-scale experimental studies with bilingual first-grade students at risk for reading problems (two studies in Spanish and two studies in English), we were able to determine that bilingual students made gains on reading and reading-related outcomes when provided intensive (50 minutes daily) interventions. By following students through second grade, we found that students who engaged in the intervention in first grade maintained many of their reading gains over the comparison students even through the end of second grade. To determine whether the effects of these interventions are maintained over an extended time, we are following these students through fourth grade (Vaughn et al., 2008).

RELATIONSHIP OF RESEARCH TO PRACTICE

The instructional framework we are applying in both our standardized and individualized interventions is based on two critical components that reflect research on effective interventions: (1) mapping sound elements to print (letter–sound correspondence in beginning reading and then phonology of sound combinations for older readers) to build and read words rapidly and accurately (Beck, 2006) and (2) word and concept meaning, as well as reading comprehension strategies, to enable students to derive meaning from words and text (Beck & McKeown, 2006; Beck, McKeown, & Kucan, 2002; Klingner, Vaughn & Boardman, 2007).

One premise guiding our instructional design is that students with significant reading problems lack mastery of accurate word reading (Paulesu et al., 2001). Instruction, therefore, also addresses learning to read "sight words," or words that are less phonetically regular in English (Ehri & Wilce, 1983; Rayner, Foorman, Perfetti, Pesetsky, & Seidenberg, 2002). This approach applies a "buildup of reading skills" from easy to more difficult. However, even the easier reading skills are taught within the context of complex multisyllable words that are suitable for older readers.

A second part of our instructional design involves teaching comprehension through improving vocabulary and concept knowledge and increasing knowledge of how to understand and interpret expository and narrative texts. Thus the intervention is aligned with current research on developing vocabulary and comprehension (Beck & McKeown, 2006; Beck et al., 2002; Gersten & Baker, 2000; Jetton & Dole, 2004; Snow, 2002; Ulanoff & Pucci, 1999). The framework has compatible interwoven elements that include building and increasing skills related to word reading—including complex word types and regular and irregular words—along with daily instruction in vocabulary and comprehension with an emphasis on information text.

Finally, the instruction developed for both components of our framework is based on converging research on the benefits of explicit and systematic instruction in reading that provides many opportunities for students to read and engage in text and to respond with feedback while the teacher scaffolds instruction. Such instruction provides for the integration of word study, word recognition, and text processing, as well as construction of meaning, vocabulary, spelling, and writing, throughout lessons (see Baumann & Kame'enui, 2004; Beck & McKeown, 2006; Berninger et al., 2003; Foorman & Torgesen, 2001; Pressley, 1998; Rayner et al., 2002; Torgesen, Rashotte, Alexander, Alexander, & MacPhee, 2003). The instruction is intensive, as reflected in activities that require high levels of student engagement in learning critical content and opportunities to practice and apply new learning while reading and writing connected text.

Most reasonable reading researchers agree with what Isabel Beck has known for a long time: that is, that the debates about the appropriate content of reading instruction often consist of simplistic interpretations of whether phonics or whole language is superior. Consensus reports of research on effective reading instruction and effective practices for teaching students with reading difficulties and disabilities concur that learning to read requires instruction that integrates components of reading that involve decoding words accurately and understanding their meaning, fluency, and comprehension (Biancarosa & Snow, 2004; Donovan & Cross, 2002; National Institute of Child Health and Human Development, 2000; RAND Reading Study Group, 2002; Snow, Burns, & Griffin, 1998; Swanson, 1999a, 1999b; Swanson, Hoskyn, & Lee, 1999; Vaughn, Gersten, & Chard, 2000). For example, the National Research Council Report (Snow et al., 1998) stated that if students are to become successful in reading, teachers must *integrate* instruction involving the alphabetic principal (word recognition), teaching for meaning (comprehension), and opportunities to read (fluency). Similarly, research suggests that effective instruction for students with reading difficulties and disabilities should include explicit and strategic word recognition and reading comprehension strategies, with scaffolded instruction that provides modeling and feedback (Foorman & Torgesen, 2001; Swanson, 1999a, 1999b).

Even students with severe problems reading words correctly and automatically benefit from early and ongoing instruction that includes a focus on understanding and access to a variety of text types, as well as word reading. Indeed, integration of instructional elements at the word and text levels was identified as an essential feature of instruction in Denton, Vaughn, and Fletcher's (2003) summary of multiple syntheses of reading difficulties.

Interventions may vary in how they integrate these critical aspects of reading instruction and in how intensely they teach different components of word recognition, fluency, and comprehension. But it is the integration of these components that appears to be critical. We believe that there is now compelling evidence that no one component of reading instruction in isolation will yield superior results (e.g., either phonics-only or literature-only instruction). Rather, the issue is how to integrate components of learning to read so that the individual needs of students can be met.

FUTURE DIRECTIONS

From my research perspective, I think that future directions in reading will need to address two compelling issues: (1) how to improve word knowledge and world knowledge for students whose language and experiences do not adequately prepare them to understand and learn from text and (2) the development of effective interventions for students who are truly dyslexic and for whom learning to read is a lifelong process. Although these two issues are not directly related, they identify two vexing problems that have been unsuccessfully addressed up to this point.

From my practice perspective, I think that future directions will require a more knowledgeable cadre of qualified teachers who will be asked to teach students representing a broader range of backgrounds, languages, cultures, and contexts than teachers in America have ever been asked to educate. This will require a level of knowledge, skills, expertise, and sensibility that will be very difficult to find but that will be essential if teachers are to make the kind of impact we need to ensure a future nation of readers.

From a personal perspective, I can imagine education only improving with the steady influence of Isabel Beck. Whether she is breathing life into typically tired practices such as phonics instruction, helping teachers think about words and the myriad of ways throughout the day we can infuse vocabulary instruction into learning, or facilitating students' thinking about understanding text by questioning the author, future teachers and their students are in good hands with the guidance of Isabel Beck. Similarly, the research, policy, and practice fields depend on her wisdom, which we expect to see considerably more of through her continued research and writing. The following refrain, written by James Dammann (my husband) and me, summarizes some of my thinking on the powerful influence and sage advice consistently provided by Isabel Beck:

> Ode to Isabel
>
> A curious career is the study of reading
> It has wrong turns and byways and pitfalls exceeding.
> The Yellow Brick Road looks inviting beside it
> And we Tin Men and Scarecrows can hardly abide it.
>
> But if the "Wars about Reading" make the road look uncertain
> There's been Dorothy ... well, Isabel ... to hold back the curtain.
> She's shown us the way through this dread Poppy Field
> And developed new signs when the way was revealed.
>
> "What 'flying monkeys'? They're critters with wings.
> We'll just sit' em down and teach'em some things!
> Pay no attention to that face on the screen....
> Bring a bucket of water ... if you know what I mean."
>
> A career like this ... there's no way to frame it.
> To say "Isabel Beck" is the only way to name it.
> A tornado of talents that has kicked up the sand
> And pulled us along to find a new land.

REFERENCES

Batsche, G., Elliott, J., Graden, J. L., Grimes, J., Kovaleski, J. F., Prasse, D., et al. (2005). *Response to intervention: Policy considerations and implementation.* Alexandria, VA: National Association of State Directors of Special Education.

Baumann, J. F., & Kame'enui, E. J. (Eds.). (2004). *Vocabulary instruction: Research to practice.* New York: Guilford Press.

Beck, I. L. (2006). *Making sense of phonics: The hows and whys.* New York: Guilford Press.

Beck, I. L., & McKeown, M. G. (2006). *Improving comprehension with Questioning the Author.* New York: Scholastic.

Beck, I. L., McKeown, M. G., & Kucan, L. (2002). *Bringing words to life: Robust vocabulary instruction.* New York: Guilford Press.

Berninger, V. W., Nagy, W. E., Carlisle, J., Thomson, J., Hoffer, D., Abbott, S., et al. (2003). Effective treatment for children with dyslexia in grades 4–6: Behavioral and brain evidence. In B. R. Foorman (Ed.), *Preventing and remediating reading difficulties: Bringing science to scale* (pp. 381–418). Baltimore: York Press.

Biancarosa, G., & Snow, C. E. (2004). *Reading next: A vision for action and research in middle and high school literacy.* Washington, DC: Alliance for Excellent Education.

Cook, B. G., & Schirmer, B. R. (2003). What is special about special education? Overview and analysis. *Journal of Special Education, 37*(3), 200–205.

Denton, C. A., Vaughn, S., & Fletcher, J. M. (2003). Bringing research-based practice in reading intervention to scale. *Learning Disabilities Research and Practice, 18*(3), 201–211.

Donovan, M. S., & Cross, C. T. (Eds.). (2002). *Minority students in special and gifted education.* Washington, DC: National Academy Press.

Ehri, L. C., & Wilce, L. S. (1983). Development of word identification speed in skilled and less skilled beginning readers. *Journal of Educational Psychology, 75*(1), 13–18.

Fletcher, J. M., Coulter, W. A., Reschly, D. J., & Vaughn, S. (2004). Alternative approaches to the definition and identification of learning disabilities: Some questions and answers. *Annals of Dyslexia, 54*(2), 304–331.

Fletcher, J. M., Lyon, G. R., Barnes, M., Stuebing, K. K., Francis, D. J., Olson, R. K., et al. (2002). Classification of learning disabilities: An evidence-based evaluation. In R. Bradley, L. Danielson, & D. P. Hallahan (Eds.), *Identification of learning disabilities: Research to practice* (pp. 185–250). Mahwah, NJ: Erlbaum.

Fletcher, J. M., Shaywitz, S. E., Shankweiler, D. P., Katz, L., Liberman, I. Y., Stuebing, K. K., et al. (1994). Cognitive profiles of reading disability: Comparisons of discrepancy and low achievement definitions. *Journal of Educational Psychology, 86*(1), 6–23.

Foorman, B. R., & Torgesen, J. (2001). Critical elements of classroom and small-group instruction promote reading success in all children. *Learning Disabilities Research and Practice, 16*(4), 203–212.

Francis, D. J., Shaywitz, S. E., Stuebing, K. K., Shaywitz, B. A., & Fletcher, J. M. (1996). Developing lag versus deficit models of reading disability: A longitudinal, individual growth curve analysis. *Journal of Educational Psychology, 88*(1), 3–17.

Fuchs, D., Mock, D., Morgan, P. L., & Young, C. L. (2003). Responsiveness to intervention: Definitions, evidence, and implications for the learning disabilities construct. *Learning Disabilities Research and Practice, 18*(3), 157–171.

Gersten, R., & Baker, S. (2000). What we know about effective instructional practices for English language learners. *Exceptional Children, 66*(4), 454–470.

Gresham, F. M. (2002). Responsiveness to intervention: An alternative approach to the identification of learning disabilities. In R. Bradley, L. Danielson, &

D. P. Hallahan (Eds.), *Identification of learning disabilities: Research to practice* (pp. 467–519). Mahwah, NJ: Erlbaum.

Hammill, D. D., & Larsen, S. C. (1974). The effectiveness of psycholinguistic training. *Exceptional Children, 41*(1), 5–14.

Ikeda, M. J., Tilly, D. W., Stumme, J., Volmer, L., & Allison, R. (1996). Agency-wide implementation of problem-solving consultation: Foundations, current implementation, and future directions. *School Psychology Quarterly, 11*(3), 228–243.

Individuals with Disabilities Education Improvement Act of 2004, 20 U.S.C. § 1400 *et seq.* (2004).

Jenkins, J. R., & O'Connor, R. E. (2002). Early identification and intervention for young children with reading/learning disabilities. In R. Bradley, L. Danielson, & D. P. Hallahan (Eds.), *Identification of learning disabilities: Research to practice* (pp. 99–149). Mahwah, NJ: Erlbaum.

Jetton, T. L., & Dole J. A. (Eds.). (2004). *Adolescent literacy research and practice.* New York: Guilford Press.

Kirk, S. A., McCarthy, J. J., & Kirk, W. D. (1968). *Examiner's manual: Illinois Test of Psycholinguistic Abilities: Revised edition.* Urbana: University of Illinois Press.

Klingner, J. K., Vaughn, S., & Boardman, A. (2007). *Teaching reading comprehension to students with learning difficulties.* New York: Guilford Press.

Larsen, S. C., Parker, R. M., & Hammill, D. D. (1982). Effectiveness of psycholinguistic training: A response to Kavale. *Exceptional Children, 49*(1), 60–66.

Linan-Thompson, S., Vaughn, S., Prater, K., & Cirino, P. T. (2006). Response to intervention for English language learners. *Journal of Learning Disabilities, 39*(5), 390–398.

Lovett, M. W., Borden, S. L., DeLuca, T., Lacarenza, L., Benson, N. J., & Brackstone, D. (1994). Treating the core deficits of developmental dyslexia: Evidence of transfer of learning after phonologically and strategy-based reading training programs. *Developmental Psychology, 30*(6), 805–822.

Lovett, M. W., Lacerenza, L., Borden, S. L., Frijters, J. C., Steinbach, K. A., & DePalma, M. (2000). Components of effective remediation for developmental reading disabilities: Combining phonological and strategy-based instruction to improve outcomes. *Journal of Educational Psychology, 92*(2), 263–283.

Marston, D., Muyskens, P., Lau, M., & Canter, A. (2003). Problem-solving model for decision making with high-incidence disabilities: The Minneapolis experience. *Learning Disabilities Research and Practice, 18*(3), 187–200.

McCarthy, J. J., & Kirk, S. A. (1968). The Illinois Test of Psycholinguist Abilities: Its origin and implications. In J. Hellmuth (Ed.), *Learning disorders* (Vol. 3, pp. 395–427). Seattle, WA: Special Child Publications.

McMaster, K. L., Fuchs, D., Fuchs, L. S., & Compton, D. L. (2005). Responding to nonresponders: An experimental field trial of identification and intervention methods. *Exceptional Children, 71*, 445–463.

National Institute of Child Health and Human Development. (2000). *Report of the National Reading Panel: Teaching children to read: An evidence-based assess-*

ment of the scientific research literature on reading and its implications for read-ing instruction (NIH Publication No. 00-4769). Washington, DC: U.S. Gov-ernment Printing Office.

Paraskevopoulos, J. N., & Kirk, S. A. (1969). *The development and psychometric characteristics of the Revised Illinois Test of Psycholinguistic Abilities.* Urbana: University of Illinois Press.

Paulesu, E., Demonet, J. F., Fazio, F., McCrory, E., Chanoine, V., Brunswick, N., et al. (2001). Dyslexia: Cultural diversity and biological unity. *Science, 291,* 2165–2167.

Pressley, M. (1998). Comprehension strategies instruction. In J. Osborn & F. Lehr (Eds.), *Literacy for all: Issues in teaching and learning* (pp. 113–133). New York: Guilford Press.

RAND Reading Study Group. (2002). *Reading for understanding: Toward an R&D program in reading comprehension.* Santa Monica, CA: RAND.

Rayner, K., Foorman, B. R., Perfetti, C. A., Pesetsky, D., & Seidenberg, M. S. (2002). How should reading be taught? *Scientific American, 286*(3), 84–91.

Shaywitz, B. A., Fletcher, J. M., Holahan, J. M., & Shaywitz, S. E. (1992). Dis-crepancy compared to low achievement definitions of reading disability: Results from the Connecticut Longitudinal Study. *Journal of Learning Dis-abilities, 25*(10), 639–648.

Snow, C. E. (2002). Second language learners and understanding the brain. In A. M. Galaburda & S. M. Kosslyn (Eds.), *Languages of the brain* (pp. 151–165). Cambridge, MA: Harvard University Press.

Snow, C. E., Burns, M. S., & Griffin, P. (1998). *Preventing reading difficulties in young children.* Washington, DC: National Academy Press.

Swanson, H. L. (1999a). Instructional components that predict treatment out-comes for students with learning disabilities: Support for a combined strategy and direct instruction model. *Learning Disabilities Research and Practice, 14*(3), 129–140.

Swanson, H. L. (1999b). Reading research for students with LD: A meta-analysis in intervention outcomes. *Journal of Learning Disabilities, 32*(6), 504–532.

Swanson, H. L., with Hoskyn, M., & Lee, C. (1999). *Interventions for students with learning disabilities: A meta-analysis of treatment outcomes.* New York: Guilford Press.

Torgesen, J. K., Alexander, A. W., Wagner, R. K., Rashotte, C. A., Voeller, K. K. S., & Conway, T. (2001). Intensive remedial instruction for children with severe reading disabilities: Immediate and long-term outcomes from two instructional approaches. *Journal of Learning Disabilities, 34*(1), 33–58, 78.

Torgesen, J. K., Rashotte, C., Alexander, A., Alexander, J., & MacPhee, K. (2003). Progress toward understanding the instructional conditions necessary for remediating reading difficulties in older children. In B. Foorman (Ed.), *Preventing and remediating reading difficulties: Bringing science to scale* (pp. 275–297). Baltimore: York Press.

Ulanoff, S. H., & Pucci, S. L. (1999). Learning words from books: The effects of read aloud on second language acquisition. *Bilingual Research Journal, 23*(4), 409–422.

Vaughn, S., Cirino, P. T., Linan-Thompson, S., Mathes, P. G., Carlson, C. D., Cardenas-Hagan, E., et al. (2006). Effectiveness of a Spanish intervention and an English intervention for English language learners at risk for reading problems. *American Educational Research Journal, 43*(3), 449–487.

Vaughn, S., Cirino, P. T., Tolar, T., Fletcher, J. M., Cardenas-Hagan, E., Carlson, C. P., et al. (2008). Long-term follow-up for Spanish and English interventions for 1st grade English language learners at risk for reading problems. *Journal of Research on Educational Effectiveness, 1*(4), 179–214.

Vaughn, S., Fletcher, J. M., Francis, D. J., Denton, C. A., Wanzek, J., Wexler, J., et al. (2008). Response to intervention with older students with reading difficulties. *Learning and Individual Differences, 18*(3), 338–345.

Vaughn, S., Gersten, R., & Chard, D. J. (2000). The underlying message in LD intervention research: Findings from research syntheses. *Exceptional Children, 67*(1), 99–114.

Vaughn, S., Linan-Thompson, S., & Hickman, P. (2003). Response to instruction as a means of identifying students with reading/learning disabilities. *Exceptional Children, 69*(4), 391–409.

Vaughn, S., Linan-Thompson, S., Mathes, P. G., Cirino, P. T., Carlson, C. D., Pollard-Durodola, S. D., et al. (2006). Effectiveness of Spanish intervention for first-grade English language learners at risk for reading difficulties. *Journal of Learning Disabilities, 39*(1), 56–73.

Vaughn, S., Mathes, P. G., Linan-Thompson, S., Cirino, P. T., Carlson, C. D., Pollard-Durodola, S. D., et al. (2006). First-grade English language learners at risk for reading problems: Effectiveness of an English intervention. *Elementary School Journal, 107*(2), 153–180.

Vaughn, S., Mathes, P. G., Linan-Thompson, S., & Francis, D. J. (2005). Teaching English language learners at risk for reading disabilities to read: Putting research into practice. *Learning Disabilities Research and Practice, 20*(1), 58–67.

Vaughn, S., Wanzek, J., & Fletcher, J. M. (2007). Multiple tiers of intervention: A framework for prevention and identification of students with reading/learning disabilities. In B. M. Taylor & J. Ysseldyke (Eds.), *Effective instruction for struggling readers, K–6* (pp 173–195). New York: Teachers College Press.

Vaughn, S., Wanzek, J. W., Linan-Thompson, S., & Murray, C. (2007). Monitoring response to intervention for students at risk for reading difficulties: High and low responders. In S. R. Jimerson, M. K. Burns, & A. M. Van Der Heyden (Eds.), *Handbook of response to intervention: The science and practice of assessment and intervention* (pp. 236–245). New York: Springer.

Vellutino, F. R., Scanlon, D. M., Sipay, E. R., Small, S. G., Pratt, A., Chen, R., et al. (1996). Cognitive profiles of difficult-to-remediate and readily remediated poor readers: Early intervention as a vehicle for distinguishing between cognitive and experiential deficits as basic causes of specific reading disability. *Journal of Educational Psychology, 88*(4), 601–638.

Wanzek, J., & Vaughn, S. (2007). Research-based implications from extensive early reading interventions. *School Psychology Review, 36*(4), 541–561.

Wise, B., Ring, J., & Olson, R. K. (1999). Training phonological awareness with and without attention to articulation. *Journal of Experimental Child Psychology, 72*(4), 271–304.

Woodcock, R. W. (1987). *Woodcock Reading Mastery Test—Revised.* Circle Pines, MN: American Guidance Service.

4

LESSONS FROM THE READING REFORM FIELD

Janice A. Dole

This is not a research report but, instead, a report of a professional journey. It seems to me that, in my case, the journey is at least as interesting as the research itself. In this chapter I report briefly on research results, but then I turn to the more interesting story of the lessons I learned on a 15-year journey into school reform in reading. This professional journey involved more than three dozen urban and rural schools in reform because of low reading test scores. I have been involved in these elementary and middle schools at different levels—as a state office administrator, a technical assistant, a professional developer and an evaluator.

OVERVIEW

Although Isabel Beck and I have many interests in the field of reading in common, one aspect of the field that Isabel never wanted to deal with was the headache associated with the sheer scale of reform in reading. I am not sure just why this became a passion of mine, but it did.

My journey followed a path similar and parallel to the one laid out by states and the federal government in the late 1990s after the seeming failure of whole-language programs to have an impact on students' reading performance. At that time a flurry of activity began at the state and federal levels regarding reading. States began their own literacy initiatives, each state having an initiative titled with its own name—Utah Reads, Maine Reads, Florida Reads, California Reads— and so forth for all 50 states. These initiatives appeared about the same time that *Preventing Reading Difficulties in Young Children* (Snow, Burns, & Griffin, 1998) was being written and that the work of the National Reading Panel (National Institute of Child Health and Human Development [NICHD], 2000) was taking place. This large national reform effort was launched, in part, by at least three concerns: (1) the alarming decline in students' reading test scores in California, (2) lack of growth on the Nation's Report Card (National Center for Educational Statistics, 2009), and (3) growing research evidence that enough was now known about beginning reading instruction to assist all teachers in delivering a much higher quality of instruction than was currently being delivered (Snow et al., 1998).

It was in this context that I shifted my research interests and work. My own journey on the road of reading reform began with a small grant from the Utah State Office of Education (USOE) in the mid-1990s and continued with the design, development, and administration of the Utah Governor's Initiative on Reading (Utah Reads). While I was working under this small grant, the request for proposal came out for the Reading Excellence Act (REA; 1998) under the Clinton administration in the late 1990s. The goal of this federal project was to improve the reading abilities of K–3 children in high-poverty schools across the country. Funds were awarded to successful state grant applicants to implement school reform in local districts. USOE colleagues and I designed, developed, and wrote a proposal for that grant. When funding was awarded, I assisted in its implementation. Finally, in the early 2000s, a state office colleague and I developed and wrote Utah's Reading First grant. Reading First had the same goal as the REA—to improve the reading abilities of children in high-poverty schools across the country at the K–3 levels. I, along with colleagues John Hosp, now at the Florida Center for Reading Research, and Michelle Hosp, codirected the evaluation of Reading First in Utah over the 5 years of the project.

Learning Anew

Throughout most of my career as a teacher and researcher, I had not worked in high-poverty schools. As a teacher, I worked in working-class schools in Massachusetts, California, and Colorado. This work was quite comfortable for me, as it matched my own working-class background. As a teacher educator and researcher, almost all the work I did was conducted in middle- and upper-middle-class schools. My journey into a different kind of school began with the USOE grant, which involved my working specifically with high-poverty, low-performing schools. This grant eventually took me to a series of urban schools with largely minority students and to rural schools with poor white and minority students across the state of Utah. Although Utah does not have the same kind of urban poverty that exists in the most densely populated cities in the country—such as Los Angeles or New York—it does have both urban and rural poverty typical of many states in the country. Our minority students are mostly Hispanic, with a large contingency of native Spanish speakers and with many Native American students as well.

My work in the early grades of these high-poverty schools led me on a new learning curve. Up to that point, my own expertise and research had been on comprehension instruction. But now I had to look at a much broader range of issues in reading instruction. It forced me to gain expertise in early reading instruction. Although I had taught early reading in the classroom and I knew, at a practical level, how young children learn to read, I did not know the research, a fact that Isabel pointed out to me repeatedly: "You really need to know the research on early reading instruction." My new interest in reading reform forced me to learn a whole body of research I had not known. Of course, as usual, Isabel was right.

Another area I needed to learn much more about was systemic change. Although I was somewhat familiar with Fullan's (1991) work and the professional development literature (Guskey, 1995; Hargreaves, 1995; Hawley & Valli, 1999; Smylie, 1995), I did not know the research on systemic change nor on various school reform efforts, a body of work largely in the policy area (for reviews, see Berman & McLaughlin, 1977; Borman, Hewes, Overman, & Brown, 2003). It is this body of work that focuses on questions such as: What needs to be in place in order for schools to reinvent themselves? What needs to happen in chronically low-performing schools (Snow et al., 1998) to change the culture of the school? Just as I intuitively knew that it was not a simple matter to change instruction, I also knew that it was not easy to change schools and districts. I remembered quite vividly Goodlad's (1984) argument that change happens at the school level, but it was not clear just how it happened or what trigger points were needed to make it happen.

Finally, I needed more information about research on professional development, a disparate and sometimes fragmented body of work with few firm conclusions. The body of research is not scientifically rigorous, but it did offer some general principles to guide educators who wanted to design professional development to assist and support teachers in their work with students.

THE RESULTS OF SYSTEMIC READING REFORM

In the projects on which I have worked, some small growth has been evident, but huge changes have not. In all projects, districts were not as interesting as individual schools. Results vary considerably at the school level, with some schools profiting from the reform and others stagnating or yo-yoing. We have seen the yo-yoing effect in many schools, in which they make progress in the first 2 years and decline the next, only to go up again and then back down. A discernable pattern of steady, incremental progress does not emerge across the years.

In our REA project, gains or losses were measured at the kindergarten level by a state-developed kindergarten pre- and postassessment and at grades 1–3 by the state's criterion-referenced (CRT) language arts scores and the third-grade SAT-9 reading test scores. The SAT-9 was administered to third-grade students routinely in the state. REA schools were compared with a set of comparison schools, matched on test scores, socioeconomic status (SES), percentage of minority children, and size of school.

Results from 2 years of the REA project were mixed (Nelson, Fox, & Gardner, 2001). At the kindergarten level, there were no differences among kindergarten children on the kindergarten pretest between the REA schools and the comparison schools. However, REA kindergartners significantly outperformed the comparison kindergartners at the end of the 2 years of the project. On the CRTs, at the first-grade level, REA schools significantly outperformed comparison schools. At the second- and third-grade levels, however, there were no significant differences on the CRTs between REA schools and comparison schools at the end of the 2 years of the project. Also, no differences were found among third grades in REA and comparison schools on the SAT-9.

Thus the gains made by one grade were offset by lack of gains at other grades. What does it mean when test scores for kindergarten and grade 1 increased significantly from one year to the next and were significantly higher for REA schools than for comparison schools when grades 2 and 3 did not increase across years and were not significantly different from comparison schools? Is the project successful or not? These types of results might make sense to researchers, but they do not make sense to school administrators and legislators. Furthermore, they do not lend themselves to easy conclusions.

Outcome measures for the Reading First project have included the state CRTs as well as two different norm-referenced tests administered to grade 3 only. According to the state CRTs, Reading First students outperformed students in the comparison group and made greater gains than students in the state overall. In grade 1 across the 5 years for all three groups, students in Reading First gained 12% in terms of the percentage of students meeting the criterion for proficiency (43 to 55%) as compared to a gain of 5% for comparison schools (49 to 54%) and a drop of 4% for the state average (76 to 72%). In grade 2 across all 5 years, students in Reading First gained 4% (61 to 65%) as compared to 0% for comparison schools (both at 60%) and a 1% drop for the state average (77 to 76%). In grade 3 across all 5 years, students in Reading First gained 11% (49 to 60%) as compared to a 1% gain for comparison schools (56 to 57%) and a 1% gain for the state average (75 to 76%). These gains suggested at least some success on the part of Reading First to improve reading achievement for the state's most needy children and some success in reducing the achievement gap as well.

WHAT I LEARNED ABOUT SYSTEMIC READING REFORM

My work under the REA and with Utah's Reading First forced me to be concerned about a whole set of educational issues about which, as a reading researcher and educator, I had never been concerned. Although I knew how to deliver professional development for high-quality reading instruction at the school and district levels, there were many other components of large-scale systemic school reform in reading for which I was unprepared. I learned firsthand the substantial difference between the field of research and the field of evaluation. Issues that, prior to now, had never been important all of a sudden took on huge significance. For example, with which schools do we compare Reading First schools? Exactly who was being tested in Reading First? How will the professional development be delivered to the people who need it? Which programs and instructional approaches are acceptable and which are not? How do we engage the commitment of principals and keep that level of commitment? Where do we find high-quality reading coaches and how do we distribute them? How do we keep teachers in the buildings? What do we do with resistant teachers? In this section I discuss these important issues.

Comparison Schools Are in Reform, Too

One critically important issue arose for me when we interviewed principals in the comparison schools in Reading First. What became clear was that reading reform does not take place in a vacuum. In fact, all Title I schools, especially here in the 2000s, are in reform. When we compare REA or Reading First schools with "comparison schools," we are not comparing them with "control schools" doing nothing. Comparison schools were hard at work at reform as well (see also Mesmer & Karchmer, 2003). For example, we found out that almost all the comparison schools in the Reading First project had reading coaches at the school level. Comparison schools all used different core reading programs and, in addition, other professional development and intervention programs as well. Finally, they all used some kind of informal assessment with their students.

Thus, when all was said and done, many of the critically important Reading First components—a reading coach, a core reading program, extensive professional development, some type of intervention, assessment-driven instruction—were also in use in the comparison schools. This makes sense in that, as soon as Reading First districts saw something that appeared to work—for example, a reading coach, an intervention program, assessment-driven instruction—they immediately implemented that same instructional component into their non–Reading First schools. And, in fact, this was what we found. Thus the lines between Reading First and non–Reading First schools became blurred.

Interestingly, the *Reading First Impact Study: Interim Report* (National Center for Education Evaluation and Regional Assistance [NCEE], 2008) found that Reading First schools performed no better than a set of selected schools used for comparison purposes. My own experiences led me to agree with a major criticism of the report that many of the Reading First components were placed in the comparison schools.

Therefore, the study reported in the *Interim Report* was not a real "test" of Reading First. As G. R. Lyon (Shaughnessy, 2007) argued,

> Many non-Reading First schools were implementing the same programs and professional development opportunities as the Reading First schools. This impact evaluation is not a true experiment which could have certainly been done given the tremendous financial resources allocated for the evaluation. As Tim Shanahan has pointed out, the comparisons made were not Reading First with non-Reading First schools, but Reading First with less-Reading First schools.

Testing All Students

The question of who was tested on the outcome measures became an issue over the years of the Reading First project. This question never arose during the REA study. At that time we examined the test scores of students that the districts reported testing, assuming that all students were tested. In Reading First, a big issue became a definitive counting up and matching of the students who were actually tested as opposed to the students who were currently enrolled in the districts. Over the years, as districts have become more accountable for their students' test scores, some schools and districts began to alter the criteria for just who was tested. In some districts students who speak English as a second language (ELLs) were not tested, nor were students with learning disabilities (LD). Not testing these students obviously affects overall test scores and changes significantly the reported progress of the districts in teaching all students to read.

It took a period of 2 years for the districts to alter their testing procedures so that almost all enrolled students were tested. At the beginning of the project, about 90% of enrolled students in grades 1–3 were tested—both in Reading First schools and in comparison schools. In the third and fourth years of the project, 99–100% of students in Reading First schools were tested, whereas 95–98% of students in comparison schools were tested. The increase in the percentage of students tested is sure to have an impact on test scores. Although we do not know which students were not tested during those first 2 years, they are unlikely to have been students who happened to score the highest on the state CRTs. It is far more likely that the districts' lowest scoring students were not tested. This issue affected how Reading First reported prog-

ress to the federal government from year to year. In our case, the testing issue arose in both Reading First and comparison schools. We do
not know the extent to which differences in the percentages of students
tested affected comparisons made between Reading First and comparison schools. We do know that across the 5 years of the project, a higher
percentage of students were tested in Reading First schools than in
comparison schools.

Rural Schools

One of the most difficult issues I wrestled with was thinking about
delivering professional development and high-quality reading instruction to rural schools. Half of the schools and districts with whom we
worked were located hours away from the metropolitan area. One of
our most needy rural districts, located partly on a Navajo reservation,
was a 6-hour drive away—with no way to get there faster than by car.
So how will the knowledge needed to provide high-quality professional
development get there? How can the districts entice highly skilled reading professionals to these rural areas? What ended up happening was
that some of the rural districts hired any live bodies to fill slots because
there simply were no people available with enough knowledge about
reading instruction to deliver that instruction or to deliver the high-
quality professional development to enable teachers in the districts
to deepen their knowledge base about reading and to improve their
instruction.

Nevertheless, the USOE and the district were eventually successful in bringing in high-quality professional development. It was very
difficult to convince educators to move to this district full time. But the
USOE was successful at enticing professional developers to travel to the
district and spend a week at a time with the different schools. This was
no easy feat; some schools within these rural districts were located 30–45
minutes apart from each other. These larger issues were ones I had not
thought about, but they were essential to setting up the infrastructure
for the delivery of high-quality reading instruction in schools.

Reading Programs and Instructional Approaches

Another important lesson for me was the difficulty of mandating programs and instructional approaches to districts. It is one thing to talk

to colleagues or even other educators at a given school about preferred programs and instructional methods. It is quite another to be responsible for mandating a particular program or instructional method. The REA grant was one of the first federal grants to states and districts that came with assurances, restrictions, and requirements about instruction itself. It must be remembered that Congress authorized the REA grant in the late 1990s, just after the apparent collapse of the whole-language approach. The terms *scientifically based reading research* and *evidence-based practice* were coined and defined around this point in time. Programs and instructional approaches that were not "scientifically based" were discouraged from being used.

At that time, though, which programs and instructional approaches were and were not scientifically based was a debated issue (as it still is today). Even within the area of phonics, now accepted in the field as an essential part of reading instruction, there is still some debate about how best to deliver the instruction in phonics. Experts can look at two different phonics programs and not necessarily agree about whether either one is "acceptable."

In the initial meetings with the districts for the REA grant, most fought to keep the programs and instructional approaches they already had in place. This was foreseeable, of course, because the districts had paid considerable sums of money for these programs and were obviously committed to them. Although in general the actual requirements for "acceptable programs" were fuzzy, some programs clearly were not in the best interests of children.

Rural districts have often been vulnerable to home-grown, self-produced programs whose developers are mostly interested in financial success. State departments of education often helplessly watch as these programs are adopted by districts eager to implement anything that they think will make a difference. During the REA project, one district wanted to keep in place a professional development model that trained all teachers in a regionally but not nationally known tutoring program. The professional development provided teachers with knowledge about how to tutor individual students in reading. Then teachers were removed from their classrooms to provide the instruction to one student at a time while substitute teachers taught the rest of the class. However, approximately 85% of the students in the schools needed individual tutoring, as they were well below grade level. Because so many of the students needed tutoring, then, it was impossible for teachers to reach all needy students. In addition, substitute teachers, not regularly certified teachers, taught the rest of the class while the teacher was out of the classroom tutoring.

Eventually, the district did give up its tutoring program and invested instead in the kind of professional development model advocated by the project. It was a hard sell for the project administrators, but the district did come around and learn a better way to deliver professional development to their teachers, at the same time keeping them in their classrooms throughout the school day.

Because of problems such as these, the Department of Education tightened up its notion of acceptable programs and instructional approaches from the REA grant to Reading First, believing that the REA left too many doors open for schools and districts to use anything they wanted. Reading First therefore required, among other things, that districts faithfully follow a "core reading program." Serious problems plagued Reading First developers within the Department of Education as they tried to identify acceptable "core reading programs" and instructional and assessment materials (Bell, 2003). I have learned to appreciate that developing policy about acceptable and unacceptable programs is no easy thing to do.

Turnover

Teachers often lament the fact that so many students in Title I classrooms leave during the school year. Teachers say that if there were less turnover among students, then test scores would be higher, an idea that certainly makes sense. However, what I learned was that a significant factor in school reform was the turnover of the teachers, reading coaches, and principals. Throughout the 5 years of Reading First, we experienced about a 30% turnover in the teachers and reading coaches in the project. The percentage of turnover among principals has been lower but important, as well.

What that means is that each year about one-third of the teachers leave and new teachers come in. This is also true for reading coaches. Thus the strong professional development that takes place each year in Reading First for both teachers and reading coaches is diluted, thereby diminishing the overall knowledge base about reading. We have seen this more clearly with reading coaches because we are in the process of examining, through coaches' logs and direct observations, how coaches spend their time. Our observers remark that some coaches have little knowledge about their jobs, having missed the strong professional development of coaches that took place in the first few years of the project. The strongest coaches appear to be the ones who have participated in the project since it started.

Leadership

The role of principals is clearly one of the most important ones in terms of the success or failure of school reform (Berman & McLaughlin, 1977). The REA project and the Reading First grant found a range of interest and commitment to the project among the different principals who were involved. I learned about three important issues related to principals: (1) the principal's level of commitment; (2) the principal's sense of continuity and focus, both necessary to sustain change; and (3) stability in the position of principal.

First, principals involved in the REA project and Reading First differed in their commitment to the projects from the beginning. The level of commitment sometimes varied depending on who was most involved in applying for the grants. When the driving force occurred at the district administrative level, without much assistance from the principals, then the commitment of some principals tended to be less strong than it was when the driving force for the grant occurred at the school level. Districts were required to demonstrate participation from principals and teachers. However, the extent to which that actually happened varied by district. This makes sense, as a reluctant principal should not diminish enthusiasm for a project. However, because the principal is so important to school reform, such a move can eventually do more harm than good.

Although the level of commitment by principals varied greatly throughout the projects, certainly all principals were committed to improving their students' reading abilities. However, some were not convinced that REA and Reading First were the way to go to accomplish this. After all, when REA and Reading First were initiated, the targeted high-poverty schools were already heavily invested in school reform of some sort. So, in all the buildings involved in REA and Reading First, school reform already existed. Giving up what already was in place was difficult for principals.

As well, it was difficult for many principals to keep the focus on reading across the years. As soon as the second year of the project began, several principals in the REA project introduced other programs and projects into their schools—along with professional development for teachers that was in addition to the extensive professional development to which they were already committed. One principal had a keyboarding program all set to introduce in year 2 of the REA project, with additional professional development for teachers and additional time being used for keyboarding by primary-grade students. It was a difficult sell to convince principals that attention needed to stay focused on reading every year.

Still another issue related to the important leadership in the district was principal stability. Although the districts in Reading First assured us that principals would be placed in buildings for a period of 3 years, turnover was higher than that. New principals most often came in knowing little about the project in which the school was immersed. For some, their commitment to the projects was less than that of those who had been with the project from the beginning. Because the principal is so important to school reform, a less than fully committed principal makes reform far more difficult; in fact, a less than fully committed principal can be a serious barrier to reform.

Throughout both REA and Reading First, I never saw a successful school with a less than fully committed principal. Principals do not necessarily need to be instructional leaders themselves, but they must have a full commitment to change and to the particular approach to change being offered. However, a principal's commitment is necessary but not sufficient. We saw some schools with fully committed principals that still were not able to make the kinds of changes and gains we would have expected.

Reading Coaches

For some reason, reading coaches became a part of the REA project and Reading First. My guess is that state departments of education saw a need for professional development for teachers beyond the typical "one-shot" workshop and inservice sessions to which teachers have been exposed for decades. Educators and researchers alike are quite critical of this traditional professional development model for teachers (Fenstermacher & Berliner, 1985; Fullan, 1991; Hawley

& Valli, 1999). Very few studies have been conducted to determine the extent to which traditional professional development results in changes in teaching behavior or student achievement. For the most part, professional development is measured, when it is measured, by teacher evaluations at the end of the session (Hawley & Valli, 1999). The extent to which teachers actually change their behavior in their classrooms based on their professional development is largely unknown. So, despite the fact that there has been very little research on reading coaches, they became the standard for professional development in both projects.

What limited research there is on reading coaches suggests the important role that reading coaches can play in assisting teachers in implementing high-quality instruction in reading (Joyce & Showers, 1995). Reading coaches are master teachers who visit classrooms and support teachers in their daily workplace. The reason coaches can be so important is that they can bridge the divide between professional development sessions and teachers' workplace, the classroom (Dole, 2004). It is likely that the very best professional development is a good reading coach to assist teachers in learning new skills and strategies to teach. That coach has the opportunity to work with teachers in their classrooms, where the learning is most meaningful and where the transfer of learning is most likely.

In order for reading coaches to play a critically important role in helping teachers change their behavior in classrooms, coaches need to be in teachers' classrooms. That is the heart of the notion of reading coaches, yet that is a very difficult thing to do. The prevailing belief among many teachers and the classroom culture in general is that classrooms are private spaces, not public places.

One of the hardest things to do as a coach is to go into teachers' classrooms. This is often the rub. Some coaches, nervous that they may not be welcome in teachers' classrooms, choose to act more as managers of information and support staff to teachers than as instructional mentors. In their cluster analysis of how coaches spend their time, Deussen, Coskie, Robinson, and Autio (2007) found that reading coaches can take on many different roles—from manager-oriented to data oriented to student-oriented to teacher-oriented at the individual level to teacher-oriented at the group level. In the schools with which I have worked, only the most confident and competent coaches actually take on the teacher-oriented roles. It is far easier to take on the roles of managers or data experts in which coaches are supporting teachers but not mentoring them.

Resistance

A critical issue in school reform arises from the source of the proposed change—whether it be bottom-up, in which teachers decide to change a program or take on a new innovation, or top-down, in which district administrators decide to adopt a new program or innovation. I have directly observed bottom-up rather than top-down reform for most of my professional career. With REA and Reading First, I have learned much about top-down reform, especially about resistance.

First, I was surprised at how much passive resistance could be generated in response to reform. I had expected to see, and was not surprised at, active resistance to top-down projects. But I had not expected to see the more common passive resistance that was evident in the REA and Reading First projects. One aspect of the successful reform effort, Success for All (SFA) (Madden, Slavin, Karweit, Dolan, & Wasik, 1993), that intrigued me was the idea that teachers in schools needed to commit to a project and actually cast a vote to approve it. I had been impressed by SFA's requirement of an 80% approval rate before they would go in to a school to institute reform. Therefore, in the projects in which I was a part, I initiated a requirement that teachers in schools discuss the project and actually vote on it (a blind vote). In fact, in all the reform projects in which I have been involved, schools voted on their participation in the project. I believed this to be an important aspect of teacher buy-in.

What surprised me was the amount of passive resistance that I saw, even with the supposed buy-in. I first became cognizant of this phenomenon when I found out that virtually every school in which a reform project was implemented had voted 100% to implement it— but, months later, I would always find a few teachers who were resistant to the project. Why would this be so, when the teachers had voted for the project? Did the resistant teachers vote for it? Of course they did. These teachers had the options of leaving the building or changing grades, but they chose not to. Instead, they chose to passively resist the reform effort. This passive resistance was clearly visible to me in the REA project in the first year when one teacher, seeing me in my role as a technical assistant on the project, closed her door after she watched me go into neighboring classrooms. As I reached for her classroom door next to observe her, I found she had locked the door of her classroom.

In the annual end-of-year interviews we conducted with Reading First, most districts reported that a weakness of, or problem within, the project was teacher resistance. At the end of the first year of Reading First, I had a meeting with all the principals. At that time, I shared with them our first-year findings from the interviews about the barrier of teacher resistance, and I suggested that principals might want to think about removing these teachers from the K–3 classrooms. Principals balked at the idea; not one principal was receptive to the idea of removing or reassigning a teacher. Toward the end of years 2 and 3 of the project, however, we found that several resistant and/or incompetent teachers had been shuffled around and reassigned out of the K–3 classrooms. In years 3 and 4 of the project, teacher resistance remained an issue mentioned by some districts, but not all.

A SUCCESS STORY ... ALMOST

So, after many sojourns into reading reform, what do I believe now? They say that inside every pessimist is an optimist, and though I may appear to be outwardly pessimistic, I remain fairly optimistic in the hope of reform in reading. It is clear that we are having success in this country in improving the reading abilities of primary-grade children. Scores on the recent reading fourth-grade tests were higher than they have been since NAEP began in 1971 and significantly higher than they were in 1999 (National Center for Education Statistics, 2009). I attribute this increased performance to the rising interest and initiatives by states and the federal government in reading reform beginning in the late 1990s, including new reviews of research (e.g., NICHD, 2000; Snow et al., 1998), and accompanying funding at both the state and federal levels. Congress bolstered the amount of funds available at the state level, not only through the REA but also through Reading First, Early Reading First, and additional Title I funding and support. For all the criticisms of these programs, and there are many, NAEP scores suggest that they are having an effect on student primary-grade reading achievement nationally.

An Example of Success

Interestingly, one of my very first journeys into school reform in reading occurred at a middle school that was powerfully successful in reforming its reading program during the life of the project (Jetton & Dole, 2004). This success story occurred in a high-poverty urban middle school that had a large number of Hispanic students, many of whom spoke English as a second language. Although this is a middle school example, there are multiple success stories like this one across the country.

There were many things that differentiated this school from others from the very beginning. Interestingly, it was not the students who differentiated this school from others; the students were similar. It was the administration and the teachers who were different. The project began in the English Department with an energetic department head, as well as an enthusiastic vice principal determined to do whatever it took to get his school on track. Teachers in the department were also an energetic group who actively sought help and support for their English classrooms. These English teachers had a unifying sense of responsibility to their students, and they knew that what they had been doing for many years was no longer working with the current students they had. Perhaps most important, the teachers did not take this fact personally; they saw it as a part of changing times, and they wanted to do something about it. Additionally, they were uniformly grateful for the funds awarded to them to purchase books and for the reading coach who had come to help them. It was the only time in my 15 years of work on reading reform when the teachers, at the first introductory session, asked, "How soon can you come into my classroom?"

The vice principal, who gave his full support to the project, began with a critical question and a promise to teachers: "What will it take to implement this new program in your classrooms?" and "Tell me the barriers you are encountering and I'll find ways to fix them." His own personal support for the teachers and the numerous ways he eliminated barriers that came up were huge factors in the success of the project. For example, the teachers needed assistance in organizing the book orders for the library of novels and nonfiction books they had ordered; the vice principal provided secretarial support to order the books. Teachers could not find a place to store the books they had purchased; the vice principal found empty space for the books. Funds were not forthcoming for the third year of the project. The vice principal hounded the USOE for those funds to continue the project. In numerous ways throughout the project, the vice principal provided the support needed for teachers to be successful.

The reading coach and I developed a model for reading and writing instruction for the middle school grades, and the reading coach worked through elements in the model in a series of professional development classes for the English teachers, who received university credit for the classes. In addition, the reading coach worked with the teachers in their classrooms each month for 3 years. She modeled reading and writing lessons for them, observed them teach, and provided them with feedback.

The eighth-graders' scores on the SAT-9, the annual standardized test administered to all eighth-graders, reflect the success of the project. Prior to the USOE project coming into the school, the school's average on the test was at the 29th percentile. During the 3 years of the project, test scores more than doubled, going up from 29% in 1996 to 59% in 1997, 59% in 1998, and 61% in 1999, the final year of the project.

The Caveat

This particular project was funded for 3 years. Three years after that, as I was writing about the project, I looked up the school's reading test scores to see whether the school had maintained its growth in reading. To my amazement, I found that since the project ended, scores had declined each year for the following 3 years. At the end of 3 years after the project ended, scores actually fell below the level at which they had been at the beginning of the project (see Table 4.1).

I went back to talk with the English Department head to find out what had changed over the course of the 3 years since the project had ended. First, she indicated that there had been a more than 30% turnover in the teachers in the department. The new teachers did not have a history with the project, nor did they have a commitment to continue a project in which they had had no part. Over time, the goals and purposes of the project were lost. In addition, the vice principal had retired. He had been a significant linchpin in the success of the project. With him gone, there was no longer a leader with the vision and support so needed for the school's success.

The support provided by the reading coach and the vice principal, as well as the critical mass of teachers who began the project together, appeared to have been decisive factors in the school's success. The department head suggested that the momentum that the department

TABLE 4.1. Average Percentile for Eighth-Grade Students at One Middle School Reading at or above Grade Level According to the SAT-9 the Year the Intervention Began up to 3 Years after the Intervention, 1996–1998

1996	1997	1998	1999	2000	2001	2002
29%	59%	59%	61%	52%	36%	26%

Note. The SAT-9 was administered in the fall of each year. The intervention began in the fall of 1996 and ended in the spring of 1998.

had made had been gradually diluted without the teachers who had been a part of the project and without the vice principal and reading coach. Minus that support and consistency, the existing teachers who had been a part of the project were not able to sustain the momentum and the strong gains they had once made.

For 3 years, this middle school "beat the odds" (Langer, 2001; Taylor, Pearson, Clark, & Walpole, 2000). Other schools in the REA and Reading First projects did, too. It is possible. And the possibilities add up and make a difference. Despite all the unknowns and hardships inherent in reading reform, it still makes sense to use the best available evidence now known to try to influence schools in reading. The price of not trying is too high.

REFERENCES

Bell, M. (2003). The International Reading Association's review of Reading First grant recipients. *The Reading Teacher, 56*(7), 670–675.

Berman, P., & McLaughlin, M. (1977). *Federal programs supporting educational change: Vol. II. Factors affecting implementation and continuation.* Santa Monica, CA: RAND.

Borman, G. D., Hewes, G. M., Overman, L. T., & Brown, S. (2003). Comprehensive school reform and achievement: A meta-analysis. *Review of Educational Research, 73*(2), 125–230.

Deussen, T., Coskie, T., Robinson, L., & Autio, E. (2007). *"Coach" can mean many things: Five categories of literacy coaches in Reading First* (Issues and Answers Report REL 2007 No. 005). Washington DC: U.S. Department of Education, Institute of Education Studies, National Center for Educational Evaluation and Regional Assistance, Regional Educational Laboratory Northwest. Retrieved June 1, 2008, from *ies.ed.gov/ncee/edlabs.*

Dole, J. A. (2004). The changing role of the reading specialist in school reform. *The Reading Teacher, 57,* 462–471.

Fenstermacher, G. D., & Berliner, D. C. (1985). Determining the value of staff development. *Elementary School Journal, 85*(3), 281–314.

Fullan, M. G. (1991). *The new meaning of educational change.* New York: Teachers College Press.

Goodlad, J. E. (1984). *A place called school.* New York: McGraw-Hill.

Guskey, T. R. (1995). Professional development in education: In search of an optimal mix. In T. R. Guskey & M. Huberman (Eds.), *Professional development in education: New paradigms and practices* (pp. 114–131). New York: Teachers College Press.

Hargreaves, A. (1995). Development and desire: A postmodern perspective. In T. R. Guskey & M. Huberman (Eds.), *Professional development in education: New paradigms and practices* (pp. 9–34). New York: Teachers College Press.

Hawley, W. D., & Valli, L. (1999). The essentials of effective professional development: A new consensus. In L. Darling-Hammond & G. Sykes (Eds.), *Teaching as a learning profession* (pp. 127–150). San Francisco: Jossey-Bass.

Jetton, T. L., & Dole, J. A. (2004). Improving literacy through professional development: Success and sustainability in a middle school. In D. S. Strickland & D. E. Alvermann (Eds.), *Bridging the gap: Improving literacy learning for pre-adolescent and adolescent learners grades 4–12* (pp. 164–182). New York: Carnegie Corporation.

Joyce, B., & Showers, B. (1995). *Student achievement though staff development.* White Plains, NY: Longman.

Langer, J. A. (2001). Teaching middle and high school students to read and write well. *American Educational Research Journal, 38,* 837–880.

Madden, N. A., Slavin, R. E., Karweit, N. L., Dolan, L. J., & Wasik, B. A. (1993). Success for All: Longitudinal effects of a restructuring program for inner-city elementary schools. *American Educational Research Journal, 30*(2), 123–148.

Mesmer, H. A. E., & Karchmer, R. A. (2003). REAlity: How the Reading Excellence Act took form in two schools. *The Reading Teacher, 56*(7), 636–645.

National Center for Education Evaluation and Regional Assistance. (2008). *Reading First impact study: Interim report.* Washington, DC: Institute of Education Sciences. Retrieved June 4, 2008, from *http://ies.ed.gov/ncee/pubs/20084016/execsumm.asp.*

National Center for Education Statistics (2009). *NAEP Data Explorer.* Retrieved June 2009 from *nces.ed.gov/nationsreportcard/lttdata/report. aspx?p=1-RED-1-20083,20043,20041,19991,19961,19941,19921,19901,19881,19841, 19801,19751,19711-RRPSCT-TOTAL- NT-MN_MN-Y_J-0-0-5.*

National Institute of Child Health and Human Development. (2000). *Report of the National Reading Panel: Teaching children to read: Report of the subgroups.* Washington, DC: Author.

Nelson, D. E., Fox, D. G., & Gardner, J. L. (2001). *An evaluation of the Utah Reading Excellence Act Project: Vol. I. Total project report.* Salt Lake City, UT: Institute for Behavioral Research in Creativity.

Reading Excellence Act of 1998; Pub. L. No. 105–277.

Shaughnessy, M. F. (2007, June). *An Interview with G. Reid Lyon: About Reading First.* Retrieved June 2, 2008, from *http://74.125.113.132/search?q=cache:-_*

zBxCUqEsoJ:www.ednews.org/articles/13767/1/An-Interview-with-G-Reid-Lyon-About-Reading-First/Page1.html.

Snow, C. E., Burns, M. S., & Griffin, P. (Eds.). (1998). *Preventing reading difficulties in young children.* Washington, DC: National Academy Press.

Smylie, M. A. (1995). Teacher learning in the workplace: Implications for school reform. In T. R. Guskey & M. Huberman (Eds.), *Professional development in education: New paradigms and practices* (pp. 92–113). New York: Teachers College Press.

Taylor, B. M., Pearson, P. D., Clark, K., &Walpole, S. (2000). Effective schools and accomplished teachers: Lessons about primary grade reading instruction in low-income schools. *Elementary School Journal, 101,*121–165.

5

THE WORD GAMES

William E. Nagy

When I was first preparing for the talk on which this chapter is based, three words came to me as a possible starting point: *strong, attractive,* and *stubborn.* I was thinking, of course, about the correlation between vocabulary knowledge and reading comprehension.

Numerous studies have found there to be very strong correlations between measures of vocabulary knowledge and reading comprehension (Anderson & Freebody, 1981), with some of them as high as .83 (Nagy, Berninger, & Abbott, 2006). Correlations this high are also attractive, seductively so. Of course, even moderately well-trained researchers know that correlations do not establish causation. But it is also true that correlations of this magnitude are not likely to occur without there being a causal relationship at work somewhere. Thus the correlation between vocabulary and reading comprehension tempts one to infer a causal relationship, and the temptation is all the stronger because the causal links that come to mind are so plausible. Probably the first causal link one would think of is that having a big vocabulary enhances comprehension. Another, perhaps equally plausible, is that good readers, in virtue of their higher levels of comprehension, read more and gain more vocabulary through their reading.

However, the correlation between vocabulary and reading comprehension has also proven to be stubborn. Not that there has not been substantial progress and much knowledge gained about vocabulary instruction. However, I would say that we have had remarkably little success in our attempts to provide definitive answers to some of the most basic causal questions, such as, Does vocabulary instruction increase students' reading comprehension? and Does wide reading increase students' vocabulary size?

One theme for this chapter, then, is that, despite much hard work and many important gains, vocabulary has proven a rather stubborn area. However, in keeping with the purpose of this book, I want to emphasize even more the context for some of the hard work that has been done in this stubborn area—in particular, the friendly rivalry in vocabulary research between Urbana and Pittsburgh. At the Center for the Study of Reading at the University of Illinois, Urbana-Champaign, Dick Anderson spearheaded an extended program of vocabulary research that involved numerous colleagues and graduate students and that resulted in more than 30 technical reports, most of which were subsequently published as articles or book chapters. Likewise, at the Learning Research and Development Center (LRDC), Isabel Beck led a team of scholars in an extremely productive and influential body of vocabulary research.

These two teams of researchers managed to disagree at one point or another on almost every issue in the area of vocabulary learning and instruction. Of course, debate is hardly unexpected in literacy research. The phrase *the reading wars* has often been used to capture the tone of the disagreements that swept the field of early reading over the past 30 years. However, I chose the title "The Word Games" for this chapter because I think that the Olympics are a better metaphor for the debates on the topic of vocabulary during the same time frame. As a participant in this piece of research history, I would like to believe that the research teams at Urbana and Pittsburgh made a powerful contribution to our understanding of vocabulary acquisition and instruction, not just because of the excellent research done at each site but also because of the spirited though amicable competition between the two teams. In the next sections of this chapter, I sketch two main issues on which we have taken opposite sides: the role of learning word meanings from context while reading in vocabulary acquisition and the efficacy of vocabulary instruction as a means of improving reading comprehension.

Before getting to the issues, though, I'd like to give just a bit more personal context. I received my PhD in linguistics from the University of California, San Diego, in 1974. In the first few years out of grad school, I did not seem to be making any progress toward finding a niche in the world of theoretical linguistics. Then, through a series of improbable (I would also say providential) circumstances, I came to the Center for the Study of Reading at the University of Illinois, Urbana-Champaign, in 1978. This was the same year that Dick Anderson and Peter Freebody's classic article "Vocabulary Knowledge" came out as a Center for the Study of Reading technical report. My first year at the Center was spent analyzing a large corpus of oral language with William Hall. Soon afterward, I joined Dick Anderson's research team and began working on an analysis of printed school English (eventually published as Nagy & Anderson, 1984). It was about at this same time that Isabel and her colleagues were beginning work on their program of vocabulary instruction (first described in print in Beck, McCaslin, & McKeown, 1980).

I think that my initial contact with the Pittsburgh team was meeting Moddy McKeown at a round table at the American Educational Research Association (AERA) annual meeting in New York in 1981. I think we were the only two there, aside from the presenter; and after the presenter left, we continued the conversation. It must have been pretty soon after that point that Moddy began planning the colloquium at the 1984 AERA meeting, where the Urbana team's paper on the "futility" of vocabulary instruction was countered with the Pittsburgh team's paper on the "fertility" of vocabulary instruction.

I wasn't able to make it to that session, but I did get to participate in a one-on-one debate with Isabel at the National Council of Teachers of English (NCTE) meeting in Philadelphia in 1986. As I remember it, we did a good job of debating, disagreeing in public even more than we would have disagreed in private. The disagreements didn't stop us from going out to dinner together afterward and—at least as I remember it—enjoying each other's company.

It might have been 10 years or so before I ever read anything published by Isabel and her colleagues. Not that I didn't read their work, but waiting for it to be published would have been absurd. We were continually sending each other prepublication versions of our papers and benefiting from each other's friendly but critical scrutiny. I know that I benefited greatly from this exchange; I had entered the vocabulary research enterprise with a PhD in linguistics, but no background in education, and with numerous blind spots. Along the way, I believe I have become more eclectic, or perhaps better said, more nuanced, in my thinking about vocabulary. And there is another kind of benefit that comes from having a friend disagree with you: Competition is invigorating.

Now let's turn to some of the points of content in our disagreements.

LEARNING WORD MEANINGS
FROM CONTEXT

One of the seemingly simple questions about vocabulary that has stubbornly resisted a simple answer is, Does wide reading increase students' vocabulary size? A slightly more general version of this question is, How much vocabulary do students pick up simply while reading, without any deliberate attempt to learn word meanings?

The Urbana team started with a predisposition to believe that individuals with large vocabularies had gained them largely through reading. There was reason to believe that not much vocabulary instruction was being done in schools (Durkin, 1978; Jenkins & Dixon, 1983) and that traditional vocabulary instruction was not especially effective (Jenkins, Pany, & Schreck, 1978; Mezynski, 1983). Although some researchers had examined students' ability to infer word meanings from context, in 1980 there did not seem to be a definitive answer to the question of to what extent vocabulary acquisition could be attributed to reading.

Our first study on learning from context during normal reading (Nagy, Herman, & Anderson, 1985) revealed a modest but statistically significant level of learning from context. Furthermore, the amount of learning from context did not seem to vary significantly much by the nature or leniency of the measure of word knowledge used. In subsequent studies, we addressed a variety of questions, such as: Is there any evidence of learning words incidentally a week after reading? Are the results different for different kinds of words and different kinds of texts (Nagy, Anderson, & Herman, 1987)? What types of text modifications increase learning (Herman, Anderson, Pearson, & Nagy, 1987; Diakidoy, 1998)? Does asking children to pay attention to the words increase their rate of learning (Kilian, Nagy, Pearson, Anderson, & García, 1995)?

Most important, we found that children do learn the meanings of words while reading, even when they are not reading with the purpose of learning these words. A meta-analysis by Swanborn and de Glopper (1999) later confirmed the picture that emerged from our work—that children learn a modest percentage (about 15%) of the unknown words that they encounter while reading.

We interpreted our results as supporting a positive answer to the question of whether wide reading could be a means of increasing students' vocabularies. One might estimate, for example, that (1) if a student read 500,000 words a year (25 minutes a day, 100 words per minute, 200 days a year), (2) if 2% of these words were unknown, and (3) if the student learned 15% of the unknown words, then the vocabulary gain would amount to 1,500 words a year. This estimate admittedly depends on some extrapolation, but the numbers that go into them seem plausible. (Carver, 1994, presents evidence that 2% is an overestimate of the words not known by students, but it could also be argued that his method of identifying unknown words—self-report by students—is an underestimate.) If our extrapolations are anywhere close to accurate, the modestly ambitious goal of increasing student reading to an hour a day could produce gains matching even generous estimates of the average students' annual vocabulary growth (Beck & McKeown, 1991)

In their 1991 review of vocabulary research, Beck and McKeown (1991) did not challenge our findings, but they certainly did question our interpretation, on several grounds. Beck, McKeown, and McCaslin (1983) had already entered the context arena with the assertion that "all contexts are not created equal." Their examination of texts from two widely used basal reading series revealed that the contexts of words to be learned by students varied greatly in the amount of information they provided, some being nonsupportive and others even misleading. This finding is, of course, not inconsistent with our claim that a small percentage of words learned from context can have large cumulative effects; the point of that article is more to address unrealistic expectations that teachers may have about the effectiveness of context as a strategy for figuring out the meanings of new words that students encounter while reading. We would agree that in this regard it is important not to overestimate the power of context.

However, Beck and McKeown (1991) also called into question our optimism about the effectiveness of context as a contributor to long-term vocabulary growth. Deftly using a quote from other researchers to voice the sharpest part of this criticism, they pointed out that the effect of context in our studies might be characterized as "statistically significant—but minute" (Schatz & Baldwin, 1986, p. 448). Schatz and Baldwin's (1986) interpretation of our results is understandable, given that it comes in an article reporting null results; the students in their study learned nothing at all about the meanings of low-frequency words they encountered in context.

We would, of course, want to make a case for considering Schatz and Baldwin's (1986) findings to be an underestimate. For example, in their study they used relatively brief contexts and low-frequency words, that is, words that were likely to be quite unfamiliar to students. If words are learned incrementally, one small step at a time, more learning would be found in a study such as ours, which used natural texts in which a number of words would be partially known to students. When readers encounter partially known words in context, it is likely that even a modest level of contextual support could nudge a few of these words over whatever threshold of word knowledge is adopted for the test.

The most serious challenge to our optimism about learning from context as a source of vocabulary growth is the fact that those who need most to learn more words are the least likely to be able to benefit from it. McKeown (1985) had found (as had others; e.g., Shefelbine, 1990; Sternberg, 1987; van Daalen-Kapteijns & Elshout-Mohr, 1981) that the ability to infer the meanings of new words from context is strongly related to reading ability. It might be true that good readers pick up large amounts of vocabulary from context while reading. However, for less proficient readers, there are a number of factors that make reading a less promising source of vocabulary knowledge: They read less, they learn a smaller proportion of the unknown words they do encounter, and they may spend less of their reading time in texts that are intellectually challenging. So to advocate reading as the main channel of vocabulary growth would be to leave some students on the short end of the "Matthew effect" phenomenon.

Finally, those who were suspicious of our extrapolations suggested that the argument for reading as a major source of vocabulary growth was primarily a default argument: Vocabulary must be learned through reading because it wasn't clear where else it was learned. It seems reasonable to believe that persons with large vocabularies acquired them through wide reading because of the lack of other possible sources. In particular, it has been argued that vocabulary instruction in schools covers only a small number of words, perhaps 300 per year under good circumstances (Jenkins & Dixon, 1983), and that oral language—at least normal conversation, even among college-educated adults—is relatively impoverished in its vocabulary (Hayes & Ahrens, 1988).

Admittedly, the default argument is not a strong one, because, as Beck and McKeown (1991) pointed out, we know relatively little about how much vocabulary might be acquired through oral language in the classroom. Though normal conversation may not be rich in rare words (Hayes & Ahrens, 1988), it is quite likely that classroom talk, both lectures and discussions, is much richer than out-of-school conversations. And the number of words that teachers explicitly teach or explain during a school day undoubtedly far exceeds the number covered in "vocabulary instruction," narrowly construed.

Where Are We Now?

Swanborn and de Glopper's (1999) meta-analysis could be said to have resolved the question of the rate of learning word meanings from context while reading. However, the question of the efficacy of inferring word meanings from context while reading as a source of vocabulary growth remains unresolved. In the National Reading Panel report (National Institute of Child Health and Human Development [NICHD], 2000), for example, it is acknowledged that students learn words from context while reading. However, the National Reading Panel also found no evidence that increasing students' volume of reading had a significant impact on their vocabulary size. This is one reason that I would characterize vocabulary as a stubborn area to research: We know that children can learn words from context while reading, and we have a fairly good idea of the rate at which they do so. And yet the jury is still out on the question of whether having children read more is an effective way of increasing their vocabulary size.

One of the interesting differences between the Urbana and Pittsburgh lines of research on context was the relationship between learning from context and reading ability. McKeown, in line with the majority of researchers who had investigated this question, found there to be a strong relationship between reading ability and success at inferring the meanings of unfamiliar words. In my research with colleagues at the Center for the Study of Reading, on the other hand, ability effects were relatively weak and, in one study, not even statistically significant. For example, Pat Herman's 1985 dissertation—published as Herman and colleagues (1987)—showed a significant interaction of learning from context with ability, but students in the 99th percentile would have learned only a little over twice as much as students in the 3rd percentile. If the amount of learning from context reported in our studies could be described as "statistically significant but minute," ability effects of this magnitude might warrant the same description.

This discrepancy in results—the fact that Urbana studies on learning from context tended to find small or no ability effects, whereas studies done in Pittsburgh and elsewhere found a strong relationship between reading ability and learning from context—might be attributed to differences in methodology. One of the key distinctions is between incidental learning of word meanings and deriving word meanings. The Urbana studies focused on incidental learning: Students were given texts to read, in most cases without being told that word learning was the purpose of the task. Students were tested on their knowledge of word meanings from the text after an interval (of from 15 minutes to a week) without the text present. In McKeown's (1985) study, and in many others that found a strong relationship between reading ability and learning words from context, the task was deriving word meanings: Students were asked to infer the meanings of words with the texts present.

I would speculate that incidental learning from context and deliberately deriving meanings from context rely to a large extent on different learning mechanisms. Truly incidental learning might, for example, rely more heavily on associative learning, as exemplified by Landauer's latent semantic analysis model (Landauer & Dumais, 1997). A simulation based on this model succeeded in "learning" the meanings of words from context with no constraints, prior knowledge, or metacognitive abilities. Roughly equivalent to a connectionist network, this model simply gathers information about which words occur in the proximity of which other words. Such associative learning might be only weakly related to reading ability.

Deriving word meanings from context, on the other hand, is explicitly metacognitive: Students make hypotheses about the meanings of unfamiliar words they encounter and evaluate these hypotheses on the basis of the information the context provides. As Sternberg and Powell (1983) point out, the processes required to make and test inferences about the meanings of new words overlap substantially with those required for reading comprehension in general, so one would expect a strong relationship between reading ability and the ability to derive word meanings from context.

As far as I know, the hypothesis that truly incidental learning from context shows smaller ability effects than deliberate inferring of word meanings from context is consistent with the available research. Another reason I find this hypothesis appealing is the success that most children experience in oral language acquisition, which presumably relies substantially on their ability to learn word meanings incidentally from context. Studies that show large ability effects for learning from context tend to portray less able readers (McKeown, 1985) or younger learners (Werner & Kaplan, 1952) as having such difficulty with using context that one wonders how they have managed to acquire any language at all.

VOCABULARY INSTRUCTION AS A WAY TO INCREASE READING COMPREHENSION

A second stubborn question about the relationship between vocabulary and reading comprehension is, Does vocabulary instruction increase students' understanding of text? This question was addressed in a series of studies by Isabel and her colleagues on rich and intensive vocabulary instruction (Beck, Perfetti, & McKeown, 1982; McKeown, Beck, Omanson, & Perfetti, 1983; McKeown, Beck, Omanson, & Pople, 1985).

This line of research represents the most thorough examination of the impact of vocabulary instruction on reading comprehension that has been conducted. In addition to the high quality of the instruction used in the interventions, the work was exemplary in its use of multiple dependent measures (including accuracy of word knowledge, fluency of lexical access, and comprehension of text) and in the comparison of different levels of instructional intensity. This series of studies and additional publications that have sprung from it (e.g., Beck, McKeown, & Kucan, 2002) have been extremely influential.

The main finding from this series of studies was a confirmation of the instrumentalist hypothesis (Anderson & Freebody, 1981)—that is, that vocabulary instruction can in fact increase reading comprehension. Some might take these results as having put the final nail in the coffin of Urbana talk about the "futility" of vocabulary instruction. However, in the world of research, it is the sworn duty of colleagues to disagree with each other, and we in Urbana did not shrink from our duty.

As I mentioned earlier, in the debate over learning vocabulary from context during reading, Urbana researchers came up with findings that were challenged as being statistically significant but educationally irrelevant. In the debate over the effects of vocabulary instruction on reading comprehension, it could be said that the roles were reversed.

One of the critiques of the vocabulary studies of Beck and her colleagues was that the intensity of instruction was higher than could (or at least would) be maintained in classrooms. In the first two studies (Beck et al., 1982; McKeown et al., 1983), there were approximately 22 minutes of instruction for each of the 104 words taught (averaging across words in the "some" and "many" conditions, the latter taking part in at least twice as many instructional encounters).

In a third study—perhaps in response to this problem—the amount of time per word was less: 15 minutes per word averaged across the high- and low-encounter conditions (12 and 4 instructional encounters, respectively). It is likely that the high-encounter words received about 20 minutes of instructional time per word and that the low-encounter words received less than 10. However, the low-encounter condition did not produce significant gains in reading comprehension, despite the high quality of instruction. Thus these studies demonstrated that vocabulary instruction can improve reading comprehension, but there is no clear indication that this can be done with less than 20 minutes of instruction per word.

A related criticism is the small number of words that could be covered by instruction of this intensity. The first two studies covered 104 words. Furthermore, most of these words were relatively low in frequency or else (as in the case of *fast* meaning "to abstain from food") represented a rather low-frequency meaning of a common word. If one adds up the frequencies of all these words and includes all their morphological relatives, the total is less than 1,000 occurrences per million words of text. That means that after more than 37 hours of high-quality vocabulary instruction spread out over 6 months, students would know one more word per thousand words of text that they read than would comparable students who had not received this instruction.

It seemed unlikely to us in Urbana that knowing one additional word out of a thousand words of text would result in a measurable gain in reading comprehension. If vocabulary instruction were to result in gains on standardized measures of reading comprehension, the effect might be due to generalization of the instruction to knowledge of uninstructed words or to gains in metalinguistic awareness produced by the instruction (Nagy, 2007).

In fact, the initial study (Beck et al., 1982) did show generalized effects, with the treatment group experiencing greater gains on standardized measures of both vocabulary and reading comprehension. However, such generalization was apparently not examined in two subsequent studies (McKeown, Beck, Omanson, & Perfetti, 1983; McKeown, Beck, Omanson, & Pople, 1985).

Another possible critique of the Pittsburgh vocabulary instruction studies concerned the type of texts used. Reading comprehension was measured in terms of recall, and the texts being recalled were written specifically to incorporate the words that had been targeted in instruction. It is likely that these texts involved a higher density of low-frequency words and the use of low-frequency words in more crucial positions than would texts written for other purposes. These studies thus do not demonstrate that high-quality vocabulary instruction would produce comprehension gains for normal text.

Where Are We Now?

The Pittsburgh vocabulary instruction studies are an example of high-quality vocabulary instruction and a powerful demonstration that the instrumentalist hypothesis is, at least under some circumstances, true. However, maintaining my stance of collegial skepticism, I would argue that the impact of vocabulary instruction on reading comprehension is another case in which vocabulary has proved to be a very stubborn field to research. There have certainly been some very promising studies, and the Stahl and Fairbanks (1986) meta-analysis certainly comes down on the instrumentalist side. But published studies since then showing an impact of vocabulary instruction on reading comprehension are rare. Mary Beth Curtis reports vocabulary interventions that have led to substantial gains on standardized measures of reading comprehension (Curtis & Longo, 2001), but the recent large-scale published studies I am aware of either did not use standardized measures of comprehension (Carlo et al., 2004) or did not find significant effects for such measures (Foorman, Seals, Anthony, & Pollard-Durodola, 2003).

Furthermore, even when there is some evidence of the impact of teaching words on generalized measures of comprehension, I don't think we have any clear idea of what the mechanism is. Is it because students became familiar with key high-utility academic vocabulary? Is it because they have become more familiar with how the academic register works? Is it because they are more aware of words?

Having stressed what I see to be the lack of a clear resolution on this issue, I must hasten to add that I think the debate has been highly profitable. In particular, the debate over the futility or fertility of vocabulary instruction has led to a far more focused discussion about the choice of words for instruction, as seen, for example, in the last three chapters of Hiebert and Kamil's (2005) book (Beck, McKeown, & Kucan, 2005; Biemiller, 2005; Hiebert, 2005) or in the symposium on choosing words at AERA in 2006. Although serious differences of opinion remain in this more focused debate, as well, I believe that it will have very concrete and practical benefits for future approaches to vocabulary instruction.

POINTS OF CONVERGENCE

Controversy is more intellectually stimulating than unanimity, and we have certainly enjoyed taking opposite positions as often as possible. However, I would guess that the number of points that we agree on is increasing and also greater than the number of points we disagree on. I remember my conversation with Isabel right after our 1986 debate at NCTE in Philadelphia. We realized that our respective positions—when we got to sit down and work on the details a little—were far closer than our debate would have suggested.

There are numerous points at which lines of research done in Pittsburgh and Urbana have been complementary. Here I'd like to mention just one example: the way that both have demonstrated the incremental nature of word learning.

It might seem obvious that word learning, like any other type of learning, is a matter of many small steps rather than a single leap. I think that there will always be a temptation for those who already know a word to expect others to get up to speed fairly quickly, if given a reasonable explanation and a few good examples. However, work done both in Urbana and in Pittsburgh has made it clear what a gradual process word learning is.

In the learning-from-context studies done in Urbana, we experimented with tests that were sensitive to different levels of word knowledge. In our first study, we used multiple-choice items at three levels of difficulty and scored students' attempts to explain word meanings on a scale with three levels. The following is an example of three levels of item difficulty from Nagy and colleagues (1985):

Level 1: *gendarme* means: a) to trick or trap someone
                                        b) policeman
                                        c) spoken as if one was out of breath or having trouble breathing
                                        d) the secret collection of information about another country
                                        e) the illegal transportation of goods across a border

Level 2: *gendarme* means: a) the illegal transportation of goods across a border
                                        b) weapon
                                        c) policeman
                                        d) face
                                        e) bravery during wartime

Level 3: *gendarme* means: a) policeman
                                        b) bellboy
                                        c) bodyguard
                                        d) spy
                                        e) waiter

One of the original motivations for looking at different levels of word knowledge was to test the hypothesis that readers gain only relatively vague or general information about words from context and require definitions to get a more precise knowledge of the word's meaning. If that were true, we would have found greater amounts of learning from context for the more lenient measures of word knowledge. However, there were no significant differences in amount of learning among the different criteria for word knowledge used. The results thus supported a picture of word learning in which word knowledge is acquired from context gradually, one small step at a time.

A later study with a test that measured five levels of word knowledge (Kilian et al., 1995) gave similar results. In this test, students were asked to respond *yes, no,* or *don't know* to five brief, randomly ordered questions containing the target word that represented five different levels of specificity, as in the following examples:

Do *toss* like to fish?
Can a bell *toss*?
Can a person *toss* a real house?
Is *tossing* a way of throwing?
Is *tossing* something you do gently?

Interestingly, when the word was used as the level of analysis, such a combination of items was more highly correlated with an interview-based assessment of word knowledge than was a single item from a standardized measure of vocabulary knowledge (Stallman et al., 1995).

The instructional studies at LRDC likewise demonstrated word learning to be a process of many small steps. In this case, the incremental nature of word learning was dramatically illustrated by the number of high-quality instructional encounters students can have with words before reaching a ceiling. In these studies, some measures featured significant differences between the "many" and "some" conditions, in which the "some" condition involved 10–18 instructional encounters with a word and the "many" condition 26–40 instructional encounters. That is, even after 18 encounters with a word, in vocabulary instruction of much higher quality than is normally found in schools, students still have room to grow in their knowledge of a word.

Both lines of research thus support a thoroughly incremental model of word learning (Nagy & Scott, 2000), underlining the importance of repetition and review in vocabulary instruction. More generally, I think it is safe to say that the Urbana–Pittsburgh vocabulary rivalry helped contribute to a "both/and," multifaceted conception of vocabulary instruction (Graves, 1986, 2000, 2006).

SOME FUTURE DIRECTIONS

I think that one of the most promising directions for vocabulary research in the future is to explore the role of metalinguistic awareness in word learning. How does students' (and teachers') awareness of language and knowledge about language contribute to their vocabulary growth?

Metalinguistic awareness in the area of vocabulary is commonly referred to as *word consciousness* (Graves & Watts-Taffe, 2002). In fact, this is the name of one of Mike Graves's (2000, 2006) four components of an effective vocabulary program. Although I am certainly in favor of promoting word consciousness, one concern I have about the use of this term is the possibility that it might be understood too narrowly. When I hear the term *word consciousness*, the first thing that comes to mind is wordplay—puns, hink pinks, word histories. These are all good things and can be very motivating. A certain level of frivolity may sometimes help counterbalance the hard work that is involved in learning words. Learning to use new words is also an emotionally risky enterprise—making mistakes in front of one's peers can be painful—so an attitude of playfulness concerning language may be crucial in enabling students to take appropriate linguistic risks that are necessary to expanding one's productive vocabulary.

However, I would hope that we can communicate an understanding of word consciousness that puts more of a value on appreciation than on entertainment. It's fun to learn about odd names for streets and towns and about words such as *boycott* and *sandwich* that can be traced back to the names of specific individuals (see Johnson, Johnson, & Schlichting, 2004, for an excellent overview of many fascinating aspects of words). However, I would like to see an even stronger emphasis on helping students experience the power of words (see Scott & Nagy, 2004).

A related problem I have with the term *word consciousness* is the danger of focusing only at the level of individual words. I certainly believe that looking at words in isolation is a legitimate activity. One wouldn't want to stop in the middle of a story, for example, to explore all the words that could be derived from the word *act* by adding prefixes and suffixes. On the other hand, neither can word consciousness be divorced from other aspects of language appreciation. Figurative language and other types of polysemy have to be explored in context. And I would also want teachers and students to understand that the power of words can involve not just the use of interesting words but also the skilled use of seemingly ordinary words. To me, perhaps the single best "word consciousness" prompt is "Write down a line you wish you had written" (Johnston, 2004, p. 16).

Word Wizard

One promising instructional application of word consciousness is the "Word Wizard" instruction, one of the components of the high-quality instruction in the Pittsburgh vocabulary interventions. Students were given Word Wizard points for bringing in evidence that they had seen, heard, or used one of the instructed words outside of the classroom. In one study (McKeown et al., 1985), this component was factored out, as the contrast between the "rich" and "extended rich" conditions, and was found to have a significant impact on some of the outcome measures.

To me, one of the most striking findings of this study was the effect that this component had on reaction times in the semantic decision task. As far as this measure was concerned, what they found was that four instructional encounters, plus the Word Wizard activities, got students to ceiling on this task. Four instructional encounters plus Word Wizard was not significantly different from 12 instructional encounters plus Word Wizard and better than 12 instructional encounters of rich instruction without Word Wizard.

I would like to see this finding replicated. I'd also like to see someone try to explain it. What is it about seeing or hearing a word outside of class that increases fluency of lexical access more than do eight additional instructional encounters inside the classroom?

Morphological Awareness

One aspect of word consciousness that I have been especially interested in recently is morphological awareness, the ability to reflect on and manipulate meaningful parts of words, such as prefixes, roots, and suffixes. Anglin (1993) has provided good evidence that children's morphological awareness plays an important role in their vocabulary development. One task that measures this ability is asking students about relationships among words: Does the word *teacher* come from the word *teach*? Does the word *corner* come from the word *corn*? Another task requires students to choose which version of a word best fits in a sentence context on the basis of suffixes: He had trouble making a (*decide, decided, decision, decisive*).

In the past several years I have been doing research on morphological awareness with Ginger Berninger and her colleagues at the University of Washington (Nagy et al., 2006; Nagy, Berninger, Abbott, Vaughan, & Vermeulen, 2003). Our findings indicate that morphological awareness makes a significant unique contribution to reading comprehension even when other important variables (e.g., phonological decoding and vocabulary knowledge) have been controlled for. These findings add to a growing body of research demonstrating the importance of morphology in reading (see Carlisle, 2003, for a recent review).

Perhaps one of the most striking findings from our research has been the strong correlation between morphological awareness and vocabulary knowledge—as high as .85 for the fourth- and fifth-grade students in our most recent study (Nagy et al., 2006). It raises any number of questions. Is our measure of morphology really just a measure of vocabulary? Or is our understanding of vocabulary knowledge too static, not recognizing the important role of metalinguistic awareness both in acquiring vocabulary knowledge and in taking vocabulary tests? Why does the correlation decrease between fifth grade and eighth grade?

Because it is so high, this correlation between morphological awareness and vocabulary knowledge is very attractive; there must be some important causal links lurking behind it. And no doubt this correlation will also prove as stubborn as that between vocabulary knowledge and reading comprehension. I am eager to explore it further. And I can approach this research challenge with confidence, knowing that I have some good friends in Pittsburgh who will be happy to point out where I'm wrong.

REFERENCES

Anderson, R. C., & Freebody, P. (1981). Vocabulary knowledge. In J. Guthrie (Ed.), *Comprehension and teaching: Research reviews* (pp. 77–117). Newark, DE: International Reading Association.

Anglin, J. M. (1993). Vocabulary development: A morphological analysis. *Monographs of the Society for Research in Child Development, 58* (Serial No. 238).

Beck, I. L., McCaslin, E. S., & McKeown, M. G. (1980). *The rationale and design of a program to teach vocabulary to fourth-grade students.* Pittsburgh, PA: University of Pittsburgh, Learning Research and Development Center.

Beck, I., & McKeown, M. G. (1991). Conditions of vocabulary acquisition. In R. Barr, M. Kamil, P. Mosenthal, & P. D. Pearson (Eds.), *Handbook of reading research* (Vol. 2, pp. 789–814). New York: Longman.

Beck, I. L., McKeown, M. G., & Kucan, L. (2002). *Bringing words to life: Robust vocabulary instruction.* New York: Guilford Press.

Beck, I. L., McKeown, M. G., & Kucan, L. (2005). Choosing words to teach. In E. Hiebert & M. Kamil (Eds.), *Teaching and learning vocabulary: Bringing research to practice* (pp. 207–222). Mahwah, NJ: Erlbaum.

Beck, I. L., McKeown, M. G., & McCaslin, E. S. (1983). Vocabulary development: All contexts are not created equal. *Elementary School Journal, 83,* 177–181.

Beck, I. L., Perfetti, C., & McKeown, M. (1982). Effects of long-term vocabulary instruction on lexical access and reading comprehension. *Journal of Educational Psychology, 74*(4), 506–521.

Biemiller, A. (2005). Size and sequence in vocabulary development: Implications for choosing words for primary grade vocabulary instruction. In E. Hiebert & M. Kamil (Eds.), *Teaching and learning vocabulary: Bringing research to practice* (pp. 223–242). Mahwah, NJ: Erlbaum.

Carlisle, J. F. (2003). Morphology matters in learning to read: A commentary. *Reading Psychology, 24,* 291–322.

Carlo, M., August, D., McLaughlin, B., Snow, C. Dressler, C., Lippman, D., et al. (2004). Closing the gap: Addressing the vocabulary needs of English-language learners in bilingual and mainstream classrooms. *Reading Research Quarterly, 39*(2), 188–215.

Carver, R. P. (1994). Percentage of unknown vocabulary words in text as a function of the relative difficulty of the text: Implications for instruction. *Journal of Reading Behavior, 26*(4), 413–437.

Curtis, M. E., & Longo, A. M. (2001, November). Teaching vocabulary to adolescents to improve comprehension. *Reading Online, 5*(4). Available at *www.readingonline.org/articles/art_index.asp?HREF=curtis/index.html.*

Diakidoy, I. N. (1998). The role of reading comprehension in word meaning acquisition during reading. *European Journal of Psychology of Education, 13*(2), 131–154.

Durkin, D. (1978). What classroom observations reveal about reading comprehension instruction. *Reading Research Quarterly, 14,* 481–533.

Foorman, B., Seals, L., Anthony, J., & Pollard-Durodola, S. (2003). A vocabulary enrichment program for third and fourth grade African-American students: Description, implementation and impact. In B. Foorman (Ed.), *Preventing and treating reading disabilities: Bringing science to scale* (pp. 419–441). Timonium, MD: York Press.

Graves, M. (2000). A vocabulary program to complement and bolster a middle-grade comprehension program. In B. Taylor, M. Graves, & P. van den Broek (Eds.), *Reading for meaning: Fostering comprehension in the middle grades* (pp. 116–135). Newark, DE: International Reading Association.

Graves, M. (2006). *The vocabulary book.* New York: Teachers College Press.

Graves, M., & Watts-Taffe, S. (2002). The place of word consciousness in a research-based vocabulary program. In A. Farstrup & S. J. Samuels (Eds.), *What research has to say about reading instruction* (3rd ed., pp. 140–165). Newark, DE: International Reading Association.

Graves, M. F. (1986). Vocabulary learning and instruction. In E. Z. Rothkopf & L. C. Ehri (Eds.), *Review of research in education* (Vol. 13, pp. 49–89). Washington, DC: American Educational Research Association.

Hayes, D. P., & Ahrens, M. G. (1988). Vocabulary simplification for children: A special case of "motherese"? *Journal of Child Language, 15*(2), 395–410.

Herman, P. A., Anderson, R. C., Pearson, P. D., & Nagy, W. (1987). Incidental acquisition of word meanings from expositions with varied text features. *Reading Research Quarterly, 22,* 263–284.

Hiebert, E. (2005). In pursuit of an effective, efficient vocabulary curriculum for elementary students. In E. Hiebert & M. Kamil (Eds.), *Teaching and learning vocabulary: Bringing research to practice* (pp. 243–263). Mahwah, NJ: Erlbaum.

Hiebert, E., & Kamil, M. (Eds.). (2005). *Teaching and learning vocabulary: Bringing research to practice.* Mahwah, NJ: Erlbaum.

Jenkins, J., & Dixon, R. (1983). Vocabulary learning. *Contemporary Educational Psychology, 8,* 237–260.

Jenkins, J. R., Pany, D., & Schreck, J. (1978, August). *Vocabulary and reading comprehension: Instructional effects* (Tech. Rep. No. 100). Urbana-Champaign: University of Illinois, Center for the Study of Reading.

Johnson, D. D., Johnson, B. v. H., & Schlichting, K. (2004). Logology: Word and language play. In J. F. Baumann & E. J. Kame'enui (Eds.), *Vocabulary instruction: Research to practice* (pp. 179–200). New York: Guilford Press.

Johnston, P. H. (2004). *Choice words: How our language affects children's learning.* Portland, ME: Stenhouse.

Kilian, A. S., Nagy, W., Pearson, P. D., Anderson, R. C., & García, G. E. (1995). *Learning vocabulary from context: Effects of focusing attention on individual words during reading* (Tech. Rep. No. 619). Urbana-Champaign: University of Illinois, Center for the Study of Reading.

Landauer, T. K., & Dumais, S. T. (1997). A solution to Plato's problem: The latent semantic analysis theory of acquisition, induction, and representation of knowledge. *Psychological Review, 104*(2), 211–240.

McKeown, M. (1985). The acquisition of word meaning from context by children of high and low ability. *Reading Research Quarterly, 20,* 482–496.

McKeown, M., Beck, I., Omanson, R., & Perfetti, C. (1983). The effects of long-term vocabulary instruction on reading comprehension: A replication. *Journal of Reading Behavior, 15*(1), 3–18.

McKeown, M. G., Beck, I. L., Omanson, R. C., & Pople, M. T. (1985). Some effects of the nature and frequency of vocabulary instruction on the knowledge and use of words. *Reading Research Quarterly, 20,* 522–535.

Mezynski, K. (1983). Issues concerning the acquisition of knowledge: Effects of vocabulary training on reading comprehension. *Review of Educational Research, 53*(2), 253–279.

Nagy, W. (2007). Metalinguistic awareness and the vocabulary-comprehension connection. In R. K. Wagner, A. Muse, & K. Tannenbaum (Eds.), *Vocabulary acquisition and its implications for reading comprehension* (pp. 52–77). New York: Guilford Press.

Nagy, W., & Anderson, R. C. (1984). How many words are there in printed school English? *Reading Research Quarterly, 19,* 304–330.

Nagy, W., Anderson, R. C., & Herman, P. A. (1987). Learning word meanings from context during normal reading. *American Educational Research Journal, 24,* 237–270.

Nagy, W., Berninger, V., & Abbott, R. (2006). Contributions of morphology beyond phonology to literacy outcomes of upper elementary and middle school students. *Journal of Educational Psychology, 98*(1), 134–147.

Nagy, W., Berninger, V., Abbott, R., Vaughan, K., & Vermeulen, K. (2003). Relationship of morphology and other language skills to literacy skills in at-risk second grade readers and at-risk fourth grade writers. *Journal of Educational Psychology, 95*, 730–742.

Nagy, W. E., Herman, P., & Anderson, R. (1985). Learning words from context. *Reading Research Quarterly, 19*, 304–330.

Nagy, W. E., & Scott, J. A. (2000). Vocabulary processes. In M. L. Kamil, P. B. Mosenthal, P. D. Pearson, & R. Barr (Eds.), *Handbook of reading research* (Vol. 3, pp. 269–284). Mahwah, NJ: Erlbaum.

National Institute of Child Health and Human Development. (2000). *Report of the National Reading Panel: Teaching children to read: An evidence-based assessment of the scientific research literature on reading and its implications for reading instruction.* Washington, DC: National Institute of Child Health and Human Development.

Schatz, E. K., & Baldwin, R. S. (1986). Context clues are unreliable predictors of word meanings. *Reading Research Quarterly, 21*(4), 439–453.

Scott, J. A., & Nagy, W. (2004). Developing word consciousness. In J. F. Baumann & E. J. Kame'enui (Eds.), *Vocabulary instruction: Research to practice* (pp. 201–217). New York: Guilford Press.

Shefelbine, J. (1990). Student factors related to variability in learning word meanings from context. *Journal of Reading Behavior, 22*, 71–97.

Stahl, S., & Fairbanks, M. (1986). The effects of vocabulary instruction: A model-based meta-analysis. *Review of Educational Research, 56*, 72–110.

Stallman, A., Pearson, P. D., Nagy, W., Anderson, R. C., & García, G. E. (1995). *Alternative approaches to vocabulary assessment* (Tech. Rep. No. 607). Urbana-Champaign: University of Illinois, Center for the Study of Reading.

Sternberg, R. (1987). Most vocabulary is learned from context. In M. G. McKeown & M. E. Curtis (Eds.), *The nature of vocabulary acquisition* (pp. 89–105). Hillsdale, NJ: Erlbaum.

Sternberg, R., & Powell, J. (1983). Comprehending verbal comprehension. *American Psychologist, 38*, 878–893.

Swanborn, M. S. L., & de Glopper, K. (1999). Incidental word learning while reading: A meta-analysis. *Review of Educational Research, 69*(3), 261–285.

van Daalen-Kapteijns, M. M., & Elshout-Mohr, M. (1981). The acquisition of word meanings as a cognitive learning process. *Journal of Verbal Learning and Verbal Behavior, 20*(4), 386–399.

Werner, H., & Kaplan, E. (1952). The acquisition of word meanings: A developmental study. *Monographs of the Society for Research in Child Development, 15*.

6

THE ROLE OF WORD MEANINGS IN COMPREHENSION

Mary E. Curtis

At the core of Isabel Beck's work has always been her keen awareness of and abiding respect for education's need to connect research and practice. Given that, it is not so surprising that the contributors to a volume in her honor would all have histories rich in teaching and learning as a profession, as well as a topic for scientific inquiry. Many of the authors began their careers in educational settings, and they moved into research because they were stimulated by questions that arose in their classrooms or in the schools or school systems in which they worked. In my own case, just the opposite is true. I began my professional life thinking that I would spend it doing research in cognitive psychology. As opportunities came along, however, I found myself making choices that pulled me closer and closer to trying to figure out how to get better outcomes for learners through improving the practices of their teachers.

I began graduate school in 1972 as a research assistant to Alan Lesgold, working at the Learning Research and Development Center (LRDC) at the University of Pittsburgh. This was not long after Ulric Neisser's *Cognitive Psychology* (1967) had come out, and I was intrigued by the notion that complex tasks could be conceptualized in terms of the mental operations they involved and that engaging in some operations might affect task performances in different ways than others. Isabel was already working at LRDC, and she and Donna Mitroff had just published their monograph describing the rationale and design of the new primary-grades reading system, a phonics-based beginning reading curriculum they had developed (Beck & Mitroff, 1972). But for me at that point, a curriculum didn't hold as much interest as a theory; I was in psychology, after all, not education.

As part of Alan's group, I assisted on research projects related to the role of mental imagery on memory for prose. This was right after Allan Paivio had published *Imagery and Verbal Processes* (1971), and we were interested in seeing whether imagery would facilitate learning from prose. The results from a series of studies (Lesgold et al., 1974), including my master's thesis (Curtis, 1975), kept pointing us to the conclusion that any positive effect found from instructing readers to image was more likely due to increasing their depth of processing than to making a second nonverbal coding system available to them. For me personally, though, the imagery studies produced another, even more compelling finding. Regardless of what we instructed them to do, quite a few of the undergraduates who participated in the research demonstrated a great deal of difficulty in remembering much from what they had read. This came as a surprise to me, and from that time forward, reading stopped being worthy of study just because it was a complex cognitive process. I now had new questions that I needed answers for, starting with how reading develops, and what fails to develop—or develops differently—in those who have reading difficulties.

IDENTIFYING DEVELOPMENTAL AND INDIVIDUAL DIFFERENCES IN READING ABILITY

My first venture into the study of reading as an educational process was as a research assistant on a longitudinal study of children at different points as they learned to read. The children were being taught with the reading curriculum mentioned earlier that Isabel had developed (Beck & Mitroff, 1972), one that the National Reading Panel would later include in its evaluation of the effects of systematic and explicit phonics instruction (National Institute of Child Health and Human Development [NICHD], 2000). In the study we tested children as they completed various portions of their curriculum, and among the tasks we used were ones that assessed children's rate of processing words in isolation, as well as their accuracy and rate in reading aloud from text. One aspect of their oral reading we were interested in was the kinds of reading errors that the children made. Because of its emphasis on phonics, some had wondered whether the program would end up producing children who were not making sense of what they were reading. We found little cause for any concern, however, as a miscue analysis of the children's errors showed them to be contextually appropriate the majority of the time (Lesgold & Curtis, 1981). A second aspect of interest—and one that turned out to be significant in terms of the children's later reading achievement—was their oral reading rate. We found that although nearly all of the children increased their reading rates fairly rapidly as they proceeded through the curriculum, a great deal of variation existed among their actual rates. And when we looked at the children's scores on a standardized test of reading achievement at the beginning of third grade, we found that we could have predicted their test performances solely on the basis of their oral reading rates during their first year of reading instruction. The higher ability readers were faster than the lower ability readers as early as November of the first grade, and they remained so throughout the first few years of their reading instruction (see also Lesgold, Curtis, Roth, Resnick, & Beck, 1980).

Our work on the longitudinal study was taking place within the context of larger discussions at LRDC and elsewhere about how efficiency in lower level, print-based skills affects the success of higher level, meaning-based processing (see, e.g., Perfetti & Lesgold, 1979). According to what came to be called *verbal efficiency theory*, accuracy in reading words was viewed as a necessary but not a sufficient requisite for skilled comprehension. Beyond being accurate, word reading needed to happen in a more or less effortless way (i.e., without requiring conscious processing) in order for readers to be able to devote attention to comprehending what they read.

This led me to wonder whether lower ability readers started out with adequate comprehension ability and just were not getting the opportunity to demonstrate it because of inadequate print skills or whether less-skilled readers were also less skilled at comprehending. So in my thesis I took an initial look at how print and meaning skills might account for differences in reading ability by comparing younger and less-skilled readers with older skilled readers (Curtis, 1980). Isabel arranged for me to assess children from two schools that she had been working with, both from a working-class, racially balanced urban district. I selected 100 children to participate, based on their prior year's reading achievement scores. Students reading at the level expected for their grade placement made up three of the groups: 20 second-graders,

20 third-graders, and 20 fifth-graders. Students reading below grade level made up the other two groups: 20 third-graders reading at about a second-grade level and 20 fifth-graders reading at about a third-grade level.

I assessed print skills using matching and vocalization tasks. In the matching tasks, the children were shown upper- and lowercase pairs of stimuli that included letters, words, and nonsense words and asked to say whether the pairs matched. The dependent variable was the speed with which the child made a correct judgment. In the vocalization task, the children were shown letters, words, and nonsense words and asked to read them out loud. This time the dependent variable was the speed with which the child said the name of an item. (Children were also asked to match dot patterns and to pronounce the names of letters they had already identified in order to control for differences that could affect the print-tasks results.)

I assessed meaning skills with a listening comprehension task. Children listened to graded passages and answered questions until reaching the point at which less than 60% of the questions were answered correctly. I estimated listening comprehension ability as the grade level reached immediately prior to the passage on which testing was stopped.

The results supported the view that development of skill in reading depends on development of efficiency in dealing with print. Consistent with the results from the longitudinal study, children's speed in matching verbal stimuli and in reading the names of letters, words, and pseudowords aloud increased with their age and was highly correlated with reading ability at all three grade levels. But the results also showed that, as speed in processing print increased, the amount of variance in reading ability attributable to performance on all of the print tasks decreased (from about 70% in grade 2 to about 30% in grade 5).

Listening comprehension also improved as reading ability did but did not vary between groups of children at different ages reading at about the same grade level. More significantly, however, the role that meaning skills played in explaining differences in reading ability seemed to increase as age and reading ability increased. For the second-graders reading at grade level, the correlation between reading and listening comprehension was −.26; for the third-graders reading at the second-grade level, $r = .34$; for the third-graders reading at grade level,

$r = .50$; for the fifth-graders reading at the third-grade level, $r = .57$; and for the fifth-graders reading at grade level, $r = .72$.

To find out to what extent a shift from print to meaning skills might underlie the differences in reading ability among the groups, I used a form of regression called commonality analysis. In a commonality analysis, the unique contribution that a variable makes is determined by the change in variance that is accounted for when the variable is forced to enter last into the regression equation. Among the second-graders, speed in reading words aloud made the largest unique contribution, accounting for 13% of the total variance explained (78%). Among the third-graders, listening comprehension was the largest single contributor, uniquely accounting for 23% of the total variance explained (71%). And among the fifth-graders, listening comprehension again made the largest unique contribution, this time accounting for 35% of the total variance explained (67%).

I interpreted this all to suggest that, although print processing efficiency may still be an important correlate of reading achievement at the higher grade levels, something underlying the connection between low-level and high-level processing explains reader differences as children grow older. At that point my focus turned to vocabulary, because both print and meaning are significant factors in vocabulary. On the one hand, accuracy and speed in decoding a word affects the probability and rate at which knowledge about a word's meaning is activated. On the other hand, the extent of knowledge about that word's meaning can affect how well it will be understood in context.

Isabel, along with Chuck Perfetti and Moddy McKeown (1982), had already begun investigating the relationship between print and meaning via an instructional intervention that came to be known as "robust vocabulary instruction." I began by comparing the performances of adults who had scored high and low on a multiple-choice vocabulary test on two tasks. On the first task, I asked the adults to read aloud the words from the test. This task yielded two scores: the accuracy and the speed with which participants identified the words. On the second task, I asked the adults to provide definitions for the words they were able to read aloud. The definition task also yielded two scores. The first score reflected participants' familiarity with the meanings of the words. To calculate that, I counted the number of words about which participants could produce any accurate semantic associations (e.g., "*confiscate* would be like smuggling—they confiscate it from you when they find it"). The second score reflected the precision of participants' knowledge of word meanings, and to calculate that I kept track of the words for which participants were able to provide synonyms or explicit definitions (e.g., "to *vacillate* means to waver").

Participants with high and low vocabulary scores differed significantly on all four measures. Relative to the high-skill group, individuals low in skill were not only less accurate in reading words but were also slower in vocalizing the words they could decode correctly. In addition, the individuals with low skill were familiar with the meanings of fewer words, and they were less precise in the way they defined the words with which they were familiar. Particularly striking was the tendency of the individuals with low skill to tie their definitions of the words to the particular contexts in which the words occurred. For example, *surveillance* was often defined as "what the police do in crime situations."

But when I looked at the relationship among all four of the measures and performance on the vocabulary test, I found that one measure was, by far, the most important: familiarity with word meanings. Getting a multiple-choice item right or wrong appeared to be a matter of whether participants had any accurate information about a word's meaning or not. Precision, or depth of word meaning knowledge, did not seem to matter on the test.

Because correct responses on a vocabulary test were possible with only a moderate amount of knowledge, it followed that raising vocabulary test scores required only increasing the number of word meanings that students were familiar with (i.e., their breadth of word knowledge). This in turn suggested a possible reason that efforts to improve comprehension through vocabulary instruction had not always been successful. Whereas raising vocabulary scores seemed to require only increasing word familiarity, improving comprehension likely required increasing the precision of knowledge associated with words whose meanings are known (exactly what "robust vocabulary instruction" was doing). Because those who scored low on vocabulary knew the meanings of fewer words—their knowledge about the meanings of the words they knew was less complete and frequently tied to specific contexts—it seemed plausible that their comprehension might also be less complete, even when a text contained words about which they had knowledge.

We explored this possibility in a study comparing adults who had more and less decontextualized knowledge of word meanings (Curtis,

Collins, Gitomer, & Glaser, 1983). We constructed pairs of paragraphs that created both a familiar and an unfamiliar context for the same word. For example, for *surveillance,* the familiar context read as follows:

> Two men were arrested yesterday after they led detectives to a warehouse containing stolen goods. The arrests were the result of information given by an anonymous phone caller. After receiving this tip, police watched the whereabouts of the men very closely.

The paragraph with the less familiar context read:

> State wildlife officials have been successful in their adoption plan for a laboratory-born eagle. The baby was introduced into the nest of adult eagles with the hope that they would accept it. After placing the chick, the officials watched the actions of the adults very closely.

Each of the paragraphs was then followed by the same sentence. The sentence was:

> This *surveillance* lasted 2 weeks.

We hypothesized that, even though the sentence was the same, comprehension of that sentence would be more challenging in the second instance than in the first, especially for those individuals who had less precise knowledge of the meaning of the target word.

To test this hypothesis, we asked adults to give us definitions for the target words. Based on their definitions, we placed the participants into two groups. One group—the higher knowledge group—was familiar with the meanings of almost all of the words and gave precise definitions for most of them. The other group—the lower knowledge group—was familiar with the meanings of most of the words but gave precise definitions for less than a third of them.

We then assessed comprehension of the paragraphs and target sentence by measuring the reading time and recall of both groups. Participants read an equal number of familiar and unfamiliar passages.

In terms of time to read the context paragraphs, the higher knowledge group read faster than the lower knowledge group, but the reading time within each group did not differ between the two kinds of paragraphs. In terms of time to read the target sentence, we found a difference based on context. But it was not the difference we had expected. For the higher knowledge group, the difference in target sentence reading time between the familiar and less familiar conditions was much greater than for the lower knowledge group. It was almost as if the more precise an individual's knowledge of a word's meaning was, the more concerned, or perhaps even more aware, he or she was about how the final sentence fit with the text that had preceded it.

After reading all of the passages, we tested everyone's memory for what they had read. We began by simply providing the target word as a prompt (e.g., "Tell me about the paragraph that contained *surveillance*"). The higher knowledge group recalled more than the lower knowledge group did, and passages that provided the more familiar context for the word were better recalled than the unfamiliar ones, but there was no interaction. For the paragraphs about which participants were unable to remember anything, we provided a content prompt (e.g., *police* or *wildlife*). The content prompt improved recall for both groups and eliminated the difference between the familiar and unfamiliar contexts for the higher knowledge group. The lower knowledge group still recalled fewer of the less familiar contexts than the familiar ones. Finally, for those paragraphs that the participants recalled, we asked them to tell us what the meaning of the target word had been. For about half of the passages recalled in the less familiar condition, the lower knowledge group either could not recall or recalled incorrectly the way that the target word was used. Similar to what we had seen when we looked at reading time, the lower knowledge group seemed less likely to try to integrate the target word into their understanding of the passage.

Of particular interest to me from this work was the potential link between the skill groups' differences in how they modified their processing of text as a function of prior knowledge and what they remembered from what they read. I wanted to know more about how to design instruction, and I decided to pursue professional opportunities through which I could learn more. Schools of education seemed to be my best route, especially because national attention had begun to be focused on ways that research on learning, thinking, and motivation might provide a knowledge base for more effective educational practice and policy (e.g., see Glaser & Takanishi, 1986). In preparation for my search, I gave my "job talk" in front of my colleagues, professors, and advisors at LRDC. To this day, I remember Isabel's feedback. Her comments were encouraging ("a solid talk"), cautionary ("don't get too carried away with the educational implications"), and comprehensive ("What are you going to wear?"). With her help and that of others, I made my move from LRDC to Harvard's Graduate School of Education.

INTERVENTIONS FOR STUDENTS
WITH READING DIFFICULTIES

While at Harvard I developed and taught graduate courses on comprehension and writing. My greatest professional development came from the work I did with Jeanne Chall in the Harvard Reading Laboratory. Jeanne had founded the lab in 1966 as a way to prepare reading specialists to work with children and adults with reading difficulties. Each semester about 30 teacher–student pairs worked in the lab, and, under her direction, the teachers learned how to identify a student's reading difficulty, to develop a plan for remediation, to plan and teach twice-weekly sessions developed according to that plan, to assess the student's progress at the end of the semester, and to prepare reports that summarized their work.

Although the clinical aspect of the lab's work was completely new and somewhat intimidating for me, I was relieved to discover that its major assumptions were quite consistent with what I had learned at LRDC from Isabel and others: first, that reading is best conceived of as a set of interrelated components, consisting of knowledge, processes, and strategies; and second, that the relationship among these components changes as reading ability develops.

Working with Jeanne, I learned several guidelines for the design of successful remediation (Chall & Curtis, 1987, 1990, 1992, 2003a, 2003b), some of which are:

- *Instructional time is best spent on the causes (not the consequences) of a reading difficulty.* Using strategy instruction to improve comprehension when decoding or fluency or vocabulary is the most pressing need will rarely yield the desired results.
- *The greater the reading difficulty, the more direct and explicit the instruction should usually be.* Instruction for students with a history of reading failure is most effective when it proceeds in stages, beginning with teacher explanation and modeling, followed by guided application and independent practice.
- *Students should feel challenged by instructional materials and tasks.* The biggest gains are realized when the difficulty of instruction surpasses what students are able to do on their own.

- *Teachers should participate in instructional activities with their students.* Collaboration offers the opportunity for the teacher to model and builds an environment for learning that is both comforting to and comfortable for students.

While developing my knowledge and skills as a diagnostician, I kept up my interest in vocabulary (Curtis, 1987a, 1987b). I continued to look at vocabulary assessment, furthering my understanding of the reasons that improving vocabulary test scores did not always improve comprehension and of the kind of vocabulary instruction that improving comprehension would require. This was also when Jeanne Chall and Catherine Snow and their students were looking at the home and school influences on the reading, writing, and language development of children from low-income families (Chall et al., 1982). They followed three groups of children for 2 years: from grades 2 to 3, from grades 4 to 5, and from grades 6 to 7. Included as part of the data collection were interviews about literacy practices at home and in school, home and classroom observations, and a battery of language and literacy tests.

A number of compelling findings emerged from this work that have been described and explored in two companion volumes (Chall, Jacobs, & Baldwin, 1990; Snow, Barnes, Chandler, Goodman, & Hemphill, 1991). One result that was especially important for my own thinking had to do with the achievement differences found among the groups. The children they followed from grade 2 through grade 3 performed particularly well on all the reading tests, as well as in their knowledge of word meanings. By grade 4, however, an intense "slump" in reading and language ability had begun to occur for some of the children, and by grade 6, about half of the children's reading and language scores were almost 2 years below their grade levels in school.

The slump started earlier on some tests than on others, and the first to slip was vocabulary. Although the second-graders had done well in defining common, high-frequency words, fourth-graders experienced difficulty in defining the more abstract, academic, and literary words that were beginning to be included as part of language testing at that grade level. By grade 7, the students were more than 2 years below norms on word meanings.

Around the same time, of course, Isabel and her colleagues (Beck, McKeown, & Omanson, 1987) were spelling out these differences among kinds of word meanings and the implications for vocabulary instruction via their notion of "word tiers." In their first tier they included the common, high-frequency words, words about which they said, "It would be difficult to argue that any direct instruction be devoted to the meanings of these words in school" (p. 155). These were the words that the second- and third-graders tested by Chall and her colleagues had no difficulty in defining.

Tier 2 included "words of high frequency for mature language users" (Beck et al., 1987, p. 155), the ones "toward which the most productive instructional efforts can be directed" (p. 155). This was consistent with Chall and colleagues' (1990) finding that lack of knowledge of the meanings of such words was the first sign of a deceleration, or "slump," in the reading and language development of the low-income students they studied.

As Isabel and her group continued their groundbreaking work on the design and validation of tier 2 vocabulary instruction, I decided to pursue the opportunity to combine my newly gained diagnostic and remedial skills with my interest in vocabulary by accepting the position as director of the Reading Center, an applied research and development center at Boys Town.

Founded in 1917, Boys Town provides treatment and care for adolescents who are socially and emotionally at risk because of such factors as school failure, broken homes, chronic neglect and abuse, and antisocial and illegal behaviors. My center was charged with evaluation of the reading instruction being provided to the more than 700 youths enrolled in Boys Town's schools and with development and testing of new methods that could be disseminated to improve the reading ability of older, at-risk adolescents nationwide.

UNDERSTANDING AND IMPROVING ADOLESCENTS' READING ABILITY

As a first step, I extended the diagnostic approach we had used at the Harvard Reading Lab to look at the reading abilities of students in an inner-city, alternative high school run by Boys Town. I tested 30 students selected from among those who were part of a larger random sample that was being followed (Curtis, 1991). The students' grade placement in school ranged from the 9th to 12th grades, with the average being 11.3. On a standardized test of reading ability that had been administered a few months prior to the diagnostic testing, the group scored an average of 2.5 grade levels below their grade placement in school (with a median percentile of 18).

The diagnostic testing involved assessing students using three different sets of graded word lists for strengths and needs in word identification, spelling ability, and listening vocabulary, along with two different sets of graded passages to assess oral reading accuracy, rate, and listening comprehension. In addition, I asked the students some questions about their attitudes toward reading and their sense of how their reading compared with that of their peers. The students were tested individually, in a single sitting, for 30–40 minutes.

In terms of alphabetics, the average grade level of students' skills in identifying words in isolation was grade 7; they achieved at grade level 8 for accuracy of oral reading in context. This would suggest to some that decoding was the likely a bottleneck for these students in reading. Results from the spelling assessment suggested otherwise, however. Most people who have problems in reading words have even more difficulty when it comes to spelling them. But this was not the case. These students' average grade-level attainment in spelling was a full grade level higher than their average grade-level performance on reading words in isolation.

Why were the students able to go from sounds to letters with more facility than they were able to from letters to sounds? Analysis of the errors they made in word reading provided some clues. When students erred in pronouncing words, the mistakes tended to be in the way they chose to segment the words and the syllables they emphasized (e.g., *un - an´ - im - ous, hy - po´ - the - ses, de - so´ - late*). I knew from my work in the Harvard Lab that errors such as these stem more from a lack of familiarity with words than from deficits in the knowledge and skills used to decode them.

Results from the listening tasks supported the view that the underlying nature of the students' reading difficulties was related to their knowledge of words rather than to print-related skills. Texts too difficult for the students to read aloud were texts that were also too difficult for them to understand through listening. And, when asked to define words presented to them aurally, the majority of the students were unable to provide meanings for words beyond the sixth-grade level.

In addition to lack of familiarity with words, fluency was also identified as a need for the students. For purposes of the study, I defined fluent reading as the ability to read text aloud at a rate of 150 words per minute or better. Only 10% of the students could read high school-level texts at this rate. The average fluency grade level was equivalent to the fifth-grade level.

Because vocabulary and fluency can influence people's feelings about reading and the enjoyment they get out of doing it, I was interested in students' reading attitudes and self-assessments. I presented them with 20 statements about reading—some positive and some negative—and asked them to rate their level of agreement using a 5-point scale. Overall, the students tended to agree with the positive statements (e.g., "Reading is a good way to spend spare time") and disagree with the negative ones (e.g., "There is nothing to be gained from reading books"). Students were also asked to compare themselves with other people their own age in each of the following areas: how well they thought they read; how much they liked to read; and how much reading they felt they did. Compared with their peers, nearly all of the students (87%) thought they read at least as well; 67% felt that they liked to read at least as much; and 70% felt that they did at least as much reading.

Summing up, the diagnostic profile for the students suggested that their strengths were their positive attitudes toward reading and their knowledge of symbol–sound correspondences. Their area of needs included increased knowledge of word meanings, improved oral reading fluency, and better understanding of their current level of functioning.

Based on these results, Boys Town made several decisions. First, within a week or two of their arrival at one of its schools, every youngster would receive a diagnostic assessment in reading. Second, the reading test results would be shared with each student's teachers and used to make instructional decisions. And third, a specific reading curriculum would be designed for those students who needed a more focused and robust intervention than was currently in place.

The reading curriculum we developed consists of four one-semester courses that students are placed in based on their current level of functioning in reading (Curtis & Longo, 1999). The first two courses provide instruction for students who are experiencing difficulties in alphabetics and fluency. The third and fourth courses are designed for those with comprehension difficulties, with the third focusing on building vocabulary knowledge and the fourth on strategies.

In our vocabulary course, we relied very heavily on Isabel's previous vocabulary research and instructional programming, finding that five principles were essential (Curtis & Longo, 2008):

- Every word and its meaning are introduced directly and explicitly, followed by a discussion of the contexts in which the word and its meaning can be applied.
- Emphasis is placed on students' ability to use the words, as well as to recognize their meanings.
- Opportunities are provided to use the word meanings in a variety of contexts, and students get feedback on their success in doing so.
- Encounters with the word meanings occur in which students solve problems and explain their reasoning in ways that lead to deeper understanding of the words and their meanings.
- Students and teachers review progress on a frequent and regular basis.

During my association with Boys Town, the vocabulary course was offered 39 times in various secondary school settings, with an average of 26 students participating in each replication. Based on the results from standardized reading tests, the students in these replications made an average gain of about one reading grade level in both vocabulary and comprehension over the course of the 16-week intervention. Central to a gain of this magnitude, however, were teachers who had a clear and deliberate focus on helping students to create the meaningful contexts for the word meanings they were acquiring, as well as their frequent and consistent emphasis on assisting them in making connections to what they already know.

The significance that teachers (vs. programs) have in reversing reading failure became even more apparent to me as I began to shift some of my attention to the area of adult literacy. I made this move in part to respond to others' interests in whether the approaches we had found to be effective with older adolescents could make a similar difference for adults. In addition, though, the older adolescents whose reading abilities I had now become the most concerned about appeared to be leaving the K–12 system and seeking help instead from adult literacy programs (Welch & DiTommaso, 2004).

FACTORS AFFECTING
ADULT LITERACY INSTRUCTION

Together with John Strucker and Marilyn Adams, I joined a project in 2004 that sought to improve the reading instruction of adult basic education (ABE) students whose reading was between grade equivalent 4 (GE 4) and grade equivalent 8 (GE 8). Known as "intermediate adult readers," this group is the largest among adult literacy learners. Based on our review of descriptive studies, we knew that their reading difficulties were likely caused by dysfluent word recognition and/or lack of a literate meaning vocabulary. But little research had taken place on approaches to improving the fluency and vocabulary knowledge of these adult GE 4–8 readers. In our research, we made the first systematic attempt to assess the value of the kind of approach that had worked at Boys Town for improving adult reading. In addition, because the lack of practice time is a persistent problem for ABE students, we evaluated the effectiveness of Soliloquy Learning's Reading Assistant, a speech-recognition reading tutor, as a means of providing distributed practice in fluency and vocabulary.

Data analyses from this project are still under way, but some preliminary results have proven to be interesting. First, with regard to our intervention, the experimental group increased their vocabulary by a significant amount when compared with the control group. Second, this improvement was apparent in learners' ability to use the vocabulary appropriately, as well as to recognize the words' meanings. Third, after 10 weeks of instruction, the improvement in vocabulary had not resulted in significant differences between the experimental and control groups' performance on a standardized reading test. And finally—and perhaps of most importance—we found a great deal of variation among the teachers in their fidelity to implementation of the intervention. Differences among teachers that appeared to be linked to implementation fidelity were observed on each of the following factors: (1) teachers' beliefs about the learners and their judgments about the appropriateness of the intervention for them, (2) teachers' ability and willingness to provide the structure and do the planning needed for the intervention, and (3) the level of verbal facility and agility required on the teachers' part to do the intervention.

As a result of this work, I came to appreciate more than ever how much good teaching matters *and* how complex it is to develop and to sustain good teachers. This is the main thrust of an initiative I am now working on, developed and funded by the Office of Vocational and Adult Education, U.S. Department of Education, known as the Student Achievement in Reading project (STAR). The goal of STAR is to translate reading research into a comprehensive package of professional development for teachers and administrators that will improve reading instruction for adult basic education students.

Our focus in STAR has been on instruction for intermediate-level adult learners, those who are reading at the fourth- to ninth-grade levels. We decided to target this group for two reasons. First, as I noted earlier, among adults (16 years and older) who are enrolled in adult literacy programs in the United States, nearly half are reading at these grade levels. Second, gains for intermediate-level adult readers have not been as great as they need to be, suggesting that these readers have not been receiving the instruction they need (Office of Vocational and Adult Education, 2007).

For the evidence base in adult reading instruction, we have relied on two sources for STAR: a review of the research on adult reading that identified the principles and trends in the results from empirical studies (Kruidenier, 2002) and a summary of the consensus among experts about the instructional implications of the research (McShane, 2005). From the evidence base, we identified five practices that hold the most promise:

- Assessment of learners' strengths and needs in each of the following components of reading: alphabetics, fluency, vocabulary, and comprehension
- Use of the assessment results to inform decisions at the program and classroom levels, including placement of learners in classes and instructional planning
- Direct and explicit instruction, consisting of teachers who explain and model reading skills and provide students with opportunities for guided practice and application
- Instruction that maximizes learners' engagement with each other, their teachers, and their reading materials and that helps learners to recognize the value of what is being taught
- Continuous monitoring by teachers and learners of instructional effectiveness

In our pilot dissemination with six states (Maine, Connecticut, Ohio, Illinois, South Dakota, and California), we have provided professional development for state and local program staff, along with technical assistance that supported the use of the practices being trained. Over the course of 8–12 months, participants in the states attended two

2-day institutes and received technical assistance to help them in implementing the instructional strategies they were learning and in changing the instructional policies that were limiting effectiveness.

Evaluation of the pilot focused on establishing the extent of change that occurred in practices in classrooms, programs, and states (Keenan, Curtis, Lanier, Meyer, & Bercovitz, 2008). Participants in STAR reported increases in the amount of time they spent on reading instruction, in their use of diagnostic reading assessment and evidence-based instructional techniques, in the quality and quantity of feedback that teachers received about their instruction, and in the amount of time that teachers and administrators spent discussing reading instruction. Some problems and concerns were also identified in the pilot. Classroom observations indicated that the extent and quality of implementation of evidence-based practices was uneven across classrooms, with alphabetics and fluency presenting teachers with the most challenge. And, although the vast majority of participants agreed that STAR had changed the way that they thought about reading and reading instruction, they did not make changes in program features—such as when learners are placed in classes and how learners are grouped for instruction—that were necessary to make the best use of the evidence-based practices they had learned.

Following up on the pilot results, we made some changes to the STAR package, revisions that we hope will improve the quality of implementation and facilitate programs' ability to maintain improvements. The first change has to do with the training. STAR is now being delivered in three 2-day institutes delivered over a 9-month period, giving participants more time to reflect during training on what they are learning and more opportunities to practice and make changes in between the institutes. We are also using a polling technology during training that allows us to assess participants' knowledge, skills, experiences, and dispositions on the spot and to adjust training accordingly.

The second change has to do with the materials provided to participants, which we have switched from paper to a Web-based delivery (*www.startoolkit.org*). Included on the website are access to the research articles that support the strategies, techniques, methods, and materials that we recommend; lists of materials and access to tools that support diagnostic assessment and instruction in alphabetics, fluency, vocabulary, and comprehension; video and audio clips of teachers and students demonstrating and supporting the use of evidence-based approaches; recommendations for how administrators can support planning for and implementation of reading instruction; and follow-up activities for practice after training.

The third change has to do with the technical assistance we are providing. We learned in the pilot how difficult it was for participants to recognize and make the changes needed to promote the use of evidence-based practices. Technical assistance has now been designed to help teachers, program directors, and state leaders to critically examine their existing practices and to identify new practices that will improve reading instruction.

STAR will be disseminated to 14 more states over the next 2 years. A quasi-experimental evaluation is under way, funded by the Department of Education, to assess the initiative's effect on learner outcomes.

CLOSING COMMENT

A few years back Isabel accepted an invitation from Lesley University to speak with area teachers and administrators about the role of vocabulary instruction in improving comprehension. The auditorium was packed, and the feedback from those who attended was glowing. The event reminded me of something I have known for 30 years: Isabel has a profound capacity and desire to engage and connect with educators. The occasion also helped to solidify a lesson that it has taken me almost as long to learn: our ability to improve students' learning rests ultimately as much on our will to improve our instruction as on our knowledge and skills in doing so.

REFERENCES

Beck, I. L., McKeown, M. G., & Omanson, R. C. (1987). The effects and uses of diverse vocabulary instructional techniques. In M. G. McKeown & M. E. Curtis (Eds.), *The nature of vocabulary acquisition* (pp. 147–163). Hillsdale, NJ: Erlbaum.

Beck, I. L., & Mitroff, D. (1972). *The rationale and design of a primary grades reading system for an individualized classroom.* Pittsburgh: University of Pittsburgh, Learning Research and Development Center.

Beck, I. L., Perfetti, C. A., & McKeown, M. G. (1982). The effects of long-term vocabulary instruction on lexical access and reading comprehension. *Journal of Educational Psychology, 74,* 506–521.

Chall, J. S., & Curtis, M. E. (1987). What clinical diagnosis tells us about children's reading. *The Reading Teacher, 40,* 784–788.

Chall, J. S., & Curtis, M. E. (1990). Diagnostic achievement testing in reading. In C. R. Reynolds & R. W. Kamphaus (Eds.), *Handbook of psychological and educational assessment of children* (pp. 405–418). New York: Guilford Press.

Chall, J. S., & Curtis, M. E. (1992). Teaching the disabled or below average reader. In A. E. Farstrup & S. J. Samuels (Ed.), *What research has to say about reading instruction* (pp. 253–276). Newark, DE: International Reading Association.

Chall, J. S., & Curtis, M. E. (2003a). Children with reading difficulties. In J. Flood, D. Lapp, J. Jensen, & J. R. Squire (Eds.), *Handbook of research on teaching English language arts* (2nd ed., pp. 413–420). Mahwah, NJ: Erlbaum.

Chall, J. S., & Curtis, M. E. (2003b). Diagnostic achievement testing in reading. In C. R. Reynolds & R. W. Kamphaus (Eds.), *Handbook of psychological and educational assessment of children: Intelligence, aptitude, and achievement* (2nd ed., pp. 405–417). New York: Guilford Press.

Chall, J. S., Jacobs, V. A., & Baldwin, L. E. (1990). *The reading crisis: Why poor children fall behind.* Cambridge, MA: Harvard University Press.

Chall, J. S., Snow, C. E., Barnes, W. S., Chandler, J., Goodman, I. F., Hemphill, L., et al. (1982). *Families and literacy: The contribution of out-of-school experiences to children's acquisition of literacy.* Cambridge, MA: Harvard University. (ERIC Document Reproduction Service No. ED 234345)

Curtis, M. E. (1975). *The effects of strategy and structure on retention of prose.* Unpublished master's thesis, University of Pittsburgh.

Curtis, M. E. (1980). Development of components of reading skill. *Journal of Educational Psychology, 72,* 656–669.

Curtis, M. E. (1987a). Cognitive analyses of verbal aptitude tests. In R. O. Freedle & R. Duran (Eds.), *Cognitive and linguistic analyses of test performance* (pp. 151–161). Norword, NJ: Ablex.

Curtis, M. E. (1987b). Vocabulary testing and vocabulary instruction. In M. G. McKeown & M. E. Curtis (Eds.), *The nature of vocabulary instruction* (pp. 37–51). Hillsdale, NJ: Erlbaum.

Curtis, M. E. (1991). *Reading skills at Father Flanagan High School.* Unpublished manuscript, Boys Town, NE.

Curtis, M. E., Collins, J., Gitomer, D., & Glaser, R. (1983). *Word knowledge influences on comprehension.* Pittsburgh, PA: Learning Research and Development Center. (ERIC Document Reproduction Service No. ED 229747)

Curtis, M. E., & Longo, A. M. (1999). *When adolescents can't read: Methods and materials that work.* Cambridge, MA: Brookline Books.

Curtis, M. E., & Longo, A. M. (2008). Teaching academic vocabulary to adolescents to improve comprehension. In L. Denti & G. Guerin (Eds.), *Effective practice for adolescents with reading and literacy challenges* (pp. 45–64). New York: Routledge.

Glaser, R., & Takanishi, R. (1986). Creating a knowledge base for education: Psychology's contributions and prospects. *American Psychologist, 41,* 1025–1028.

Keenan, C., Curtis, M. E., Lanier, L. C., Meyer, J., & Bercovitz, L. (2008). *STAR: Improving adult literacy through the use of evidence-based reading instruction.*

Paper presented at the International Reading Association annual convention, Atlanta, GA.

Kruidenier, J. (2002). *Research-based principles for adult basic education reading instruction.* Washington, DC: Partnership for Reading. Retrieved January 23, 2008, from *www.nifl.gov/partnershipforreading/publications/html/adult_ed/adult_ed_1.html.*

Lesgold, A. M., & Curtis, M. E. (1981). Learning to read words efficiently. In A. M. Lesgold & C. A. Perfetti (Eds.), *Interactive processes in reading* (pp. 329–360). Hillsdale, NJ: Erlbaum.

Lesgold, A. M., Curtis, M. E., DeGood, H., Golinkoff, R., McCormick, C., & Shimron, J. (1974). *The role of mental imagery in text comprehension: Preliminary studies.* Pittsburgh, PA: University of Pittsburgh, Learning Research and Development Center.

Lesgold, A. M., Curtis, M. E., Roth, S. F., Resnick, L. B., & Beck, I. L. (1980). *A longitudinal study of reading acquisition.* Paper presented at the meeting of the American Educational Research Association, Boston.

McShane, S. (2005). *Applying research in reading instruction for adults: First steps for teachers.* Washington, DC: Partnership for Reading. Retrieved January 23, 2008, from *www.nifl.gov/partnershipforreading/publications/mcshane/index.html.*

National Institute of Child Health and Human Development. (2000). *Report of the National Reading Panel: Teaching children to read: An evidence-based assessment of the scientific research literature on reading and its implications for reading instruction* (NIH Publication No. 00-4769). Washington, DC: U.S. Government Printing Office. Retrieved March 29, 2008, from *www.nichd.nih.gov/publications/nrp/smallbook.cfm.*

Neisser, U. (1967). *Cognitive psychology.* New York: Appleton-Century-Crofts.

Office of Vocational and Adult Education. (2007). *Adult education annual report to Congress year 2004–05.* Washington, DC: U.S. Department of Education.

Paivio, A. (1971). *Imagery and verbal processes.* New York: Holt, Rinehart, & Winston.

Perfetti, C. A., & Lesgold, A. M. (1979). Coding and comprehension in skilled reading and implications for reading instruction. In L. B. Resnick & P. Weaver (Eds.), *Theory and practice of early reading* (pp. 57–85). Hillsdale, NJ: Erlbaum.

Snow, C. E., Barnes, W. S., Chandler, J., Goodman, I. F., & Hemphill, L. (1991). *Unfulfilled expectations: Home and school influences on literacy.* Cambridge, MA: Harvard University Press.

Welch, J. R., & DiTommaso, K. (2004). Youth in ABE: The numbers. *Focus on Basics, 7,* 18–21. Retrieved March 17, 2008, from *www.ncsall.net/?id=123.*

7

WHAT IS A GOOD QUESTION?

Art Graesser, Yasuhiro Ozuru,
and Jeremiah Sullins

Isabel Beck's contributions to education have spanned a broad landscape, including monumental advances in vocabulary learning, deep comprehension, discourse coherence, communication, classroom interaction, and questions. Questions are the focus of this chapter, in recognition of the book published by Isabel and her colleagues, *Questioning the Author* (Beck & McKeown, 2006; Beck, McKeown, Hamilton, & Kucan, 1997). This work is both a scholarly advance and a practical solution to improving reading comprehension. Students learn to read text at deeper levels of comprehension by having teachers model and prompt the readers to ask good questions, such as the following:

What is the author trying to tell you?
Why is the author telling you that?
Does the author say it clearly?
How could the author have said things more clearly?
What would you say instead?

These are indeed excellent questions. They encourage students to reflect on the process of communication through text, on the quality of the text in meeting communication goals, on text coherence, and on the possibility of a text having alternative forms of expression. Instead of being viewed as a perfect artifact that has been cast in stone, text can be viewed as a fallible and flexible medium of communication that merits critical scrutiny. The process of inquiry helps the reader shift his or her mindset from viewing text as a static object to viewing it as part of a fluid communication process. This shift in the reader's mental model of the reading process results in deeper comprehension.

Questions have an important status in the work of Beck, in that of many of her contemporaries, and in our research, as well. However, it is important to appreciate the fact that all questions do not have equal impact. Questions vary in quality with respect to the support they offer for thinking, learning, and discovery. This fact motivates the core research question of this chapter: *What makes a good question?* An answer has the potential to profoundly improve the processes of classroom learning, tutoring, reading, exploration, hypothesis testing, motivation, and a host of other activities in the educational enterprise (Graesser & McMahen, 1993; Graesser, McNamara, & VanLehn, 2005; Graesser & Olde, 2003; Graesser & Person, 1994; Wisher & Graesser, 2007).

I (A. G.) have been obsessed for over three decades with understanding the mechanisms of question asking and answering. The obsession emerged early in my career from a number of unsettling observations. I noticed that students asked very few questions. Students were essentially bankrupt in displays of curiosity and genuine inquiry. Even the accomplished students appeared to have broken question generators. I would routinely invite new graduate students who wanted to work with me to spend 1 week formulating a couple of research questions that they felt passionate about. The questions needed to be so interesting to them that they would spend hundreds of hours in the libraries or laboratories in search of an answer. I discovered that approximately half of the students could not think of a single genuine question within a 1-week time span. These were the high-percentile students, the cream of the crop, the ones who had the explicit goal of building a career in *research*. For half, not a single research question came to mind.

Another observation motivated my obsession with investigating questions. My mentors in graduate school would sometimes accuse me or my peers of exhibiting faulty inquiry. The mentors would dramatically assert, "The problem here is that you are asking the wrong question." Unfortunately, the guidance was always flimsy on what the right question was or, more to the point, what principles should guide the generation of good research questions. It is fascinating that even most professors are quite muddled about the nature of good questions.

Many of us were convinced that the cognitive science revolution of the 1970s would come to the rescue and correct the problems of question bankruptcy and misspecification. The models of representing world knowledge and associated cognitive processes were systematic, organized, and elegant. There were models of semantic networks (*is–a* hierarchies), goal–plan–script–action structures, causal networks, and spatial hierarchies; each of these had its own unique set of constraints and affiliated questions. The models were structurally and computationally precise rather than ad hoc collages formulated entirely by researchers' intuitions. For the first time in history, knowledge and questioning were not a complete mystery, and there could be principled recommendations not only on how to generate questions but also on how to generate *good* questions.

Investigations of question asking and answering are alive and well today in this age of Google. For the first time in history, a person can ask a question on the Web and receive answers in a few seconds. Twenty years ago it would take hours or weeks to receive answers to the same questions as a person hunted through documents in a library. The Google generation is destined to have more inquisitive minds than the generations that relied on libraries. In the future, the textbooks on learning and cognition are likely to have chapters on question asking and answering, in addition to chapters on perception, memory, decision making, problem solving, and so on.

This chapter begins by defining a landscape of questions and using it to examine some alternative frameworks for categorizing questions and scaling them on quality. The subsequent section reviews some research that supports the claim that helping students to generate better questions can promote learning at deeper levels. Next we describe some learning technologies that encourage the asking and answering of high-quality questions. The chapter ends with a plea for someone to develop a "Question-Authoring Workbench." The workbench would train instructors, students, textbook writers, curriculum developers, test constructors, and other educational communities to compose better questions and thereby elevate the standards of comprehension beyond the current shallow standards.

THE LANDSCAPE OF QUESTIONS

One initial step toward improving question quality is to consider the broad landscape of question types, the levels of knowledge tapped by a question, and the cognitive processes involved in answering questions. We have defined a *landscape of questions* as the distribution of questions that tap different categories of knowledge and different cognitive proficiencies. If there are Q question categories, K categories of knowledge, and P cognitive processes, then there are $Q \times K \times P$ *cells* in the total space of questions, as illustrated in Figure 7.1. Most question writers focus on a very narrow terrain, resulting in questions that do not prompt students to think deeply. In offering the landscape, we aim to promote a broader vision of question design, marked by deeper analysis of learning objectives and questions that better match learning goals.

Types of Questions

Schemes for classifying questions have been proposed in the fields of psychology, education, and artificial intelligence (Dillon, 1988; Graesser & Person, 1994; Lehnert, 1978; Mosenthal, 1996). We discuss two that we think show promise—one that was developed by our research team (Graesser & Person, 1994) and the other by Mosenthal (1996).

Graesser–Person Taxonomy

The Graesser–Person taxonomy (Graesser & Person, 1994) classifies questions according to the nature of the information being sought in a good answer to the question. Table 7.1 lists and defines these categories. The 16 question categories can be scaled on depth, which is

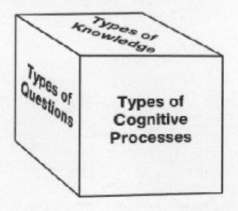

FIGURE 7.1. Landscape of questions.

TABLE 7.1. Question Taxonomy Proposed by Graesser and Person (1994)

Question category	Generic question frames and examples
1. Verification	Is X true or false? Did an event occur? Does a state exist?
2. Disjunctive	Is X, Y, or Z the case?
3. Concept completion	Who? What? When? Where?
4. Example	What is an example or instance of a category?
5. Feature specification	What qualitative properties does entity X have?
6. Quantification	What is the value of a quantitative variable? How much? How many?
7. Definition	What does X mean?
8. Comparison	How is X similar to Y? How is X different from Y?
9. Interpretation	What concept or claim can be inferred from a static or active pattern of data?
10. Causal antecedent	What state or event causally led to an event or state? Why did an event occur? Why does a state exist? How did an event occur? How did a state come to exist?
11. Causal consequence	What are the consequences of an event or state? What if X occurred? What if X did not occur?
12. Goal orientation	What are the motives or goals behind an agent's action? Why did an agent do some action?
13. Instrumentalprocedural	What plan or instrument allows an agent to accomplish a goal? How did an agent do some action?
14. Enablement	What object or resource allows an agent to accomplish a goal?
15. Expectation	Why did some expected event *not* occur? Why does some expected state *not* exist?
16. Judgmental	What value does the answerer place on an idea or advice? What do you think of X? How would you rate X?

defined by the amount and complexity of content produced in a good answer to the question. In some of our analyses, we have differentiated simple *shallow* questions (categories 1–4), *intermediate* questions (5–8), and complex *deep* questions (9–16). This scale of depth is validated to the extent that it correlates significantly ($r = .60 \pm .05$) with both Mosenthal's (1996) scale of question depth and the original Bloom (1956) taxonomy of cognitive difficulty.

Although the Graesser–Person scheme has some degree of validity, we cannot claim that it has a perfect scale for depth. For example, one can readily identify *disjunctive* questions that require considerable thought and reasoning, as in the case of the difficult physics question: *When the passenger is rear-ended, does the head initially (1) go forward, (2) go backward, or (3) stay the same?* Generating an answer to this question requires a causal analysis, which corresponds to question categories 10 and 11, so this question may functionally be a hybrid question. But hybrid questions present a problem if we are trying to create a unidimensional scale of depth.

As another problematic example, consider the category *instrumental/procedural*, which falls on the complex, deep end of our scale. Yet some of these questions require minimal thought and reasoning, such as, *How do you open a refrigerator?* The Graesser–Person scale of depth of question categories is somewhat crude and approximate because it is also important to consider the knowledge representations and cognitive processes that are recruited during the course of question answering.

Mosenthal's Taxonomy

Mosenthal (1996) developed a coding system to scale questions on abstractness, which reasonably corresponds to depth. Mosenthal's levels of abstractness range from most concrete (which targets explicit information) to an intermediate level that identifies information such as procedures and goals that may or may not be explicit to abstract levels that tap identification of causes and effects, reasons, and evidence. As in the taxonomy of the Graesser–Person scheme, Mosenthal's classification scheme is based on the information sought in the answer and does not systematically consider the world knowledge and cognitive processes needed to generate answers to questions. Indeed, both of the classification schemes conflate a number of dimensions that are conceivably separable, such as depth, complexity, abstractness, and explicitness. However, both schemes have some degree of validity in scaling questions on quality with respect to promoting learning.

Types of Knowledge

Knowledge Representations in Artificial Intelligence and Cognitive Science

Researchers in cognitive science and artificial intelligence in the 1970s through 1990s spent considerable effort dissecting the formal and psychological properties of different classes of knowledge (Lehmann, 1992; Lenat, 1995; Schank, 1999; Sowa, 1983). These theories identified and specified the formal properties of particular elements, relations, and classes of knowledge. The goal of dissecting knowledge in this way was to develop a systematic understanding of knowledge that would displace reliance on intuition and folklore. The question categories (e.g., in Table 7.1) were found to operate systematically on particular types of knowledge in various computational models of question answering, such as QUALM (Lehnert, 1978) and QUEST (Graesser, Gordon, & Brainerd, 1992).

As an illustration of some different types of knowledge, consider the categories proposed in Wisher and Graesser (2007):

Agents and entities: These are organized sets of people, organizations, countries, and entities.

Class inclusion: One concept is a subtype or subclass of another concept.

Spatial layout: This involves spatial relations among regions and entities in regions.

Compositional structures: Components have subparts and subcomponents.

Procedures and plans: A sequence of steps/actions in a procedure accomplishes a goal.

Causal chains and networks: An event is caused by a sequence of events and enabling states.

Others: These include property descriptions, quantitative specifications, rules, and mental states of agents.

Each of these types of knowledge has a unique set of properties, relations, and constraints. For example, an *is–a* relation connects concept nodes in class inclusion knowledge—for example, *a robin is a bird, a bird is an animal*—whereas a *cause* relation would connect event nodes in a causal network. Question categories of the sort in Table 7.1 are systematically aligned with the types of knowledge illustrated here. Definition questions have a close affinity with class-inclusion structures, whereas goal-orientation questions have a close affinity with procedures and plans. The QUEST model of question answering (Graesser et al., 1992) provided a systematic mapping between the types of knowledge and many of the question classes in Table 7.1.

Knowledge Representation in Discourse Processing

Researchers in the field of discourse processing postulate that cognitive representations of texts can be separated into levels of explicit information, referential mental models (sometimes called situation models), rhetorical structure, and pragmatic communication (Graesser, Millis, & Zwaan, 1997; Kintsch, 1998; Perfetti, Britt, & Georgi, 1995; Snow, 2002). The *explicit information* preserves the wording, syntax, and semantic content of the material that is directly presented. The *mental model* is the referential content of what the explicit material is about. In a technical text that explains a device, for example, the mental model would include the components of the device, the spatial arrangement of components, the causal chain of events by which the system successfully unfolds, the mechanisms that explain each causal step, the functions of components, and the plans of humans who manipulate the system for various purposes. The *rhetorical structure* is the more global composition and genre that organizes the discourse. For example, the structure of a story is very different from that of an expository text with a claim + evidence rhetorical structure. The *pragmatic communication* specifies the main messages or points that the author is trying to convey to the reader.

These four levels of discourse can be ordered on depth. More inferences and deeper levels of processing are needed as one moves from the explicit information to the mental models to the rhetorical and pragmatic communication levels. For example, Bloom's (1956) taxonomy is a popular traditional taxonomy for scaling cognitive tasks on cognitive difficulty and skill (as discussed further later). The Bloom categories of recognition and recall correspond to explicit information, whereas the Bloom category of comprehension closely aligns with the mental models that result from the integration of explicit information with preexisting knowledge. The questions in Beck and colleagues' (1997) *Questioning the Author* have alignments to rhetorical structure and pragmatic communication, which are at the deep end of the continuum.

Types of Cognitive Processes

Cognitive processes need to operate on the knowledge in order for the knowledge to have an impact on a person's question-answering behavior. It is therefore important to identify the types of cognitive processes during question answering and how different types of knowledge are recruited in these processes (Goldman, Duschl, Ellenbogen, Williams, & Tzou, 2003; Graesser, Lang, & Roberts, 1991; Guthrie, 1988; Kyllonen & Roberts, 2003; Reder, 1987; Rouet, 2006; Singer, 2003). There is a rich cognitive literature on process models of question asking and answering. Here we briefly discuss two older models that are widely recognized in the field of education: Bloom's (1956) taxonomy and Carroll's (1976, 1987) coding scheme for cognitive tasks.

Bloom's Taxonomy

Bloom's (1956) taxonomy is one of the early analyses of cognitive processes in the field of education. The major categories in the original system are recognition, recall, comprehension, application, analysis, synthesis, and evaluation. This order of categories is meant to represent progressively greater difficulty. Recognition and recall are the easiest, comprehension is intermediate, and application, analysis, synthesis, and evaluation are the most difficult. However, the relative ordering within the highest four categories is not necessarily clear-cut.

Bloom's taxonomy may not provide a perfect classification of cognitive processes, but the scheme has survived in many educational circles for several decades. Recognition and recall would be the primary processes associated with questions that access facts and events stored in long-term memory, such as *What is the value of gravity on the earth's surface?* or *When did Lance Armstrong first win the Tour de France?* However, comprehension and synthesis would be needed when a question inquires about a character's hidden intentions in a novel, and application is needed when a person inquires about possible causes of equipment breakdown.

Carroll's Coding Scheme for Cognitive Tasks

Carroll's (1976, 1987) coding scheme for items from cognitive tasks may be used to label some the cognitive processes involved in answering questions. The general elements of Carroll's scheme include characteristics of the stimuli in the task, types of responses, the primary memory stores (e.g., short-term vs. long-term memory stores) used during task completion, and the elementary information processes that are likely to be executed in specific tasks. The elementary information processes are segregated into necessary *operations* versus more probabilistic *strategies*. The operations and strategies that are most relevant to typical questions that tap deep knowledge include: (1) educing identities or similarities between two or more stimuli, (2) retrieving general information from memory, (3) retrieving or constructing hypotheses, (4) examining different portions of memory, (5) performing serial operations with data from memory, (6) recording intermediate results, (7) reinterpreting ambiguous items, (8) comprehending and analyzing language stimuli, and (9) judging stimuli with respect to specified characteristics.

The landscape of questions discussed in this section has included example theoretical schemes for classifying questions, knowledge representations, and cognitive processes. The categories can be weakly ordered on depth so there is some principled foundation for evaluating the quality of questions in promoting learning. We present these schemes for purposes of illustration rather than asserting that they are ideal theoretical schemes. Future research will no doubt provide improvements in the classifications and theoretical analyses.

A Peek at the Quality of Multiple-Choice Questions of Textbook Writers

The benefit of using our landscape concept to guide the generation of questions may be illustrated in a recent study we conducted. We analyzed a corpus of multiple-choice questions on psychology in college textbooks and in a Graduate Record Examination (GRE) practice book (written by a commercial publisher, not the Educational Testing Service [ETS]). We randomly selected 30 multiple-choice questions from the test banks associated with three textbooks and the GRE practice book, yielding 120 questions altogether. Cognitive psychologists and graduate students in cognitive psychology coded the questions on two different theoretical schemes on question depth. One was the question taxonomy of Graesser and Person (1994), which has a depth classification that significantly correlates with Bloom's (1956) taxonomy of cognitive objectives ($r = .64$). The other was Mosenthal's (1996) scale of question depth, which correlates well ($r = .59$) with the Graesser–Person taxonomy. The analyses revealed that only 23% of the questions were classified as deep questions according to the Graesser–Person taxonomy and that 21% were classified as deep questions according to the Mosenthal scale.

Our results are a dramatic example of the difficulty that even experts have in generating deep questions. Quite clearly, the textbook industry, teachers, and other question designers need assistance in generating deep questions because it is hardly a natural inclination to generate them. The distribution of questions needs to be shifted to attain greater depth and relevance to the learning objectives of our school systems.

STUDENTS ASKING QUESTIONS: THE REALITY AND THE POTENTIAL

There is an idealistic vision that students are curious question generators who actively self-regulate their learning. They identify their own knowledge deficits, ask questions that focus on these deficits, and answer the questions by exploring reliable information sources. Unfortunately, this idealistic vision of intelligent inquiry is an illusion at this point in educational practice. Most learners have trouble identifying their own knowledge deficits (Baker, 1985; Hacker, Dunlosky, & Graesser, 1998) and ask very few questions (Dillon, 1988; Good, Slavings, Harel, & Emerson, 1987; Graesser & Person, 1994). Graesser and Person's (1994) estimate from available studies revealed that the typical student asks less than 0.2 questions per hour in a classroom and that the poverty of classroom questions is a general phenomenon across cultures. The fact that it takes several hours for a typical student to ask one question in a classroom is perhaps not surprising, because it would be impossible for a teacher to accommodate 25–30 curious students. The rate of question asking is higher in other learning environments (Graesser, McNamara, & VanLehn, 2005). For example, an average student asks 26 questions per hour in one-on-one human tutoring sessions (Graesser & Person, 1994) and 120 questions per hour in a learning environment that forces students to ask questions in order to access any and all information (Graesser, Langston, & Baggett, 1993).

Given the poverty of student questions, particularly questions at deeper levels, researchers in cognitive science and education have often advocated learning environments that encourage students to generate questions (Beck et al., 1997; Collins, 1988; Edelson, Gordin, & Pea, 1999; Palincsar & Brown, 1984; Pressley & Forrest-Pressley, 1985; Schank, 1999; Van der Meij, 1994; Zimmerman, 1989). There are several reasons why question generation might play a central role in learning (Wisher & Graesser, 2007). The learner actively constructs knowledge in generating questions rather than passively receiving information. The act of generating questions should encourage learners to become more sensitive to their own knowledge deficits and comprehension failures.

The learner is presumably more motivated and engaged in the material when the experience is tailored to the learner's own needs. Learners are normally tested by answering questions, so the learner's generating questions should improve the overlap between the cognitive representations built during comprehension and the ideal representations that teachers test.

Empirical evidence supports the claim that improvements in the comprehension, learning, and memory of technical material can be achieved by training students to ask questions during comprehension (Ciardiello, 1998; Davey & McBride, 1986; Gavelek & Raphael, 1985; King, 1989, 1992, 1994; Palincsar & Brown, 1984; Rosenshine, Meister, & Chapman, 1996; Van der Meij, 1994; Wong, 1985). The process of question generation accounts for a significant amount of these improvements from question-generated learning, over and above the information supplied by answers. Rosenshine and colleagues (1996) provided the most comprehensive analysis of the impact of question generation on learning in their meta-analysis of 26 empirical studies that compared question-generation learning with conditions with appropriate controls. The outcome measures in these studies included standardized tests, short-answer or multiple-choice questions prepared by experimenters, and summaries of the texts. The median effect sizes were 0.36 for the standardized tests, 0.87 for the experimenter-generated tests, and 0.85 for the summary tests.

Training students to ask deep questions would, of course, be desired in the interventions. One of the key predictors of deep questions during inquiry is the existence of goals, tasks, or challenges that place individuals in *cognitive disequilibrium.* Learners face cognitive disequilibrium when they encounter obstacles to goals, anomalies, contradictions, incompatibilities with prior knowledge, salient contrasts, obvious gaps in knowledge, and uncertainty in the face of decisions (Chinn & Brewer, 1993; Collins, 1988; Festinger, 1957; Flammer, 1981; Graesser & McMahen, 1993; Schank, 1999). Graesser and his colleagues have developed a cognitive model of question asking called PREG (Graesser, Lu, Olde, Cooper-Pye, & Whitten, 2005; Graesser & Olde, 2003; Otero & Graesser, 2001) that embraces cognitive disequilibrium in its foundation. The term PREG stems from part of the word *pregunta,* which means "question" in Spanish. The PREG model has a set of rules that predict the particular questions that readers should ask on the basis of the characteristics of the text, the type of disequilibrium, the reader's background knowledge, and metacognitive standards of comprehension (Otero & Graesser, 2001). It is beyond the scope of this chapter to describe the PREG model in detail, however.

It is important to acknowledge that questions are not always generated by knowledge deficits and cognitive disequilibrium. Graesser, Person, and Huber (1992) identified four very different types of question-generation mechanisms that occur in naturalistic settings. Whereas the first category consists of bona fide *knowledge deficit* questions, the other three mechanisms address communication and social interaction processes. *Common-ground* questions are asked when the questioner wants to establish or confirm whether knowledge is shared between participants in the conversation (such as "Are we working on the third problem?" "Did you mean the independent variable?"). *Social coordination* questions are indirect requests for the addressee to perform an action or for the questioner to have permission to perform an action in a collaborative activity (e.g., "Could you graph these numbers?" "Can we take a break now?"). *Conversation-control* questions are asked to manipulate the flow of conversation or the attention of the speech participants (e.g., "Can I ask you a question?"). Sometimes it is ambiguous whether a student's question is a knowledge-deficit question or an attempt to get attention from a teacher, tutor, or peer.

Many, if not most, questions posed by students and teachers are not sincere information- seeking (SIS) questions. Van der Meij (1987) identified 11 assumptions that need to apply for a question to qualify as an SIS question:

1. The questioner does not know the information he or she asks for with the question.
2. The question specifies the information sought after.
3. The questioner believes that the presuppositions to the question are true.
4. The questioner believes that an answer exists.
5. The questioner wants to know the answer.
6. The questioner can assess whether a reply constitutes an answer.
7. The questioner poses the question only if the benefits exceed the costs.
8. The questioner believes that the respondent knows the answer.

9. The questioner believes that the respondent will not give the answer in absence of a question.
10. The questioner believes that the respondent will supply the answer.
11. A question solicits a reply.

A question is not an SIS question if one or more of these assumptions are not met. For example, a physics teacher grilling students with a series of questions in a classroom (e.g., *What forces are acting on the vehicle in the collision? What are the directions of the forces? What is the mass of the vehicle?*) is not asking SIS questions because the questions violate assumptions 1, 5, 8, and 10. Teachers know the answers to most questions they ask during these grilling sessions, so they are not modeling bona fide inquiry. Similarly, assumptions are violated by rhetorical questions (*When does a person know when he or she is happy?*), gripes (*When is it going to stop raining?*), greetings (*How are you?*), and attempts to redirect the flow of conversation in a group (a hostess asks a silent guest, *So when is your next vacation?*). In contrast, when a person's computer is malfunctioning, the following questions asked of a technical assistant are SIS questions: *What's wrong with my computer? How can I get it fixed? How much will it cost?*

The social and pragmatic mechanisms that underlie questions are sometimes important in education on dimensions other than deep learning of academic subject matter. They are important for acquiring skills of socialization and communication. Their significance may do little to clear the picture of what constitutes a good question, but it is essential to understand the social and communication processes when questions are embedded in educational practice. Aside from these pragmatic concerns, if the goal is to learn deep knowledge of academic content, then good questions are at the deeper levels of Graesser–Person taxonomy and more abstract levels of Mosenthal's taxonomy and use such question stems or expressions as *why, how, what caused, what are the consequences, what if, what if not,* and *so what.*

LEARNING TECHNOLOGIES THAT CAN IMPROVE QUESTIONS AND LEARNING

Most teachers, tutors, and student peers do not ask a high density of deep questions (Dillon, 1988; Graesser & Person, 1994), so students have limited exposure to high-quality inquiry. There are few role models in school environments through which students can learn good question asking and answering skills vicariously. This situation presents a golden opportunity for turning to technology to help fill this gap.

In the early 1990s, Graesser, Langston, and Baggett (1993) developed and tested Point & Query (P&Q) software that pushed the limits of learner question asking and that exposed the learner to a broad profile of question categories. College students learned about musical instruments entirely by asking questions and interpreting answers to questions. This system was a combination of a hypertext/hypermedia system and a question-asking and -answering facility (see Graesser, Hu, Person, Jackson, & Toth, 2004, for a recent application of P&Q to the subject matter of research ethics). In order to ask a question, the student points to a hot spot on the display (e.g., the double reed of an oboe) and clicks a mouse. Then a list of questions about the selected object or area of an object (e.g., the double reed of an oboe) is presented. Example questions are: *What does a double reed look like? What does an oboe sound like?* and *How does a double reed affect sound quality?* The learner subsequently clicks on the desired question, and an answer immediately appears. Therefore, the learner can ask a question very easily by two quick clicks of a mouse.

Research on the P&Q software proved to be quite illuminating from the standpoint of the quantity and quality of questions. Regarding quantity, learners ended up asking a mean of 120 questions per hour, which is approximately 700 times the rate of questions in the classroom (Graesser & Person, 1994). This is a dramatic increase in the rate of question asking, but the quality of question asking is also important to consider. The students in all conditions were exposed to both low-quality (shallow) and high-quality (deep) questions on the menu of question options on the P&Q software. The results revealed that the quality of student questions did not improve by simply exposing the students to menus of high-quality questions associated with hot spots in hypertext/hypermedia pages. When students explored the hypertext space on their own, they overwhelmingly tended to pose questions that tapped shallow knowledge much more often than deep knowledge. The only way to get the students to ask and explore deep questions was to give them task objectives that directly required deep learning, such as "Your goal is to design a new instrument that has a deep, pure tone." A satisfactory solution to this task required an understanding of how the dynamics of air reeds causes changes in the quality of sound and how the size of an instrument determines the resulting pitch. The questions selected by the students were highly skewed to the shallow end of the continuum unless there was a task goal that required an understanding of the science of sound.

A different approach to using technology is to use animated pedagogical agents to model good inquiry and to have the student vicariously observe such skills. The student could observe a curious learner agent who asks good questions while narrating a journey through the learning materials. The student could observe two agents having a conversation, with one asking good, deep questions about the learning materials and the other agent giving deep explanation-based answers. Instead of relying on humans to do this, computerized agents can provide the training both rigorously and tirelessly.

Animated pedagogical agents have become increasingly popular in recent advanced-learning environments (Atkinson, 2002; Baylor & Kim, 2005; Graesser, Lu, et al., 2004; McNamara, Levinstein, & Boonthum, 2004; Moreno & Mayer, 2004; Reeves & Nass, 1996). These agents interact with students and help them learn either by modeling good pedagogy or by holding a conversation directly with the student. The agents may take on different roles: mentors, tutors, peers, players in multiparty games, or avatars in the virtual worlds. In some systems, such as AutoTutor (Graesser, Lu, et al., 2004), the students hold a conversation with the computer in natural language. In other systems, the students vicariously observe agents that either present information in monologues, interact with each other in dialogues, or hold conversations with three or more agents.

One recent system with agents was designed with the explicit goal of modeling the asking of deep questions during learning. The system is called *iDRIVE,* which stands for *Instruction with Deep-level Reasoning questions In Vicarious Environments* (Craig, Gholson, Ventura, Graesser, & the Tutoring Research Group, 2000; Craig, Sullins, Witherspoon, & Gholson, 2006; Driscoll et al., 2003). iDRIVE has dyads of animated agents train students to learn science content by modeling deep-reasoning questions in question–answer dialogues. A student agent asks a series of deep questions (based on the Graesser–Person taxonomy) about the science content, and the teacher agent immediately answers each question. For example:

STUDENT AGENT: How does the earth's gravity affect the sun?

TUTOR AGENT: The sun experiences a force of gravity due to the earth, which is equal in magnitude and opposite in direction to the force of gravity on the earth due to the sun.

STUDENT AGENT: How does the gravitational force of the sun affect the earth?

TUTOR AGENT: The force of the sun on the earth will be equal and opposite to the force of the earth on the sun.

Learning gains on the effectiveness of iDRIVE on question asking, recall of text, and multiple-choice questions have shown effect sizes that range from 0.56 to 1.77 compared with a condition in which students listen to the monologue on the same content without questions. The version of iDRIVE that asks deep questions produced better learning than (1) a version that asked shallow questions instead of deep questions and (2) a version that gave a monologue and substituted questions with silence to control for time on task (Craig et al., 2006).

AutoTutor is another computer system that is motivated by theories of question-based inquiry and deep learning. AutoTutor is an intelligent tutoring system with an animated pedagogical agent that helps students learn by holding a conversation with them in natural language (Graesser, Lu, et al., 2004). One way of viewing AutoTutor is that it stimulates and continuously maintains an optimal level of cognitive disequilibrium in learners' minds by presenting thought-provoking challenging questions, sustaining goal-driven inquiry through continuous dialogue, and providing deep answers that exhibit explanations of the material. AutoTutor presents a series of questions or problems that require deep reasoning, as in the case of the following conceptual physics problem:

When a car without headrests on the seats is struck from behind, the passengers often suffer neck injuries. Why do passengers get neck injuries in this situation?

Composing an answer is challenging for most students when the ideal answer is lengthy or requires deep explanatory reasoning. A typical student produces only one or two sentences when initially asked one of these conceptual physics problems, whereas an ideal answer would be a paragraph in length (roughly 10 sentences). AutoTutor assists the learner in the evolution of an improved answer that draws out more of the learner's knowledge, that fills in missing information, and that corrects the learner's misconceptions. The dialogue between AutoTutor and student typically takes between 50 and 200 *turns* (i.e., the learner expresses something, then the tutor, then the learner, and so on) before a good answer to this single physics question emerges.

Four interesting results emerge from the AutoTutor research with respect to questions and learning. Three of the findings present optimistic news, but one suggests that there are limitations in this technology. First, assessments of AutoTutor on learning gains in 15 experiments have shown effect sizes of approximately 0.8 standard deviation units in the areas of computer literacy (Graesser et al., 2004) and Newtonian physics (VanLehn et al., 2007) compared with suitable control conditions (e.g., pretests, textbook reading control). These evaluations place Auto-Tutor somewhere between an untrained human tutor (Cohen, Kulik, & Kulik, 1982) and an intelligent tutoring system with ideal tutoring strategies (Corbett, 2001). Second, the interactive conversational aspects of AutoTutor show advantages over noninteractive content control conditions, but this advantage in interactivity occurs only when the subject matter content is more advanced than what the student already knows; otherwise, the interactive AutoTutor and noninteractive control conditions produce equivalent learning gains (VanLehn et al., 2007). Third, AutoTutor is effective in modeling deep questions because the proportion of student questions that are deep increases as a consequence of the interactions with AutoTutor (Graesser, McNamara, & VanLehn, 2005). Fourth, the modeling of deep questions is limited if AutoTutor provides poor answers to the questions. In fact, many students stop asking questions altogether if they are not satisfied with the quality of the answers that AutoTutor provides. An intelligent interactive learning environment may not be the best choice when the quality of the automated responses is poor or marginal. The more suitable alternative would be a choreographed dialogue between agents (such as iDRIVE) that exhibits excellent inquiry from which the student can vicariously learn.

A QUESTION-AUTHORING WORKBENCH

The previous sections in this chapter have made a number of claims about the relationships between questions and learning. Available research indicates that: (1) most students ask few questions in most learning settings; (2) questions of students, teachers, and textbook writers tend to be shallow rather than deep; (3) training students to ask deeper questions facilitates comprehension and learning; (4) a number of psychological models specify how to stimulate more and deeper questions—for example, teachers or agents modeling deep questions or presenting challenges that place the students in cognitive disequilibrium. Given this research context, the time is ripe for a research team to develop a *Question-Authoring Workbench* (QAW). The workbench would train instructors, students, textbook writers, curriculum developers, test constructors, and other educational communities to compose better questions that elevate standards of learning in the educational enterprise. The workbench would train question developers on theoretical principles of quality questions, present examples of high-quality questions, and guide the user of the workbench in creating questions in different cells of a large landscape of questions.

A Sketch of the Question–Authoring Workbench

The proposed workbench would have several modules that vary in the degree of interactivity with the user and in the sophistication of its computational components that automatically analyze language, discourse, and world knowledge. For example, a *didactic instruction* module in the workbench would be a repository of guidelines for the creation of different categories of questions, at varying levels of depth and relevance to the learning objectives. This might be organized according to the landscape of questions in Figure 7.1. A *scripted exemplar* module would augment the didactic instruction module by presenting and explaining questions that cover the broad landscape of question categories, types of knowledge, and cognitive skills. A *scripted interactive* module would go a step further by guiding the question writer in composing questions for a preselected corpus of texts, including explanatory feedback on the writer's contributions. A *question evaluation* module would critique questions created by the question writers on a preselected sample of texts. The four modules would hopefully create a learning environment that could be used by students in addition to researchers, teachers, textbook writers, and other professions in education.

Our workbench vision is compatible with research efforts at Educational Testing Service that draw on the expertise of multidisciplinary research teams with backgrounds in cognitive science, artificial intelligence, linguistics, and education (Bejar, 1993, 2002; Deane & Shee-han, 2003; Graff, Steffen, & Lawless, 2004). There are reasons for being optimistic that workbench modules can to some extent analyze language and provide adaptive feedback because there have been major advances in computational linguistics (Jurafsky & Martin, 2000), statistical representations of world knowledge (Landauer, McNamara, Dennis, & Kintsch, 2007), and discourse processes (Graesser, Gernsbacher, & Goldman, 2003). I (A. G.) have been involved with developing a number of systems that automatically analyze natural language, in addition to the AutoTutor system described earlier. For example, QUAID (Question Understanding Aid) is a Web tool that analyzes questions on the difficulty of the words, syntactic complexity, and working memory load (Graesser, Cai, Louwerse, & Daniel, 2006). Coh-Metrix (Graesser, McNamara, Louwerse, & Cai, 2004) is a tool on the Web that analyzes texts on hundreds of measures of words, syntactic complexity, referential cohesion, coherence of mental models, and genre. A QAW would be a feasible extension of these projects that integrate advances in computational linguistics, discourse processes, education, and cognitive science.

We imagine a QAW that could accommodate questions in a multiple-choice (MC) format, in addition to questions without response options. Nearly all sectors of education and training have relied on the MC question format: K–12 teachers, university professors, the textbook industry, the College Board and ETS (e.g., SAT, GRE), online universities, and training materials for business, industry, government, and the military. MC questions prevail in the formative assessments that occur during the learning process, in addition to the summative assessments that occur at the end of training and the completion of education milestones. Assessment methods are currently moving toward more constructive response formats, such as open-ended questions (Leacock & Chodorow, 2003), essays (Burstein, 2003; Foltz, Gilliam, & Kendall, 2000), mathematical derivations, and voice recordings (Zechner, Bejar, & Hemat, 2005), but these assessments are not likely to replace MC questions entirely. Moreover, the case can be made that (1) MC questions are more advantageous relative to open-ended questions under certain circumstances and (2) most of the criticisms of MC questions are largely based on the poor quality of MC items existing in the field, not necessarily because the MC question format is intrinsically unsuitable for assessment of deep knowledge or higher level cognitive skills.

Quality of MC Questions

Most readers of this chapter will have completed thousands of MC tests during their academic histories and will have constructed thousands of such questions themselves. However, the technical properties of good MC questions are not widely known. MC questions typically have a question *stem* and a list of *response options*. The *key* is the most accurate response option, whereas *distracters* are incorrect response options.

The quality of the MC questions can be evaluated with respect to the landscape of questions described in the first section of this chapter. However, an important additional consideration is the selection of the response options. To what extent is each response option a plausible answer and to what extent can the response options be differentiated? It is recommended that the distracters should vary by degree (Downing & Haladyna, 1997). For example, one distracter should be the *near miss*. This option is the most seductive distracter that reflects a common misconception that learners have. The discrimination between the key and the near miss should reflect an important learning objective or pedagogical point rather than testing an obscure, arbitrarily subtle, or unenlightening detail. The *thematic distracter* has content that is related to the topic at hand but that is not correct. A learner who quickly scans the learning materials would have trouble discriminating the thematic distracter from the key and near miss. The *unrelated distracter* would seem reasonable to someone who never read the material and might be plausible according to folklore and world knowledge. Our analyses of the corpus of MC questions about psychology (reported earlier) indicated that distracters rarely followed such systematic principles. As a result, the items were quite vulnerable to guessing or other unwanted processes that help learners identify the target without appropriately understanding the material. Instructors and question writers for textbooks rarely implement systematic methods of generating questions that are routinely implemented, at great expense, in the College Board and ETS.

There are circumstances in which MC questions with appropriate answer options are more discriminating in assessment of learning than questions with open-ended formats without response options. As an example, in one of our research projects we compared AutoTutor with various control conditions, such as reading yoked chapters from a textbook or reading a text that has information equivalence to AutoTutor. Learning gains for AutoTutor versus comparison conditions were assessed with over a dozen measures: (1) MC questions that tap shallow knowledge, such as definitions, facts, and properties of concepts; (2) MC questions that tap deep knowledge, such as causal reasoning, justifications of claims, and functional underpinnings of procedures; (3) written essays; (4) cloze tasks that require students to fill in missing words in texts to articulate explanatory reasoning on the subject matter; and (5) assessment tasks requiring problem solving (Graesser, Lu, et al., 2004; VanLehn et al., 2007). We were happy to document the advantages in learning of AutoTutor over various controls (Graesser, Lu, et al., 2004), but the important question arises as to which measures of evaluation were most sensitive in showing differences between Auto-Tutor and comparison conditions.

We have found that the MC questions that tap deep knowledge have consistently been the most sensitive measures of learning. However, this claim should be qualified by the constraints that we imposed on the construction of the MC questions. We adopted a principled framework for generating MC questions that taps the mental models that underlie science content. The framework was inspired by the field of qualitative physics (Forbus, 1984) and instantiated in the Force Concept Inventory for Newtonian physics (Hestenes, Wells, & Swackhamer, 1992). Suppose there is a set of components (e.g., object, event, action, or process) in a scientific system and that each component influences each other component in either a positive, negative, or neutral manner. A student with a deep understanding of the underlying mental model would be able to keep track of how all of the components would influence other components. Questions can be asked to tap this relational knowledge, such as the following:

When the passenger in a car is rear-ended, does the head initially (1) go forward, (2) go backward, or (3) stay the same?

A deep comprehender is able to trace the causal antecedents and causal consequences of an event, whereas a poor comprehender is undiscriminating in tracking the impact of one event on other events in the scientific system.

The strong form of our claim, based on the preceding finding, is that well-constructed MC questions that tap deep knowledge can be a more sensitive measure than open-ended questions and essays. MC questions can be composed to be more discriminating and can permit the researcher to target particular ideas and misconceptions. This may be particularly true when target knowledge involves groups of concepts that have formally defined conceptual relations. Each distracter option can represent different (sometimes erroneous) conceptual relations with the target knowledge, the question stem, or both, as in the case of science or mathematics. In contrast, recall tests and open-ended questions run the risk of allowing students to get by with vague or verbose answers that sidestep subtle discriminations among interrelated concepts in scientific explanatory systems. MC questions can potentially assess mastery of a broad diversity of content and skills that vary in subtlety, granularity, and depth. It is an empirical question, of course, whether the MC questions can achieve these ambitious goals. Ideally, MC questions could be developed that are firmly grounded in cognitive and learning sciences, as in the case of evidence-centered design (Mislevy, Steinberg, & Almond, 2003), tree-based regression (Sheehan, 2003), and rule space procedures (Buck, Van Essen, Tatsuoka, & Kostin, 1997).

FINAL COMMENTS

In this chapter we have advocated the development of a Question Authoring Workbench that would assist students, teachers, textbook writers, and researchers in composing better questions. The current questions prepared by teachers and textbook writers are often both shallow and poorly crafted, which in part explains why so many students have shallow standards for what it means to comprehend. The College Board and ETS have much better questions, but it is extremely expensive to design questions that satisfy constraints that serve psychometric engineering goals, theoretical components in the cognitive and learning sciences, and the standards articulated in educational communities. There needs to be an interdisciplinary confluence among cognitive science, psychometrics, computational linguistics, and education in order to solve this problem.

The QAW would expose the users to a landscape of questions that cross types of questions, knowledge, and cognitive processes. A simple QAW would provide didactic instruction on the landscape of questions and would present examples of both good and bad questions in the landscape. A traditional hypertext/hypermedia system would provide an adequate technology for providing these facilities. A more sophisticated QAW would prompt the user to generate questions and would give feedback on the quality of generated questions. This would require more sophisticated technologies from computational linguistics, discourse processes, artificial intelligence, and cognitive science.

The value of the workbench is bolstered by available research that has investigated relationships between learning and questions. Available research indicates that most students ask few questions in most learning settings; that the questions of students, teachers, and textbook writers tend to be shallow rather than deep; that training students to ask deeper questions facilitates comprehension and learning; and that an abundance of cognitive, discourse, and pedagogical theories exist that specify how to stimulate deeper questions.

It should be apparent that there is not a simple answer to *What is a good question?* We hope that this chapter provides the reader with some new perspectives and a comprehensive snapshot of our fundamental and unending quest. And Isabel Beck's *Questioning the Author* (Beck et al., 1997; Beck & McKeown, 2006) is positioned smack dab in the center of the puzzle.

ACKNOWLEDGMENTS

The research on AutoTutor was supported by the National Science Foundation (SBR 9720314, REC 0106965, REC 0126265, ITR 0325428, REESE 0633918), the Institute of Education Sciences (R305H050169, R305B070349), and the Department of Defense Multidisciplinary University Research Initiative (MURI), administered by the Office of Naval Research under grant N00014-00-1-0600. The Tutoring Research Group (TRG) is an interdisciplinary research team made up of researchers from psychology, computer science, physics, and education (visit *www.autotutor.org*). The research on QUAID was supported by the National Science Foundation (SES 9977969), and the research on Coh-Metrix was supported by the Institute for Education Sciences (IES R3056020018-02). Any opinions, findings, and conclusions or recommendations expressed in this material are those of the authors and do not necessarily reflect the views of National Science Foundation, Institute for Education Sciences, or Department of Defense.

REFERENCES

Atkinson, R. K. (2002). Optimizing learning from examples using animated pedagogical agents. *Journal of Educational Psychology, 94,* 416–427.
Baker, L. (1985). How do we know when we don't understand? Standards for evaluating text comprehension. In D. L. Forrest-Pressley, G. E. Mackinnon,

& T. G. Waller (Eds.), *Metacognition, cognition and human performance* (pp. 155–205). New York: Academic Press.

Baylor, A. L., & Kim, Y. (2005). Simulating instructional roles through pedagogical agents. *International Journal of Artificial Intelligence in Education, 15,* 95–115.

Beck, I. L., & McKeown, M. G. (2006). *Improving comprehension with Questioning the Author: A fresh and expanded view of a powerful approach.* New York: Scholastic.

Beck, I. L., McKeown, M. G., Hamilton, R. L., & Kucan, L. (1997). *Questioning the Author: An approach for enhancing student engagement with text.* Newark, DE: International Reading Association.

Bejar, I. I. (1993). A generative analysis of a three-dimensional spatial task. *Applied Psychological Measurement, 14,* 237–245.

Bejar, I. I. (2002). Generative testing: From conception to implementation. In S. H. Irvine & P. C. Kyllonen (Eds.), *Generating items from cognitive tests: Theory and practice* (pp. 199–217). Mahwah, NJ: Erlbaum.

Bloom, B. S. (1956). *Taxonomy of educational objectives: The classification of educational goals. Handbook 1. Cognitive domain.* New York: McKay.

Buck, G., Van Essen, T., Tatsuoka, K., & Kostin, I. (1997). *Identifying the cognitive attributes underlying performance on the PSAT Writing Test.* Unpublished manuscript.

Burstein, J. (2003). The *e-rater* scoring engine: Automated essay scoring with natural language processing. In M. D. Shermis & J. Burstein (Eds.), *Automated essay scoring: A cross-disciplinary perspective* (pp. 113–121). Hillsdale, NJ: Erlbaum.

Ciardiello, A. V. (1998). Did you ask a good question today? Alternative cognitive and metacognitive strategies. *Journal of Adolescent and Adult Literacy, 42,* 210–219.

Carroll, J. B. (1976). Psychometric tests as cognitive tasks: A new structure of intellect. In L. B. Resnick (Ed.), *The nature of intelligence* (pp. 27–56). Hillsdale, NJ: Erlbaum.

Carroll, J. B. (1987). Psychometric approaches to cognitive abilities and processes. In S. H. Irvine & S. E. Newstead (Eds.), *Intelligence and cognition: Contemporary frames of reference* (pp. 217–251). Boston: Martinus Nijhoff.

Chinn, C., & Brewer, W. (1993) The role of anomalous data in knowledge acquisition: A theoretical framework and implications for science instruction. *Review of Educational Research, 63,* 1–49.

Cohen, P. A., Kulik, J. A., & Kulik, C. C. (1982). Educational outcomes of tutoring: A meta-analysis of findings. *American Educational Research Journal, 19,* 237–248.

Collins, A. (1988). Different goals of inquiry teaching. *Questioning Exchange, 2,* 39–45.

Corbett, A. T. (2001). Cognitive computer tutors: Solving the two-sigma problem. In M. Bauer, P. J. Gmytrasiewlcz, & J. Vassileva (Eds.), *User Modeling 2001: Eighth International Conference, UM 2001* (pp. 137–147). Berlin: Springer.

Craig, S. D., Gholson, B., Ventura, M., Graesser, A. C., & the Tutoring Research Group. (2000). Overhearing dialogues and monologues in virtual tutoring sessions: Effects on questioning and vicarious learning. *International Journal of Artificial Intelligence in Education, 11,* 242–253.

Craig, S. D., Sullins, J., Witherspoon, A., & Gholson, B. (2006). Deep-level reasoning questions effect: The role of dialog and deep-level reasoning questions during vicarious learning. *Cognition and Instruction, 24*(4), 563–589.

Davey, B., & McBride, S. (1986). Effects of question generation on reading comprehension. *Journal of Educational Psychology, 78,* 256–262.

Deane, P., & Sheehan, K. (2003). *Automatic item generation via frame semantics: Natural language generation of math word problems.* Available at *http://ccl.pku. edu.cn/doubtfire/Semantics/AutomaticItemGenerationViaFrameSemantics=by= deane.pdf.*

Dillon, J. (1988). *Questioning and teaching: A manual of practice.* New York: Teachers College Press.

Downing, S. M., & Haladyna, T. M. (1997). Test item development: Validity evidence from quality assurance procedures. *Applied Measurement in Education, 10,* 61–82.

Driscoll, D. M., Craig, S. D., Gholson, B., Ventura, M., Hu, X., & Graesser, A. C. (2003). Vicarious learning: Effects of overhearing dialog and monolog-like discourse in a virtual tutoring session. *Journal of Educational Computing Research, 29,* 431–450.

Edelson, D. C., Gordin, D. N., & Pea, R. D. (1999). Addressing the challenges of inquiry-based learning through technology and curriculum design. *Journal of the Learning Sciences, 8,* 391–450.

Festinger, L. (1957). *A theory of cognitive dissonance.* Evanston, IL: Row, Peterson.

Flammer, A. (1981). Towards a theory of question asking. *Psychological Research, 43,* 407–420.

Foltz, W., Gilliam, S., & Kendall, S. (2000). Supporting content-based feedback in on-line writing evaluation with LSA. *Interactive Learning Environments, 8,* 111–128.

Forbus, K. D. (1984). Qualitative process theory. *Artificial Intelligence, 24,* 85–168.

Gavelek, J. R., & Raphael, T. E. (1985). Metacognition, instruction, and the role of questioning activities. In D. L. Forrest-Pressley, G. E. MacKinnon, & G. T. Waller (Eds.), *Metacognition, cognition, and human performance: Instructional practices* (Vol. 2, pp. 103–136). Orlando, FL: Academic Press.

Goldman, S. R., Duschl, R. A., Ellenbogen, K., Williams, S., & Tzou, C. T. (2003). Science inquiry in a digital age: Possibilities for making thinking visible. In H. van Oostendorp (Ed.), *Cognition in a digital world* (pp. 253–284). Mahwah, NJ: Erlbaum.

Good, T. L., Slavings, R. L., Harel, K. H., & Emerson, M. (1987). Students' passivity: A study of question asking in K–12 classrooms. *Sociology of Education, 60,* 181–199.

Graesser, A. C., Cai, Z., Louwerse, M., & Daniel, F. (2006). Question Understanding Aid (QUAID): A web facility that helps survey methodologists improve the comprehensibility of questions. *Public Opinion Quarterly, 70,* 3–22.

Graesser, A. C., Gernsbacher, M. A., & Goldman, S. (Eds.). (2003). *Handbook of discourse processes.* Mahwah, NJ: Erlbaum.

Graesser, A. C., Gordon, S. E., & Brainerd, L. E. (1992). QUEST: A model of question answering. *Computers and Mathematics with Applications, 23,* 733–745.

Graesser, A. C., Hu, X., Person, P., Jackson, T., & Toth, J. (2004). Modules and information retrieval facilities of the Human Use Regulatory Affairs Advisor (HURAA). *International Journal on eLearning, 3,* 29–39.

Graesser, A. C., Lang, K. L., & Roberts, R. M. (1991). Question answering in the context of stories. *Journal of Experimental Psychology: General, 120,* 254–277.

Graesser, A. C., Langston, M. C., & Baggett, W. B. (1993). Exploring information about concepts by asking questions. In G. V. Nakamura, R. M. Taraban, & D. Medin (Eds.), *The psychology of learning and motivation: Vol. 29. Categorization by humans and machines* (pp. 411–436). Orlando, FL: Academic Press.

Graesser, A. C., Lu, S., Jackson, G. T., Mitchell, H., Ventura, M., Olney, A., et al. (2004). AutoTutor: A tutor with dialogue in natural language. *Behavioral Research Methods, Instruments, and Computers, 36,* 180–193.

Graesser, A. C., Lu, S., Olde, B. A., Cooper-Pye, E., & Whitten, S. (2005). Question asking and eye tracking during cognitive disequilibrium: Comprehending illustrated texts on devices when the devices break down. *Memory and Cognition, 33,* 1235–1247.

Graesser, A. C., & McMahen, C. L. (1993). Anomalous information triggers questions when adults solve problems and comprehend stories. *Journal of Educational Psychology, 85,* 136–151.

Graesser, A. C., McNamara, D. S., Louwerse, M. M., & Cai, Z. (2004). Coh-Metrix: Analysis of text on cohesion and language. *Behavioral Research Methods, Instruments, and Computers, 36,* 193–202.

Graesser, A. C., McNamara, D. S., & VanLehn, K. (2005). Scaffolding deep comprehension strategies through Point&Query, AutoTutor, and iSTART. *Educational Psychologist, 40,* 225–234.

Graesser, A. C., Millis, K. K., & Zwaan, R. A. (1997). Discourse comprehension. *Annual Review of Psychology, 48,* 163–189.

Graesser, A. C., & Olde, B. A. (2003). How does one know whether a person understands a device? The quality of the questions the person asks when the device breaks down. *Journal of Educational Psychology, 95,* 524–536.

Graesser, A. C., & Person, N. K. (1994). Question asking during tutoring. *American Educational Research Journal, 31,* 104–137.

Graesser, A. C., Person, N., & Huber, J. (1992). Mechanisms that generate questions. In T. Lauer, E. Peacock, & A. C. Graesser (Eds.), *Questions and information systems* (pp. 167–187). Hillsdale, NJ: Erlbaum.

Graff, E. A., Steffen, M., & Lawless, R. (2004). *Statistical and cognitive analysis of quantitative item models.* Paper presented at the annual conference of the International Association for Educational Assessment (IAEA), Philadelphia.

Guthrie, J. T. (1988). Locating information in documents: Examination of a cognitive model. *Reading Research Quarterly, 23,* 178–199.

Hacker, D. J., Dunlosky, J., & Graesser, A. C. (Eds.). (1998). *Metacognition in educational theory and practice.* Mahwah, NJ: Erlbaum.

Hestenes, D., Wells, M., & Swackhamer, G. (1992). Force Concept Inventory. *Physics Teacher, 30,* 141–158.

Jurafsky, D., & Martin, J. H. (2000). *Speech and language processing: An introduction to natural language processing, computational linguistics, and speech recognition.* Upper Saddle River, NJ: Prentice-Hall.

King, A. (1989). Effects of self-questioning training on college students' comprehension of lectures. *Contemporary Educational Psychology, 14,* 366–381.

King, A. (1992). Comparison of self-questioning, summarizing, and notetaking-review as strategies for learning from lectures. *American Educational Research Journal, 29,* 303–323.

King, A. (1994). Guiding knowledge construction in the classroom: Effects of teaching children how to question and how to explain. *American Educational Research Journal, 31,* 338–368.

Kintsch, W. (1998). *Comprehension: A paradigm for cognition.* Cambridge, UK: Cambridge University Press.

Kyllonen, P. C., & Roberts, R. D. (2003). Cognitive process assessment. In R. Fernandez-Ballesteros (Ed.), *Encyclopedia of psychological assessment* (pp. 200–203). London: Sage.

Landauer, T., McNamara, D. S., Dennis, S., & Kintsch, W. (Eds.). (2007). *Handbook on latent semantic analysis.* Mahwah, NJ: Erlbaum.

Leacock, C., & Chodorow, M. (2003). C-rater: Scoring of short-answer questions. *Computers and the Humanities, 37,* 389–405.

Lehmann, F. (1992). *Semantic networks in artificial intelligence.* New York: Elsevier Science.

Lehnert, W. G. (1978). *The process of question answering: A computer simulation of cognition.* Hillsdale, NJ: Erlbaum.

Lenat, D. B. (1995). Cyc: A large-scale investment in knowledge infrastructure. *Communications of the ACM, 38,* 33–38.

McNamara, D. S., Levinstein, I. B., & Boonthum, C. (2004). iSTART: Interactive strategy trainer for active reading and thinking. *Behavioral Research Methods, Instruments, and Computers, 36,* 222–233.

Mislevy, R. J., Steinberg, L. S., & Almond, R. G. (2003). On the structure of educational assessments. *Measurement: Interdisciplinary Research and Perspectives, 1,* 3–62.

Moreno, R., & Mayer, R. E. (2004). Personalized messages that promote science learning in virtual environments. *Journal of Educational Psychology, 96,* 165–173.

Mosenthal, P. (1996). Understanding the strategies of document literacy and their conditions of use. *Journal of Educational Psychology, 88,* 314–332.

Otero, J., & Graesser, A. C. (2001). PREG: Elements of a model of question asking. *Cognition and Instruction, 19,* 143–175.

Palincsar, A. S., & Brown, A. (1984). Reciprocal teaching of comprehension-fostering and comprehension-monitoring activities. *Cognition and Instruction, 1,* 117–175.

Perfetti, C. A., Britt, M. A., & Georgi, M. (1995). *Text-based learning and reasoning: Studies in history.* Hillsdale, NJ: Erlbaum.

Pressley, M., & Forrest-Pressley, D. (1985). Questions and children's cognitive processing. In A. C. Graesser & J. B. Black (Eds.), *The psychology of questions* (pp. 277–296). Hillsdale, NJ: Erlbaum.

Reder, L. (1987). Strategy selection in question answering. *Cognitive Psychology, 19,* 90–138.

Reeves, B., & Nass, C. (1996). *The media equation: How people treat computers, televisions, and new media like real people and places.* Cambridge, UK: Cambridge University Press.

Rosenshine, B., Meister, C., & Chapman, S. (1996). Teaching students to generate questions: A review of the intervention studies. *Review of Educational Research, 66,* 181–221.

Rouet, J. (2006). *The skills of document use: From text comprehension to web-based learning.* Mahwah, NJ: Erlbaum.

Schank, R. (1999). *Dynamic memory revisited.* New York: Cambridge University Press.

Sheehan, K. M. (2003). Tree-based regression: A new tool for understanding cognitive skill requirements. In H. F. O'Neal & R. S. Perez (Eds.), *Technology and applications in education* (pp. 222–227). Mahwah, NJ: Erlbaum.

Singer, M. (2003). Processes of question answering. In G. Rickheit, T. Hermann, & W. Deutsch (Eds.), *Psycholinguistics* (pp. 422–431). Berlin: de Gruyter.

Snow, C. (2002). *Reading for understanding: Toward an R&D program in reading comprehension.* Santa Monica, CA: RAND.

Sowa, J. F. (1983). *Conceptual structures: Information processing in mind and machine.* Reading, MA: Addison-Wesley.

Van der Meij, H. (1987). Assumptions of information-seeking questions. *Questioning Exchange, 1,* 111–118.

Van der Meij, H. (1994). Student questioning: A componential analysis. *Learning and Individual Differences, 6,* 137–161.

VanLehn, K., Graesser, A. C., Jackson, G. T., Jordan, P., Olney, A., & Rose, C. P. (2007). When are tutorial dialogues more effective than reading? *Cognitive Science, 31,* 3–62.

Wisher, R. A., & Graesser, A. C. (2007). Question asking in advanced distributed learning environments. In S. M. Fiore & E. Salas (Eds.), *Toward a science of distributed learning and training* (pp. 209–234). Washington, DC: American Psychological Association.

Wong, B. Y. L. (1985). Self-questioning instructional research: A review. *Review of Educational Research, 55,* 227–268.

Zechner, K., Bejar, I. I., & Hemat, R. (2005, January). *Towards an understanding of the role of speech recognition in non-native speech assessment.* Paper presented at the Review of Assessment Design Capabilities Initiative, Educational Testing Service, Princeton, NJ.

Zimmerman, B. J. (1989). A social cognitive view of self-regulated academic learning. *Journal of Educational Psychology, 81,* 329–339.

8

DEVELOPING A MODEL OF QUALITY TALK ABOUT LITERARY TEXT

Ian A. G. Wilkinson, Anna O. Soter,
and P. Karen Murphy

Having Australian roots, I (I. W.) had the good fortune (or misfortune) to complete three theses or dissertations over the course of my academic apprenticeship. My honor's qualifying thesis focused on students' sentence-level processing in reading as demonstrated by their oral reading errors (Wilkinson & Brown, 1983). My master's thesis focused on students' discourse-level processing of narrative texts (Wilkinson, Elkins, & Bain, 1995). My doctoral dissertation focused on the dynamics of reading groups during teacher-guided instruction (Wilkinson & Anderson, 1995). With each successive study, I investigated students' processing of larger units of text, and I moved closer to understanding the instructional contexts that shaped students' learning.

My "discovery" of reading instruction stemmed from my experience as a research assistant for the Commission on Reading, charged with writing *Becoming a Nation of Readers* (Anderson, Hiebert, Scott, & Wilkinson, 1985). Isabel Beck was a member of the commission, and a fearsome one at that (at least for a first-year doctoral student). In the course of my interactions with Isabel, I learned that, contrary to my image, gained from a promotional photograph, the building that housed the Learning Research and Development Center (LRDC) was *not* in fact cascading down a hill (it is indeed quite stable). Some years later, I was told in no uncertain terms by Isabel that my doctoral advisor, Richard C. Anderson, and I put too many variables in our regression equations (she was right). These were important lessons!

On a more serious note, I learned from Isabel that text matters. Indeed, Isabel has spent her career investigating the properties of successively larger units of text and demonstrating their cognitive consequences for students' comprehension and learning. I also learned from Isabel that, just as text matters, so does instruction. Of necessity, students in their day-to-day classroom instruction deal with texts of varying quality. As Isabel and her colleagues have convincingly demonstrated in their work on "Questioning the Author," teachers play an important role in mediating students' understanding and learning when students are reading texts that are not always considerate in terms of the cognitive demands they place on students.

Since my doctoral work, I have become increasingly interested in the role of language as one of the most important instructional factors mediating learning. In my doctoral work, I viewed talk in small-group lessons as an "extended text" that served as a resource for students and a means of rehearsal of text information (a curiously behavioral interpretation). Indeed, one of the more interesting results in my dissertation was the finding that students' reinstatement of text propositions in discussion had significant positive effects on students' recall of the text (Wilkinson & Anderson, 1995). In a more recent review of research on peer influences on learning, I came to view talk as a cognitive tool to help students organize their thoughts, to reason, to plan, and to reflect on their actions (Wilkinson & Fung, 2002). The research I reviewed on peer-led, heterogeneous ability groups showed that group interactions and discourse helped promote students' cognitive restructuring, problem solving, and other forms of higher level thinking. In my most recent work, I have come to view talk as a sociocultural tool for thinking together, or what Mercer (2000, 2002) calls "interthinking." According to this view, talk offers students a means to combine their intellectual resources to collectively make sense of experience and to solve problems.

In what follows, I report on one part of a recent 4-year project that my colleagues and I completed that builds on this view of talk as a sociocultural tool. The work investigates discussions as a means of fostering students' high-level comprehension of narrative text and examines the kinds of talk that mediate students' understanding and learning. As will be seen, it stands on the shoulders of Isabel and her colleagues, in their work on Questioning the Author, as well as on those of other leading researchers who have studied text-based discussions.

OVERVIEW

Talk is a central feature of social-constructivist pedagogy, and research is beginning to reveal those aspects of talk that can be relied on as either agents or signals of student learning. Select empirical and theoretical research shows that the quality of classroom talk is closely connected to the quality of student problem solving, understanding, and learning (e.g., Mercer, 1995, 2002; Nystrand, Gamoran, Kachur, & Prendergast, 1997; Wegerif, Mercer, & Dawes, 1999). This research indicates that there is sufficient reliability in language use to enable us to make valid inferences about the productiveness of talk for student learning (see also Anderson, Chinn, Chang, Waggoner, & Yi, 1997; Applebee, Langer, Nystrand, & Gamoran, 2003). Assuredly, the discourse–learning nexus is complex and highly situated, and the mapping between discourse and learning is imperfect. Nevertheless, my colleagues and I believe that the research has reached a level of maturity at which we can identify those aspects of discourse and attendant classroom norms that shape student learning.

In 2002, we embarked on a journey to investigate an important issue concerning social-constructivist pedagogy in reading, the impact of classroom discussions on students' high-level comprehension of text. We used the term *high-level comprehension* to refer to critical, reflective thinking about and around text. Borrowing from Chang-Wells and Wells's (1993) idea of literate thinking, we viewed high-level comprehension as requiring students to engage with text in an epistemic mode to acquire not only knowledge of the topic but also knowledge about how to think about the topic and the capability to reflect on one's own thinking. We regarded it as very similar to what Resnick (1987) defined as higher order thinking, a process that involved "elaborating, adding complexity, and going beyond the given" (p. 42). We were aware that there were already a considerable number of approaches to conducting classroom discussions. What we thought was lacking in the literature on these approaches was an overarching framework to help educators make sense of the myriad methods, their similarities and differences, and their strengths and weaknesses. We sought to bring some order to the field by identifying converging evidence on the use of discussion to promote high-level comprehension of text and to advance understanding of how teachers can use discussions in ways that are sensitive to their instructional goals and to the contexts in which they work.

Over the next 4 years, we conducted an exhaustive synthesis of the research on text-based discussions.[1] We identified nine approaches to conducting discussion that demonstrated potential to promote students' high-level comprehension of text. We developed and validated a conceptual framework describing similarities and differences among the nine approaches in terms of parameters that pertain to key decisions teachers make to define the instructional frame for discussion. We conducted a comprehensive meta-analysis of 42 quantitative studies to examine the effects of the discussion approaches on teacher–student talk and on individual student comprehension and learning outcomes. We also analyzed the discourse arising from the discussions and evaluated the approaches on a common set of discourse features known to characterize quality discussions to provide a richer understanding of the nature of students' thinking.

To qualify for inclusion in our synthesis of research, an approach to discussion had to demonstrate consistency of application and have an established place in educational research or practice based on a record of peer-reviewed empirical research conducted in the past three decades. Nine approaches qualified for inclusion in our synthesis: Instructional Conversations (ICs; Goldenberg, 1993), Junior Great Books Shared Inquiry (JGB; Great Books Foundation, 1987), Questioning the Author (QtA; Beck & McKeown, 2006; Beck, McKeown, Hamilton, & Kucan, 1997) Collaborative Reasoning (CR; Anderson, Chinn, Chang, Waggoner, & Nguyen, 1998), Paideia Seminars (PS; Billings & Fitzgerald, 2002), Philosophy for Children (P4C; Sharp, 1995), Book Club (BC; Raphael & McMahon, 1994), Grand Conversations (GCs; Eeds & Wells, 1989), and Literature Circles (LCs; Short & Pierce, 1990). These approaches serve various purposes depending on the goals teachers set for their students: to acquire information on an efferent level, to adopt a critical–analytic stance, and/or to respond to literature on an aesthetic or expressive level. Nevertheless, in our judgment, all had

---

[1] This project was funded by the Institute of Education Sciences, U.S. Department of Education, under PR/Award No. R305G020075, "Group Discussions as a Mechanism for Promoting High-Level Comprehension of Text."

potential to help students develop high-level thinking and comprehension of text.

Rather reluctantly, as an outcome of this 4-year endeavor, we developed a model of discussion for promoting high-level comprehension that we called Quality Talk. This model combined the best features of the nine approaches while foregrounding features of those approaches that, we came to learn, gave prominence to the critical–analytic stance (CR, PS, and P4C). At the time, we were not sure the field needed yet another approach to classroom discussions. Nor were we certain that our model offered anything new above and beyond what other approaches offered. By definition of the way we developed Quality Talk, it shared many features with existing approaches. Nevertheless, by developing the model, we were able to test our ideas about what makes for productive discussions about text.

In this chapter, we describe the journey we took in developing Quality Talk. First, we describe the four elements of the model and explain where each of the elements came from. Second, we present an integrative view of the model such as we might present to teachers. Third, we describe the approach to professional development that is key to teachers' implementation of the model. Fourth, we illustrate what the model looks like in the classroom. Fifth, we reflect on what the model has to offer over and above extant models.

As a backdrop to describing this journey, it is worth noting that development of our model was informed by the results of our meta-analysis of discussion approaches. One of the major findings from the meta-analysis was that the approaches to discussion differentially promoted high-level comprehension of text. Many of the approaches were highly effective at promoting students' comprehension, especially those that we categorized as more efferent in nature, namely QtA, IC, and JGB. Moreover, some of the approaches were effective at promoting students' critical thinking, reasoning, argumentation, and metacognition about and around text, especially CR and JGB. Critical thinking, reasoning, argumentation, and metacognition aligned well with our notion of high-level comprehension. A second major finding was that increases in student talk did not necessarily result in concomitant increases in student comprehension. Rather, it seemed that a particular kind of talk was necessary to promote comprehension. As we looked for what were the operative features in extant approaches, these findings steered us toward those approaches that were more critical–analytic in nature and to the kinds of talk that seemed to promote high-level thinking and reasoning.

FOUR ELEMENTS OF QUALITY TALK

Quality Talk is an approach to classroom discussion premised on the belief that talk is a tool for thinking and that certain kinds of talk can contribute to high-level comprehension of text. We describe our model in terms of four elements: (1) an ideal instructional frame for discussion; (2) discourse tools and signs to promote productive talk about text; (3) conversational moves for teacher modeling and scaffolding; and (4) a set of pedagogical principles.

Ideal Instructional Frame

We developed what we call an "ideal" instructional frame for conducting productive discussions from our analysis of the nine discussion approaches. This frame represents a set of conditions that we think are important for promoting quality talk about text; there is room for variation from these conditions, but they reflect what we think is ideal. To develop this frame, we read all available documents and viewed videos describing the approaches and coded them on various parameters of discussion. The parameters related to key decisions that teachers make to define the instructional frame for discussion. We began by describing the approaches in terms of the parameters identified by Chinn, Anderson, and Waggoner (2001): To what extent does the orientation toward the text correspond to an *aesthetic, efferent,* and *critical–analytic stance?* Who has *interpretive authority?* Who has *control of the topic?* Who *controls turns* for speaking? To these, we added parameters suggested by Hanssen (1990), as well as others, that we thought captured important variation among the approaches: Who *chooses the text?* What *genre* is used? When does *reading* occur? Is discussion *whole class or a small group?* Is the group *homogeneous or heterogeneous* in ability? Is the group *teacher- or peer-led?* To what degree is discussion focused on *authorial intent?* In total, we coded the approaches on 13 parameters.

We found it was relatively easy to code the approaches in terms of stance. We agreed that LCs, GCs, and BC gave prominence to the expressive stance; QtA, ICs, and JGB gave prominence to the efferent stance; and PS, CR, and P4C gave prominence to the critical–analytic stance. Our understanding of stance was informed by Rosenblatt's (1978) characterization of the aesthetic and efferent stance. However, we took issue with the term *aesthetic* as applied to these discussions because, in our judgment, few actually attained a truly aesthetic response (see Soter & Shen, 2005, for a discussion of this issue). Instead, we chose to use the term *expressive,* after Jakobson (1987), to describe a reader-focused response. In this stance, discussion gives prominence to the reader's affective response to the text, to the reader's own spontaneous, emotive connection to all aspects of the textual experience. We defined an efferent stance as a text-focused response in which discussion gives prominence to reading to acquire and retrieve information. The focus is on "the ideas, information, directions, conclusions to be retained, used, or acted on after the reading event" (Rosenblatt, 1978, p. 27). Drawing on the work of Wade, Thompson, and Watkins (1994), we defined a critical–analytic stance as a more objective, critical response in which discussion gives prominence to interrogating or querying the text in search of the underlying arguments, assumptions, worldviews, or beliefs. This stance engages the reader's querying mind, prompting him or her to ask questions.

As we coded the approaches on the parameters, we had two major revelations. One revelation was that there seemed to be a relation between the stance realized in the discussions and the control exerted by teachers versus students. Discussions that gave prominence to an expressive stance (LCs, GCs, and BC) were ones in which students seemed to have the greatest control. By contrast, discussions that gave prominence to an efferent stance (QtA, ICs, and JGB) were ones in which teachers seemed to have the greatest control. And discussions that gave prominence to the critical–analytic stance (PS, CR, and P4C) were ones in which teachers and students seemed to share control. We noted that, in the more critical–analytic approaches, the teacher had considerable control over text and topic, but students had considerable interpretive authority and control over turn taking (i.e., a more open participation structure).

Another revelation was that at least a moderate degree of emphasis on the efferent and the expressive stances seemed necessary for discussion to foster a high critical–analytic orientation to text. There were not enough degrees of freedom among the nine approaches for us to be sure about this conjecture, but it was, at least, consistent with other theory on the role of knowledge and affect in learning. Piaget (1954/1981), for instance, thought of interest as the "fuel" for constructive activity and argued that both emotional and intellectual engagement were necessary for sustained inquiry.

We speculated that the shared control between teacher and students in the more critical–analytic approaches helped foster the knowledge-driven and affective engagement. Indeed, we thought of the shared control as the "group-level substrate" that helped give rise to the efferent and expressive responses that, in turn, fueled the critical–analytic stance.

Thus our ideal instructional frame for conducting productive discussions includes shared control between teacher and students, in which the teacher has control over choice of text and topic but students have interpretive authority and control of turns (i.e., there is an open participation structure). Another important feature is a moderate to high degree of emphasis on the expressive and efferent stances toward the text. As indicated, we believe at least a moderate degree of knowledge-driven and affective engagement is necessary (though not sufficient) for students to interrogate or query text in search of its underlying arguments, assumptions, worldviews, or beliefs. Students need to be encouraged to make spontaneous, emotive connections to the textual experience (i.e., a personal, expressive response) while reading to acquire and retrieve information (i.e., an efferent stance). Having connected with the text and gained a general understanding, students are well positioned to adopt a critical–analytic stance. These features and other parameter values of our ideal frame for conducting discussions about text are shown in Table 8.1.

Discourse Tools and Signs

Our understanding of the discourse tools and signs for productive talk about text came from our analysis of the discourse of the nine discussion approaches. We sought to analyze transcripts of the discussions in terms of discourse features that might serve as proximal indicators of high-level comprehension. First, we scoured the research literature on classroom discourse and student learning to identify features of discourse that were linked to high-level comprehension. We looked for features for which there was good theoretical warrant for believing that they were linked to high-level thinking and comprehension and good empirical research demonstrating that connection.

TABLE 8.1. Parameter Values of an Ideal Instructional Frame for Productive Discussion about Text

Parameter	Ideal value
Prediscussion activity	Yes, to promote individual response
Choice of text	Teacher
Control of topic	Teacher
Interpretive authority	Students
Control of turns	Students
Whole class/small group	Small group
Teacher-/peer-led	Either, but begin with teacher-led
Grouping by ability	Heterogeneous
Reading before/during	Before
Genre	Narrative fiction
Expressive stance	Medium to high
Efferent stance	Medium to high
Critical–analytic stance	High
Postdiscussion activity	Yes; sometimes content, sometimes process

After several months of searching the literature and testing candidate discourse features on samples of transcripts, we arrived at a set of features that we thought might serve as proximal indicators of students' high-level comprehension. These were: teachers' and students' use of authentic questions, uptake, and questions that elicit high-level thinking (i.e., generalization, analysis, speculation) (Nystrand et al., 1997; Nystrand, Wu, Gamoran, Zeiser, & Long, 2003); teacher and students' use of questions that elicit extratextual connections (i.e., affective, intertextual, and shared knowledge connections) (Allington & Johnston, 2002; Applebee et al., 2003; Bloome & Egan-Robertson, 1993; Edwards & Mercer, 1987; Shuart-Faris & Bloome, 2004; Taylor, Pearson, Peterson, & Rodriguez, 2003); students' elaborated explanations (Chinn, O'Donnell, & Jinks, 2000; Webb, 1989); and students' exploratory talk (Mercer, 1995, 2000). We also identified a number of "reasoning words," words that, when used in appropriate contexts, signal reasoning (Wegerif & Mercer, 1997; Wegerif, Mercer & Dawes, 1999). Table 8.2 provides definitions and examples of these features.

Next, we analyzed full transcripts of discussions from the nine approaches for these features. Following Nystrand and colleagues (1997),

TABLE 8.2. Discourse Tools and Signs for Productive Classroom Discussion about Text

Discourse feature	Teacher (T) Student (S)	Definition	Examples
Authentic question	T&S	Answer is not prespecified; speaker is genuinely interested in knowing how others will respond.	"How do you think annoying them would do that?"
Uptake	T&S	A speaker asks a question about something that another speaker has uttered previously. Often marked by use of pronouns.	"How did it work?" "What causes this?"
High-level thinking question	T&S	Marked by analysis, generalization, speculation: "How?" "Why?" "What if?"	"So how did Fulton's success affect river travel?"
Affective response question	T&S	Makes connections between text and student's own feelings or life experiences.	"What did you feel?"
Intertextual response question	T&S	Makes connection between text and another text, or other works of art, media, TV, newspapers, etc.	"How is that like another book we read?"
Shared knowledge response question	T&S	Makes connection between current discussion and previous discussions or knowledge that has been shared.	"What did we talk about last week that relates to this?"
Elaborated explanation	S	Thinking is explained in some detail through extension, building on an idea step by step, giving reasons for a statement, expanding on a statement.	"I agree with Joseph, because he keeps annoying them by saying 'shut up,' and I think he is trying to just get them to let him play because they wouldn't let him play because he didn't have his glove."

(*continued*)

TABLE 8.2. (*continued*)

Discourse feature	Teacher (T) Student (S)	Definition	Examples
Exploratory talk	S	Coreasoning in which students build and share knowledge over several turns, evaluate evidence, consider options. Use language to "chew" on ideas, to think collectively. Typically contains clusters of reasoning words.	S1: "But why do you think she wants to be a kid?" S2: "Because she likes to swim and be around lots of kids." S3: "And she likes playing a lot, with kids and stuff." S1: "Yes." S4: "And I agree, because if she wasn't swimming, she'd probably be sitting back in a rocking chair. She's having a lot of fun, just like the children."
Reasoning words	S	Conjunctions and phrases that indicate a reasoning process is at work (e.g., adverbial conjunctions).	*Because, if, so, I think, agree, disagree, would, could, maybe, might, how, why*

we coded questions based on what they elicited from students rather than based on their form; in other words, we coded "question events." In Nystrand and colleagues' view, questions are "sites of interaction" (p. 144) at which students' responses to questions reflect their understandings of the interactions as manifest in their discourse moves.

One insight we gained from this analysis was that the more critical–analytic and more expressive approaches seemed to offer the greatest opportunities for students to engage in high-level thinking and reasoning. These approaches showed high incidences of authentic questions and uptake—discourse moves that Nystrand and colleagues (1997) viewed as providing epistemological space in which students can construct knowledge. Commensurate with this pattern of findings, these approaches also showed high incidences of questions that elicited high-level thinking (analysis, generalization, speculation) and high incidences of elaborated explanations and/or exploratory talk.

However, what distinguished the more critical–analytic approaches from the more expressive approaches were differences in the opportunities for individual and collective reasoning. The more critical–analytic approaches, especially CR and P4C, showed high incidences of both elaborated explanations and exploratory talk (JGB also fared quite well in this regard). By contrast, the more expressive approaches showed high incidences of exploratory talk but somewhat lower incidences of elaborated explanations. We think the shared control between teachers and students in the more critical–analytic discussions is responsible for the richer reasoning. The shared control provides space for students to engage in extended episodes of collective reasoning, but it still affords teachers opportunities to model, scaffold, and prompt students' individual reasoning.

This explanation is supported by the pattern of findings within the expressive approaches. In BC, in which the teacher is absent in the small-group discussions, we found that there were more opportunities for exploratory talk than in LC and GC. Conversely, in LC and GC, where the teacher is usually present, we found that there were more elaborated explanations (though still not as much as in the critical–analytic approaches).

Taken together, our findings support the view that productive discussions are structured and focused yet not dominated by the teacher. They suggest that productive discussions occur where students hold the floor for extended periods of time, where students are prompted to discuss texts through open-ended or authentic questions, and where discussion incorporates a high degree of uptake. Our findings also suggest that a certain amount of modeling and scaffolding on the part of the teacher is necessary to prompt elaborated forms of individual reasoning from students.

In our Quality Talk model, we call the discourse features "tools and signs" to help teachers promote productive discussion and understand when it might be occurring. Following Vygotsky (1978), we refer to them as *tools* and *signs* to emphasize that some act as external agents to promote productive talk among students and some serve as internal signs of students' high-level thinking and comprehension. Some of them are epistemological tools teachers can use to give students greater control over the flow of information: asking authentic questions that invite a range of responses from students; employing uptake to build on students' contributions; and asking questions that elicit students' high-level thinking (i.e., generalization, analysis, and speculation). Some are signs of individual and collective reasoning that teachers can look for and encourage, such as students giving elaborated explanations and engaging in exploratory talk. Reasoning words provide another index of elaborated explanations and exploratory talk. Over time, the distinction between tools and signs becomes blurred as students internalize certain discourse tools and use them to support and foster not only their own thinking but also that of their peers.

Teacher Modeling and Scaffolding

Conversational moves for teacher modeling and scaffolding productive talk about text, the third element of our model, grew out of our professional development work with teachers. We were at first reluctant to prescribe specific techniques for use by teachers because of our desire to make the model applicable in a wide range of contexts. However, it soon became apparent that some teachers could benefit from having a repertoire of conversational moves to initiate students into the kinds of talk that promote critical–reflective thinking about text. Teacher moves are key features of QtA, CR, and PS. They appear to provide a useful, temporary aid for teachers in the early stages of conducting discussions (P. D. Pearson, personal communication, April 30, 2005), and research suggests that such prompts help mediate student learning and problem solving (King, 1999; Wegerif, 2006). Table 8.3 provides examples of teacher moves that model and scaffold productive talk about text.

Pedagogical Principles

The pedagogical principles, the fourth element of our model, comprise understandings about language and pedagogy that we think are essential to fostering a culture of dialogic inquiry in the classroom. These were developed from our review of the research literature on discussions and from our experience working with teachers who were learning to implement Quality Talk discussions. As we sifted through the literature on extant discussion approaches, we noticed some commonalities in pedagogy that were not reflected in the other elements of our model. Our experience working with teachers confirmed that the principles were indeed important for conducting productive discussions.

The first set of principles comprises basic notions about conducting discussions about text:

• *Use rich, interesting texts that permit a variety of interpretations, opinions, or positions on the part of students on a topic with which students have some familiarity (i.e., background knowledge).* Texts suited to discussion have a dialogic quality that affords students opportunities to engage

TABLE 8.3. Examples of Teacher Moves that Model and Scaffold Productive Talk about Text

- *Summarizing.* Teacher slows group down and summarizes what has been discussed. Builds coherence.

  Example: "Let's just pause here and summarize what we've all said."

- *Modeling.* Teacher models a move she or he would like students to make.

  Example: "I'm a little confused as to how that fits in with your argument. Can you say that more clearly?" "Brian, do you have something to add to that?"

- *Prompting.* Teacher helps student construct a longer response or a response that includes evidence from the text, thereby supporting more sophisticated talk.

  Example: "Why do you think that?" "So why does that mean Victor was an angel?"

- *Marking.* Teacher makes explicit or reinforces a good move a student made.

  Example: "Did you notice what Mary did? She went back to the text to find evidence for her point of view. I really like the way Mary did that."

- *Challenging.* Teacher challenges students to consider an alternative point of view.

  Example: "Some people might say ... " "Does what you're talking about happen for everyone?" "Do you think that makes sense?"

- *Participating.* Teacher participates as a group member to share his or her own ideas about the text; she or he displays a willingness to think and talk with the students.

with them from expressive, efferent, and critical–analytic stances. Our experience suggests that discussions are facilitated by texts that are somewhat challenging for students yet that cover topics with which they have some familiarity.

- *Establish collaboratively with students norms or "ground rules" for discussion.* Ground rules for discussion are a feature of CR and, to some extent, BC and LCs. They help promote a more open participation structure by giving students more control over turn taking. They are also important in helping foster exploratory talk (Mercer, 1995).

- *Initiate discussion by asking a "big question."* A big question is a question of central importance to understanding the story, and it is an authentic question in that there is no one right answer. Big questions, sometimes called *interpretive questions*, are a feature of CR, P4C, GCs, and JGB. A good big question establishes the overall goal for the discussion and helps motivate the expressive, efferent, and critical–analytic stances toward text. It elicits differences of opinion about the text and encourages students to offer well-founded, reasoned responses—and it is these differences of opinion and reasoned responses that pull students into a closer reading and more critical–analytic thinking about the text.

The second set of principles comprises larger ideas about language and pedagogy:

• *Language is a tool for thinking and for "interthinking."* It is important for teachers to understand that language serves dual functions when it comes to learning and problem solving in discussion. As Vygotsky (1934/1962) proposed, language functions as a psychological tool to help us organize our thoughts, to reason, to plan, and to reflect on our actions. As he proposed, it also functions as a social and cultural tool for sharing information and jointly constructing knowledge. Language gives us a vehicle for combining our intellectual resources to collectively make sense of experience and to solve problems. As indicated earlier, Mercer (2000, 2002) calls this use of language as a social mode of thinking "interthinking."

• *Productive discussions involve balancing the conflicting demands of maintaining a clear structure and focus yet being responsive to students' contributions.* Several discussion approaches (e.g., ICs, QtA) call attention to the difficult balancing act that teachers face when conducting discussion. For talk to be productive, it needs to be structured and focused but not so much as to prohibit generative learning (cf. Cohen, 1994; King, 1999).

• *Over time, there needs to be a gradual release of responsibility for control of the discussion from teacher to students.* Gradual release of responsibility is a principle of almost all good teaching (cf. Pearson & Gallagher, 1983). In the context of discussions, it might mean moving from teacher-generated questions to student-generated questions; moving from the teacher sharing interpretive authority with his or her students to students having full interpretive authority; and moving from teacher-led, whole-class discussion to student-led, small-group discussion. Ultimately, the goal is for students to take responsibility for coconstructing their own interpretations of and responses to text, to build their understandings together.

PUTTING IT ALL TOGETHER

In preparation for our professional development with teachers in the final phase of our project, we developed an integrative model to help teachers understand how the four elements of Quality Talk fit together. The relationships among the four elements are illustrated in Figure 8.1. We used a tree metaphor to convey the organic nature of classroom discussions.

The inspiration for this illustration came from Guthrie and colleagues' (Guthrie, 2003; Guthrie, Wigfield, & Perencevich, 2004) work on concept-oriented reading instruction (CORI; see Wilkinson, 2005). CORI is a comprehensive instructional program for students in grades 3–5 to foster reading engagement and comprehension. It combines sup-

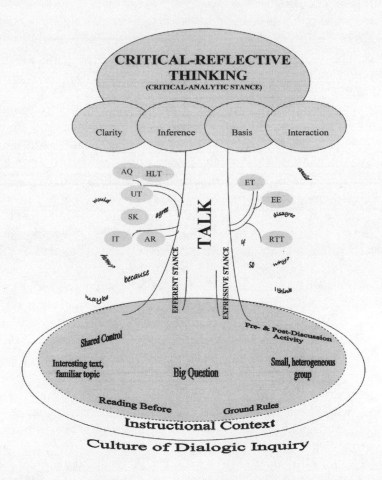

FIGURE 8.1. Quality Talk model. AQ, authentic questions; HLT, high-level thinking questions; UT, uptake; SK, shared-knowledge questions; IT, intertextuality questions; AR, affective response questions; ET, exploratory talk; EE, elaborated explanations; RTT, reference to text.

port for students' background knowledge, reading strategy instruction, and motivation. One of the key features of CORI is that it is taught within an instructional context that supports both the cognitive and motivational aspects of reading engagement. Some of the features of the instructional context for CORI were similar to the parameters of our instructional frame, and the way Guthrie and colleagues construed the cognitive and motivational aspects of reading as working together in support of engagement and comprehension was similar to the way we saw the efferent and expressive stances working together in support of a critical–analytic orientation toward text. Moreover, the primary support for the cognitive and motivational aspects of reading engagement in CORI comes from the conceptual knowledge goals for reading (from which CORI derives its name). These conceptual knowledge goals in CORI function in much the same way as big questions do in classroom discussions.

In Figure 8.1, the instructional context is portrayed as the foundation for quality talk about text, and this context is embedded within a classroom culture of dialogic inquiry. The instructional context incorporates the salient features of our ideal instructional frame, as well as the basic notions about conducting discussions about text, as listed in our first set of pedagogical principles. Talk develops out of this instructional context and supports students' critical–reflective thinking about and around text. As described earlier, critical–reflective thinking does not derive from just any kind of talk but from talk characterized by discourse tools and signs that are linked to high-level comprehension: authentic questions (AQ); uptake (UT); questions that promote high-level thinking (HLT), affective response (AR), intertextual connections (IT), and connections to shared knowledge (SK); elaborated explanations (EE); exploratory talk (ET); and reasoning words (*because, I think, how, why,* etc.). Making references to text (RTT) in support of ideas or positions is another feature of talk that we later added to our model. The culture of dialogic inquiry, shown at the base of the tree, embodies the larger notions about language and pedagogy in our second set of pedagogical principles. We think this culture is necessary to nurture productive talk about text. Although authentic questions, uptake, and other features of productive discussions have potential for promoting high-level comprehension, their potential may be lost unless they are used within a culture that values students' contributions to the construction of knowledge and understanding (cf. Nystrand et al., 1997).

These kinds of talk, when embedded within an appropriate instructional context, can help foster the desired classroom culture, but, in our experience, it can take some time for teachers and students to acquire the corresponding beliefs and values.

From our experience, we found that teachers needed some specificity as to what constituted critical–reflective thinking about text—that is, to know what good thinking "looked like"—so they knew when to enter a discussion to model and scaffold productive talk. We therefore added the four attributes shown toward the top of the tree. Following Ennis (1987), we defined critical–reflective thinking as "reasonable reflective thinking that is focused on deciding what to believe or do" (p. 10). We characterized critical–reflective thinking about text in terms of Ennis's four attributes: *clarity*, being clear about what is being said; *inference*, making deductive and inductive inferences and value judgments; *basis*, having a reasonable basis for those inferences; and *interaction*, engaging in cooperative interaction with peers. Other discussion approaches (e.g., CR) characterize critical–reflective thinking in this way.

Not shown in the figure are the modeling and scaffolding moves teachers can use to initiate students into the kinds of talk that promote critical–reflective thinking. We envision modeling and scaffolding as temporary supports to guide growth of Quality Talk in the early stages of implementing the model.

PROFESSIONAL DEVELOPMENT
FOR QUALITY TALK

Implementing Quality Talk requires that teachers view talk as more than giving students the floor. Rather, our model suggests the need for a comprehensive understanding and commitment to viewing extended student talk as both a context and a vehicle for learning. The model underscores our view that sustained and scaffolded professional development is fundamental to the implementation of Quality Talk, in that we are not simply introducing isolated strategies that can be adopted in a relatively short period of time. For most teachers, becoming familiar with the four elements of the model requires a substantial shift in their knowledge and beliefs about the role of talk in learning and its potential benefit for students' high-level comprehension.

In conceptualizing our professional development for Quality Talk, we drew on Richardson and Placier's (2001) notion of "normative reeducative change," Dole's (2003) principles of professional development for comprehension instruction, and Duckworth's (1996) research on teacher learning. Richardson and Placier's notion of normative reeducative change suggested that teachers' practices change when their personal norms change. Personal norms included how teachers habitually conduct instruction, as well as their goals and beliefs about instruction and student learning. Dole's analysis helped us expand on this notion by identifying principles of successful professional development programs. These principles included: a focus on students and students' performance; involvement of teachers in planning and undertaking professional development; school-based instruction; collaborative problem solving on the part of teachers; ongoing and sustained support; and instruction in the theoretical underpinnings of teaching and learning. Duckworth extended this notion of professional development to specify the importance of having teachers do and experience what they will have their students do and experience.

Based on this conceptualization, our professional development in Quality Talk included an initial five-session workshop followed by several follow-up sessions and a period of in-class coaching. In the workshop, we engaged teachers in Quality Talk discussions to enable them to experience what their students would experience. We had them observe videotapes of successful and not-so-successful Quality Talk discussions. And we encouraged teachers to critically analyze and reflect on what they observed and to use the metalanguage (talk about talk) of Quality Talk. Our discussions about discussions themselves took the form of Quality Talk (cf. Saunders, Goldenberg, & Hamann, 1992). In the follow-up sessions, we provided opportunities for teachers to engage in collaborative problem solving regarding their use of Quality Talk. Teachers collectively viewed videotapes of discussions drawn from their own classrooms and explored ways to enhance the quality of the discussions. In the in-class coaching, teachers worked individually with a "discourse coach" who observed their discussions and provided one-on-one assistance in using the discussion model.

An integral part of the coaching was helping teachers to analyze videotapes of their discussions using an instrument we developed called the Talk Assessment Tool for Teachers (TATT) (Wilkinson, Soter, & Reninger, 2006). This tool afforded teachers the opportunity to reflect on the nature of the talk and to explore ways to enhance the quality of their discussions. Working in conjunction with a discourse coach, teachers selected a 10-minute segment of videotaped discussion to analyze; they viewed the video segment twice, making notes on a worksheet; then they made an assessment of the quality of the talk in the 10-minute sample on a 4-point scale using a series of detailed rubrics. They also answered a number of questions about the discussion to help them reflect on the extent to which it might have benefited students' learning and comprehension. These techniques enabled teachers to gain both a global understanding of the discussion and a deeper understanding of the specific discourse features (e.g., authentic questions, uptake, and elaborated explanations) that indicated high-level thinking and comprehension.

WHAT DOES QUALITY TALK LOOK LIKE IN THE CLASSROOM?

In this section, we present two vignettes illustrating how two teachers instantiated the Quality Talk model in their classrooms. They come (with some adaptation for the purposes of illustration) from a doctoral dissertation by Reninger (2007), who studied the discussion practices of two teachers who were in their second year of using Quality Talk. The first vignette describes a discussion conducted by Mrs. Reinhart with a small group of fourth-grade students, heterogeneous in ability, who were discussing a short story called *Victor* by James Howe. The story is about a young boy, Cody, who is incapacitated and lying in a hospital bed on his 13th birthday. Cody creates an imaginary world, inspired by the ceiling tiles in the hospital, to help him get through the illness. He refers to the world as "The Land Above" and invents characters that inhabit this world. Cody is also visited by a mysterious man named Victor who tells Cody stories about what his life will be like when he grows up, and these stories give Cody the hope and strength to overcome his illness.

Mrs. Reinhart chose the story and read it to the class 2 days earlier. The day before the discussion, students read the story in pairs. Then, as a prediscussion activity, Mrs. Reinhart had students make Post-it notes about points from the story that they thought would be important to discuss. On the day of the discussion, Mrs. Reinhart had assembled the notes on a chart that the students could refer to during the discussion.

Mrs. Reinhart began the discussion with a review of the ground rules for conversation, which she and the students created together in September. She asked the group, "What do we need to remember today as we're talking?" Several students responded: "Listen to each other," "don't need to raise hands," "respect each other," "if someone's not talking, ask them a question," and "it's okay to disagree." One of the goals Mrs. Reinhart had set for herself, after analyzing her previous discussion using the TATT, was to be less dominant to encourage students to engage in exploratory talk. So she added: "And try to talk to the group, not just to me." She then began the discussion. "Okay, let's get started. Yesterday, many of us wrote questions about Victor, so let's start there and see where we go. So, who is Victor?" The students began their conversation about Victor, suggesting he was someone from The Land Above, a real person, or an imaginary friend. One girl said she thought Victor was an angel. Mrs. Reinhart replied, "You think Victor is an angel. That's an interesting perspective. Can you tell me why you think so?" The girl then gave an elaborated explanation of the reasons she thought Victor was an angel. Another girl said she thought Victor was from The Land Above. Mrs. Reinhart held back. The students then engaged in an episode of exploratory talk, thinking together through the merits of this opinion. A boy challenged this view: "How could he be talking from The Land Above, because remember in the story it said Cody could hear the screeching on the floor from when Victor was pulling up a chair to keep Cody company. So how could he be talking from The Land Above?" A boy replied, "Yeah, but how do you know people can't travel from and to The Land Above?" A girl commented: "This isn't realistic, this isn't like nonfiction, this is fiction, so anything could happen." The students then engaged in another episode of exploratory talk in which they reasoned together about what could be true and not true in the story. The discussion lasted 25 minutes. As a postdiscussion activity, Mrs. Reinhart asked students in the group to summarize everyone's views about who Victor was. She then thanked the group and got ready for her next discussion.

The second vignette describes a discussion conducted by Mrs. Pearson, a fifth-grade teacher, also about Victor. At this stage in the year, Mrs. Pearson's discussions were all peer-led. She generally circulated among five groups of four or five students who simultaneously discussed a story.

Mrs. Pearson informed students of the discussion question, "Who is Victor?" and wrote the question on the board. Mrs. Pearson then instructed students to write other questions or thoughts they had about the story on the copies of the text as they read. Mrs. Pearson passed out copies of the story and instructed students to read either independently or in pairs. She waited for everyone to finish and then told the students about the prediscussion assignment. She asked students to each write a paragraph, answering the question, "Who is Victor?" Students wrote for about 10 minutes. Mrs. Pearson then gave the directions for the small-group discussions:

> "Before we get into groups, I would like you to write two or three goals you have for yourself during the discussion on the same paper you wrote about Victor. I know many of you have been trying to talk more, some of you are trying to talk less, and we have all talked about backing up what we say when we give our opinions. So write what you want to do during the discussion and what you want to have happen during the discussion."

One of the goals Mrs. Pearson had set for this discussion, based on her analysis of her last few discussions using the TATT, was for her students to provide more elaborated explanations for their ideas or opinions. All students wrote for about a minute, and then Mrs. Pearson asked, "How can you push people's thinking a little in the discussions?" Nicole said, "Ask them why," and Justin said, "Challenge them and give your own reasons." At this, Mrs. Pearson remarked, "And try to back up what you say with reasons or evidence from the text or your experience. Remember, the strength of support is what gets people to listen to your ideas." Mrs. Pearson then asked students to form into their groups. Mrs. Pearson's voice rose above the shuffling sounds of students getting into their groups. "Remember to do a goal whip-around before you start talking about the big question." Mrs. Pearson walked around the room, briefly stopping at the groups, reminding them to share goals. As the students got into their conversations, Mrs. Pearson circulated among the groups, sitting with each for several minutes and listening to the conversations before moving to another group. In one group, a student, Kyle, offered an opinion about Victor but did not elaborate on his reasoning. Mrs. Pearson asked, "What makes you think so?" Kyle responded, "Somewhere in the story it said … maybe on page 80 … it said … " [reads from text]. Mrs. Pearson prompted, "So are you saying that's evidence? … [Kyle nodded]. Interesting." After 22 minutes of discussion, Mrs. Pearson initiated a 10-minute debriefing meeting from the front of the room. Several students raised their hands in order to share their goals and tell the class how they believed they met the goals they had written at the beginning of the discussion. Mrs. Pearson also asked for feedback from the students about making the next discussions better. Students then returned to their desks.

We note that in both vignettes there were pre- and postdiscussion activities (some about content, some about process) and that students met in small groups. In both vignettes, teachers chose the story and were in charge of the topic, but students controlled turn taking and evaluated each others' ideas (i.e., they had interpretive authority). Students asked most of the questions and did most of the thinking. They were genuinely invested in the conversations (affective stance), had built sufficient knowledge to understand the story (efferent stance), and came to the discussion well prepared to interrogate the text (critical–analytic stance).

REFLECTIONS ON THE MODEL

Does the field of social-constructivist pedagogy in reading need another approach to conducting classroom discussions? In asking ourselves this question, we have vacillated in how to position our model. On the one hand, because of the way we developed the model, it shares many features of extant approaches and might be viewed as a more generic description of these approaches. On the other hand, no one approach incorporates all aspects of the instructional frame that we have identified as ideal for conducting productive discussions. Moreover, in developing the model, we have given more weight to features of those approaches that are more critical–analytic in their orientation toward text. So there is reason to believe use of Quality Talk could yield outcomes on students' high-level comprehension of text that are as good as if not better than those of some current approaches to discussion.

Throughout our development of the model, we have been at pains not to impose a prescriptive routine on teachers. Rather, we have sought to give teachers a conceptual understanding of how and why talk might support students' thinking about text and to provide them with a general model that they can instantiate in a variety of ways. What makes our model unique is that *talk* is the primary focus.[2] Indeed, as the name implies, our model moves the focus of discussion away

[2] There are interesting similarities between Quality Talk and Accountable Talk[SM] (see *www.instituteforlearning.org*). However, we learned of Accountable Talk only toward the end of our project and developed Quality Talk quite independently of it. Accountable Talk comprises a set of standards for productive conversation in academic contexts and forms part of the New Standards Project (Resnick & Zurawsky, 2005).

from prescriptive routines to a focus on the quality of the talk and the epistemological moves teachers make via their discourse (e.g., authentic questions, uptake) to foster students' individual and collective reasoning. This approach affords teachers some freedom to implement the model in different ways (e.g., teacher-led or student-led) depending on their needs and the contexts in which they work. Thus there is reason to believe that the model might be more sustainable than some other approaches.

We have some evidence that Quality Talk can enable teachers to make sustained shifts in their discourse practices. Reninger (2007) studied the practices of two teachers (fourth and fifth grades) who worked with us on an earlier version of the model and who continued to use the model for a second year. Her research showed that the teachers incorporated the model into their everyday classroom practices, and she documented instances in which the discourse practices were taken up in other aspects of literacy instruction (e.g., guided reading groups), as well as in other areas of the curriculum.

We also have some evidence that use of the model can yield effects that align with our notion of high-level comprehension. In 2004–2005, we conducted a preliminary investigation of Quality Talk using a quasi-experimental design. Fourteen language arts teachers in fourth-, fifth-, and sixth-grade classrooms from three suburban school districts and a Catholic archdiocese participated. All teachers took part in five sessions of professional development at the beginning of the school year. Following these sessions, seven teachers were assigned to the experimental group (ongoing professional development) and seven to a comparison group, matching as far as possible on grade, school sector, and socioeconomic status. Teachers in the experimental group attended three follow-up sessions and were given in-class coaching throughout the year; teachers in the comparison group received only the initial professional development. Results revealed variability in implementation of text-based discussions in both conditions. Nevertheless, we found statistically significant effects on a transfer test assessing students' persuasive essay writing in favor of the experimental group. Students in the experimental group more often articulated their positions and repeated their positions in writing their arguments.

The journey we took in developing the model has taught us much about conducting discussions with literary texts. We note, however, that we have learned much less about conducting discussions with informational texts. Quality Talk was specifically designed for use with narrative fiction because this is the predominant genre used in the nine discussion approaches we analyzed (only QtA was designed specifically to help students grapple with the meaning of expository text, although other approaches—e.g., PS and CR—have been tried with more expository texts) (see Jadallah et al., Chapter 9, this volume). We have reason to believe that elements of the model may need some modification for use with other genres. In the next leg of our journey, we hope to examine systematically how Quality Talk can be adapted to promote high-level comprehension with informational texts.

REFERENCES

Allington, R. L., & Johnston, P. H. (2002). *Reading to learn: Lessons from exemplary fourth-grade classrooms.* New York: Guilford Press.

Anderson, R. C., Chinn, C., Chang, J., Waggoner, J., & Yi, H. (1997). On the logical integrity of children's arguments. *Cognition and Instruction, 15*(2), 33.

Anderson, R. C., Chinn, C., Waggoner, J., & Nguyen, K. (1998). Intellectually stimulating story discussions. In J. Osborn & F. Lehr (Eds.), *Literacy for all: Issues in teaching and learning* (pp. 170–186). New York: Guilford Press.

Anderson, R. C., Hiebert, E. H., Scott, J. A., & Wilkinson, I. A. G. (1985). *Becoming a nation of readers: The report of the Commission on Reading.* Washington, DC: National Institute of Education. (Available from the University of Illinois, Becoming a Nation of Readers, P. O. Box 2774, Station A, Champaign, IL 61820-8774)

Applebee, A., Langer, J., Nystrand, M., & Gamoran, A. (2003). Discussion-based approaches to developing understanding: Classroom instruction and student performance in middle and high school English. *American Educational Research Journal, 40,* 685–730.

Beck, I. L., & McKeown, M. G. (2006). *Improving comprehension with Questioning the Author: A fresh and expanded view of a powerful approach.* New York: Scholastic.

Beck, I. L., McKeown, M. G., Hamilton, R. L., & Kucan, L. (1997). *Questioning the Author: An approach for enhancing student engagement with text.* Newark, NJ: International Reading Association.

Billings, L., & Fitzgerald, J. (2002). Dialogic discussion and the Paideia Seminar. *American Educational Research Journal, 39*(4), 907–941.

Bloome, D., & Egan-Robertson, A. (1993). The social construction of intertextuality in classroom reading and writing lessons. *Reading Research Quarterly, 28,* 305–333.

Chang-Wells, G. L. M., & Wells, G. (1993). Dynamics of discourse: Literacy and the construction of knowledge. In E. A. Forman, N. N. Minick, & C. A.

Stone (Eds), *Contexts for learning: Sociocultural dynamics in children's development* (pp. 58–90). New York: Oxford University Press.

Chinn, C. A., Anderson, R. C., & Waggoner, M. (2001). Patterns of discourse in two kinds of literature discussions. *Reading Research Quarterly, 36,* 378–411.

Chinn, C. A., O'Donnell, A. M., & Jinks, T. S. (2000). The structure of discourse in collaborative learning. *Journal of Experimental Education, 69,* 77–97.

Cohen, E. G. (1994). Restructuring the classroom: Conditions for productive small groups. *Review of Educational Research, 64*(1), 1–35.

Dole, J. A. (2003). Professional development in reading comprehension instruction. In A. P. Sweet & C. E. Snow (Eds.), *Rethinking reading comprehension* (pp. 176–206). New York: Guilford Press.

Duckworth, E. (1996). *"The having of wonderful ideas" and other essays on teaching and learning.* New York: Teachers College Press.

Edwards, D., & Mercer, N. (1987). *Common knowledge: The development of understanding in the classroom.* New York: Methuen.

Eeds, M., & Wells, D. (1989). Grand conversations: An exploration of meaning construction in literature study groups. *Research in the Teaching of English, 23*(1), 4–29.

Ennis, R. H. (1987). A taxonomy of critical thinking dispositions and abilities. In J. B. Baron & R. J. Sternberg (Eds.), *Teaching thinking skills: Theory and practice* (pp. 9–25). New York: Freeman.

Goldenberg, C. (1993). Instructional conversations: Promoting comprehension through discussion. *Reading Teacher, 46*(4), 316–326.

Great Books Foundation. (1987). *An introduction to shared inquiry.* Chicago: Author.

Guthrie, J. T. (2003). Concept-oriented reading instruction: Practices of teaching reading for understanding. In A. P. Sweet & C. E. Snow (Eds.), *Rethinking reading comprehension* (pp. 115–140). New York: Guilford Press.

Guthrie, J. T., Wigfield, A., & Perencevich. K. C. (Eds.). (2004). *Motivating reading comprehension: Concept-oriented reading instruction.* Mahwah, NJ: Erlbaum.

Hanssen, E. (1990). Planning for literature circles: Variations in focus and structure. In K. G. Short & K. M. Piece (Eds.), *Talking about books: Creating literate communities* (pp. 199–209). Portsmouth, NH: Heinemann.

Jakobson, R. (1987). *Language in literature* (K. Pomorska & S. Rudy, Eds.). Cambridge, MA: Harvard University Press.

King, A. (1999). Discourse patterns for mediating peer learning. In A. M. O'Donnell & A. King (Eds.), *Cognitive perspectives on peer learning* (pp. 87–116). Mahwah, NJ: Erlbaum.

Mercer, N. (1995). *The guided construction of knowledge: Talk amongst teachers and learners.* Philadelphia: Multilingual Matters.

Mercer, N. (2000). *Words and minds: How we use language to think together.* London: Routledge.

Mercer, N. (2002). The art of interthinking. *Teaching Thinking, 7,* 8–11.

Nystrand, M., Gamoran, A., Kachur, R., & Prendergast, C. (1997). *Opening dialogue: Understanding the dynamics of language and learning in the English classroom.* New York: Teachers College Press.

Nystrand, M., Wu, A., Gamoran, A., Zeiser, S., & Long, D. A. (2003). Questions in time: Investigating the structure and dynamics of unfolding classroom discourse. *Discourse Processes, 35*(3), 135–198.

Pearson, P. D., & Gallagher, M. C. (1983). The instruction of reading comprehension. *Contemporary Educational Psychology, 8*, 317–344.

Piaget, J. (1981). *Intelligence and affectivity: Their relation during child development.* Palo Alto, CA: Annual Reviews. (Original work published 1954)

Raphael, T. E., & McMahon, S. I. (1994). Book Club: An alternative framework for reading instruction. *Reading Teacher, 48*(2), 102–116.

Reninger, K. (2007). *Intermediate-level, lower-achieving readers' participation in and high-level thinking during group discussions about literary texts.* Unpublished doctoral dissertation, Ohio State University.

Resnick, L. B. (1987). *Education and learning to think.* Washington, DC: National Academy Press.

Resnick, L., & Zurawsky, C. (2005). Getting back on course: Standards-based reform and accountability. *American Educator, 29*(1), 8–46.

Richardson, V., & Placier, P. (2001). Teacher change. In V. Richardson (Ed.), *Handbook of research on teaching* (4th ed., pp. 905–947). Washington, DC: American Educational Research Association.

Rosenblatt, L. (1978). *The reader, the text, the poem: The transactional theory of the literary work.* Carbondale: Southern Illinois University Press.

Saunders, W., Goldenberg, C., & Hamann, J. (1992). Instructional conversations beget instructional conversations. *Teaching and Teacher Education, 8,* 199–218.

Sharp, A. M. (1995). Philosophy for children and the development of ethical values. *Early Child Development and Care, 107*, 45–55.

Short, K. G., & K. M. Pierce (Eds.). (1990). *Talking about books: Creating literate communities.* Portsmouth, NH: Heinemann.

Shuart-Faris, N., & Bloome, D. (Eds.). (2004). *Uses of intertextuality in classroom and educational research.* Greenwich, CT: Information Age.

Soter, A. O., & Shen, V. (2005, February). *Deconstructing the "aesthetic" in students' responses to literary texts.* Paper presented at the annual conference of the National Council of Teachers of English, Columbus, Ohio.

Taylor, B. M., Pearson, P. D., Peterson, D. S., & Rodriguez, M. C. (2003). Reading growth in high-poverty classrooms: The influence of teacher practices that encourage cognitive engagement in literacy learning. *Elementary School Journal, 104*(1), 3–28.

Vygotsky, L. S. (1962). *Thought and language.* Cambridge, MA: MIT Press. (Original work published 1934).

Vygotsky, L. S (1978). *Mind in society: The development of higher psychological processes.* Cambridge, MA: Harvard University Press.

Wade, S., Thompson, A., & Watkins, W. (1994). The role of belief systems in authors' and readers' constructions of texts. In R. Garner & P. A. Alexander (Eds.), *Beliefs about text and instruction with text* (pp. 265–293). Hillsdale, NJ: Erlbaum.

Webb, N. M. (1989). Peer interaction and learning in small groups. *International Journal of Education Research, 13*, 21–39.

Wegerif, R. (2006). Towards a dialogic understanding of the relationship between teaching thinking and CSCL. *International Journal of Computer Supported Collaborative Learning, 1*(1), 143–157.

Wegerif, R., & Mercer, N. (1997). Using computer-based text analysis to integrate qualitative and quantitative methods in research on collaborative learning. *Language and Education, 11*(4), 271–286.

Wegerif, R., Mercer, N., & Dawes, L. (1999). From social interaction to individual reasoning: An empirical investigation of a possible socio-cultural model of cognitive development. *Learning and Instruction, 9*, 493–516.

Wilkinson, I., & Brown, C. (1983). Oral reading strategies of year one children as a function of level of ability and method of instruction. *Reading Psychology, 4*, 1–9.

Wilkinson, I. A. G. (2005). Motivating reading on motivating reading [Review of the book *Motivating reading comprehension: Concept-oriented reading instruction*]. Retrieved from *PsycCRITIQUES database, 50*(14), Article 19.

Wilkinson, I. A. G., & Anderson, R. C. (1995). Sociocognitive processes in guided silent reading: A microanalysis of small-group lessons. *Reading Research Quarterly, 30*, 710–740.

Wilkinson, I. A. G., Elkins, J., & Bain, J. D. (1995). Individual differences in story comprehension and recall of poor readers. *British Journal of Educational Psychology, 65*, 393–408.

Wilkinson, I. A. G., & Fung, I. Y. Y. (2002). Small-group composition and peer effects. *International Journal of Educational Research, 37*, 425–447.

Wilkinson, I. A. G., Soter, A. O., & Reninger, K. B. (2006). *Talk assessment tool for teachers.* Unpublished manuscript, Ohio State University.

9

COLLABORATIVE REASONING ABOUT A SCIENCE AND PUBLIC POLICY ISSUE

May Jadallah, Brian Miller, Richard C. Anderson,
Kim Nguyen-Jahiel, Jie Zhang,
Anthi Archodidou, *and* Kay Grabow

Dick Anderson, the senior member of this research team, grew up in a farm town of 2,800 people in west central Wisconsin. Dick recalls:

"My high school had the faint smell of a dairy barn. About half the students rode a school bus in from the country. They did morning farm chores and had no time to change clothes before climbing on the bus. During my senior year, I looked through Lovejoy's guide to American colleges and universities at the little town library. It was clear that, statistically speaking, Harvard was our greatest university. No one from my town had ever gone to Harvard or, as far as I knew, to any Ivy League school. Naively, I applied to Harvard and only to Harvard. After all, I was valedictorian of my high school class! I was accepted at Harvard, but I had no idea how challenging a major university would be. There were 400 high school valedictorians in my class from such places as Exeter, Choate, the Bronx High School of Science, and New Trier. My grades at the end of my first semester were a B, a C, a D, and an F. Fortunately for me, freshman classes were year-long back then, and first-semester grades did not become part of one's permanent record. A harbinger of my current interest in argumentation was my involvement in intercollegiate debate while at Harvard. I took part in, perhaps, a hundred debates with teams from other colleges and universities."

The Collaborative Reasoning project was launched in the early 1990s. A decade earlier Anderson and colleagues had initiated a program of research to methodically examine the major parts of the conventional reading lesson. Studies of attention during oral reading, oral reading errors, and teacher feedback following errors had just been completed (Chinn, Waggoner, Anderson, Schommer, & Wilkinson, 1993; Imai, Anderson, Wilkinson, & Yi, 1992). These studies were tedious for the students, tedious for the research team, and evidently tedious for the larger educational research community, as the papers have seldom been cited. The research team moved on to tackle discussion. Martha Waggoner, a member of the team and an experienced elementary school teacher, lamented that the typical story discussion is boring, unproductive, and not worth studying. She persuaded us to try to design a better approach to discussion. Within a few months, Collaborative Reasoning had begun to take shape, and we left behind the tedium of oral reading errors.

COLLABORATIVE REASONING
AND QUESTIONING THE AUTHOR

Collaborative Reasoning is an approach to classroom discussion intended to be intellectually stimulating and personally engaging. Students meet in heterogeneous groups of five to eight students in which they are expected to take positions on a "big question" raised by a text they have read, to present reasons and evidence for their positions, and to challenge one another when they disagree. Previous research on Collaborative Reasoning has primarily involved stories addressing ethical dilemmas. The project described in this chapter is an effort to extend the approach to an environmental science and public policy issue.

Collaborative Reasoning features open participation in which students talk freely without raising their hands. The teacher is supposed to allow students to operate the discussion as independently as possible. Ideally, students have control over what to say and when to say it, control over the topic, and the interpretive authority to evaluate the ideas that are presented. Collaborative Reasoning discussions are characterized by long stretches in which the teacher says nothing (Chinn, Anderson, & Waggoner, 2001). During these stretches, students look at each other when they are speaking, sometimes addressing each other by name. They pick up on and respond to each others' contributions. Although the discussions are student led, the teacher is present to foster the development of reasoning and positive social dynamics.

Collaborative Reasoning was designed as an alternative to recitation. Although it is commonly called a "discussion," during a recitation the teacher expresses over half the words that are spoken and maintains firm control over topic and turn taking (Cazden, 2001; Chinn et al., 2001). Recitation is an entrenched classroom practice in which teachers play a dominant role (Beck, McKeown, Worthy, Sandora, & Kucan, 1996; Bellack, Kliebard, Hyman, & Smith, 1966; Cazden, 2001). The manifest purpose of a discussion that takes the form of a recitation is to ensure that the students know the story, or textbook assignment, detail by detail. Most questions are simple, and the answers come directly from the text or, at most, require a limited inference.

The trouble is that recitations do not enable genuine dialogue (Nystrand, Wu, Gamoran, Zeiser, & Long, 2003). Students do not have the chance to express extended ideas; their answers often consist of only a word or a phrase (Cazden, 2001). Students follow the teacher during a recitation; they have little opportunity to ask questions, redirect the topic, or otherwise take initiative. Recitations provide few openings for critical or reflective thinking.

Isabel Beck, whose distinguished career we are celebrating with this volume, has also designed an alternative to recitation, called Questioning the Author. The genesis of Questioning the Author and that of Collaborative Reasoning are similar. Both approaches to discussion arise from dissatisfaction with superficial classroom talk and shallow engagement with texts. Isabel Beck and her colleagues investigated the reasons that school texts are frequently difficult to comprehend and then created systematic methods for making them better. Despite modifications of text that clearly improved coherence, readability, and voice, they found that students still frequently showed a disappointing lack of deep understanding. "In characterizing the problem [of lack of deep understanding], we turned to our observation that students tend to *resist* digging in and grappling with text ideas. It seemed as if students often took very little time to work through what they were reading and actually consider the ideas" (Beck & McKeown, 2001, p. 229). Beck and her colleagues developed Questioning the Author to encourage students to approach reading as a dialogue with the author of the text in a search for meaning.

A major feature that Questioning the Author and Collaborative Reasoning have in common is that both strive to make students active agents in their own learning. Teacher and student roles change, and both approaches affect classroom discourse. Teachers talk considerably less and ask fewer questions that call for students to retrieve details from the text; teachers start to construct their questions around students' responses (Beck & McKeown, 2001; Chinn et al., 2001). At the same time, students' level of participation increases greatly, and students move from providing answers lifted from the text to reflecting about ideas.

Although both approaches to discussion aim to promote more thoughtful engagement with text, the two approaches are designed to achieve somewhat different goals. In Questioning the Author, the primary goal of discussion is to construct the meaning of the text based on what a "fallible" author has expressed. In Collaborative Reasoning, the primary goal is to construct reasoned arguments about issues raised in the text. Because of these different goals, participants in discussions take different stances. Questioning the Author assumes primarily an efferent stance (Rosenblatt, 1994), meaning that students are reading and discussing the text in order to acquire concepts and information. Collaborative Reasoning assumes primarily a critical–analytic stance, meaning that students are reading and discussing the text in order to come to a reasoned decision about a dilemma (Anderson, Chinn, Waggoner, & Nguyen, 1998). The two approaches also have somewhat different modes of operation. In particular, in Questioning the Author the management of turn taking is controlled by the teacher via a series of teacher-posed questions, whereas in Collaborative Reasoning students talk freely around a single "big question."

COLLABORATIVE REASONING
ABOUT SCIENCE AND PUBLIC POLICY

Previous research suggests that being involved in argumentation helps people learn science and social science concepts. For example, Wiley and Voss (1999) found that students who were asked to write arguments rather than narratives, summaries, or explanations outperformed other students in inference and analogy tasks. Previous research also supports the idea that collaborative group work meshes well with science and social science learning and engenders deeper thinking. For example, Okada and Simon (1997) found that, compared with students who worked alone, those who worked in pairs entertained hypotheses and considered alternative ideas more frequently and talked about justification more actively. Rivard and Straw (2000) documented that talk is important for sharing, clarifying, and distributing knowledge among peers and that asking questions, hypothesizing, explaining, and formulating ideas are all important mechanisms for science learning during peer discussions. Similarly, Mercer, Dawes, Wegerif, and Sams (2004) showed that working together in small groups enabled students to improve their language and reasoning skills and to reach higher levels of attainment in science.

We have designed a multidisciplinary unit, featuring Collaborative Reasoning and other forms of small-group collaboration, about how wolves that live near a community should be handled—an issue that is controversial and highly interesting for elementary-age students. The Wolf Unit uses a variety of informational texts and a modified jigsaw structure (Aronson, 1978) to help students learn about issues surrounding wolf reintroduction and management. Students read texts that incorporate different genres (e.g., expository text, newspaper articles, and formal letters). Working collaboratively, "expert panels" of students learn about a specific wolf-related issue (i.e., ecology, economics, or livestock and pets) and then share what they have learned with the rest of the class. The unit incorporates two Collaborative Reasoning discussions, one early in the unit and one later when the students know more about wolves and their interactions with man. The Wolf Unit has been used successfully in a number of fourth- and fifth-grade classrooms. In this chapter, we focus on two fourth-grade classrooms.

On the first day, students are asked to imagine that they are officials at the Wolf Management Agency. The agency has received a letter from the city council of a fictitious town called Winona that is concerned because wolves have been sighted near the town. Students get to know Winona better by studying a pictorial map of the town and reading an edition of its weekly newspaper, the *Winona Messenger*. They learn general information about wolves, such as their habitat, social behavior, and biology. Then, on the second day, students gather for their first

Collaborative Reasoning discussion to decide whether they, as officials of the Wolf Management Agency, should give the people of Winona permission to hire hunters to kill the wolves. The initial discussions we have observed were lively. Almost all of the students are against killing the wolves. Most of the ideas they exchange focus on relocating wolves and separating wolves from humans.

On later days, groups of students do research about wolves. They watch a *National Geographic* video documentary, read magazines and books, and browse the Internet. Students learn from all these resources, but they find the video especially engaging and informative.

Over a period of several days, students work in expert panels to examine one of three facets of the wolf management problem: the ecosystem, the economy, or livestock and pets. Students become "experts" on these facets by reading and discussing booklets that we have written. The booklets provide information on both sides of the wolf reintroduction controversy. For example, in the information booklet on economy, students read that the presence of wolves may affect the tourism industry. The booklet suggests that wolves may attract wildlife fanciers who want to see wolves but, on the other hand, campers might stay away because they are worried about possible wolf attacks. Students read these booklets collaboratively with minimal teacher input. They find this section of the Wolf Unit, in its current form, to be the most difficult and least interesting.

The expert panels complete several graphing, calculation, and research activities. Each panel then constructs a poster and gives a presentation sharing their expertise with the class. Students love making the poster together and think this is the most interesting and engaging activity in the whole unit. They also enjoy giving the presentation.

In the last session, students participate in their second and final small-group Collaborative Reasoning discussion. They reconsider the question of whether Winona should be allowed to kill the wolves. New discussion groups are formed, mixing students from the three expert panels. Students say that they appreciate getting to hear ideas from other expert panels. As we detail later, the students often use information from the posters they have created to support their arguments in this discussion. After the final discussion, students write individual letters to the citizens of Winona, each student explaining his or her own decision about whether the town should be allowed to kill the wolves.

EVALUATION OF THE WOLF
REINTRODUCTION AND MANAGEMENT UNIT

Our evaluation is based on videos and transcriptions of Wolf Unit activities, especially the two Collaborative Reasoning discussions; on field notes of participant–observers; on analysis of students' work during the unit, especially their individual decision letters; and on attitudes toward the unit as revealed in responses to questionnaires and interviews with children and teachers.

All of the foregoing data were collected in two classrooms in different schools. One school served a low-income urban neighborhood, in which 82% of the students were Latino/a, 14% were African American, and 4% were European American; 80% were eligible for free or reduced-price lunch, and 50% had limited English proficiency. The average normal curve equivalent (NCE) on the Gates–MacGinitie reading comprehension test was 37.2 in the participating classroom from this school. The other school served a mixed low- to middle-income urban neighborhood, in which 58% of the students were European American, 22% were Latino/a, 11% were African American, and 9% were Asian American or reported mixed ethnicity. Half of the students, 52%, were eligible for free or reduced-price lunch, and 17% of them had limited English proficiency. The mean Gates–MacGinitie NCE was 65.8. A total of 31 students across both schools were involved in the evaluation study.

However, one analysis described in this chapter included 47 students from two additional classrooms in a third school serving a homogeneous rural community. In this school, 99.6% of the students were European American, and 20% were eligible for free or reduced-price lunch. The mean Gates–MacGinitie NCEs were 58.5 and 54.7. The reason for including these classrooms was to get a larger and more representative set of individual decision letters. Videos of discussions and other Wolf Unit activities were not obtained in the rural classrooms.

The participating classes had engaged in nine Collaborative Reasoning discussions before the Wolf Unit. Each class was taught by a veteran elementary school teacher who had training and experience in moderating Collaborative Reasoning discussions. Teachers implemented the Wolf Unit in 10–11 hours over a 3-week period near the end of the school year. In the following sections, teachers and students are identified with pseudonyms.

THEMES IN THE COLLABORATIVE REASONING DISCUSSIONS

Both the first and final discussions of the five discussion groups in the two urban classrooms were examined turn by turn to identify the themes students talked about. Through an iterative process, a list of 21 themes was generated. Next, discussions were chunked into episodes. An episode is a sequence of turns that deals mainly with a single theme or topic (Gee, 2005). Two researchers independently chunked and coded two discussions; the resulting interrater agreement reached 89%. The remaining discussions were chunked and theme coded by one researcher. For each theme, the percentage of words related to the theme was calculated. Episodes dealing with group dynamics were excluded from the calculations.

Sixteen out of the 21 themes were found in both the first and final discussions, with an average of 10 themes per group, as indicated in Table 9.1. Many of the same themes occurred across groups and discussions; however, several shifts in emphasis took place from the first to the final discussion. In the first discussion, students' talk centered on themes drawn from prior knowledge and common sense. Their main concerns were about two issues. First, students were concerned about whether wolves are truly dangerous; whether wolves attack livestock, people, and other wild animals. Second, students discussed solving Winona's problem by separating wolves from people and how that could be achieved. In the final discussion, these two issues continued to be addressed, but students talked significantly more about ecological and economic concepts derived from the Wolf Unit. The most prominent theme shifted from "Should wolves be relocated?" in the first discussion to "Will the food chain be affected if wolves are killed?"

MODES OF REASONING DURING DISCUSSIONS

Discussions were examined for the use of three modes of reasoning: (1) arguments, counterarguments, and rebuttals; (2) multistep causal reasoning; and (3) systems thinking. Of special interest is whether there was a change in the kind and quality of students' reasoning from the first to the second Collaborative Reasoning discussion.

TABLE 9.1. Number of Words Devoted to Themes in Two Collaborative Reasoning Discussions

Discussion themes	First discussion	Second discussion	$\chi^2(1)$
1. Will the food chain be affected if wolves are killed?	68	1002	13.32**
2. Do wolves (have the right to) attack livestock and pets? Should people kill wolves if wolves kill their livestock or pets? Do wolves affect ranchers' livelihood?	896	989	0.04
3. Should wolves be separated from people by relocating the wolves into a zoo, park, or preserve and/or building a fence around the wolves?	1,519	854	3.54[†]
4. Do wolves attack people if people do not threaten them? Should people/children be afraid of a wolf attack?	1,126	707	1.59
5. Should wolves be tranquilized?	196	670	4.03*
6. Do wolves affect the economy negatively (or positively)?	71	661	6.74**
7. Do wolves have the right to live on land if they were there before people? Should people be allowed to kill wolves if wolves go on people's property? Should people move if wolves go onto their property? Do wolves have the right to attack people if people go onto their land or threaten them?	174	587	3.80[†]
8. Should wolves be saved because they are endangered and might become extinct?	209	311	0.15
9. Do wolves have the right to kill other wild animals to survive (circle of life)? Do wolves have the right to live because they are part of nature?	662	291	2.06
10. Do humans destroy wolves' habitat?	0	214	3.05
11. Are wolves at the top of the food chain? Are humans wolves' predators?	90	141	0.34
12. Should people feed wolves to keep them away from the town?	804	98	8.87**
13. Do wolves come into the town because they don't have enough food in the wild? Do humans kill wolves' prey?	213	56	1.02
14. Would hunters be able to kill the wolves if they tried?	0	49	1.01
15. Is it against the law for people to kill wolves without a permit? Should there be rules against killing wolves?	261	48	1.85

16.	Should people be educated about wolves?	0	46	1.01
17.	Do wolves have the right to live because they are living creatures just like people? (if explicitly stated)	216	44	1.02
18.	Do people/wolves have the right to kill wolves/animals without using their pelts or meat? Do people have the right to kill wolves if they use their pelts?	175	40	0.34
19.	Should people hire rangers/police to protect wolves (or put up signs to warn people)?	236	5	3.05
20.	Should wolves be taught/trained to behave in a way that is safe for humans?	21	0	0.00
21.	Are wolves useful?	111	0	2.02

Note. Themes are sorted based on the number of words devoted to that theme in the final discussion.

$^{\dagger}.05 < p \le .06$; $^{*} p < .05$; $^{**} p < .01$.

If at least one student in a discussion advanced a counterargument to challenge another student's argument and a student responded to the counterargument with a rebuttal, then this discussion was coded as containing the core Argument → Counterargument → Rebuttal sequence. It should be noted that this category includes instances in which the counterargument being rebutted was not explicitly stated.

We defined multistep causal reasoning as having occurred when students reached a conclusion after considering a series of cause–effect relationships. If students decided that wolves should not be killed because X will happen, and then students explained in some detail how killing wolves affects A, A affects B, and then B affects X, this was considered a discussion with three-step reasoning. If a discussion had at least one example of a chain with two or more steps, the discussion was said to contain multistep reasoning.

A systems-thinking approach requires that students connect different facets of a problem to achieve an integrated evaluation. We considered a discussion to contain systems thinking if students connected two or more facets, including economy, ecology, livestock and pets, and/or moral or legal considerations, together at least once. We were not satisfied if students simply considered more than one perspective during a discussion. Only instances in which students explicitly asserted a relationship between two or more facets were credited as systems thinking.

All 10 discussions (five groups, two discussions per group) were coded for these three modes of reasoning. The raters had 93% agreement for each of the three categories. Disagreements were easily resolved through discussion. Table 9.2 indicates that in the first and final discussions all groups used Argument → Counterargument → Rebuttal; however, only in the final discussion did all the groups use multistep causal reasoning. One group in the first discussion used a systems-thinking approach; however, four groups in the final discussion incorporated it. To give a clearer sense of these modes of reasoning, the remaining portion of this section presents several examples of each type.

Argument → Counterargument → Rebuttal

Examples of Argument → Counterargument → Rebuttal are ubiquitous. The fact that students spontaneously challenged each other is not surprising, considering that respectfully challenging others is part of the Collaborative Reasoning approach. In the following episode from the first discussion, students are arguing about whether people have good reasons to kill the wolves. The students had read an article in the *Winona Messenger* that a sheepdog, named Elmo, had been found dead. Although the people had incomplete evidence, they speculated that wolves had attacked and killed Elmo. This segment of the discussion focuses on the conditions under which killing a wolf or a dog might be permissible.

> GALENO: They [people] are killing them because the wolves killed Elmo, who was trying to protect the sheep.
>
> ADDISON: Supposedly. It [Elmo] might have wandered off and then the wolf chased it off to that place. It [Elmo] might have started something against the wolf.
>
> GALENO: He [Elmo] was trying to protect the sheep.
>
> ADDISON: That is as far as they [people] know!
>
> GALENO: Yeah, we don't know if the wolves did or did not [kill the dog]. If they did, then that's their [people's] reason to kill the wolves.

This segment contains an Argument → Counterargument → Rebuttal sequence. The sequence begins with Galeno advancing the

TABLE 9.2. Number and Percentage of Uses of Three Modes of Reasoning in Discussions and Individual Decision Letters

Activity	Core argument sequence	Multistep reasoning	Systems thinking
First discussion[a]	5/5 (100%)	1/5 (20%)	1/5 (20%)
Second discussion[a]	5/5 (100%)	5/5 (100%)	4/5 (80%)
Urban decision letters[b]	8/26 (31%)	4/26 (15%)	0/26 (0%)
Rural decision letters[b]	25/44 (57%)	17/44 (39%)	4/44 (9%)

[a]The unit of analysis is the discussion group.
[b]The unit of analysis is the individual student.

argument that the people do have a legitimate reason to kill the wolves: Wolves killed Elmo, and Elmo was trying to protect the sheep. Addison advances a counterargument that Elmo may have initiated the conflict with the wolves and also questions whether the people had complete or accurate knowledge about what really happened. Galeno qualifies his argument by conceding that people might not have complete knowledge about the incident but maintains that the principle is still valid.

This discussion segment excerpted here illustrates that students' talk is often elliptical and that they frequently use pronouns in a vague way. Anderson, Chinn, Chang, Waggoner, and Yi (1997) found that students' naturally occurring arguments are filled with unclear referring expressions. They maintained, however, that unclear referring expressions are common in the unrehearsed everyday talk of adults, as well as the talk of young students. Furthermore, they asserted that students who are active participants in discussions generally seem to understand what is being said. We have clarified ambiguous expressions [in square brackets] to make the excerpts easier to understand.

Multistep Causal Reasoning

During the second Collaborative Reasoning discussion, students in all of the groups used multistep reasoning to construct explanations of ecological and economic phenomena. In a segment of their final discussion, one group focused on the food-chain theme. To provide an explanation for the stance that wolves should not be killed, Haben envisioned two causal chains. The first one focused on scavengers, and the other focused on plants. In both cases, he maintains that if the wolves became extinct the entire food chain would be disrupted.

HABEN: If the food chain, like if the wolf be um be extinct then the um, you know, as you know, like the um the hawks, the eagles eat the um leftovers from a wolf when they kill the moose and deers and the elk, and once the um the um the um the wolves become extinct, then I think the eagles would become extinct.

AMY: We are not talking about eagles.

HABEN: But I know that. I was talking about the food chain.

.
.
.

HABEN: Okay, Anana, um what I said, like if they keep killing the wolves pretty soon the wolves will become extinct. Well, it is already becoming extinct. But um, but Anana said that we are at the top of the food chain, and if like we … we eat plants, right? And we use the trees but (…) and if the um, the plants, the tree eaters eat the um trees and plants and we eat the plants and we use the trees, so more likely the tree, and like the plants will become like gone, but then they will grow back, like I said. Like I said, in a while.

The first multistep argument captured in this episode started with wolves killing large herbivores, followed by scavengers feeding on the leftovers of the wolves' kills. Without wolves, Haben predicted that the food chain would be broken and scavengers would become extinct. The second multistep argument in the episode is less complete. Haben was trying to explain how wolves affect the producers (plants) of an ecosystem. His causal chain was developed as follows: wolves are becoming extinct, so implicitly there will be no species to control the population of large herbivores; humans eat plants and use trees; herbivores eat plants and trees; humans and herbivores will eat up all plants and trees. Based on this causal reasoning, Haben decided that wolves should not be killed because if wolves became extinct, then trees will become extinct, too. However, Haben failed to connect all the ideas in this chain. Although Haben's arguments were not always complete, he demonstrated a serious attempt to engage in multistep reasoning. Furthermore, while it is not apparent in this example, Haben did incorporate ideas from other students, demonstrating a collaborative process.

The previous example might leave the impression that students were able to achieve multistep arguments only by using the science content introduced in the unit. However, the following example shows that they were able to integrate moral arguments into their consideration of the wolf dilemma. This is a critical process, because arguing about public policy controversies requires deliberations of technical, moral, and social dimensions. In this excerpt, the group decided that protecting ranchers' livelihood by giving ranchers a "conditional right" to kill wolves should be balanced by giving wolves a similar "conditional right" to kill humans. That is, wolves should also have the right to kill humans, but only if humans attempted to kill them.

HABEN: Um, why should they [people], they um, they only ... like I said they should only kill the wolves really if they [wolves] invade they [people] property because you know they [people] have the right to um, like like when you see the sign on the streets say um ...

MIGUEL: No trespassing?

HABEN: Yeah, well it's just like the wolves doing that and then they [people] have the right to protect they property.

ANANA: But the wolves don't know any better.

HABEN: I know that, but, but ... I know that the wolves don't know any better, but, they [people] just protect they property. I know that the wolves tryna eat, you know and they don't know. And the wolves, I think that the wolves should protect they selves by attacking human who try to kill 'em.

ANANA: ... So, if the person just like what Haben said ... I understand that they might invade the property, wolves don't know better and like say if [a] wolf just like walks through, then the wolf doesn't know any better, and the wolf doesn't know what to do when the person like threatens them. So if a person threatens them, I think that there will be human attack. Because a person just can't be like aim a gun at them and just say "Get out of my property or I will shoot you." And the wolf might just think that they [people] wana fight or something, and they [wolves] might attack them.

HABEN: I think that they [wolves] should attack like um humans only if they [humans] try um kill 'em [wolves] but not like for food or nothing, but only if they try to kill them.

ADRIANO: To defend themselves.

HABEN: Yeah, to defend they selves. Every man or woman have the right to defend they selves [inaudible].

In this episode Haben made a moral argument based on the premise of equal human–wolf rights, but Anana thought that giving humans and wolves conditional permission to kill each other was wrong. She thought that wolves were at a disadvantage because they were not able to communicate with humans. To support her argument, she imagined a hypothetical scenario involving a rancher and a wolf and used hedging phrases (e.g., *I think, might*) to indicate what could possibly take place if this scenario happened. The coconstruction of this multistep moral argument shows the children refining their evolving ideas about the wolf management controversy.

Unlike the multistep reasoning common in the second Collaborative Reasoning discussions, the first discussions contained mostly single-step reasoning. In the following utterance from the first discussion, Anana makes an analogy between people and wolves in that both eat other animals. She does not further examine chains of predator–prey relationships.

> ANANA: Well, yeah, I agree with Haben because, that's how it goes, it is just the circle of life and like many people like eat birds and stuff so we eat other animals and the wolves can eat other animals too, so it is just a circle of life, it is just how it goes, so....

Systems Thinking

The final set of examples illustrates students' use of systems thinking. Two students from the livestock and pets panel in the following example weigh the advantages and disadvantages of killing the wolves to the economy of Winona. Lewis combines ideas about ranching with ideas about economy. He considers ranching and the timber industry as two subsystems of a larger economic system and integrates them together. However, in order for Lewis to make this connection, he needed the information from Galeno to understand that ranchers need wood to build fences to protect their livestock.

> GALENO: Because if they [people] kill them [wolves], they will really help the farmers and the animals and the sheep. Because then the farmers or whatever they are [ranchers] have to go and buy the logs ... it is expensive. It will save them more amount of money to buy more sheep.

LEWIS: But that will give the timber industry more money, and this benefits the whole community. So, there is more advantages than less advantages if they [people] don't kill the wolves.

In this section we showed how students incorporated the core themes of the unit into their discussions and how their reasoning developed from simple direct relationships to more complex multi-step causal arguments and systems-thinking approaches. In the next section, we analyze the students' decision letters to explore the extent to which these modes of thinking may have been internalized by individual students.

SOURCES OF INFORMATION AND REASONING IN INDIVIDUAL DECISION LETTERS

The individual decision letters that students wrote to the Winona town council at the end of the Wolf Unit were analyzed for (1) the source of concepts and information, (2) thematic content, (3) modes of reasoning, and (4) the level of students' understanding of selected scientific concepts. Due to absences, letters were obtained from 70 of the 78 students. The form on which students from the urban classrooms wrote their letters had a limited amount of space to write, and one classroom had a limited amount of time to write; as a result, the average length of the letters from the urban classrooms was only 42 words. The students in the rural classrooms were given a form with much more space, they had enough time to write, and their letters averaged 120 words in length. The letters were chunked into idea units and coded in several ways, detailed in the following, with interrater agreement about coding decisions equal to or greater than 89%.

An interesting question is whether students were able to pick up ideas from listening to presentations and participating in discussions with students from other expert panels or whether they acquired concepts and information available only to their own expert panels. Both the jigsaw model and the Collaborative Reasoning approach are based on the assumption that students learn from each other. This question can be answered by examining the sources of concepts and information students included in their decision letters. Table 9.3 displays the percentage of words in idea units uniquely associated with the three expert panels. As might be expected, students wrote more statements based on information available to their own panels. However, it is fascinating to see that about half of the information students included in their letters came from expert panels of which they were not members. This result indicates that jigsaw grouping, poster presentations, and the final discussion were effective activities for disseminating information widely throughout the classrooms.

Table 9.3 further indicates that students in general wrote less about the economic ramifications of wolf reintroduction than about the impact on ecology and on livestock and pets. One explanation is that economic considerations are not salient in students' life experience at this young age.

The analysis of themes indicated that students included in their decision letters the same themes they talked about in the discussions. The aggregate percentage of words devoted to the various themes in the letters written by the students were highly correlated with the aggregate percentage of words devoted to these themes in their final discussion (urban classrooms, $r = .85$; rural classrooms, $r = .86$). These very high correlations must mean that students had similar concerns and acquired similar understandings across groups and classroom settings. The themes in the letters had much lower correlations with the themes in the first discussion (urban classrooms, $r = .20$; rural classrooms, $r = .56$). This indicates that the Wolf Unit strongly influenced students' thinking about wolf reintroduction and management.

Although in the final Collaborative Reasoning discussion all groups included the Argument → Counterargument → Rebuttal sequence and at least one multistep argument, Table 9.2 shows that these modes of reasoning were not prominent in students' individual letters. The limited space for writing provided to the students from the urban classrooms might have been one reason for this result. Students from the rural classrooms, who had more space, considered more counterargu-

TABLE 9.3. Percentage of Words in Decision Letters Devoted to Three Topics by Students from Different Expert Panels

Panel	Topic			
	Livestock	Ecology	Economy	$\chi^2(2)$
Livestock and pets panel	57%	29%	14%	33.1**
Ecology panel	37%	51%	13%	42.9**
Economy panel	33%	16%	50%	26.1**

** $p < .01$.

ments, were more likely to offer rebuttals, and displayed more multistep reasoning: 57% of these students included the core sequence of argument moves and 39% presented at least one multistep argument. The fact that groups engaged in systems thinking when discussing the wolf controversy illustrates the power of collaboration in raising the level of reasoning. However, we were disappointed that this type of reasoning was seldom evident in the individual decision letters.

Students' Employment of Reasoning Strategies

An excerpt from the letter written by Nadin, a member of the economy expert panel, contains an example of the Argument → Counterargument → Rebuttal reasoning strategy. Nadin drew evidence-based arguments from all three expert panels to construct a persuasive reply to the people of Winona. In the second paragraph of her letter, Nadin addresses ranchers' worries about possible wolf attacks by giving them factual information she learned from the livestock and pets panel.

> *The agency and I looked at the economy of Winona. We [tried] to*
> *determine which industries would gain more money and which*
> *would lose money. We are glad to inform you that almost 3/4 of the*
> *industries we looked at would either increase or stay the same.*
>
> *We know that the ranchers are worried about livestock and*
> *pets. However, wolves do not kill very many pets or livestock.*
> *We determined that 8 in 10,000 sheep were killed last year. We*
> *recommend building fences or small buildings to secure your*
> *animals. The last thing we considered was about the ecosystem. If*
> *we kill the wolves, deer, elk, moose and other large mammals will*
> *overpopulate. Wolves are an essential part of the food chain.*
>
> *However, we are aware that you are worried for your children*
> *and families. We are planning to relocate the wolves to your near*
> *by state park in mountain state. Thank you for alerting [us] about*
> *this problem.*

In the second paragraph, Nadin not only provided a rebuttal to a possible counterargument, but she also suggested a solution for ranchers who might not be totally convinced by her evidence. The recommendation she provided was a solution she herself had brought up during the final discussion.

Although all groups in the final discussion used at least one multistep causal argument, the majority of the students did not use this form of reasoning in their individual decision letters. The following letter is a good example by one student, Zane, who did use a multistep argument. His letter demonstrates an increased understanding of ecological concepts while also illustrating an amazing misconception:

I think you should not kill the wolves because they are just like dogs and they are harmless as long as you don't bother them. They are helping tree growth. Because they kill Elk and the Elk drink water, which doesn't give trees enough. But when they are dying, water gets to the roots of trees and they grow. And beaver population will go up too, because they can make dams. Plus there are only 441,000,000 turkeys and only 1,200 were killed. There are only 2,301,000 cattle and only 26 were killed. There is only 68,000 dogs 10 were killed. There is 1,600 sheep 20 were killed.

The letter contains a multistep argument, with a causal chain going from wolves killing elk, to elk drinking less water, to trees having more water, to trees growing. This argument is an attempt by Zane to describe the mechanism that explains the effect of wolves on trees. Although it is partly fallacious, the explanation has the characteristics of good scientific reasoning. Zane has learned that there are many indirect ecological relationships. He also has learned that some keystone species have important effects on species throughout a food chain. Zane was a member of the livestock and pets group, so he did not read the ecosystem text that explains the effects of wolves on other species. His understanding is a combination of what he learned from the presentation of the ecology panel, the reasoning he heard during the final discussion, and his own attempts at constructing a conception of these ecosystem relationships. Although he did not succeed in constructing a conception that is scientifically sound, his letter demonstrates that he has thought deeply about the topic and has learned several important ecological ideas through group activities.

Another aspect of Zane's letter is his shaky number sense. Zane and many other students revealed in their final discussions and letters that they understood that wolves kill just a small number of livestock out of the total number living in Mountain State. However, they were insensitive to the order of magnitude of the actual numbers. Zane was off by a factor of 10 in reporting the numbers of turkeys, cattle, and sheep, despite the fact that the numbers were displayed on a poster visible to the students when they wrote their essays.

Systems thinking was the least applied mode of reasoning in students' letters. Mike's essay following is a rare example of systems thinking. He is also the rare example of a student arguing for having the wolves killed. Mike was a member of the economy expert panel; however, he was strongly influenced by the livestock and pets information. He combined economic and livestock and pets arguments seamlessly to support his position. For example, Mike combined his knowledge of the reasons wolves might hurt tourism with the idea of government reimbursement for damage by wolves that he learned about from the livestock and pets group.

> *Yes, I think you should hire professional hunters to kill the wolves around your city of Winona. I read the packet that you sent us and you said that the wolves were getting some of your town businesses go out because wolves scared people out of town so people heard about it and didn't want to go back to Winona because they didn't like the wolves and people and farms loose sheep and cattle from wolves that's why you should kill the wolves so that the government don't have to pay for what the wolves killed and according to the poster we made I think tourism will go down because people made complaints about wolves in their camp site so if you don't kill the wolves they might hurt other people or animals in the forest then the government will have to pay for the damage against the animal or person so make sure you pick the best choice.*

We found that 41% of the students from rural classrooms considered arguments from two facets; however, only 9% were able to combine the two facets and weigh them seamlessly to come to a wider systems-based understanding of the issue. The ambiguity of real-life problems, the social dimension of the wolf controversy, the uncertainty about wolves' effects, and the scattered data about wolves in the different activities of the unit are some reasons that may explain the lack of systems thinking in students' letters. It was only during the discussions, when they were actively collaborating with other students who held different perspectives, that some groups were capable of achieving systems thinking.

In general, the decision letter results suggest that the poster presentation and final mixed-group discussions were effective learning
activities for information acquisition and knowledge sharing. They also
indicate that these indirect learning experiences are suitable platforms
for exposing students to multiple perspectives and different modes of
reasoning.

MOTIVATION AND ENGAGEMENT
DURING THE WOLF UNIT

Children in urban classrooms were given questionnaires following each
session of the Wolf Unit to evaluate their motivation and engagement.
The results indicate that children were highly engaged in the different
activities. Over all the sessions, 88% of the children said that the Wolf
Unit was either interesting or very interesting, 90% said the Wolf Unit
was either personally engaging or very personally engaging, and 94%
said that they were excited or very excited to learn more about wolves.
Children especially liked group activities, such as making posters. A
topic and an approach to lesson design that are engaging for children
was one criterion for developing the Wolf Unit. The results from the
questionnaire corroborated the impressions we had based on classroom
observation, videos, field notes, and postproject interviews. The Wolf
Unit was exciting to children, and it helped them think deeply about a
current controversial issue.

CONCLUDING REMARKS

To recapitulate, in a 10-lesson unit on wolf reintroduction and management, fourth-graders role-played being members of a government
agency deciding whether a town should be allowed to shoot wolves
sighted near its outskirts. Students read background material, saw a
video, formed "expert panels" that studied one of three topics related
to wolf management, and then made presentations to the whole class.
Small groups within classrooms, composed of students from different
expert panels, held two Collaborative Reasoning discussions, one near
the beginning of the unit and the other near the end.

Comparison of the two discussions indicated that in the final discussion students talked more about ecology and economics and talked

less about simplistic themes. Discussions were analyzed for the presence of three modes of reasoning: the core Argument → Counterargument → Rebuttal sequence, multistep causal reasoning, and systems thinking, as represented by simultaneous coordination of two or more perspectives. All groups used the core sequence of argument moves in both discussions, but in most groups multistep reasoning and systems thinking appeared only in the final discussion.

Two of the modes of reasoning were found in many of the decision letters that students wrote at the end of the unit: the core sequence of argument moves and multistep causal reasoning. The themes students included in their letters matched the themes they emphasized in the final discussion. About half of the information students included in their decision letters came from expert panels of which they were not members, indicating broad dissemination of information throughout the classrooms.

We were disappointed in the small percentage of students who were able to use in their decision letters the modes of reasoning that they had displayed in their final discussions. One reason for this was procedural. The students in the urban classrooms were not given enough space to write. Probably, a more general reason is that writing is hard work for students, and they may forgo the elaborations that we take to be markers of types of reasoning. Expressing themselves in writing may be especially challenging for students who are English language learners.

A surprise to us, but undoubtedly not a surprise to most mathematics and science educators, is students' tenuous sense of number. Order-of-magnitude errors were common. No surprise to us (Anderson et al., 1997), but perhaps a surprise to some, is that students' oral and written arguments can be incredibly vague. Their discourse is elliptical and filled with pronouns whose references are unclear. We have found in other current work that, when greater clarity is scaffolded by the teacher, Collaborative Reasoning provides a forum in which students learn to express themselves more clearly. Although at the present time we do not have enough evidence to reach a firm conclusion, it stands to reason that extended opportunities for open discussions of complex issues, such as those afforded by Collaborative Reasoning, could have exceptionally positive effects on the language development of students with limited English proficiency.

Of course, during the Wolf Unit, students sometimes expressed scientific or socioeconomic misconceptions. It is inevitable that, when students are given the social and intellectual space to think for themselves, sometimes their thinking will go in directions that adults believe are wrong. But we do not consider that good teaching consists of stamping out errors. Rather, we would prefer an educational environment that enables students to become self-improving, alert to dubious assumptions, ready to question, determined to make judgments on best available evidence, and able to find their own errors and correct them.

In summary, an integrated environmental science and public policy unit, featuring cooperative learning and collaborative discussions, led to forms of thinking not often seen in elementary school classrooms. Students were highly engaged—not just having fun but having fun thinking about hard issues. African American and Latino/a students had an especially positive response to the unit. Our next major goal is to further document instructional practices that give a large boost to the conceptual understanding, thinking skills, language, and motivation of nonmainstream children.

REFERENCES

Anderson, R. C., Chinn, C., Chang, J., Waggoner, M., & Yi, H. (1997). On the logical integrity of children's arguments. *Cognition and Instruction, 15,* 135–167.

Anderson, R. C., Chinn, C., Waggoner, M., & Nguyen, K. (1998). Intellectually stimulating story discussions. In J. Osborn & F. Lehr (Eds.), *Literacy for all: Issues in teaching and learning* (pp. 170–186). New York: Guilford Press.

Aronson, E. (1978). *The jigsaw classroom.* Beverly Hills, CA: Sage.

Beck, I. L., & McKeown, M. G. (2001). Inviting students into the pursuit of meaning. *Educational Psychology Review, 13,* 225–241.

Beck, I. L., McKeown, M. G., Worthy, J., Sandora, C. A., & Kucan, L. (1996). Questioning the Author: A year-long classroom implementation to engage students with text. *Elementary School Journal, 96,* 385–414.

Bellack, A., Kliebard, M., Hyman, T., & Smith, L. (1966). *The language of the classroom.* New York: Teachers College Press.

Cazden, C. B. (2001). *Classroom discourse: The language of teaching and learning* (3rd ed.). Portsmouth, NH: Heinemann.

Chinn, C. A., Anderson, R. C., & Waggoner, M. A. (2001). Patterns of discourse in two kinds of literature discussion. *Reading Research Quarterly, 36,* 378–411.

Chinn, C. A., Waggoner, M. A., Anderson, R. C., Schommer, M., & Wilkinson, I. A. (1993). Situated action in the small-group reading lesson: A microanalysis of oral reading error episodes. *American Educational Research Journal, 30,* 361–392.

Gee, J. P. (2005). *An introduction to discourse analysis: Theory and method* (2nd ed.). New York: Routledge.

Imai, M., Anderson, R. C., Wilkinson, I., & Yi, H. (1992). Properties of attention during reading lessons. *Journal of Educational Psychology, 84,* 160–173.

Mercer, N., Dawes, L., Wegerif, R., & Sams, C. (2004). Reasoning as a scientist: Ways of helping children to use language to learn science. *British Educational Research Journal, 30,* 359–377.

Nystrand, M., Wu, L., Gamoran, A., Zeiser, S., & Long, D. (2003). Questions in time: Investigating the structure and dynamics of unfolding classroom discourse. *Discourse Processes, 35,* 135–198.

Okada, T., & Simon, H. A. (1997). Collaborative discovery in a scientific domain. *Cognitive Science Society, 21,* 109–146.

Rivard, L. P., & Straw, S. B. (2000). The effects of talk and writing on learning science: An exploratory study. *Science Education, 84,* 566–593.

Rosenblatt, L. M. (1994). *The reader, the text, the poem: The transactional theory of the literary work.* Carbondale: Southern Illinois University Press. (Original work published 1978)

Wiley, J., & Voss, J. F. (1999). Constructing arguments from multiple sources: Tasks that promote understanding and not just memory for text. *Journal of Educational Psychology, 91,* 301–311.

10

COMPREHENSION PROCESSES
AND CLASSROOM CONTEXTS

Walter Kintsch

During all the years I have known Isabel Beck I have thought of her as the ideal educational researcher: someone who is on top of the research, with respect to experimental methods as well as theory, but whose work derives directly from her concerns about classroom practice. She understands what students need and what teachers need, not only in the general way we all do but also very concretely in terms of their day-to-day activities. She has been a teacher herself, and she has managed to smoothly integrate her experiences as a teacher and as a researcher. I have also been a teacher and have also ended up in educational research, but with a different trajectory.

My teaching career began long ago in the mountains of Austria. I taught second grade in my first year, then was transferred to a one-room school, where I stayed for 3 more years. I had students from first to eighth grade in my classroom, but not very many of them—in one year only 9, and never more than 14. I mostly supervised the older kids as they taught the younger ones. They all liked me, because they were farm kids who had hard work to do at home, so school was fun. I liked teaching, too. My approach to teaching was a fairly modern one: We really were a community of learners, jointly involved in knowledge construction rather than my delivering well-prepared lectures to my pupils. But it was kind of lonely up on that mountain. Only two other houses could be seen from my single-room schoolhouse, where I lived in a little cubbyhole under the roof. It was after the war (World War II, to be specific), and the country was in pretty bad shape. I decided that I did not want to spend the rest of my life that way; I wanted to go to the university to study psychology—clinical psychology, of course. That meant faraway Vienna, without any means of support. Then I was offered a Fulbright scholarship to the University of Kansas, which was even farther away (and totally unknown to me). That was life-changing event number 1. Number 2 was that, upon arrival in Kansas, I enrolled in experimental psychology rather than clinical, just to see what that was like, as it did not matter much what I did during my 1-year stay in the United States. So I became a psychologist, an American psychologist, moreover.

What attracted me to psychology was the idea of exploring experimentally the laws of learning. That meant rats' learning in those days. But from the very beginning I was enamored by theory: I read Hull's *Principles of Behavior* and was fascinated (Hull, 1943). What a young man who knew absolutely nothing found interesting in this weird book was the idea that you could actually state formal, testable principles of behavior. That interest stayed with me; the way it manifested itself changed a lot over the years, for my intellectual development as a psychologist during the second half of the previous century followed a convoluted path.

The starting point was behaviorism: My PhD thesis used a runway to test a fine point of Hullian theory with rats. I also did some rather good work on classical conditioning with dogs (poor dogs!). But I changed directions very quickly under the dual influence of Bill Estes and Noam Chomsky. As a postdoc in Bill's lab, I was introduced to the new mathematical psychology, which offered real tools for modeling behavior in place of Hull's pseudomath. And Chomsky's early writing not only weaned me away from behaviorism but also made me curious about language.

Mathematical models first dealt with learning, but that soon changed, as the 1960s became the decade of memory research. Memory psychology meant (and still means) recognition and recall experiments with lists of words as stimuli. Memory research flourished in the 1960s, and the journals were full of exciting discoveries and new ideas. The meetings of the Psychonomic Society were eagerly awaited events in which you could catch up on what was really new. Among the many new findings were two related ones that impressed me most: the role of organization and structure in facilitating recall and the clustering of related words that was observed when participants recalled a list. What the words meant was obviously crucial in both cases. If it was all about meaning, then why not take the next step and work with really meaningful materials, namely, text?

Psycholinguistics at that time was dominated by Chomsky's concern with syntax, not meaning. By the end of the 1960s, however, some psychologists and linguists, among them some of the best of his own students, became dissatisfied with Chomsky's approach, specifically his rejection of semantics. Psychologists began to look at what the traditional owners of that field—linguists and philosophers—had to say, and in the early 1970s, several proposals for a propositional representation of meaning emerged. My own contribution was *The Representation of Meaning in Memory* (Kintsch, 1974). The basic idea was that meaning had to be dealt with not only at the word or concept level but also at the propositional level, where proposition was a formalization of the notion of idea unit. In my own case, I began a 10-year collaboration with the Dutch linguist Teun van Dijk that was devoted to working out how readers constructed mental representations of the text they read; that is, what the process of text comprehension was like. In 1978 we published "Towards a Model of Text Comprehension and Production," a process model of text comprehension (Kintsch & van Dijk, 1978); in 1983 the book *Strategies of Discourse Comprehension* summarized the results of this collaboration (van Dijk & Kintsch, 1983). I continued this line of research, culminating in the construction–integration (CI) theory, a semiformal model that emphasizes the interplay between top-down and bottom-up processes in discourse comprehension. *Comprehension: A Paradigm for Cognition* (Kintsch, 1998) provides a comprehensive account of this work.

Eventually, this work caught the interest of some reading researchers. Reading, until fairly recently, meant decoding, but there were a few researchers whose interests went beyond that. That is, of course, how Isabel gets into that picture, because Isabel was one of the researchers focusing on comprehension at a time when it was not as fashionable as it is now.

What educational researchers needed was a way to talk and think about comprehension, and the kind of framework provided by discourse psychology was useful in that respect. Today, such concepts as *macrostructure* and *situation model* are household words. Educational researchers would have liked more, however: a formal model of discourse comprehension that could be shown to adequately describe comprehension and that had predictive power. The construction–integration model is inadequate in this respect. I think that it has been and continues to be a useful way to talk and think about comprehension, to understand the successes and failures of comprehension after the fact, and to use this understanding in designing better instructional methods, but as a formal model is it inadequate. It suffers from a very basic limitation: its unit, the proposition, is not formally defined.

When I first began this work, I did not think this was a serious problem. The triumph of artificial intelligence seemed imminent, and I expected that someone was going to solve my problems for me any day. All I needed was a parser that computed propositional representations for any arbitrary English text. It was not a problem suitable for me, but once someone built such a parser, I would use it for modeling discourse comprehension. The decades went by, somehow, and still there was no parser. Eventually I realized that there would likely be none during my lifetime.

Then something curious happened: my colleague Tom Landauer introduced me to latent semantic analysis (LSA). LSA is a machine-learning method that infers a semantic representation for word meanings from a large corpus of texts. It does so automatically, without supervision, and by relatively straightforward mathematical means. The meaning of texts could also be represented in the same "semantic space," simply as the sum of the words. LSA has its limitations: It uses only word co-occurrence information in generating its semantic space, disregarding syntax and discourse structure, although texts are not simply the sum of their words. LSA considers only verbal meaning, whereas perception and action also play a role in human meaning. Indeed, LSA was soundly rejected initially as much too simplistic. But I was impressed. Here was a formal method that required no human tinkering and that scaled up to all of human (verbal) knowledge. In spite of its limitations, it produced, under certain conditions, results that corresponded with human semantic intuitions amazingly well. The recent *Handbook of Latent Semantic Analysis* (Landauer, McNamara, Dennis, & Kintsch, 2007) provides introductions to LSA and an overview of how LSA has been used so far, both as a tool for building a semantic theory and in practical applications.

However, for me there remained a problem. The units in LSA are words, and there is no notion of proposition. I spent most of my career arguing that propositions are the units of meaning, not words. I justified my work with LSA with the same argument as the drunk who lost his keys in the dark but was looking for them under a lantern that provided some light. One could really do interesting things with LSA even though it lacks a natural way to deal with propositional units. LSA is an incomplete theory and open to improvement—but what theory is not incomplete and could not use some improvement? In the last few years I have spent my time mostly trying to develop a system that would be an improvement on LSA in that it considers syntactic information and hence has a way to deal with propositional units. I return to this work in progress later, but I do not discuss it here in detail. Instead, I describe my experience with an instructional system based on LSA that has been introduced into a number of schools and that in some ways is similar to Questioning the Author and in other ways is not.

This system, called *Summary Street*, has been described in a number of publications (Kintsch, Caccamise, Franzke, Johnson, & Dooley, 2007; Kintsch, Steinhard, Stahl, Matthews, Lamb, & LSA Research Group, 2000); several more studies (Caccamise, Franzke, Eckhoff, Kintsch, & Kintsch, 2007; Caccamise et al., in preparation; Franzke, Kintsch, Caccamise, Johnson, & Dooley, 2005; Wade-Stein & Kintsch, 2004) report the results of the scale-up and evaluation studies we did with *Summary Street* (with support from an Interagency Education Research Initiative [IERI] grant from the National Science Foundation [NSF]). Thus I can keep my discussion here informal and refer the reader to this literature for the missing specifics.

By the late 1990s Tom Landauer and his collaborators at the University of Colorado had perfected LSA. Given a very large corpus of texts—for example, an 11 million–word corpus of texts that a high school graduate might have read in the course of his or her studies— LSA constructs a semantic space in which every word and every text can be specified. A semantic space is a (high-dimensional) map of meaning in which words are vectors in that space whose distance from each other can be readily computed. This is very useful, both for theoretical work in psychology and for various applications. We began to explore various possibilities for educational uses of LSA with our graduate students, such as matching texts with students of different background knowledge so that each student reads a text that is within his or her zone of proximal learning (Wolfe et al., 1998). Eventually we—actually, Eileen Kintsch and Dave Steinhart—approached some teachers, asking them how they might want to use a method such as LSA. Two sixth-grade teachers responded (Cindy Matthews and Ronald Lamb; see Kintsch et al., 2000). They said that they frequently ask their students to summarize background reading in preparation for a class discussion. However, they rarely were able to correct these summaries, and the quality of the summaries was therefore quite low; an automated system that could provide feedback to students could be useful to them. Thus Summary Street was born. (The name was coined by an enthusiastic sixth-grader.)

It is quite interesting what happened next. Summary Street is a highly sophisticated computer system. I don't give a technical description here, but the work we had to put into the technical development of Summary Street was only a small fraction of the total development effort. What was difficult and time-consuming was to make the system usable by students and teachers. It took a lot of patient observation and talking with both students and teachers before we came up with a usable system. We started with written feedback—and much too much of it. That was a disaster. Then we experimented with point systems, but that did not work, either, because everyone wanted to have the best score, which led to unhealthy competition. Students became focused on the point scores rather than on the quality of their writing. Finally, we came up with the interface shown in Figure 10.1.

Students write their summaries on the computer, and to request feedback, they push a button that initiates a comparison between the summary they have written and the original text. A screen like the one in Figure 10.1 appears. It displays several horizontal bars and a line that designates their ideal end point for content coverage. The bars correspond to the sections of the text being summarized, and the distance of the bars from the line indicates how well each section has been covered. In our example, the content of the first two sections has been adequately covered, but the next three sections do not pass the threshold. The student can now go back to the book, reread one of the unfinished sections, and add some material about it to what she or he has already written. She or he can get new feedback then and continue in this way until all bars are above threshold. (In a newer version, yellow bars turn green when they reach the threshold; the students liked that, and "going green" became part of the culture in a number of Summary Street class-

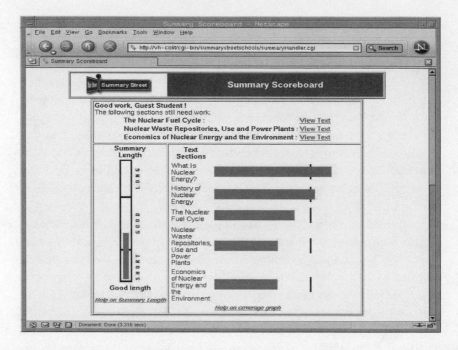

FIGURE 10.1. A screenshot of the Summary Street interface. The writer has covered the first two sections but not the other three; the length of the summary is within the specified boundaries.

rooms.) What usually happens, however, is that by the time all sections are covered, the students' summary exceeds the length threshold set by the teacher (e.g., the summary must be at least 150 but no longer than 250 words long). The vertical bar on the left indicates graphically whether the summary is within the prescribed limits. Now the student is faced with the tricky task of making his or her summary more concise. This can be done by deleting material or by rewriting material that is too detailed to make it more essential. Summary Street helps the student with that task, too. When a bar is far over the threshold line, the student knows that there is a lot about this section in what she or he has written, and hence that material might be considered for a cut. In addition, the student can ask the system to identify irrelevant or redundant sentences. To find irrelevant sentences, we compare each sentence the student has written with the text as a whole, and if the sentence is not at all similar to the text, we flag it as potentially irrelevant. To flag redundant sentences, we compare each sentence with every other and flag sentence pairs that are too similar. The student then must decide what to do: to delete one or the other sentence or parts of it; to combine the two sentences into a shorter one; or to leave things as they are if he or she disagrees with the judgment of the computer. The student can work until all sections are beyond the threshold bar and the length is within prescribed limits or quit at any point and hand what she or he has written to the teacher as it is.

In Colorado, as part of our scaling-up effort, Summary Street was used by more than 4,000 students in grades 5–11 (mostly grades 6 and 7) in school districts all over the state—urban, suburban, and rural—including a school with a predominantly Native American population. In some cases teachers were introduced to Summary Street via workshops; sometimes they received help from our group; but often, after a brief introduction, they were entirely on their own. Teachers could use Summary Street any way they wanted. A group of 1,840 students participated in a more formal year-long study in which Summary Street was used in the experimental classrooms and conventional summarization instruction was given in the control classrooms. Teachers used Summary Street in their classrooms as much as they felt like, with the result that students in the experimental group received Summary Street training from 0 to 11 times, with a mode of 5 exposures. Their summary writing ability was tested at the beginning and end of the year, when students were also given subsets of the Test of Reading Comprehension (TORC; Brown, Hammill, & Wiederholt, 1995).

The results of the evaluation studies we performed are highly positive. Students wrote better summaries with the tool than without it. With repeated use of Summary Street, students learned how to write summaries even without the tool (about five or six tries appear to be enough). The more often they have actually used Summary Street, the better their summaries became. Summary Street practice transferred to performance on the TORC, so that students who used Summary Street more often during the year received better scores on the TORC; this effect persists when ability measures (performance on the highly reliable Colorado Student Assessment Program [CSAP] test) are statistically controlled, suggesting that this finding is not merely a selection effect. All of these findings are statistically significant in analyses with classrooms as the unit of analysis, rather than students. Thus we have demonstrated that Summary Street has reliable and significant effects in classroom use.

A couple of observations help to show why Summary Street works and how it works. Generally, students liked to work with Summary Street (except for advanced high school and college students, who felt, correctly, that the system really did not have anything to teach them that they did not already know). There are two apparent reasons for the positive acceptance of Summary Street. First, students felt that the system actually helped them. Second, they appreciated the anonymity of the computer. There was no all-knowing teacher who told them that they were doing things wrong or how to do it right, just a machine that gave hints. They could screw up and try again—nobody knew. Some students in special education who, according to their teacher, never even tried to write a summary worked with Summary Street for a whole hour without frustration, and, although the product was far from a golden summary, it was an outstanding achievement for them.

But the computer is not only anonymous; it also is fallible. The advice it gives is useful but not always right. Sometimes sentences are flagged as redundant when they are not; sometimes a sentence is called irrelevant because it is expressed in a novel way. Whatever hint Summary Street gives, it is up to the writer to decide what to do about it. The fact that the writer must decide at every step what changes to make is arguably the most important feature of Summary Street pedagogically. Instructional situations differ in the degree of guidance they require. In general, when solving an algebra problem, in which there is a single correct solution and only certain steps will get you there, fairly tight control is probably optimal. But as there are many ways to write a good summary, we can let the writer explore. Guidance, however loose, is still crucial: Summary Street indicates whenever the student digresses too far from the task and provides hints about what corrective steps might be taken.

Given the draft of a summary, Summary Street reacts always in the same way, no matter who the student is, what grade or school he or she is in, or who the teacher is and what she or he does. One might conjecture, therefore, that we have here a teacher-proof system. Unlike many interventions whose implementation depends on the teacher acting out faithfully what she or he is instructed to do, Summary Street seems equally effective no matter what the teacher does. That idea is totally wrong, however. In reality, the teacher is as crucial as ever. We have observed many classes that used Summary Street and many different kinds of teachers and instructional approaches. The conclusion is compelling (although difficult to capture in a statistical analysis)—that how the teacher employs Summary Street in her or his class is crucial for its effectiveness. If it is used as it was by the original teachers who helped us design Summary Street (to prepare for a class discussion) or in some other way for a well-motivated pedagogical purpose (e.g., to introduce a new topic or to prepare for a presentation or for a test), students typically like using it, and they learn from it. However, if summary writing is not given some purpose by the teacher, Summary Street is perceived as just another meaningless chore or treated as a game to be fooled or broken, and nothing is learned about summary writing. In some notable instances, having noticed from the server records that in certain schools Summary Street did not prosper, one of our staff members drove all across the state to interview the teachers, sometimes getting them to try again but with a purpose. Thus Summary Street was used effectively in the same class that initially had rejected it a few weeks earlier. Summary Street is a useful tool, but it is up to the teacher to show the student why, when, and how to use this tool. If a teacher uses Summary Street merely as a keep-them-busy exercise, students don't take to it; if students use Summary Street to organize their thoughts for an upcoming class discussion, they appreciate it and learn from it how to write a summary.

The last thing I want to say about Summary Street concerns the importance of long-term planning. Summary Street was supported by a grant from NSF through the IERI program. The purpose of the grant was to scale up and evaluate Summary Street in Colorado schools, which we accomplished. In the fall of 2007, our IERI grant ended. We are no longer able to support the use of Summary Street in Colorado schools. We have demonstrated, at a considerable expense to the taxpayer, that Summary Street scales up and can be an effective tool. However, except for a fortunate circumstance, that would have been the end of Summary Street. In that case, it would have not been obvious that the money we have spent in testing Summary Street was wisely spent, because for all practical purposes Summary Street was dead, however successful it had been. Fortunately, things turned out differently. Tom Landauer, the inventor of LSA, had founded a company, Knowledge Analysis Technologies, to develop the use of LSA-based systems in education, business, and government. This company was a subcontractor on our IERI grant, supplying the server that analyzed students' writings. The company was later sold and operates now under the name of Pearson

Knowledge Technologies. It has integrated Summary Street into work-books distributed by Prentice Hall, combined it with other Web-based literacy tools, and is marketing it as part of their WriteToLearn system (*www.WriteToLearn.net*). Thus Summary Street lives on, even though it has lost its name; but what we have learned about it is not lost. If all goes well, students all over the country will profit from our research with Summary Street.

I have dwelt at length on our experiences with Summary Street because they are relevant to Isabel's work and perhaps have parallels in her experience with pedagogical interventions. Our approach shares with Questioning the Author the goal of teaching students a power-ful approach to comprehension through guided practice. Research on comprehension, as well as best practices, have identified what these comprehension strategies are, and further research and hands-on expe-rience have revealed good methods to get students to use them. In both our approaches, classroom use was carefully monitored, and we were rewarded by seeing our efforts succeed, at least to some extent. We learned a lot in the process of implementing Summary Street in Colo-rado schools. Perhaps the most important lesson for us was that our software need not be perfect; it is all right if the feedback is not always optimal, as long as it is helpful on the whole. Thus science-based tools can indeed benefit learning, but, like any tool, their effectiveness depends ultimately on the teacher to employ them in a meaningful learning experience.

I have heaped praise on Summary Street, and it is a fine tool, indeed. But it is a tool for a very limited purpose: It teaches middle school students how to write summaries. There is so much more to comprehension than summarization. It would be nice if we could sup-port comprehension with automated, individualized computer tools in other respects, too. LSA is not always suitable for that purpose, how-ever. It gives good results when it has long enough texts to analyze, but, because of its neglect of syntax, it fails with sentence-length texts such as we typically encounter in short-answer questions in tutoring situa-tions. What is needed is a system with all the advantages of LSA—that is, a theoretically sound system that is capable of scaling up to real-life problems—but that takes into account syntax as well as semantics. A number of people are currently working on this problem, and some progress has already been made—for example, Dennis (2005). What is so interesting about the work of Dennis is not only that it combines syntactic and semantic analysis but that, in doing so, it shifts the unit of analysis from the word (as in LSA) to propositions, extensionally defined. This is very important progress, because it has long been known that comprehension is organized in terms of propositional structures (e.g., Kintsch, 1974). We are currently working on a similar system that combines semantic and syntactic information and enables us to deal with propositional structures. The construction–integration-2, or CI-2, model retains two different types of information in long-term memory: a latent, LSA-like semantic structure and an exemplar memory of syntactic dependency units, which are the building blocks of propositions. In working memory, sentence meanings are constructed by combining these two pieces of information in a contextually appropriate way. Thus what a word means in a sentence context is determined not only by its latent semantic structure but also by the precise way it is being used in the context of that sentence (Kintsch & Mangalath, in press). Our hope is that this model will be able to score the responses of participants in tutoring situations and hence provide a basis for the construction of an automated comprehension tutor that can help students not only with summarization but also with a broad range of comprehension problems.

REFERENCES

Brown, V. L., Hammill, D. D., & Wiederholt, J. L. (1995). *Test of Reading Comprehension* (3rd ed.). Austin, TX: Pro-Ed.

Caccamise, D., Franzke, M., Eckhoff, A., Kintsch, E., & Kintsch, W. (2007). Guided practice in technology-based summary writing. In D. S. McNamara (Ed.), *Reading comprehension strategies* (pp. 375–396). New York: Erlbaum.

Caccamise, D., Snyder, L., Allen, C., DeHart, M., Kintsch, E., Kintsch, W. & Oliver, W. *Summary Street: Scale-up and evaluation.* Manuscript in preparation.

Dennis, S. (2005). A memory-based theory of verbal cognition. *Cognitive Science, 29*, 145–193.

Franzke, M., Kintsch, E., Caccamise, D., Johnson, N., & Dooley, S. (2005). Summary Street: Computer support for comprehension and writing. *Journal of Educational Computing Research, 33*, 53–80.

Hull, C. L. (1943). *Principles in behavior.* New York: Appleton-Century.

Kintsch, E., Caccamise, D., Franzke, M., Johnson, N., & Dooley, S. (2007). Summary Street: Computer-aided summary writing. In T. K. Landauer, D. McNamara, S. Dennis, & W. Kintsch (Eds.), *Handbook of latent semantic analysis* (pp. 263–278). Mahwah, NJ: Erlbaum.

Kintsch, E., Steinhart, D., Stahl, G., Matthews, C., Lamb, R., & LSA Research Group (2000). Developing summarization skills through the use of LSA-backed feedback. *Interactive Learning Environments, 8,* 87–109.

Kintsch, W. (1974). *The representation of meaning in memory.* Hillsdale, NJ: Erlbaum.

Kintsch, W. (1998). *Comprehension: A paradigm for cognition.* New York: Cambridge University Press.

Kintsch, W., & Mangalath, P. (in press). The construction of meaning. *TopiCS in Cognitive Science, 1.*

Kintsch, W., & van Dijk, T. A. (1978). Towards a model of text comprehension and production. *Psychological Review, 85,* 363–394.

Landauer, T. K., McNamara, D., Dennis, S., & Kintsch, W. (Eds.). (2007). *Handbook of latent semantic analysis.* Mahwah, NJ: Erlbaum.

van Dijk, T. A., & Kintsch, W. (1983). *Strategies of discourse comprehension.* New York: Academic Press.

Wade-Stein, D., & Kintsch, E. (2004). Summary Street: Interactive computer support for writing. *Cognition and Instruction, 22,* 333–362.

Wolfe, M. B., Schreiner, M. E., Rehder, R., Laham, D., Foltz, P. W., Kintsch, W., et al. (1998). Learning from text: Matching reader and text by latent semantic analysis. *Discourse Processes, 25,* 309–336.

11

UNDERSTANDING THE WORD-LEVEL FEATURES OF TEXTS FOR STUDENTS WHO DEPEND ON SCHOOLS TO BECOME LITERATE

Elfrieda H. Hiebert

I met Dick and Jane in the grade 1–3 room of a four-room schoolhouse in a tiny hamlet in central Saskatchewan. From my initial encounter, I was fascinated with their lives, which seemed so exotic compared with mine. We had numerous animals on the small farm that supplemented my father's meager income as a minister. But our animals were functional and *never* in the house as Puff and Spot were. Unlike Puff, our cats were there for one purpose—to kill mice in the barn. Unlike Spot, our dog's purpose was to protect the chickens and cow in the barn at night from local wildlife.

Dick and Jane's family life differed dramatically from mine, as well. I could never imagine Dick and Jane's mother marshalling the children to collect snow that she melted in a tub for the Saturday bath or the Monday clothes washing. I lay awake at night, wishing for a grandmother like theirs. My Omas demanded that we speak to them in German, even when we were proud that we had (finally) learned English at a level that pleased our teachers.

My relationship with Dick and Jane was complicated by the rules for reading about them. We had to bring a sealing jar ring from our mothers' canning supplies as part of our first-grade materials. The sealing jar ring was put around the text that the first-graders hadn't read with the teacher. While the teacher worked with students in the other two grades, we could reread the pages that had been taught that day (or the previous day). We could not, however, read any of the pages in the portion secured by the sealing jar ring. This prohibition was all that I needed to begin an illicit relationship with the basal reader. Surreptitiously, I would go into the prohibited section and read ahead. I am confident that my reading proficiency and love of reading stem, at least in part, from the thrill of opening the contraband section of the basal reader.

These were the beginnings of my interest in basal readers. As a reader, I have read thousands of other texts. As an educator, I have advocated that students be immersed in outstanding literature (Anderson, Hiebert, Scott, & Wilkinson, 1985) and information (Hiebert, 2008). As a researcher, I have studied various aspects of reading development and instruction. But consistently my work has returned to the study of the features of schoolbooks that beginning and struggling readers are given to support their reading development. In particular, this work has focused on students who, as I had, enter school as English language learners (ELLs) and/or come from homes that are challenged economically.

In this chapter, I address three topics: (1) finding a direction for work focused on school texts, (2) developing and testing a framework on critical text features for beginning and struggling readers, and (3) developing a model of strategic vocabulary selection for narrative and informational texts.

FINDING A DIRECTION

I've been fortunate to have been involved in many events that, although appearing serendipitous at the time, have created a stimulating professional life. Of a host of such experiences during the early years of my career, I focus on two—the students I taught as a classroom teacher and my involvement in *Becoming a Nation of Readers* (Anderson et al., 1985).

With an MEd from the University of Illinois at Urbana-Champaign (before the Center for the Study of Reading was created), I began teaching in California's central valley. Many of my second-graders were ELLs. Even though I had done my student teaching in the same context as that in which I taught, no part of the teacher education curriculum had dealt with the strengths and needs of ELLs. I began teaching with no information about the uniqueness of the Spanish that my ELL students spoke. At the time I was teaching, all students in the state of California read from the same textbook. Janet and Mark led the cast of characters in the Harper and Row program (O'Donnell & VanRoekel, 1966). Clothing styles fit the early 1970s, but the dilemmas that Janet and Mark faced were similar to the problems that had confronted Dick and Jane in the mid-1950s. Janet and Mark continued to deal with bruised knees, a menagerie of pets, and lost objects. By second grade— the level that I taught—the type and repetition of vocabulary was not much different from what I had read in that classroom in Saskatchewan two decades earlier.

My second-graders spent part of each class day on individually prescribed instruction (IPI; Lindvall & Bolvin, 1966), as well as in the basal reading program. IPI consisted of a set of pretests, worksheets, and posttests. Children worked independently for a half hour daily on worksheets related to items that they had failed on a pretest. Although I had some serious questions about the appropriateness of the basal reading program for my students, especially the ELLs, my issues with IPI were even more serious. Children could spend an inordinate amount of time on attempting to master an objective with a seriously flawed set of items or relating to an aspect of linguistic knowledge whose relationship to reading acquisition is uncertain (e.g., identifying numbers of syllables in unknown words).

I became very interested in how *potential* funds of knowledge could be brought to the task of school reading. Of course, it would be several decades before Luis Moll (Moll, Armanti, Neff, & Gonzalez, 1992) would put that particularly compelling label to this construct. My teaching experience influenced the choices that I made in selecting topics to pursue as I worked on my PhD at the University of Wisconsin, Madison. In my dissertation research (Hiebert, 1981), I asked what young children might know about print (in the form of environmental print and the functions of print) before they began formal instruction. I had then— and have continued to have—a strong commitment to the learning of children who depend on schools to become literate. My observations of student learning and mismatches between texts, instruction, and students also influenced the choices in my research program in my first position as a faculty member at the University of Kentucky.

Just as my teaching experience had served to galvanize me into a career in research, the next seminal experience to influence my work was a year spent at the Center for the Study of Reading. The document that resulted—*Becoming a Nation of Readers* (Anderson et al., 1985)—summarized research, much of it on text features. This report challenged many of the existing premises underlying texts, including the role of controlled vocabulary throughout a reading program and the role of readability formulas. We shouldn't have been surprised that practices change when they are challenged in a national report. However, I don't believe that any of us would have predicted the direction that things took—whole language.

DEVELOPING AND TESTING A FRAMEWORK OF TEXT FEATURES FOR BEGINNING AND STRUGGLING READERS

Within 2 years of the publication of *Becoming a Nation of Readers*, California (California English/Language Arts Committee, 1987) had mandated that textbooks adopted for use and purchased with state funds feature authentic literature rather than controlled vocabulary. This policy was extended across the elementary grades, even though the youngest students in research on the effects of texts manipulated to conform with readability requirements had been second-graders (Hiebert, 2002). By the early 1990s, after Texas (Texas Education Agency [TEA], 1990) had implemented a mandate similar to California's, all major basal programs consisted of authentic literature. The biggest change in texts was in the anthologies for first-graders. Texts in which a small set of words was repeated across selections were replaced by anthologies of literature selections with numerous unique words. Often, the selections were chosen for their repetitive text structures, with *Brown Bear, Brown Bear* (Martin, 1967) offered as the model for appropriate text. In that story, high-frequency words were repeated within the repetitive structure (e.g., *What do you see?*) in the belief that students would recognize these words automatically. When teachers saw that many students were not developing this automaticity, they asked for additional texts. More of the same kinds of texts were provided (rather than other possible types of texts, such as ones with a preponderance of phonetically regular words), and classrooms were soon flooded with "Little Books."

The Little Books were described as covering a gradient of difficulty. The leveling system initially focused on four features (Peterson, 1991): (1) book and print features, (2) content, themes, and ideas, (3) text structure, and (4) language and literary elements. Nothing was said about the consistency of letter–sound patterns or about high-frequency words. The Little Books differed substantially from the texts that had been described in *Becoming a Nation of Readers* as appropriate for first-graders. That document gave Dr. Seuss's (e.g., Geisel, 1960) texts as a prototype for texts for beginning readers. In addition to inventive, playful text and illustrations, Dr. Seuss used high-frequency words and words with consistent and common vowel patterns. Unlike the Little Books that had numerous multisyllabic words (to be deciphered using illustrations), a text such as *Green Eggs and Ham* had very few multisyllabic words.

When a publisher told me that the texts within the first-grade anthologies were intended for read-alouds and not for developing independent reading proficiencies, I was spurred into action. I began a program of work that had three phases: (1) describing the new context and its effects, (2) developing the TExT model, and (3) examining the effects of TExT interventions.

Describing the New Context and Its Effects

My first interest during this period was to describe the nature of learning and instruction in classrooms when texts were not selected or developed based on repetition of vocabulary and inclusion of phonetically regular words. With Charles Fisher, I conducted an observational study of literature- and skills-oriented classrooms in Title I schools (Fisher & Hiebert, 1990). In the literature-based classrooms, instructional experiences were remarkably similar across second- and sixth-grade classrooms. Even in second-grade classrooms (in which our assessments indicated many students were struggling as readers), opportunities to learn about the commonalities across words were few. Instruction occurred in whole-class settings through minilessons. A minilesson on reading was likely to focus on the craft of an illustrator, a comprehension strategy such as summarizing, and, sometimes, features of words (e.g., homophones). Even in second grade, students' reading occurred almost solely from self-selected texts, typically Little Books.

Educators were increasingly recognizing that many students required additional support. An intervention in tune with the prevailing zeitgeist was the response—Reading Recovery. As was the case in a number of flagship institutions, a Reading Recovery training program was proposed at my institution (the University of Colorado, Boulder), and I was asked to implement it. Before I agreed to lead a training site, I wanted to know about the efficacy of the intervention in American schools, especially high-impact ones. I was interested in how the intervention influenced students' long-term reading performances given that it used texts with no or little control and that its premise was that knowledgeable teachers would adjust texts for students. At that point, I could find no research in an archival journal on the efficacy of the intervention in American schools. I undertook to summarize the existing data gathered in American schools that was accessible to me as a non-Reading Recovery researcher. After a long and difficult search for data, I published my conclusion (Hiebert, 1994): that the effect of investing intervention dollars in this tutoring program at first grade was, at best, small on the reading performance of a grade cohort. Soon after, another review was published with a similar conclusion (Shanahan & Barr, 1995).

Concluding that one-to-one tutoring would not cover the need, particularly in high-impact schools, I began to study the effects of small-group instruction in Title I settings. A particular focus of this instruction was to ensure that students had a chance to apply information about the alphabetic system being taught in lessons to the texts that they were reading. Because the available materials were the Little Books, my colleagues and I worked hard to sort them by phonics patterns and high-frequency words (Hiebert, Colt, Catto, & Gury, 1992). Our analyses of student performances as a result of participating with the restructured Title I program showed that even a modicum of text control made a substantial difference in students' word recognition.

I was concerned with the direction that first-grade programs were taking. In a chapter for the *Handbook of Educational Psychology* (Hiebert & Raphael, 1996), Taffy Raphael and I examined the basis for different models of text for first-graders. The most dominant over the 20th century had been the high-frequency-word model based on the work of Thorndike (1921)—the model that Gray and Arbuthnot (1946) used in the *Dick and Jane* texts that had been the mainstay for numerous students in North America, including me. Clearly, there were difficulties with the high-frequency-word model and the readability formulas that reified this model. At the same time, the model that was in the foreground in the early 1990s—that of authentic text with its many unique words (including many multisyllabic words)—posed numerous challenges for teachers and their students.

I was not the only one asking questions about the characteristics of texts. The results of the first state-by-state comparison of the National Assessment of Educational Progress (Campbell, Donahue, Reese, & Phillips, 1996) had been released, and the poor performances of California's fourth-graders were interpreted to be a product of the literature-based, whole-language disposition of the state's framework (Levine, 1996). Because of textbook adoption cycles, Texas (Texas Education Agency [TEA], 1997) preceded California in mandating a shift away from authentic to decodable texts, with *decodable* defined as the match between instruction in the teachers' manuals and students' texts. Although the fit between instructional guidance and students' texts is important, the existing research was not conclusive as to this criterion. In particular, answers were nonexistent as to how many lessons beginning readers (especially ones who depend on schools to become literate) require to grasp a particularly challenging grapheme–phoneme correspondence. I was convinced that a model of text needed to address more than one element.

Developing the TExT Model

After numerous iterations based on reviews of research and observations of beginning and struggling readers, I identified a model that I labeled as *Text Elements by Task* (TExT; Hiebert, 2002). This label directs attention to the interaction between text elements and tasks. The nature of texts that students can process will differ as a function of the kinds of adult or digital scaffolding they receive. Two dimensions of texts are particularly influential on independent word identification: (1) the cognitive load represented by the number of new, unique words per 100 and (2) the linguistic content of new, unique words. *Cognitive load* refers to the number of different words that need to be recognized within a text. Consider the following two text excerpts, both of 11 words:

Excerpt A: Matt ran and ran. Matt ran far from Mom and Dad (E. H. H.).

Excerpt B: Francisco ran into the garden. His grandmother was reading a book (Tafolla, 2007).

Excerpt A has 6 different words, and Excerpt B has 11 different words. For beginning readers, Excerpt B with 11 different words is predicted to be more demanding than Excerpt A, in which three words are repeated. If teachers support students in figuring out words, beginning readers will be able to apply their knowledge of *Matt, ran,* and *and* in Excerpt A.

Linguistic content refers to knowledge about words and word components. The frequency of a word's appearance in written English is one aspect of linguistic content. I have proposed that the words that are found in school texts (Zeno, Ivens, Millard, & Duvvuri, 1995) can be classified into seven word zones according to their frequency in written English (Hiebert, 2005b). The word zones differ in size and the number of times the words in them appear in a million words of text. The number of words in the highly frequent zones (zones 0–2), in which words can be expected to occur at least 100 or more times per 1 million words of text, is relatively small (930). Approximately 4,900 words are in zones 3 and 4, in which words are predicted to appear with moderate frequency (from 10 to 99 times per 1 million words). Zones five and six are large (approximately 150,000 words). These words appear rarely in texts, with likely occurrences from .01 to 9 times per 1 million words.

The second kind of linguistic information pertains to common, consistent vowel patterns in words. To develop automaticity in reading requires generalization and application of knowledge about the relationships between letters and sounds. Excerpts A and B pose different opportunities for and demands on readers' knowledge of vowel patterns. In Excerpt A, four of the six unique words have the same vowel (short *a*) in a consonant–vowel–consonant pattern. In Excerpt B, none of the words have the same vowel pattern. Furthermore, five of the words are multisyllabic, which pose even greater demands on beginning readers than monosyllabic words (Juel & Roper/Schneider, 1985).

Initially, I used the TExT model to describe what students needed to know at particular points to be successful in reading texts. I was especially interested in how demands on student knowledge had changed over time. For this analysis (Hiebert, 2005c), I examined the only program still in existence of the two that Chall (1967/1983) described as prototypical mainstream basal programs. I examined entry first-grade and exit first- and second-grade texts from 1962 to 2000 and subsequently conducted an analysis of the 2007 copyright (Hiebert, 2008). In the 1962 and 1983 copyrights, the rate at which new words appeared was fairly consistent at the end of grades 1 and 2. A sea change occurred, however, in the rate of introduction of new words at the *beginning* of grade 1 in the 1993 copyright. From 1983 to 1993, the rate of new, unique words increased from 5 to 30 words in entry-level, grade-1 selections. Even as policies in 2000 (and again in 2007) meant that texts were evaluated by decodability, the number of unique words has remained high (23 in 2007).

In a subsequent study, my colleagues and I (Hiebert, Martin, & Menon, 2005) analyzed the shared words across components of programs that claimed different philosophical roots: a literature-based approach, a decoding-oriented approach, and a program that began with decoding and, by the middle of grade 1, emphasized literature (i.e., a decoding–meaning approach). Three components of each of the three programs were examined: anthologies, which included selections from children's literature; decodable texts, which are short books that emphasize one or more grapheme–phoneme relationships that have been presented in accompanying lessons in the teacher's guide; and Little Books or leveled texts, which are based on the premise that students can access texts through predictable text structures, illustrations, and compelling content (Fountas & Pinnell, 1999). For the literature-based and the decoding–literature programs, the percentage of shared words across the three components was exactly the same—28%. In the decoding-oriented program, the percentage was higher—40%. In all cases, the majority of shared words came from the 300 most frequent words.

A final descriptive study was to determine the ability of the TExT model to predict students' performances on texts. Charles Fisher and I (Hiebert & Fisher, 2007) gave two sets of instructional texts that differed in the number of unique words, the complexity of letter–sound correspondences of words, and the presence of high-frequency words to students at the end of the first trimester of first grade. We were almost 100% accurate in predicting the words that were, indeed, difficult and the words that were, indeed, easy. Furthermore, the differences in fluency and accuracy were substantial as a result of the complexity of letter–sound correspondences and the presence of high-frequency words.

Examining the Effects of TExT-Based Texts on Student Proficiencies

The next phase of the research involved selecting and designing texts to comply with the TExT model and to determine the effectiveness of these texts in supporting children's reading development in relation to other texts. Creating new texts is a highly costly venture. Consequently, we began with existing texts. In the first study, Shailaja Menon and I (Menon & Hiebert, 2005) took a set of existing texts and ordered them according to the phonics part of the TExT model. We tried as best we could to hold down the number of unique words, but, over that, we had little control. We did better, however, than was the case with the existing basal reading program. The students who had the reordered texts did significantly better on both the text reading and word-level reading tasks of an informal reading inventory than those with the basal reading program.

I then had the opportunity to work on designing a set of texts as part of a technology grant through which online texts could be developed. With compelling arguments, I was able to get, for experimental purposes, hard copies of the texts that were used in two studies. The first study (Hiebert & Fisher, 2006b) was implemented with ELLs during the final trimester of first grade. Students from the same class were assigned to one of three groups: (1) single-criterion (SC) text (consisting of a set of decodable texts) (Adams et al., 2000); (2) multiple-criteria (MC) text (consisting of texts written to systematically introduce words with common and consistent letter–sound patterns, high-frequency words, and high-imagery words (Hiebert, Brown, Taitague, Fisher, & Adler, 2004); or (3) control group. Project teachers used the same lesson plan that included talking about words, writing them, and reading and rereading texts for the two interventions, with the only difference being between SC and MC texts, which were the focus of approximately 40% of a half-hour session. The two intervention groups performed significantly better than the control group in rate and accuracy of reading three texts; the difference between the two intervention groups was significant on one of the texts. The second study (Hiebert & Fisher, 2006a) was similar in methods and sample to the first study but was approximately 67% longer in duration. Students who read the MC texts gained 2.8 words correct per minute on an informal reading inventory for every week of instruction, as compared with 2.4 words gained by students who read the SC texts and 2.0 words per week by the control students.

I was next interested in applying the construct to texts that could be used with struggling readers. Charles Fisher and I (Hiebert & Fisher, 2005) conducted an analysis of the texts used in the fluency studies reviewed by the National Reading Panel (NRP; National Institute of Child Health and Human Development [NICHD], 2000) that left me confident that the texts that support students' automaticity in word recognition have a high proportion of high-frequency and phonetically regular words and low proportions of rare, singly appearing, and multi-syllabic words. Many of the texts in the NRP-reviewed studies that supported fluency came from old basal reading programs that are unlikely to generate the engagement that invites repeated and extended reading or to support development of background knowledge. I chose to create informational texts because analyses I had done of science texts showed that rare words were more likely to be repeated in these texts than in narrative texts (Hiebert, 2007). I set about creating a curriculum for the development of fluency with core high-frequency words and also words with common and consistent vowel patterns. The curriculum has six levels. The first level consists of the 300 most frequent words or words with short or long vowel patterns in monosyllabic words. By the third level of texts, the words are either among the 1,000 most frequent words or monosyllabic. By the final level, the curriculum consists of the 5,000 most frequent words or all monosyllabic words. At any level, 98% of the words need to fall within the target curriculum. I chose this level because of its association with independent reading (Betts, 1946). Students need the opportunity to practice texts at a point at which they can recognize most of the words but are not reading with automaticity. I called these *scaffolded texts* in that they provide support for students who are moving to automatic word recognition.

These texts were tested in several studies (Hiebert, 2005a, 2006) in which repeated and guided reading occurred with either the texts from the basal reading anthology or the scaffolded texts. In both studies, the students who did repeated reading with the scaffolded texts had higher performances than students who read the basal texts. Although differences between the two groups were not statistically different, the scaffolded-texts group performed significantly higher on a measure of oral reading fluency than a control group that read the literature in the basal reading program but without repeated reading ($p < .04$; Hiebert, 2005a). The basal group did not perform significantly higher than the control group ($p < .2$). In studies conducted by other groups of researchers, effects have been substantially greater (Vadasy & Sanders, 2008).

DEVELOPING A MODEL OF STRATEGIC VOCABULARY SELECTION FOR NARRATIVE AND INFORMATIONAL TEXTS

Because an emphasis on automatic and accurate word recognition with critical groups of words is a necessary foundation for proficient reading, I was confident that the first line of focus for the TExT model should be on scaffolded texts that support fluency and word recognition. But increasingly, as I analyzed and wrote texts, I asked about how best to support students in their use of the many words in zones 4 and beyond, particularly the 135,000 or more words in word zone 6. Unlike with most words in zones 0–2, learning these words involves more than pronouncing the word and, in so doing, recognizing that it is in one's oral vocabulary. Many of these words are rare; most are used only in written language. I began to ask how curriculum developers, publishers, and teachers can be guided in handling vocabulary strategically. As a result of this initial work, I had what I term to be an epiphany. This epiphany has provided me with several compelling questions, the answers to which I am pursuing at present.

Foundational Work

If the gap in word knowledge with which students enter school (Hart & Risley, 1995) is not to widen, time spent in school needs to be used strategically. My work on vocabulary learning began with the goal of finding conceptually driven and strategic ways of identifying critical vocabulary—vocabulary that would make the biggest difference for students who depend on schools to become literate. I was very much aware of my status as a newcomer to research on vocabulary learning. Consequently, my first activity was to enroll colleagues who had greater background in the area to collaborate with me.

Identifying Underlying Vocabulary Curriculum

An initial collaboration with Judy Scott and Shira Lubliner (Scott, Lubliner, & Hiebert, 2006) was directed at establishing the nature of vocabulary in assessments and instruction among the studies reviewed by the NRP (NICHD, 2000). Few of the studies attended to the variables that Nagy and Scott (2000) had identified as critical to depth and breadth of vocabulary knowledge. Furthermore, few of the studies considered a criterion beyond the specific words that were taught in the instructional intervention. Staying with the words that have been taught, rather than including groups of words to which students might extend or generalize their knowledge, provides little indication of how much larger a vocabulary students can access as a result of an intervention.

While I was working on the analyses of the studies within the NRP, I was also participating in a study group on vocabulary assessment with David Pearson and Michael Kamil (the latter had been the chair of the NRP's subgroup on vocabulary). As part of our discussions, which extended over a 2-year period, we studied the words on four vocabulary assessments that had been identified by a national panel as complying with Reading First criteria (Kame'enui, 2002) and included two individually administered assessments and two group-administered assessments. Our study group wanted to use illustrative items from these tests in a paper that we were developing on the assessment of vocabulary. Because the tests were copyrighted, we could not reproduce the items from the assessments. However, the technical manuals provided no guidance or frameworks for the designation of vocabulary. The best that we could do was to develop items with words that had similar frequency ratings and phonics–syllabic patterns. In the paper that our study group eventually produced (Pearson, Hiebert, & Kamil, 2007), we concluded that psychometric requirements, rather than theoretical frameworks of vocabulary, drive the design of tests. A group of words that has been identified through various processes is administered to a sample of students. Difficulty of words is established by the percentage of students who answered the question correctly. The results of such assessments indicate how students perform relative to students at particular percentile levels but nothing about students' knowledge of a particular domain of vocabulary.

As it became apparent that the existing vocabulary assessments had few conceptual undergirdings, I began to identify possible criteria that might be applied to the selection of words. I began, as I had previously (Hiebert, 2002), with an analysis of assessments. In this case (Hiebert, 2005b), the assessments were the released items from fourth-grade, standards-based tests of three of the United States' four largest states (Texas, New York, and Florida) and the National Assessment of Educational Progress (NAEP). I was particularly interested in the vocabulary that accounted for approximately 90% of the corpora on these assessments because 90% has been cited as the level at which, if students have automatic word recognition, they should be able to use context in figuring out the additional 10% (Stahl & Kuhn, 2002). An average of 92% of the unique words on the four assessments was accounted for by words that are predicted to appear 10 or more times per 1-million-word corpus. An initial goal for a vocabulary curriculum from grades 1 through 4, it seemed to me, would be to ensure that students are facile with the approximately 5,500 words within this range (i.e., the words in zones 0–4).

I was curious as to the number of words that could be identified if two criteria were applied to this corpus: (1) They needed to belong to a semantic family of at least two words within the 5,500 most frequent words and (2) the target word needed to be unknown. To create semantic families, I used Nagy and Anderson's (1984) criteria for "semantically transparent" connections to cluster words with inflected endings, suffixes, prefixes, and compounds into semantic families. To establish whether a word was known, I began with Dale and O'Rourke's (1981) *Living Word Vocabulary* (*LWV*) and verified the placement of words in grade-level lists with *The Ginn Word Book for Teachers* (*GWBT*; Johnson & Moe, 1983). Approximately 10% of the 5,500 most frequent words are sufficiently unknown to a critical portion of an age cohort to merit instruction, and they also belonged to a semantic family. The number of unknown words in different word zones ranges from a low of approximately 50 at zone 1 to approximately 185 at word zone 4. If word zone 1 is regarded to be a focus of first grade (with subsequent zones through 4 matched to equivalent grades), it would be anticipated that the task would be doable as a portion of a vocabulary curriculum.

Vocabulary in Thematic Clusters

As I was working to identify the conceptual foundations of vocabulary curriculum in general, I was asked to participate in a project that aimed to integrate literacy into science inquiry units: Seeds of Science/ Roots of Reading (Seeds/Roots; Cervetti, Pearson, Barber, Hiebert, & Bravo, 2007). I was extremely interested in the Seeds/Roots project because it represented a way of treating the rare vocabulary that was not accounted for within the "efficient, effective vocabulary curriculum" (Hiebert, 2005b) I have just described. At one level, the selection of vocabulary in a content area such as science is fairly straightforward in that critical concepts are identified clearly in standards documents (Marzano, 2004). Within inquiry science approaches, however, vocabulary per se has often not been emphasized. We began the Seeds/Roots project with two units (Shoreline Science and Terrarium Investigations) that had been developed by science educators for inquiry-based science instruction. The developers of these original units at Lawrence

Hall of Science at the University of California, Berkeley, had identified central concepts for these two topics (e.g., *erosion and forces* for the first topic, *habitat and decomposition* for the second). For some concepts, students participated in activities that demonstrated the meaning of the words. For other concepts, clarification of the vocabulary depended on the teacher. To create the integrated literacy–science inquiry units of Seeds/Roots, we began by targeting discipline-specific concepts and words to which students had had repeated exposure in different formats. Each unit included nine nonfiction science books that highlighted many target words.

An empirical investigation (Cervetti et al., 2006) compared a science-only treatment (using the original science-inquiry units), a literacy-only treatment (involving literacy lessons that our research team developed for each of the nine texts of the Terrarium unit), a science–literacy treatment (receiving the inquiry science materials of the science-only treatment and the literacy materials of the literacy-only treatment in a combined form), and a control group. On vocabulary tasks, science–literacy students outperformed science-only students on Shoreline vocabulary. For the Terrarium unit, the science–literacy group outperformed the science-only and the no-treatment groups. There were no significant differences between the science–literacy and literacy-only groups.

An Epiphany

As I did this foundational work, I had an epiphany that, in retrospect, should not have been an epiphany at all. My insight falls into the category of "what my grandmother knew," as Hoffman and Pearson (2000) described it. Quite simply, what I understood was the substantial differences in the words that compose the unique vocabularies of informational and narrative texts. Both kinds of text share a substantial percentage of highly and moderately frequent words. But there are also words that are unique to both kinds of texts. In earlier describing my choice of an informational genre in designing a text-based intervention for struggling readers, I mentioned that rare words in informational texts are more likely to be repeated than the rare words in narrative texts. But the issue of rare words across the two genres is more than a quantitative difference. The content words of informational texts are used with precision and are repeated frequently. Authors of narrative texts repeat concepts rather than words, and, typically, students know these concepts. A second- or third-grader knows what it means to be scared. An author writing for students at this level is unlikely to use the word *scared* over and over; rather, the author will use synonyms such as *frightened, afraid, fearful,* and *terrified* to communicate the character's disposition.

I had numerous discussions with colleagues about what the distinctions between the vocabulary of informational and narrative texts mean for the selection and instruction of vocabulary. While working hard not to defuse my excitement about this newfound knowledge, Bill Nagy reminded me of an article that he had published with Dick Anderson and Patricia Herman in 1987. In this study (Nagy, Anderson, & Herman, 1987), they examined various properties of words and texts and their effects on learning words from context. Conceptual difficulty in the Nagy et al. study was determined by a 4-point scheme: (1) known concept with a one-word synonym (e.g., *fight–altercation*); (2) known concept that can be summarized in a familiar phrase (e.g., *you're sorry–apologize*); (3) unknown concept that can be learned on the basis of available experiences and information (e.g., *naive*); and (4) unknown concept that requires new factual information or learning a related system of concepts (e.g., *divide* as *boundary between drainage basins* requires information about river systems). The only word-level variable that significantly related to learning from context was conceptual difficulty. Furthermore, this variable and the average length of unfamiliar words were the text-level properties that most strongly influenced learning from context. More in-depth analyses showed that it was the contrast between words in category 4 and the combination of the three other categories that accounted for the significant differences. This contrast is one, fundamentally, between the words in content areas such as science and social studies and words in narrative texts. There will be exceptions, of course, but the kinds of words that represent unknown concepts are more prominent in informational texts than they are in narrative works. Furthermore, words representing unknown concepts occur concurrently in texts—words such as *decomposition* and *nutrients.* Such conjunction requires, Nagy and colleagues (1987) emphasized, the understanding of relationships among concepts in a text.

Also trying not to dampen my enthusiasm about my epiphany, my dear friend and mentor, Isabel Beck, reminded me of the vocabulary tiers about which she and her colleagues have written so extensively and that have been disseminated so widely (Beck, McKeown, & Kucan,

2002). A major distinction within this system is between tier 2 and tier 3. The former contains words that represent concepts that are familiar to students, although the words themselves may not be. Tier 3, on the other hand, contains words that represent unfamiliar concepts from content areas.

Current Foci

My epiphany may not have been highly original, but I have great interest in and enthusiasm for studying differences in the vocabularies of narrative and content-area texts (and the manner in which these two vocabularies require different forms of instructional treatments). My involvement in the Seeds of Science/Roots of Reading project (Cervetti et al., 2007) has left me confident that the treatment of rare vocabulary in content areas can best be done through thematic and conceptual instruction. Although sources for selecting and instructing content-specific vocabulary are available (e.g., Marzano, 2004), there is a vocabulary that is shared across content areas that is overlooked in both content-area and reading/language arts instruction: the words that have been described as general academic words (Nation, 1990) and that were prominent in my analysis of the 5,586 words—words such as *form, system,* and *process* (Hiebert, 2005b). My other current focus pertains to the vocabulary of narrative texts. Dealing with the vast numbers of rare words, many of which appear a single time in a narrative text or even an anthology of narrative texts, is an issue that I am currently addressing.

General Academic Words for the Elementary Grades

I have intensified my examination of general academic words, begun earlier (Hiebert, 2005b), because of the widespread interest in general academic vocabulary. The Academic Word List (AWL; Coxhead, 2000) that represents Nation's (1990) work was developed from university textbooks. Even though the AWL was intended to support university students learning English as a second language, it has been used in programs for elementary and middle school students in the United States (Scholastic, 2006) and in research with middle-graders (Snow, 2007). General academic vocabulary is likely an issue in the elementary school (Bailey, 2006); the words in university texts may not be precisely the same as those in elementary and middle school texts.

I (Hiebert, 2007) identified 400 morphological families (each with an average of five words) that occur across content areas and that have at least one or two members that appear with sufficient frequency to expect that the words would occur in elementary texts. I have labeled the group of morphological families as the Core Academic Word List (CAWL). In a relatively large corpus of words from reading/language arts, social studies, and science textbooks at grades 2, 4, and 6, I found that the CAWL accounts for a significant percentage of the words in science and social studies texts at grades 4 and 6 but not in narrative texts at these grades (or at grade 2).

The Vocabulary of Narrative Texts

My work on the vocabulary of narrative texts is at a stage at which I am speculating, proposing, trying things out, reading extensively, and talking with colleagues. My reason for emphasizing narrative texts is that if the vocabulary of narrative texts could be dealt with more economically than is now the case, time within the reading/language arts block would be freed up for instruction in the vocabulary from content-area texts, which often represents conceptually complex and unknown content to elementary students, as well as in general academic words. Furthermore, when vocabulary instruction treats words individually and does not encourage connections between words and to underlying semantic categories, students are not supported in a generative stance toward vocabulary.

As I have confirmed in several studies (e.g., Hiebert, 2008), numerous rare words occur a single time in narrative texts. Such words are evident in the teachers' guide for a text from a second-grade anthology (Cooper et al., 2003): *apartment, delivery, handcarts, restaurant, market*, and *celebrations*. Another 18 words from word zones 3 and higher occur in this story but are not the focus of instructional guidance in the teachers' guide—words such as *medicinal, furious, musty*, and *cobbler* and words related to Chinatown, where the story occurs (*woks, tai chi, kung fu*). There are at least three problems with the identification of words from this text. The first is that many words that are rare are not addressed. Second, the target words do not necessarily require in-depth instruction. When the conceptual difficulty scheme of Nagy and colleagues (1987) is applied to these words, all fall into the first three categories. To spend 15 or more minutes on each of these words is not making good use of students' time. Third, students are not being guided in making connections across words and concepts. In this particular lesson, the word *market* is not presented in relation to other words that authors might use for describing business areas in communities other than Chinatown, in other countries, or even historical times, such as *bazaar, mall, shopping stall, trading post,* or *dime* or *department store.*

I have been experimenting with placing concepts into larger groups. For the latter, I have used Marzano and Marzano's (1988) 61 superclusters, which I have organized into 12 megaclusters. Examples of three megaclusters are physical actions and motion, cognitive–perceptual actions, and communication.

I am particularly interested in how these megaclusters represent elements of story structure. Beck and McKeown (1981) described the manner in which the elements of narrative texts—setting, characters, plot, and resolution of conflict—can be used to enhance comprehension. Might these elements also be useful for teachers and students to organize the many rare words in the narrative texts they read? For example, characters consistently engage in actions as part of the plot. In Figure 11.1, I have illustrated how 40 verbs from the second-grade unit in the basal anthology that I referred to previously might be organized within the three megaclusters having to do with characters' actions. The verbs in this group represent concepts that are typically known by second-graders (although the specific label may not be). One word that likely falls into Nagy and colleagues' (1987) category 3 is the word *dispatched,* which, as is illustrated in Figure 11.1, would be the object of more elaborated instruction.

Figure 11.1 illustrates a possible way in which teachers and their students could attend to rare words in texts. I am confident that readers (as well as teachers and their students) will categorize these verbs in different ways. I provide this figure to illustrate how a teacher might guide students in identifying potentially new vocabulary in narrative texts and in grappling with similarities and differences in the meanings and uses of the many rare words in narrative texts. As the lessons consider a group of words such as those in Figure 11.1, students come to understand the manner in which authors of narrative texts vary their use of words to convey the nuances of their characters' thinking, actions, and communication. Such activities could be highly useful in the productive use of vocabulary—particularly writing—as much or

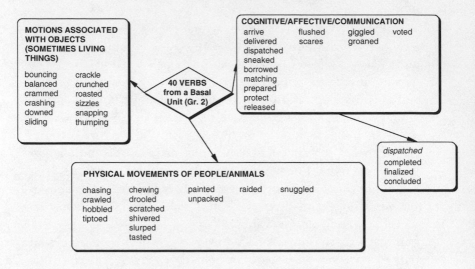

FIGURE 11.1. Forty verbs from a basal unit organized into three megaclusters.

even more so than in the receptive domain. I present this combination of megaclusters and story elements as a possibility to be put to an empirical test. In a study of this hypothesis, for example, students in some classrooms could be supported in identifying words from their narrative texts that fit into the megaclusters. Electronic technologies such as whiteboards would seem to be perfect for this purpose. In other classrooms, students would be supported in identifying words that are part of the components of stories, such as words that describe character traits or settings.

ON TO THE FUTURE

As is evident in my thinking to date on the selection and instruction of vocabulary in narrative text, I am confident that new issues will arise as I explore particular questions. I also recognize that serendipitous experiences and partnerships arise as one conducts research. Most recently, my thinking has been challenged and developed through my interactions with Bill Nagy as we wrote the chapter on vocabulary for the fourth volume of the *Handbook of Reading Research* (Nagy & Hiebert, in press). I anticipate many more years of learning as I continue to ask how school texts can support those students who most depend on schools to become highly literate.

REFERENCES

Adams, M. J., Bereiter, C., McKeough, A., Case, R., Roit, M., Hirschberg, J., et al. (2000). *Open court reading.* Columbus, OH: SRA/McGraw-Hill.

Anderson, R. C., Hiebert, E. H., Scott, J. A., & Wilkinson, I. A. G. (1985). *Becoming a nation of readers: The report of the Commission on Reading.* Washington, DC: National Institute of Education. (Available from the University of Illinois, Becoming a Nation of Readers, P. O. Box 2774, Station A, Champaign, IL 61820-8774)

Bailey, A. L. (Ed.). (2006). *Language demands of school: Putting academic English to the test.* New Haven, CT: Yale University Press.

Beck, I. L., & McKeown, M. G. (1981). Developing questions that promote comprehension: The story map. *Language Arts, 58,* 913–918.

Beck, I. L., McKeown, M. G., & Kucan, L. (2002). *Bringing words to life: Robust vocabulary instruction.* New York: Guilford Press.

Betts, E. (1946). *Foundations of reading instruction.* New York: American Book.

California English/Language Arts Committee. (1987). *English-language arts framework for California public schools (kindergarten through grade twelve).* Sacramento: California Department of Education.

Campbell, J., Donahue, P., Reese, C. M., & Phillips, G. (1996). *NAEP 1994 reading report card for the nation and the states.* Washington, D C: U.S. Department of Education.

Cervetti, G. N., Pearson, P. D., Barber, J., Hiebert, E., & Bravo, M. (2007). Integrating literacy and science: The research we have, the research we need. In M. Pressley, A. K. Billman, K. H. Perry, K. E. Reffitt, & J. M. Reynolds (Eds.), *Shaping literacy achievement: Research we have, research we need* (pp. 157–174). New York: Guilford Press.

Cervetti, G. N., Hiebert, E. H., Barber, J., Pearson, P. D., Bravo, M., Arya, D. J., et al. (2006, April). *Science and literacy learning in an integrated science/literacy program: Effects of a large-scale implementation.* Paper presented at the annual meeting of the American Educational Research Association, San Francisco.

Chall, J. S. (1983). *Learning to read: The great debate* (3rd ed.). Fort Worth, TX: Harcourt Brace. (Original work published 1967)

Cooper, J. D., Pikulski, J. J., Ackerman, P. A., Au, K. H., Chard, D. J., Garcia, G. G., et al. (2003). *Around Town: Level 2.1.* Boston: Houghton Mifflin.

Coxhead, A. (2000). A new academic word list. *TESOL Quarterly, 34*(2), 213–238.

Dale, E., & O'Rourke, J. (1981). *Living word vocabulary.* Chicago: World Book/Childcraft.

Fisher, C. W., & Hiebert, E. H. (1990). Characteristics of tasks in two literacy programs. *Elementary School Journal, 91,* 6–13.

Fountas, I. C., & Pinnell, G. S. (1999). *Matching books to readers: Using leveled books in guided reading, K–3.* Portsmouth, NH: Heinemann.

Geisel, T. S. (1960). *Green eggs and ham.* New York: Random House.

Gray, W. S., & Arbuthnot, A. H. (1946). *The new basic readers: Curriculum foundation series.* Chicago: Scott, Foresman.

Hart, B., & Risley, T. (1995). *Meaningful differences in everyday parenting and intellectual development in young American children.* Baltimore: Brookes.

Hiebert, E. H. (1981). Developmental patterns and interrelationships of preschool children's print awareness. *Reading Research Quarterly, 16,* 236–260.

Hiebert, E. H. (1994). Reading Recovery in the United States: What difference does it make to an age cohort? *Educational Researcher, 23,* 15–25.

Hiebert, E. H. (2002). Standards, assessment, and text difficulty. In A. E. Farstrup & S. J. Samuels (Eds.), *What research has to say about reading instruction* (3rd ed., pp. 337–369). Newark, DE: International Reading Association.

Hiebert, E. H. (2005a). The effects of text difficulty on second graders' fluency development. *Reading Psychology, 26,* 183–209.

Hiebert, E. H. (2005b). In pursuit of an effective, efficient vocabulary curriculum for the elementary grades. In E. H. Hiebert & M. Kamil (Eds.), *The teaching and learning of vocabulary: Bringing scientific research to practice* (pp. 243–263). Mahwah, NJ: Erlbaum.

Hiebert, E. H. (2005c). State reform policies and the task textbooks pose for first-grade readers. *Elementary School Journal, 105,* 245–266.

Hiebert, E. H. (2006). Becoming fluent: What difference do texts make? In S. J. Samuels & A. E. Farstrup (Eds.), *What research has to say about reading fluency* (pp. 204–226). Newark, DE: International Reading Association.

Hiebert, E. H. (2007). The word zone fluency curriculum: An alternative approach. In M. R. Kuhn & P. J. Schwanenflugel (Eds.), *Fluency in the classroom* (pp. 154–170). New York: Guilford Press.

Hiebert, E. H. (2007, May). *A core academic word list for the middle grades.* Paper presented at the 52nd annual meeting of the International Reading Association, Toronto, ON.

Hiebert, E. H. (2008). The (mis)match between texts and students who depend on schools to become literate. In E. H. Hiebert & M. Sailors (Eds.), *Finding the right texts: What works for beginning and struggling readers: Research-based solutions* (pp. 1–20). New York: Guilford Press.

Hiebert, E. H., Brown, Z. A., Taitague, C., Fisher, C. W., & Adler, M. A. (2004). Texts and English language learners: Scaffolding entrée to reading. In F. B. Boyd, C. H. Brock, & M. S. Rozendal (Eds.), *Multicultural and multilingual literacy and language: Context and practices* (pp. 50–73). New York: Guilford Press.

Hiebert, E. H., Colt, J. M., Catto, S., & Gury, E. (1992). Reading and writing of first-grade students in a restructured Chapter 1 program. *American Educational Research Journal, 29,* 545–572.

Hiebert, E. H., & Fisher, C. W. (2005). A review of the National Reading Panel's studies on fluency: On the role of text. *Elementary School Journal, 105,* 443–460.

Hiebert, E. H., & Fisher, C. W. (2006a, July 7). *A comparison of two types of text on the fluency of first-grade English language learners.* Paper presented at the annual meeting of the Society for the Scientific Study of Reading, Vancouver, BC, Canada.

Hiebert, E. H., & Fisher, C. W. (2006b). Fluency from the first: What works with first graders. In T. Rasinski, C. Blachowicz, & K. Lems (Eds.), *Fluency instruction: Research-based best practices* (pp. 279–294). New York: Guilford Press.

Hiebert, E. H., & Fisher, C. W. (2007). The critical word factor in texts for beginning readers. *Journal of Educational Research, 101,* 3–11.

Hiebert, E. H., Martin, L. A., & Menon, S. (2005). Are there alternatives in reading textbooks? An examination of three beginning reading programs. *Reading Writing Quarterly, 21,* 7–32.

Hiebert, E. H., & Raphael, T. E. (1996). Psychological perspectives on literacy and extensions to educational practice. In D. C. Berliner & R. C. Calfee (Eds.), *Handbook of educational psychology* (pp. 550–602). New York: Macmillan.

Hoffman, J., & Pearson, P. D. (2000). Reading teacher education in the next millennium: What your grandmother's teacher didn't know that your granddaughter's teacher should. *Reading Research Quarterly, 35,* 28–44.

Johnson, D. D., & Moe, A. J. (with Baumann, J. F.). (1983). *The Ginn word book for teachers: A basic lexicon.* Boston: Ginn.

Juel, C., & Roper/Schneider, D. (1985). The influence of basal readers on first grade reading. *Reading Research Quarterly, 20,* 134–152.

Kame'enui, E. J. (2002). *An analysis of reading assessment instruments for K–3.* Eugene: University of Oregon, Institute for the Development of Educaitonal Achievement.

Levine, A. (1996). America's reading crisis: Why the whole-language approach to teaching reading has failed millions of children. *Parents, 16,* 63–65, 68.

Lindvall, C. M., & Bolvin, J. O. (1966). The project for individually prescribed instruction (Working Paper No. 8). Pittsburgh, PA: University of Pittsburgh, Learning Research and Development Center.

Martin, B. (1967). *Brown bear, brown bear: What do you see?* New York: Henry Holt.

Marzano, R. J. (2004). *Building background knowledge for academic achievement.* Alexandria, VA: Association for Supervision and Curriculum Development.

Marzano, R. J., & Marzano, J. S. (1988). *A cluster approach to elementary vocabulary instruction.* Newark, DE: International Reading Association.

Menon, S., & Hiebert, E. H. (2005). A comparison of first graders' reading with little books or literature-based basal anthologies. *Reading Research Quarterly, 40*(1), 12–38.

Moll, L. C., Armanti, C., Neff, D., & Gonzalez, N. (1992). Funds of knowledge for teaching: Using a qualitative approach to connect homes and classrooms. *Theory into Practice, 31,* 132–141.

Nagy, W., & Scott, J. (2000). Vocabulary processing. In M. Kamil, P. Mosenthal, P. D. Pearson, & R. Barr (Eds.), *Handbook of reading research* (Vol. 3, pp. 269–284). Mahwah, NJ: Erlbaum.

Nagy, W. E., & Anderson, R. C. (1984). How many words are there in printed school English? *Reading Research Quarterly, 19,* 304–330.

Nagy, W. E., & Hiebert, E. H. (in press). Toward a theory of word selection. In M. L. Kamil, P. D. Pearson, P. A. Afflerbach, & E. B. Moje (Eds.), *Handbook of reading research* (Vol. 4). New York: Longman.

Nagy, W. E., Anderson, R. C., & Herman, P. A. (1987). Learning word meanings from context during normal reading. *American Educational Research Journal, 24,* 237–270.

Nation, I. S.P. (1990). *Teaching and learning vocabulary.* Boston: Heinle & Heinle.

National Institute of Child Health and Human Development. (2000). *Report of the National Reading Panel: Teaching children to read: An evidence-based assessment of the scientific research literature on reading and its implications for reading.* Washington, DC: U.S. Government Printing Office.

O'Donnell, M., & VanRoekel, B. H. (1966). *All through the year.* Evanston, IL: Harper & Row.

Pearson, P. D., Hiebert, E. H., & Kamil, M. L. (2007). Vocabulary assessment: What we know and what we need to know. *Reading Research Quarterly, 42,* 282–296.

Peterson, B. L. (1991). Selecting books for beginning readers. In D. E. DeFord, C. A. Lyons, & G. S. Pinnell (Eds.), *Bridges to literacy: Learning from Reading Recovery* (pp. 119–147). Portsmouth, NH: Heinemann.

Scholastic. (2006). *ReadAbout* [Computer software]. New York: Author.

Scott, J. A., Lubliner, S., & Hiebert, E. H. (2006). Constructs underlying word selection and assessment tasks in the archival research on vocabulary instruction. In J. V. Hoffman, D. L. Schallert, C. M. Fairbanks, J. Worthy, & B. Maloch (Eds.), *55th yearbook of the National Reading Conference* (pp. 264–275). Oak Creek, WI: National Reading Conference.

Shanahan, T., & Barr, R. (1995). Reading Recovery: An independent evaluation of the effects of an early instructional intervention for at-risk learners. *Reading Research Quarterly, 30,* 958–996.

Snow, C. (2007, October 2). *Word generation: An approach to promoting academic language.* Paper presentation at the conference on Academic Language and Content: A Focus on English Language Learners in Middle School, Oak Brook, IL.

Stahl, S. A., & Kuhn, M. R. (2002). Making it sound like language: Developing fluency. *Reading Teacher, 55,* 582–584.

Tafolla, C. (2007). *Mama's birthday present.* Glenview, IL: Scott, Foresman.

Texas Education Agency. (1990). *Proclamation of the State Board of Education advertising for bids on textbooks.* Austin, TX: Author.

Texas Education Agency. (1997). *Proclamation of the State Board of Education advertising for bids on textbooks.* Austin, TX: Author.

Thorndike, E. L. (1921). *The teacher's word book.* New York: Columbia University Press.

Vadasy, P. F., & Sanders, E. A. (2008). Repeated reading intervention: Outcomes and interactions with readers' skills and classroom instruction. *Journal of Educational Psychology, 100,* 272–290.

Zeno, S. M., Ivens, S. H., Millard, R. T., & Duvvuri, R. (1995). *The educator's word frequency guide.* Brewster, NY: Touchstone Applied Science Associates.

12

TEXT IN THE SCIENCE CLASSROOM

Promoting Engagement
to Facilitate Conceptual Change

Suzanne H. Broughton *and* Gale M. Sinatra

The context for the research we present in this chapter is a current line of inquiry examining the nature of the refutational text effect in promoting conceptual change. The studies we report were initiated by my (G.M.S.) former doctoral student and collaborator, Suzanne Broughton (see Broughton, 2008; Broughton, Sinatra, &, Reynolds, in press). As will become evident through reading the chapter, this work draws heavily on research by Isabel Beck and Moddy McKeown. During my time as a postdoctoral fellow with Isabel and Moddy at the Learning Research and Development Center (LRDC), our research focused on fifth-graders' challenges in comprehending their social studies textbook passages (see, e.g., Beck, McKeown, Sinatra, & Loxterman, 1991; McKeown, Beck, Sinatra, & Loxterman, 1992). We identified issues of lack of students' background knowledge and poor text coherence as factors contributing to comprehension difficulties. These issues have remained of great importance in my research over the years.

Lately, the majority of my work has been in the area of conceptual change learning, which examines how students come to change their thinking, particularly about scientific phenomena (see, e.g., Sinatra & Pintrich, 2003). Most recently, my scholarship has focused on understanding the cognitive and affective processes that inhibit or facilitate conceptual change learning (Nussbaum, Sinatra, & Poliquin, 2008; Sinatra, 2005; Sinatra & Mason, 2008). In a series of studies (e.g., Sinatra, Southerland, McConaughy, & Demastes, 2003; Southerland & Sinatra, 2003) my colleagues and I have demonstrated that beliefs can "trump" knowledge in determining students' acceptance of scientific theories when they have too little content understanding.

The issue of background knowledge (or lack thereof) has remained a central theme of my research over the years. As can be seen in this chapter, issues of text structure have come back into the foreground in my recent work through my students' research interest in the use of refutational text to promote conceptual change. In some ways, my research has come full circle, as the studies we present in this chapter are once again examining the interaction of background knowledge and text structure.

The festschrift in honor of Isabel's career, held in 2007 at LRDC and celebrated in this volume, highlighted the breadth and depth of her career contributions, from her work in beginning reading to that on vocabulary and on coherence and text comprehension through her more recent work on text discussion. Much of this work informs our current thinking in the research we present in this chapter. The threads of Isabel's work can be clearly traced through my own, as we demonstrate. Thank you, Isabel, for a lifetime of research that has inspired the researchers assembled in this volume and has made a significant and lasting impact on the field of reading.

BACKGROUND: WHY THE NEED FOR CONCEPTUAL CHANGE?

It is widely agreed that students come to the classroom with previously formed conceptions that may not align with the accepted scientific viewpoint. For example, young children may hold the misconception of a flat Earth (Vosniadou & Brewer, 1987, 1992). Learning within the science classroom often involves providing students opportunities to overcome such misconceptions by comparing their prior conceptions to the scientific perspective. The challenge for science educators is to help move students beyond their strongly held prior conceptions, rooted in experience, to adopt a scientific point of view that often is contradictory to their experience. This process of restructuring one's prior knowledge to align with the scientific perspective has been described as conceptual change (Chinn & Brewer, 1993; Dole & Sinatra, 1998; Duit, 1999; Posner, Strike, Hewson, & Gertzog, 1982; Vosniadou, 1999; Vosniadou & Brewer, 1987). Conceptual change involves the development of qualitatively different representations from those previously held by the individual (Vosniadou, Ioannides, Dimitrakopoulou, & Papademetriou, 2001).

INSTRUCTIONAL INTERVENTIONS FOR PROMOTING CONCEPTUAL CHANGE IN SCIENCE

Science educators use a variety of instructional techniques to promote change in their students' knowledge representations. These include constructing concept maps (Mason, 1992), concept webs, or Vee diagrams (Mintzes, Wandersee, & Novak, 1997) and hands-on activities, such as conducting experiments (Hodson, 1998; Hynd, McWhorter, Phares, & Suttles, 1994). Cognitive and developmental psychologists have also emphasized hands-on inquiry interventions to facilitate conceptual change. For example, Vosniadou and colleagues (2001) utilized a combination of models and small-group discussions to promote conceptual change about force and energy. Halldén and colleagues (2002) used illustrations, interviews, and manipulative models to promote conceptual change in young children's concepts of the shape of the Earth. Self-explanations of key concepts described in expository texts have also been shown to be effective in facilitating conceptual change (Chi, 2000). Computer simulations have been used as pathways to conceptual change on a variety of physics concepts (Biemans & Simons, 2002; Nussbaum & Sinatra, 2003; Wiser & Amin, 2002).

TEXTS IN THE SCIENCE CLASSROOM

Expository texts are used as a primary method of instruction across curriculum contexts. Despite their widespread usage in most domains of the curriculum, they are used less frequently in the science classroom than in some other content areas. The sparse use of texts in science classrooms has been traced to the emergence, in the early 1980s, of an inquiry-based learning approach to science (Yore, Bisanz, & Hand, 2003). Inquiry learning continues to be emphasized in national reform movements (American Association for the Advancement of Science [AAAS], 1993; National Research Council [NRC], 1996) as an effective avenue for children to learn science, with the focus of most science instruction on *doing* science (Settlage & Southerland, 2007) as preferable to reading about scientific content or process.

Not only has inquiry been emphasized, but there is also reason to speculate that text use may have been purposely deemphasized in the science classroom. The use of science textbooks does have many drawbacks. A long history of research has documented the problems with standard textbook passages. Problems that researchers have identified include the use of ambiguous references (Frederiksen, 1981) and a high density of new concepts that are introduced without providing sufficient information about the to-be-learned concepts (Kintsch, Kozminsky, Streby, McKoon, & Keenan, 1975).

A major issue identified by researchers is that expository texts do not seem to take into account the level of background knowledge of the target readers (Anderson, 1978; Beck et al., 1991; O'Reilly & McNamara, 2007). Beck and her colleagues argue this point in terms of what they call *explanatory coherence*. According to Beck and colleagues (1991), expository texts do not sufficiently explain ideas to allow young readers, who may lack background information, to draw connections among ideas and establish coherence. Thus these texts place a heavy burden on the reader to make inferences and assume that the reader has the relevant knowledge needed to make connections among text elements (Beck, Perfetti, & McKeown, 1982; Beck et al., 1991). The lack of explanatory coherence typically results in low levels of text comprehension (McKeown et al., 1992).

Lack of text coherence is a consequence of a common format for expository texts, especially science texts, in which information is presented as a series of related but discrete topics (e.g. plants, animals, cells) in a list-like manner with little or no supporting information to assist learners in connecting the content (Mikkila-Erdmann, 2002). In science classrooms, students may fail to make associations among the ideas presented in expository texts and thus fail to comprehend, precisely due to a lack of background knowledge in combination with a lack of coherent text presentations.

O'Reilly and McNamara (2007) point out that science texts assume that the reader has sufficient prior knowledge to make inferences that are necessary for comprehension. It is all too common, especially in the content area of science, that students lack sufficient background knowledge to connect ideas in a text. The characteristics of traditional expository texts discussed here may impede conceptual change because, unless the reader is able to connect the ideas in the text, the relationship between the reader's prior misconceptions and the scientific perspective presented in the text is unlikely to be detected. Researchers have demonstrated that conceptual change is less likely if the reader fails to recognize the inconsistency between his or her background knowledge and the text ideas (Chi & Roscoe, 2002; Chinn & Brewer, 1993).

The Promise of Refutational Texts

In contrast to traditional expository texts, refutational texts are designed to facilitate conceptual change through reading. The format of refutational texts addresses a major issue with traditional expository texts by explicitly prompting readers to connect their background knowledge with text concepts. First, a common misconception is stated with the intention of activating the reader's previously held beliefs. Second, the misconception is explicitly and directly refuted in an attempt to challenge the reader's beliefs. Third, the accepted scientific perspective is presented in a coherent and concise manner with the goal of having the reader perceive it as a plausible and fruitful alternative (Hynd, 2001; Limón Luque, 2003).

Refutational texts are written so that learners will find them clear and compelling (Mikkilia-Erdmann, 2002; Murphy, 2001). Moreover, examples provided within refutational texts are designed to be perceived by the reader as highly plausible. Plausibility of the scientific concept is considered a precondition for conceptual change by most models (Dole & Sinatra, 1998; Posner et al., 1982). In addition, refutational texts explain the utility of the scientific theory, which makes the text argument more compelling (Hynd, 2003).

The format of refutational texts mirrors that of texts described by Beck and colleagues (1991) as coherent and written in a causal explanatory style. Coherent texts, according to Kintsch and van Dijk (1978), are those in which the ideas within the text are clearly connected for the reader. Specifically, texts are more coherent when there is a high degree of argument overlap, or the repetition of ideas from one proposition to another. We suggest that refutational texts are written with a higher degree of argument overlap than traditional expository texts, which facilitates comprehension and thus the conceptual change process.

In their discussion of coherence and causal explanatory style, Beck and her colleagues explain that coherent, causal explanatory texts are written so that the sequencing of ideas is evident for the reader. In addition, texts written in a causal explanatory style are intended to clarify, elaborate, explain, and motivate salient information and to make relationships among text ideas explicit (McKeown et al., 1992). The sequencing of information is a central feature of refutational texts, which state first a common misconception, then the explicit refutation of that misconception, followed by the scientific explanation. The language used throughout the refutational text is intended to help the reader make connections among the ideas in the text, as well as to connect the text ideas with their own knowledge.

Refutational texts have been shown to be more effective than traditional expository texts in promoting conceptual change in science learning (Alvermann & Hynd, 2001; Hynd, 2001; Hynd, Alvermann, & Qian, 1997; Mason & Boscolo, 2004; Mason & Gava, 2007). Guzzetti, Snyder, Glass, and Gamas (1993) conducted a meta-analysis of the research in reading and science education to examine the instructional interventions developed to promote conceptual change. The meta-analysis revealed a large effect that showed refutational texts as effective tools in assisting students in identifying the discrepancies between their prior knowledge and the scientific viewpoint. Research by Beck and colleagues suggests that the coherent, causal explanatory style of refutational texts helps to make this inconsistency visible to the reader (Beck et al., 1991). When the discrepancy is identified, it may lead to cognitive dissonance for the reader. This dissonance may in turn lead to systematic, detail-oriented cognitive processing, which increases the likelihood of conceptual change (Dole & Sinatra, 1998; Petty & Cacioppo, 1986; Posner et al., 1982).

Appreciating the discrepancy between the ideas presented in a science text and one's own ideas entails understanding the content-area terminology. In another strand of their research, Beck and her colleagues have conducted extensive research in the area of vocabulary development and its relationship with text comprehension (see Beck et al., 1982; Beck, McKeown, & McCaslin, 1983). They explain that skilled comprehenders are able to access word meanings quickly and develop quality connections among concepts. Expository texts are often rife with terms that may be unfamiliar to the reader. These terms make up what Beck and her colleagues call "tier 3" vocabulary words. Tier 3 words are those "whose frequency of use is quite low, often being limited to specific domains" (Beck, McKeown, & Kucan, 2002, p. 16). Too many tier 3 words in a science passage may undermine the reader's ability to discern the relationships among the text concepts, and thus they cannot connect those ideas to their own. Refutational texts are written such that the key terms that are necessary for making these connections are defined. Ensuring that readers have the necessary vocabulary to comprehend the key concepts in the texts may be yet another reason that refutational texts have shown success in promoting conceptual change.

TEXT PROCESSING
AND CONCEPTUAL CHANGE

Researchers have begun moving from speculations about the nature of the refutational text effect to empirical investigations designed to explore the effect more directly. It has been argued that refutational texts may be effective because they facilitate the four necessary conditions of conceptual change (Hynd, 2003). These conditions include dissatisfaction with one's existing conceptions and finding the new conception to be intelligible, plausible, and fruitful for opening up additional areas of inquiry (Posner et al., 1982). We would suggest that these conditions of conceptual change are more likely to be achieved if the reader has sufficient relevant background knowledge and the ability to understand the relationships among the ideas presented in the text.

Recently, an alternative explanation for the refutational text effect has been offered that bridges these two ideas. That is, readers must both successfully activate the relevant background knowledge and have the opportunity to compare that concept with the scientific idea. A model of reading comprehension, the landscape model of reading (see van den Broek, Young, Tzeng, & Linderholm, 1999), may help to explain how this plays out with refutational texts. According to the landscape model, a balance is maintained between the reader's limited attentional resources and standards of coherence. Van den Broek and Kendeou (2008) explain: "As the reader proceeds through the text, concepts fluctuate in activation: with each new cycle, some concepts continue to be active, others decline in activation and yet others become newly reactivated" (p. 338). The fluctuations in activation are the result of four informational sources: (1) text information in the current cycle, (2) residual text information from the previous cycle, (3) the memory representation constructed thus far, and (4) the reader's prior knowledge, which can include misconceptions. Van den Broek and his colleagues postulate that readers must both coactivate (activate both their prior knowledge and the new conception simultaneously) and then integrate the text information with their prior knowledge (Kendeou & van den Broek, 2007). Moreover, only information that is coactivated can be compared and possibly integrated with the reader's conceptual framework. Thus, for conceptual change to occur, the misconception must be activated simultaneously with the accurate scientific information (van den Broek & Kendeou, 2008).

It may be the case that coactivation is facilitated through refutational texts because both the misconception and the scientific viewpoint are explicitly stated for the reader. In turn, because the text is written in a causal, explanatory style, with key terms defined, the refutational text has the potential to promote coactivation and integration.

Refutational texts may also increase the learner's engagement with the ideas in the text, both during and after reading, which increases the likelihood of conceptual change. One model of conceptual change, the cognitive reconstruction of knowledge model (Dole & Sinatra, 1998), suggests that the interaction between learner and message characteristics determines the degree of cognitive engagement the learner has with the message. Dole and Sinatra (1998) hypothesize that engagement can be described as varying on a continuum from "low cognitive engagement to high metacognitive engagement" (p. 121). High engagement is associated with central processing and involves deep, systematic processing of the new content. Higher levels of engagement increase the likelihood of conceptual change. In contrast, low cognitive engagement typically results in superficial, heuristic processes, which decrease the likelihood of change.

High cognitive engagement may be facilitated through reading refutational texts based on the reader's perceptions of personal relevance and critical weighing of the scientific explanation. For example, the reader may find the refutation sentence personally relevant because the misconception stated in the text is similar to the conceptions held by the reader. Furthermore, the refutation sentence may lead the reader to then thoughtfully and critically weigh the scientific explanation during or after reading because it explicitly rejects the misconception.

Researchers have begun examining online and offline comprehension of refutational texts in order to gain a better understanding of the nature of the refutational text effect (Kendeou & van den Broek, 2005; van den Broek & Kendeou, 2008). Online processes are those that occur during reading, such as activating background knowledge, drawing inferences, and making connections among text elements. These processes assist the reader in developing a mental representation of the text in memory. Offline processes are those that occur after reading, such as responding to questions about the text, constructing summaries, or engaging in discussions of the text content. Online measures provide insights into how the text is processed and the representation is formed. Offline measures provide insights into the reader's mental representations of the text that result from reading the text and into how they use that information in subsequent activities dealing with that text content.

In a significant step forward in investigations of the refutational text effect, Kendeou and van den Broek (2005) investigated the effects of readers' misconceptions on the cognitive processes of comprehension of science texts and whether those misconceptions are represented in the readers' recall of the text. Both online and offline measures were used within the study. The topic of the refutational text was electrical current and simple circuits. Online processes were measured by tracking participants' reading times sentence by sentence and using a think-aloud protocol. Offline processes were measured by asking comprehension questions about the main ideas presented in the text. Participants read the text as it was presented on a computer screen one sentence at a time and advanced the text by a mouse click.

Kendeou and van den Broek (2005) hypothesized that coactivation of the readers' misconceptions and the scientific explanation presented in the text would result in slower reading times of the refutation segments for those who held misconceptions about electrical current than for those readers who held accurate scientific conceptions. In addition, it was predicted that readers who held inaccurate conceptions would recall less text information and be less accurate in their recall than readers with accurate conceptions.

The findings revealed that readers with misconceptions did not spend more time reading the refutation sentences than did those without misconceptions. This suggests that online processes do not differ for readers with misconceptions and readers without misconceptions (Kendeou & van den Broek, 2005). However, the offline measure analyses revealed that readers with misconceptions recalled significantly less information from the text than readers without misconceptions and that that information was more inaccurate. This study demonstrates the potential of combining both online and offline measures to gain a deeper understanding of the refutational text effect.

In a second study, Kendeou and van den Broek (2007) investigated the effects of readers' misconceptions and text structure during reading of science texts. They focused on how the quality and quantity of readers' misconceptions affect reading. Quality referred to the accuracy of the reader's knowledge, whereas quantity was described as the amount of prior knowledge that influenced comprehension, such as the difference between novice and expert (Chi, Feltovich, & Glaser, 1981). To examine the effects of text structure, participants read a traditional expository text and a refutational text while performing a think-aloud task. Each text focused on the topic of Newton's first and third laws of motion. The text was presented using the same methodology as in the previous study.

The results showed that readers with misconceptions engaged in more conceptual change strategies when reading the refutational text than the expository text, and, as expected, readers without misconceptions did not engage in conceptual change processes. Conceptual change processes included detecting an inconsistency between one's prior knowledge and the information in the text and engaging in efforts to repair the conflict, such as contrasting one's prior knowledge with the text information. In addition, readers with misconceptions tended to generate fewer correct inferences and more inaccurate inferences than those without misconceptions.

An interesting finding from this study is that the number of correct inferences produced during the think-aloud phase was associated with higher levels of text recall for readers with misconceptions. This finding was not shown for the group without misconceptions. Kendeou and van den Broek (2007) suggest that the production of correct inferences likely increased the compatibility between the reader's prior knowledge and the text.

Analyses of the online measure, reading time, showed no significant differences between those with misconceptions and those with accurate scientific knowledge when reading the expository text. However, a difference in reading times was shown between groups when reading the refutational text, in contrast to the finding in Kendeou and van den Broek's (2005) previous study. Readers with misconceptions read the refutational sentences more slowly than readers without misconceptions.

The previous studies revealed that a full explanation of the online processes involved in reading refutational texts remains elusive. In an attempt to better understand these online processes, van den Broek and Kendeou (2008) launched a third study in which they combined empirical data (i.e., reading times and think-alouds) and computational simulations using the landscape model of reading (van den Broek, Risden, Fletcher, & Thurlow, 1996; van den Broek et al., 1999). That analysis showed that the structure of refutational text and that of traditional expository text elicit fundamentally different comprehension processes for readers with misconceptions. Refutational texts were associated with slower reading times and more online conceptual change process than were expository texts.

Van den Broek and Kendeou (2008) argue that refutational texts increase the likelihood of coactivation, which, in turn, leads readers with misconceptions to "experience conflict and engage in efforts to repair the conflict and create coherence" (p. 344). The coherence that results from the coactivation and integration of the readers' prior knowledge and the text information increases the likelihood of conceptual change. In contrast, expository texts may not elicit coactivation processes even when the reader holds misconceptions about the topic.

The series of studies conducted by Kendeou and van den Broek offer some useful insights to the nature of the refutational text effect. Refutational texts are more likely to elicit conceptual change processes among readers with misconceptions than are expository texts. Refutational texts may promote coactivation and integration of the readers' prior knowledge with the text information, thus increasing the likelihood that the reader will detect an inconsistency between his or her prior knowledge and the text. Van den Broek and Kendeou (2008) argue that coactivation of misconceptions and text information is a necessary step toward conceptual change.

The findings regarding reading times in relation to refutational texts warrant further investigation. Kendeou and van den Broek's studies show mixed results on the reading time analyses. In their series of studies, reading times were shown to have no significant differences in one study (Kendeou & van den Broek, 2005), but longer reading times for readers with misconceptions were shown in two others (Kendeou & van den Broek, 2007; van den Broek & Kendeou, 2008). This suggests that refutation texts can foster coactivation of the misconception and the correct scientific explanation, which can result in slower processing of the information for readers with misconceptions. These mixed results motivated us to explore the nature of the refutational text effect. Our research with refutational texts and reading times revealed a different trend, as described in the following section.

ATTENTION ALLOCATION

Our own interest in the nature of the refutational text effect led us to investigate the relationship between refutational text, attention allocation, and conceptual change (Broughton, Sinatra, & Reynolds, in press). Because the findings from reading time studies comparing refutational and expository texts show mixed results in regard to time spent processing the refutational material, we sought to understand how the attention allocation literature might inform this research.

In a review of the literature on text comprehension and attention allocation, Reynolds (1992) argued that readers paid extra attention to text elements that are more salient due to task instructions or perspectives or due to text structure manipulations such as argument overlap (Kintsch & van dijk, 1978). Reynolds and his colleagues demonstrated that there was a causal relationship between the extra allocated attention and increases in learning and recall (Lapan & Reynolds, 1994; Reynolds, Shepard, Lapan, Kreek, & Goetz, 1990; Reynolds, Trathen, Sawyer, & Shepard, 1993). However, research has also shown that skilled adult readers can learn new text material that they deem personally interesting even when they allocate less attention to it (Shirey & Reynolds, 1988). It is this paradox that led us to explore readers' attentional allocation when reading refutational texts.

We hypothesized that different phenomena may underlie the disparate effects of refutational text on attention allocation. For example, refutation segments are highly salient and may result in readers devoting more attention to those segments of the text than others (Reynolds, 1992). Alternatively, the refutational text effect may mirror the effect of interesting text material. Readers may find the stated misconception interesting or personally relevant if they recognize it as their own conception. However, readers do not spend additional time reading information they find interesting; indeed, they may read this information more quickly.

In a sequence of two experiments we examined whether readers would devote differential attention (as indicated by either increased or decreased reading times) to refutation segments. Furthermore, we sought to determine whether differential attention allocation could be related to promoting greater conceptual change—the traditional refutational text effect. We predicted that participants who read the refutational text would spend more time reading than participants who read the expository text. We formed this prediction based on the landscape model (van den Broek et al., 1999), expecting that the refutational text would promote coactivation of the reader's prior knowledge and the text information, leading to increased reading times. Furthermore, we expected the slower reading times of participants who read the refutational text to result in an increase in scientific understanding of the reasons that the seasons change and a decrease in misconceptions.

In Experiment 1, college undergraduates (mean age = 25.5) read either a refutational text or an expository text on the causes of seasonal change. Text passages were comparable in length and content. The texts differed only in the first paragraph, which was the refutation paragraph in the refutational text. The first sentence of the refutational text explicitly stated a common misconception about seasonal change. The third sentence in the refutational text directly refuted the misconception. Otherwise, the beginning paragraphs of both texts were comparable in terms of writing style and content. (See Figure 12.1 for the first paragraph of each text.) The text was presented sentence by sentence on a computer screen, in the same manner as the van den Broek and Kendeou studies. Participants advanced through the text by pressing the space bar. Reading times were recorded per sentence.

We initially coded data from the essay questions and participants' diagrams from the Seasons Concept Inventory by identifying idea units in the essay responses as well as in the diagram and the corresponding explanation. The idea units were then separated into two categories, misconceptions and scientific concepts. We calculated a total misconception score and a separate total science concept score for each question. For example, on the pretest, if a participant's responses indicated

Why the Seasons Change (Refutational)

Many people believe that the changing seasons are the result of the Earth being closer to the Sun during the summer months and farther away from the Sun during the winter months. Perhaps you hold similar beliefs. However, seasons do not change because the distance between the Earth and the Sun change. In fact, Earth is closer to the Sun in winter and farther away from the Sun in summer. Seasonal change is the result of two features of the Earth: its tilted axis and its elliptical orbit around the Sun.

Why the Seasons Change (Nonrefutational)

From your own experiences you know that the seasons change throughout the year. Depending on the latitude where you live, the temperatures may vary from hot to cold. The changing seasons on Earth are the result of two features of the Earth: its tilted axis and its elliptical orbit around the Sun. Earth is closest to the Sun in January (winter) and farthest from the Sun in July (summer).

FIGURE 12.1. Refutational and nonrefutational text introductory paragraphs.

three misconceptions in essay question 1, two misconceptions in essay question 2, and two misconceptions in the diagram and corresponding explanation, a total score of 7 misconceptions was given on that measure. The posttest was similarly scored.

The results showed no significant advantage for the refutational text group for conceptual change. Although participants who read the refutation segments read faster than did participants who read the comparable segments of the expository text, this difference was not statistically significant, and participants in both text conditions experienced significant increases in conceptual understanding of the reasons that the seasons change.

Given the unexpected results of experiment 1 (lack of advantage for the refutational text group), we decided to conduct a second experiment to extend the findings of experiment 1. The measures for experiment 2 were identical to those used in experiment 1, with the addition of an interview measure. We asked participants to identify the sentences they most attended to, the sentences they found most interesting, and the sentences they thought were most important. We also asked participants to identify any sentences that may have contradicted their prior knowledge. Lastly, we asked participants whether they noticed anything unique about the text.

For further analyses we combined the samples from experiment 1 and experiment 2 after statistical analyses indicated no differences between the groups. We again compared the reading times between the refutational text group and the expository text group. The results showed that the refutational text group spent significantly less time reading than the expository text group did. When this difference was examined more closely by comparing the two texts sentence by sentence, the significant differences were due to the refutational segments of the text. Furthermore, the refutation sentence was read at a significantly faster rate than the comparable sentence in the expository text. These results suggest that the decreased time participants spent reading the refutation paragraph was due to the reduction in time spent processing the refutation sentence.

When we examined learning effects, the results again showed increases in conceptual understanding for participants in both text conditions and also a significant reduction in misconceptions for both groups. The results also showed an advantage for the refutational text in that participants who read the refutational text had significantly fewer misconceptions than participants who read the expository text.

The content analyses of the interview transcripts revealed some interesting findings. Participants in the refutational text group most commonly identified the refutational sentences as the most important and the most interesting. When asked why they selected those sentences, participants most commonly replied that the sentences contradicted what they knew. Participants who read the expository text most frequently selected the explanatory sentence related to seasonal change as the most important and most interesting. The most common rationale given by participants for selecting the explanatory sentence was that the information summed up the topic.

The findings from both experiments revealed that both text types promoted increased understanding of seasonal change. However, readers in the refutational text group had significantly fewer misconceptions than those in the expository text group. As noted earlier, this effect may be the result of the refutational text's coherence, providing the opportunity for readers to form appropriate relationships among concepts (Beck et al., 1982, 1983). As those relationships among ideas are fashioned, the reader may notice the discrepancies in their prior beliefs and begin to replace the misconception with an understanding of the accepted scientific viewpoint.

Based on the landscape model, we expected increased reading times for participants who read the refutational text because the refutational text should draw readers' attention to the anomalous information and result in coactivation of the misconception and the scientific perspective. However, the findings revealed decreased reading times for the refutational paragraph. Even though participants spent less time reading the refutational segments, they still attended to them, identified them as important and interesting, and may have changed their misconceptions based on this information. We conclude that these findings may be due to the interest effect (i.e., readers find the refutational statement interesting and, therefore, read it more quickly), or it may be that the increased coherence or the causal explanatory style of the refutational text (Beck et al., 1991; McKeown et al., 1992) facilitates comprehension for the reader. Clearly, further investigations will need to examine these possibilities.

PROMOTING CONCEPTUAL CHANGE THROUGH QUESTIONING THE AUTHOR

Coherent texts have been shown to increase the reader's recall of text information, as well as improve the quality of the information recalled (Beck et al., 1991). Coherence is especially important when the text focuses on complex issues such as those typically presented in refutational texts. However, coherence does not guarantee that young readers, or readers who are novices in a content area, will be able to comprehend the complex topics presented in science texts. Beck and her colleagues (1982, 1991; Beck & McKeown, 2006) recommend incorporating discussions about the text topic that allow opportunities for elaboration on the main ideas in the text, an approach they call Questioning the Author (QtA).

In our own research, we have incorporated the use of small-group discussion based on QtA to facilitate deeper engagement with the information in refutational texts as a pathway toward promoting conceptual change. We specifically selected QtA (Beck & McKeown, 2001, 2006; Beck, McKeown, Sandora, Kucan, & Worthy, 1996) based on its approach to actively engage readers with the text and to make explicit the relationships among central ideas more visible to the reader.

The QtA activity promotes collaborative meaning-making discussions between teacher and students. The discussions take place as the teacher and students read the text together, pausing at key points to grapple with the central ideas in order to understand how the ideas relate to one another. QtA provides students the opportunity to connect their topic-relevant knowledge with what the author has written, as well as with what other students know, and then to use that information in constructing a collaborative understanding of the text (McKeown et al., 1992). Thus we hypothesized that QtA would allow students to discuss with their fellow students and the teacher how their ideas might be similar to the misconceptions stated in the text and the reasons that the author is telling them that the scientific idea is different from their own.

The rich body of research by Beck and her colleagues has demonstrated the efficacy of QtA as a tool for promoting comprehension (Beck & McKeown, 2001, 2006; Beck et al., 1996; McKeown et al., 1992). We were interested in examining whether refutational text with QtA discussions would promote greater change in students' nature of science (NOS) beliefs, attitudes, and conceptions than reading a refutational text alone. The topic of the text and discussion was the reclassification of Pluto as a dwarf planet (Broughton, 2008). We predicted that rereading and discussing the text though a QtA activity would increase the likelihood of attitude, belief, and conceptual change.

Participants were fifth- and sixth-grade students enrolled at a private school located in the intermountain West. Students' ages ranged from 10 to 12 years. These students were primarily from white, upper-middle-class families. Approximately the same number of males and females participated in the study.

Students completed pre-, post-, and delayed posttest measures, including a survey of their attitudes about Pluto (Attitudes about Pluto), a nature of science inventory (Beliefs about the Nature of Science; Conley, Pintrich, Vekiri, & Harrison, 2004), and a research-developed concept inventory about planets (Concepts about Planets). The Attitudes about Pluto survey asked students to state whether they agreed or disagreed with the scientists' recent decision to reclassify Pluto as a dwarf planet. The Beliefs about the Nature of Science survey measured students' beliefs about the certainty of scientific knowledge (e.g., "Scientific knowledge is always true") and development of scientific knowledge (e.g., "New discoveries can change what scientists think is true"). Many researchers investigating students' nature of science beliefs have found that young students typically view science knowledge as static, absolute, and consisting of isolated facts (Conley et al., 2004; Elder, 2002; Mason et al., 2008). The Concepts about Planets survey assessed students' conceptual knowledge about planets and Pluto through six open-ended questions. This format was similar to that used by other researchers investigating conceptual change (Broughton, Sinatra, & Reynolds, 2006, Hynd, 2001; Hynd, Alvermann, & Qian, 1997; Mason, 2001; Mason, Gava, & Boldrin, 2008).

The intervention for this study included a refutational text that explained the changing nature of science, the role of evidence in scientific decisions, and the history of Pluto's planetary status. The text also included information on both the old and the new definition of a planet and an explanation of Pluto's reclassification to dwarf planet status. Students in both conditions read the text twice. Students in the control group reread the text independently at their desks, whereas those in the experimental group reread the text during small-group QtA discussions. The target questions posed during the QtA discussion were intended to elicit students' NOS beliefs, attitudes toward Pluto's reclassification, and concepts about planets. For example, after reading the text segments describing the changing nature of scientific knowledge, students were asked, "What do you think the author is telling us about science theories this time?"

Results showed that the refutational text was effective in promoting belief change, attitude change, and conceptual change across both conditions. Students in both conditions showed a statistically significant shift toward acceptance of Pluto's reclassification to a dwarf planet. Additionally, students in both conditions reported a change in their NOS beliefs toward a more dynamic view of science and a greater level of acceptance about Pluto's reclassification after rereading the text. The findings also showed that conceptual change was promoted through the QtA discussions. Students in the reread-plus-discussion group showed greater conceptual change regarding the reasons for rewriting the definition of planet than those in the reread group.

This finding may be explained through Beck and McKeown's (2006) description of QtA: that participating in QtA discussions enables students to exchange ideas and to consider alternative ideas. In a similar fashion, we posit that as students discussed alternative ideas they may have been more likely to detect the inconsistency in their own prior beliefs compared with the scientific explanation as presented in the text. The findings of our study suggest that the discussion of the alternative ideas, including the scientific perspective, likely facilitated the conceptual change process. An example of how the QtA discussion facilitated students' critical weighing of alternative ideas may help to support our assertion. The following discussion excerpt occurred after students read the text segment describing the discovery of the Kuiper Belt and the subsequent redefinition of the concept of planet.

RESEARCHER: What did the author tell us about the Kuiper Belt, and how does that play into this whole discussion?

TYLER: Well, umm, with the Kuiper Belt that's really going to change. It really probably changed a lot because you'd have hundreds of planets instead of nine. So, probably many scientists thought that they should change the definition of planet to make it so that there is not hundreds, and hundreds, and hundreds of planets in our solar system.

ANNE: Because there might be more things like the Kuiper Belt out there, and we need to change the definition because there could be like thousands of planets.

RESEARCHER: Good thoughts. Yes?

AARON: Going back to science can change, science is changing, it's they're saying that they thought they had nine planets. And then when they discovered the Kuiper Belt they were just as big as Pluto. So that would make them a planet. But then with the Kuiper Belt, instead of adding hundreds and hundreds of more planets, they just deleted one.

AMY: It's sort of like, what they all said. If they kept the same definition they would have hundreds and hundreds of planets. And they changed them and that made it so that Pluto wasn't a planet.

Prior to reading the text and engaging in QtA discussions, these students held the misconception that scientists rewrote the definition of planet because they didn't like Pluto and wanted to find a way to demote it. After the intervention, most of these students experienced conceptual change as they came to understand that the definition of planet was rewritten based on the discovery of the Kuiper Belt, independent of Pluto. They experienced belief change about the changing nature of science and attitude change toward a more favorable view of the reclassification. We suggest that students engaged more deeply with this alternative idea based on the structure that QtA discussions provided. The discussion leader was able to highlight the Kuiper Belt as the central idea and encouraged students to think about its relationship to the new definition of planet. The discussion provided an avenue for students to compare and contrast the new information with their previously held concepts.

CONCLUSION

Recent investigations into the nature of the refutational text effect shed new light on the reasons that these texts may play an important role in science learning. Topics in science often necessitate that students change their thinking to adopt a scientific understanding. However, conceptual change has proven to be an elusive phenomenon that is difficult to promote. Refutational texts have been shown to support conceptual change; thus reintroducing these texts into the science classroom can provide another opportunity for students to engage with contrasting ideas.

Two key constructs emphasized by Beck and her colleagues, coherence and background knowledge, may help to explain the power of refutational texts. Refutational texts are designed to be more coherent and more explanatory than typical science texts. As we come to better understand the role these factors play in refutational texts, we may be able to generate texts that are more effective in promoting greater comprehension and more opportunities for knowledge change.

Our suggestion of promoting the use of text written in the refutational style for classroom science instruction should not be taken to indicate a lack of support for the inquiry approach—quite the contrary. Inquiry has been shown to be effective in promoting a change in students' understandings about science content, and we fully support its use in science classrooms. However, participating in a hands-on activity does not guarantee that students will understand the phenomenon demonstrated. Thus the power of inquiry activities might be increased by having students read a refutational text, discuss it using a QtA approach, and then engage in inquiry activities that emerge from the discussion. Integrating different activities may produce value-added effects in terms of high engagement, comprehension, and conceptual change.

REFERENCES

Alvermann, D. E., & Hynd, C. R. (2001). Effects of prior knowledge activation modes and text structure on nonscience majors' comprehension of physics. *Journal of Educational Research, 83,* 97–102.

American Association for the Advancement of Science. (1993). *Benchmarks for science literacy.* New York: Oxford University Press.

Anderson, R. C. (1978). Schema-directed processes in language comprehension. In A. Lesgold, J. Pelligreno, S. Fokkema, & R. Glaser (Eds.), *Cognitive psychology and instruction* (pp. 67–82). New York: Plenum Press.

Beck, I. L., & McKeown, M. G. (2001). Inviting students into the pursuit of meaning. *Educational Psychology Review, 13,* 225–241.

Beck, I. L., & McKeown, M. G. (2006). *Improving comprehension with Questioning the Author: A fresh and expanded view of a powerful approach.* New York: Scholastic.

Beck, I. L., McKeown, M. G., & Kucan, L. (2002). *Bringing words to life: Robust vocabulary instruction.* New York: Guilford Press.

Beck, I. L., McKeown, M. G., & McCaslin, E. S. (1983). Vocabulary development: All contexts are not created equal. *Elementary School Journal, 83,* 177–181.

Beck, I. L., McKeown, M. G., Sandora, C., Kucan, L., & Worthy, J. (1996). Questioning the Author: A year-long classroom implementation to engage students with text. *Elementary School Journal, 96,* 385–414.

Beck, I. L., McKeown, M. G., Sinatra, G. M., & Loxterman, J. A. (1991). Revising social studies text from a text-processing perspective: Evidence of improved comprehensibility. *Reading Research Quarterly, 26,* 251–276.

Beck, I. L., Perfetti, C. A., & McKeown, M. G. (1982). Effects of long-term vocabulary instruction on lexical access and reading comprehension. *Journal of Educational Psychology, 74,* 506–521.

Biemans, H. J. A., & Simons, P. R. J. (2002). Computer-assisted instructional strategies for promoting conceptual change. In M. Limon & L. Mason (Eds.), *Reconsidering conceptual change: Issues in theory and practice* (pp. 3–27). Dordrecht: Kluwer Academic.

Broughton, S. H. (2008). *The Pluto debate: Influence of emotions on belief, attitude, and knowledge change.* Unpublished doctoral dissertation, University of Nevada, Las Vegas.

Broughton, S. H., Sinatra, G. M., & Reynolds, R. E. (2006). *The influence of the selective attention strategy: Measuring the effects of refutation text in conceptual change.* Paper presented at the annual meeting of the European Association for Research on Learning and Instruction, SIG on Conceptual Change, Stockholm, Sweden.

Broughton, S. H., Sinatra, G. M., & Reynolds, R. E. (in press). The nature of the refutation text effect: An investigation of attention allocation. *Journal of Educational Research.*

Chi, M. T. H. (2000). Self-explaining expository texts: The dual processes of generating inferences and repairing mental models. In R. Glaser (Ed.), *Advances in instructional psychology* (pp. 161–238). Mahwah, NJ: Erlbaum.

Chi, M. T. H., Feltovich, P. J., & Glaser, R. (1981). Categorization and representation of physics problems by experts and novices. *Cognitive Science, 5,* 121–152.

Chi, M. T. H., & Roscoe, R. D. (2002). The processes and challenges of conceptual change. In M. Limon & L. Mason (Eds.), *Reconsidering conceptual change: Issues in theory and practice* (pp. 3–27). Dordrecht: Kluwer Academic.

Chinn, C. A., & Brewer, W. F. (1993). The role of anomalous data in knowledge acquisition: A theoretical framework and implications for science instruction. *Review of Educational Research, 63*(1), 1–49.

Conley, A. M., Pintrich, P. R., Vekiri, I., & Harrison, D. (2004). Change in epistemological beliefs in elementary science students. *Contemporary Educational Psychology, 29,* 186–204.

Dole, J. A., & Sinatra, G. M. (1998). Reconceptualizing change in the cognitive construction of knowledge. *Educational Psychologist, 33*(3), 109–128.

Duit, R. (1999). Conceptual change approaches in science education. In W. Schnotz, S. Vosniadou, & M. Carretero (Eds.), *New perspectives on conceptual change* (pp. 263–282). Oxford, UK: Elsevier.

Elder, A. D. (2002). Characterizing fifth grade students' epistemological beliefs in science. In B. K. Hofer & P. R. Pintrch (Eds.), *Personal epistemology: The psychology of beliefs about knowledge and knowing* (pp. 347–364). Mahwah, NJ: Erlbaum.

Frederiksen, J. R. (1981). Understanding anaphora: Rules used by readers in assigning pronominal referents. *Discourse Processes, 4,* 323–348.

Guzzetti, B. J., Snyder, T. E., Glass, G. V., & Gamas, W. S. (1993). Promoting conceptual change in science: A comparative meta-analysis of instructional interventions from reading education and science education. *Reading Research Quarterly, 28,* 117–155.

Halldén, O., Petersson, G., Scheja, J., Ehrlen, K., Haglund, L., Osterline, K., et al. (2002). Situating the question of conceptual change. In M. Limon & L. Mason (Eds.), *Reconsidering conceptual change: Issues in theory and practice* (pp. 137–148). Dordrecht: Kluwer Academic.

Hodson, D. (1998). *Teaching and learning science: Towards a personalized approach.* Buckingham, UK: Open University Press.

Hynd, C. (2003). Conceptual change in response to persuasive messages. In G. M. Sinatra & P. R. Pintrich (Eds.), *Intentional conceptual change* (pp. 1–18). Mahwah, NJ: Erlbaum.

Hynd, C., Alvermann, D., & Qian, G. (1997). Preservice elementary school teachers' conceptual change about projectile motion: Refutation text, demonstration, affective factors, and relevance. *Science Education, 81,* 1–27.

Hynd, C. R. (2001). Refutational texts and the change process. *International Journal of Educational Research, 35,* 699–714.

Hynd, C. R., McWhorter, J. Y., Phares, V. L., & Suttles, C. W. (1994). The role of instructional variables in conceptual change in high school physics topics. *Journal of Research in Science Teaching, 31,* 933–946.

Kendeou, P., & van den Broek, P. (2005). The effects of readers' misconceptions on comprehension of scientific text. *Journal of Educational Psychology, 97,* 235–245.

Kendeou, P., & van den Broek, P. (2007). The effects of prior knowledge and text structure on comprehension processes during reading of scientific texts. *Memory and Cognition, 35,* 1567–1577.

Kintsch, W., Kozminsky, E., Streby, W. J., McKoon, G., & Keenan, J. M. (1975). Comprehension and recall of text as a function of content variables. *Journal of Verbal Learning and Verbal Behavior, 14,* 196–214.

Kintsch, W., & van Dijk, T. A. (1978). Toward a model of text comprehension and production. *Psychological Review, 5,* 363–394.

Lapan, R., & Reynolds, R. E. (1994). The selective attention strategy as a time-dependent phenomenon. *Contemporary Educational Psychology, 19,* 379–398.

Limón Luque, M. (2003). The role of domain-specific knowledge in intentional conceptual change. In G. M. Sinatra & P. R. Pintrich (Eds.), *Intentional conceptual change* (pp. 133–170). Mahwah, NJ: Erlbaum.

Mason, C. L. (1992). Concept mapping: A tool to develop reflective science instruction. *Science Education, 76,* 51–63.

Mason, L. (2001). Responses to anomalous data on controversial topics and theory change. *Learning and Instruction, 11,* 453–483.

Mason, L., & Boscolo, P. (2004). Role of epistemological understanding and interest in interpreting a controversy and in topic-specific belief change. *Contemporary Educational Psychology, 29,* 103–128.

Mason, L., & Gava, M. (2007). Effects of epistemological beliefs and learning text structure on conceptual change. In S. Vosniadou, A. Baltas, & X. Vamvakoussi (Eds.), *Reframing the problem of conceptual change in learning and instruction* (pp. 165–196). Oxford, UK: Elsevier.

Mason, L., Gava, M., & Boldrin, A. (2008). On warm conceptual change: The interplay of text, epistemological beliefs, and topic interest. *Journal of Educational Psychology, 100,* 291–309.

McKeown, M. G., Beck, I. L., & Blake, R. G. K. (2009). Rethinking reading comprehension instruction: A comparison of instruction for strategies and content approaches. *Reading Research Quarterly, 44*(3), 218–253.

McKeown, M. B., Beck, I. L., Sinatra, G. M., & Loxterman, J. A. (1992). The contribution of prior knowledge and coherent text to comprehension. *Reading Research Quarterly, 27,* 79–93.

Mikkila-Erdmann, M. (2002). Science learning through text: The effect of text design and text comprehension skills on conceptual change. In M. Limon & L. Mason (Eds.), *Reconsidering conceptual change: Issues in theory and practice* (pp. 337–353). Dordrecht: Kluwer Academic.

Mintzes, J. J., Wandersee, J. H., & Novak, J. D. (1997). Meaningful learning in science: The human constructivist perspective. In G. D. Phye (Ed.), *Handbook of academic learning: Construction of knowledge* (pp. 404–447). San Diego, CA: Academic Press.

Murphy, P. K. (2001). What makes a text persuasive? Comparing students' and experts' conceptions of persuasiveness. *International Journal of Educational Research, 35,* 675–698.

National Research Council. (1996). *National science education standards.* Washington, DC: National Academy Press.

Nussbaum, E. M., & Sinatra, G. M. (2003). Argument and conceptual engagement. *Contemporary Educational Psychology, 28,* 384–395.

Nussbaum, E. M., Sinatra, G. M., & Poliquin, A. (2008). The role of epistemological beliefs and scientific argumentation in promoting conceptual change. *International Journal of Science Education, 30,* 1977–1999.

O'Reilly, T., & McNamara, D. S. (2007). The impact of science knowledge, reading skill, and reading strategy knowledge on more traditional "high stakes" measures of high school students' science achievement. *American Educational Research Journal, 44,* 161–196.

Petty, R. E., & Cacioppo, J. T. (1986). The elaboration likelihood model of persuasion. In L. Berkowitz (Ed.), *Advances in experimental social psychology* (pp. 123–205). New York: Academic Press.

Posner, G. J., Strike, K. A., Hewson, P. W., & Gertzog, W. A. (1982). Accommodation of a scientific conception: Toward a theory of conceptual change. *Science Education, 66,* 211–227.

Reynolds, R. E. (1992). Selective attention and prose learning: Theoretical and empirical research. *Educational Psychology Review, 4*(4), 1–48.

Reynolds, R. E., Shepard, C., Lapan, R., Kreek, C., & Goetz, E. T. (1990). Differences in the use of selective attention by more successful and less successful tenth-grade readers. *Journal of Educational Psychology, 82,* 749–759.

Reynolds, R. E., Trathen, W., Sawyer, M., & Shepard, C. R. (1993). Causal and epiphenomenal use of the selective attention strategy in prose comprehension. *Contemporary Educational Psychology, 18,* 258–278.

Settlage, J., & Southerland, S. A. (2007). *Teaching science to every child: Using culture as a starting point.* New York: Routledge.

Shirey, L. L., & Reynolds, R. E. (1988). The effect of interest on attention and learning. *Journal of Educational Psychology, 80,* 159–166.

Sinatra, G. M. (2005). The warming trend in conceptual change research: The legacy of Paul Pintrich. *Educational Psychologist, 40,* 107–115.

Sinatra, G. M. (2007, June). *A little knowledge is a dangerous thing: Using beliefs and dispositions to make judgments about scientific theories.* Invited keynote address presented at the first annual meeting of the Research on Learning, Center Learning Research, University of Turku, Finland.

Sinatra, G. M., & Mason, L. (2008). Beyond knowledge: Learner characteristics influencing conceptual change. In S. Vosniadou (Ed.), *International handbook of research on conceptual change* (pp. 560–582). New York: Routledge.

Sinatra, G. M., & Pintrich, P. R. (2003). The role of intentions in conceptual change learning. In G. M. Sinatra & P. R. Pintrich (Eds.), *Intentional conceptual change* (pp. 1–18). Mahwah, NJ: Erlbaum.

Southerland, S. A., & Sinatra, G. M. (2003). Learning about biological evolution: A special case of intentional conceptual change. In G. M. Sinatra & P. R. Pintrich (Eds.), *Intentional conceptual change* (pp. 1–18). Mahwah, NJ: Erlbaum.

van den Broek, P., & Kendeou, P. (2008). Cognitive processes in comprehension of science texts: The role of co-activation in confronting misconceptions. *Applied Cognitive Psychology, 22,* 335–351.

van den Broek, P., Risden, K., Fletcher, C. R., & Thurlow, R. (1996). A "landscape" view of reading: Fluctuating patterns of activation and the construction of a stable memory representation. In B. K. Britton & A. C. Graesser (Eds.), *Models of understanding text* (pp. 165–187). Hillsdale, NJ: Erlbaum.

van den Broek, P., Young, M., Tzeng, Y., & Linderholm, T. (1999). The landscape model of reading: Inferences and the online construction of a memory representation. In H. van Oostendorp & S. R. Goldman (Eds.), *The construction of mental representations during reading* (pp. 71–98). Mahwah, NJ: Erlbaum.

Vosniadou, S. (1999). Conceptual change research: State of the art and future directions. In W. Schnotz, S. Vosniadou, & M. Carretero (Eds.), *New perspectives on conceptual change* (pp. 3–13). Oxford, UK: Elsevier.

Vosniadou, S., & Brewer, W. F. (1987). Theories of knowledge restructuring in development. *Review of Educational Research, 57,* 51–67.

Vosniadou, S., & Brewer, W. F. (1992). Mental models of the earth: A study of conceptual change in childhood. *Cognitive Psychology, 24,* 535–585.

Vosniadou, S., Ioannides, C., Dimitrakopoulou, A., & Papademetriou, E. (2001). Designing learning environments to promote conceptual change in science. *Learning and Instruction, 11,* 381–419.

Wiser, M., & Amin, T. G. (2002). Computer-based interactions for conceptual change in science. In M. Limon & L. Mason (Eds.), *Reconsidering conceptual change: Issues in theory and practice* (pp. 357–388). Dordrecht: Kluwer Academic.

Yore, L. D., Bisanz, G. L., & Hand, B. M. (2003). Examining the literacy component of science literacy: 25 years of language and science research. *International Journal of Science Education, 25,* 689–725.

13

LITERACY IN THE DIGITAL WORLD

*Comprehending and Learning
from Multiple Sources*

Susan R. Goldman

with Kimberly A. Lawless, Kimberly W. Gomez,
Jason Braasch, Shaunna MacLeod, *and* Flori Manning

My (S.R.G.) contribution to this Festschrift volume emphasizes some work I am currently involved in with several colleagues at University of Illinois at Chicago. The work focuses on creating ways to assess elementary and middle school students' knowledge and skills related to comprehension of multiple information sources, including traditional print resources as well as the new media that are widely available through the World Wide Web.

The focus on assessment of multiple-source comprehension seems particularly appropriate for inclusion in a volume honoring Isabel Beck and her legacy because it brings together a number of themes that permeate Isabel's and my own work over the past 25 or so years, including the importance of creating materials and instructional strategies that support excellent literacy instruction in classrooms. In the chapter, I first describe a bit of my personal history, especially as it intersected with and was influenced by Isabel and her work. In the process, I share my theoretical perspectives on comprehension and the evolution of those in response to empirical data and developments in contemporary theories of learning. The centerpiece of the chapter is a description of the evidence-centered design process we are using to develop the assessment of multiple-source comprehension. The final sections of the chapter discuss instructional implications and future direction. Our assessment work makes direct connections to classroom instructional practices, because the audiences for the assessment are teachers and students in middle school classrooms. Simultaneously, the design process contributes to the development of a model of multiple source comprehension and raises questions for future research efforts.

PERSONAL HISTORY: GROWING UP AT THE LEARNING RESEARCH AND DEVELOPMENT CENTER

I entered the world of cognitive and instructional psychology in 1973, through the doors of the Learning Research and Development Center (LRDC). At that time, LRDC was distributed across several locations. The physical separations were emblematic of the distance between the research and development sides of the organization at that time. For example, the psychologists doing laboratory research were located a 15-minute uphill walk from the place where the work of curriculum development was going on. In 1975 or 1976, LRDC was fortunate to be able to put all the pieces together in a brand new facility, where it continues today. The cohabitation in the same physical space had a powerful impact on my own trajectory because it increased the likelihood that I would interact with folks outside of my own discipline of psychology, in particular Isabel Beck.

Interactions with Isabel had a critical, formative impact on my thinking in a number of ways. First, I became aware of the gap between classrooms and much of the psychological research that was being done and that I was studying in my own graduate program in cognitive psychology. However, the LRDC mission, norms, and organizational structures catalyzed efforts to address the gap. Isabel was among the researchers at LRDC attempting to understand the work going on outside of their own disciplinary fields and traditions. In these efforts to bridge the gap between classrooms and cognitive research on reading, Isabel exemplified the intelligent novice, and as a participant–observer in this process, I learned a second important lesson from Isabel: the value of questions for learning and understanding, especially questions that probed assumptions and pushed for conceptual clarity.

An accomplished reading educator, Isabel was full of questions about the cognitive empirical literature, and she asked them of anyone who happened to be around. She was ruthless in pursuit of explanations stripped of jargon and couched in everyday terms and examples that made sense. I know because not infrequently I was on the receiving end of those questions. I remember one conversation we had about inferences—how prevalent they were in reading, yet how little we knew about how to teach students to make inferences appropriately. At the same time, Isabel was quick to assert that reading required attention to the text and that without the knowledge and skills to "decode" that print all the inference making in the world wouldn't produce good comprehension. At that time, it was hard to foresee the progression of research questions Isabel and her colleagues would pursue over the next 20 years. However, what was obvious was that Isabel was taking up a cognitive perspective on reading. She and her colleagues described their cognitive orientation in a 1996 book chapter that traced the progression of research questions she had pursued:

> Our approach to analyzing text was based on theory and research from a cognitive perspective. The cognitive orientation to reading research had brought much progress in understanding the ways that readers interact with texts. In investigations of the reading process, emphasis turned to trying to understand the mental activities involved in reading, that is, what the reader does while reading, rather than being confined to the products of reading, that is, what the reader remembers from reading. (McKeown, Beck, & Sandora, 1996, p. 97)

In their efforts to study these mental activities, Isabel and her colleagues engaged in detailed analyses of the characteristics of classroom materials, specifically textbooks, that students were asked to learn from. They found that these texts left implicit both conceptual information and logical connections needed to create coherent mental representations of the situations described in the texts. What sense did readers make of these texts? How were they processing them? Were they getting beyond the surface to the meaning? Beck and colleagues conducted think-aloud studies to see whether readers actively engaged with such texts and, if so, how they did it. They were at the same time interested in whether there were differences related to reading ability in the impact of thinking aloud and in the "bang for the buck" of revising texts to make them more coherent. Revision generally made the causal structure more explicit and filled in background knowledge that the author assumed the reader would have (Loxterman, Beck, & McKeown, 1994).

Ultimately, in looking for ways to engage students more actively and deeply with texts, Isabel and colleagues developed the Questioning the Author strategy (Beck, McKeown, Sandora, Kucan, & Worthy, 1996). This approach emphasized interactions in the classroom among readers as they grappled with the meaning of the text: Students not only questioned the author but also engaged in spirited discussions with one another. These kinds of interactions necessitated work with teachers on changing their practice to support and create contexts in which student talk was valued and encouraged. In their work with teachers, Isabel and her colleagues engaged teachers in living the principle that "meaning is constructed through active grappling with information" (McKeown et al., 1996, p. 117). It somehow seems fitting that the process that enabled Isabel to learn and deeply understand cognitive issues in reading and comprehension is the very same process that has now proven to be so successful as a strategy for teachers and young learners in their classrooms.

THEORETICAL PERSPECTIVES AND ASSUMPTIONS

There are several points of contact between the research of Isabel Beck and her colleagues and my own research. We have both focused on complex or deep comprehension processes, how readers engage with text, how characteristics of text and instruction affect that engagement, and the kind of teaching that fosters the development of engagement in the meaning-making process. We have used think-aloud and questioning strategies as windows into learners' meaning-construction processes (e.g., Coté, Goldman, & Saul, 1998; Goldman, 1985; Wolfe & Goldman, 2005). We have collaborated with teachers on the design of instructional units and on strategies for engaging youngsters with text (Zech, Gause-Vega, Bray, Secules, & Goldman, 2000).

My current theoretical perspective on comprehension recognizes the inherently social and intertextual properties of reading and learning (Goldman, 1997, 2004; Goldman & Bloome, 2004) and examines meaning construction as a complex of processes, some of which are more individualistic, some of which are more socially based.[1] Also present is the legacy of Isabel's convictions regarding the central importance of decoding and of my own earlier work on reading skill differences in verbal memory (Goldman, Hogaboam, Bell, & Perfetti, 1980; Perfetti & Goldman, 1976; Perfetti, Goldman, & Hogaboam, 1979). In Table 13.1, I summarize my current theoretical perspectives and assumptions about comprehension and learning from text. These inform our work on the assessment of multiple-source comprehension. In referring to multiple sources, we borrow from the New London Group's (1996) notion of multiliteracies: A *source* is any form of information that a person is able to process or use. Sources may be written, oral, gestural, graphical, dynamic, static, or combinations thereof. The traditional printed text is thus one source of information. The assumptions listed in Table 13.1 indicate that comprehension is an interactive and constructive process in which prior knowledge plays a major role. Prior knowledge is of a variety of types, including what the learner already knows about the topic and the content structure of the particular text form (cf. Goldman & Rakestraw, 2000). At the same time, constructed meaning is constrained by the content of the text—by what the text says. Meaning construction occurs for specific purposes, tasks, and goals; these help the reader determine what sources are useful and, within a source, what information is relevant and important. Learners' interests and their interpretations of the task requirements affect their engagement with the task and information sources. Disciplines such as science or history have adopted specific discourse forms, or genres, for communications among members of that discipline. Knowledge of these forms and differences among disciplines is one aspect of what learners bring to the meaning-construction task. Finally, the ubiquitous electronic availability of information increases the complexity of sense making in two ways. First, it increases the likelihood that learners will be drawing on multiple sources of information to complete many of their tasks. Second, it increases the need to critically evaluate information sources for their credibility and trustworthiness.

In the next section of the chapter, we describe our approach to assessment and the role that these theoretical perspectives and assump-

---

[1] A process can be social through interaction with another or through prior knowledge developed in interactions with others. For example, remembering what someone else thought of a particular author or reading selection would be a social aspect of meaning making.

tions play in guiding what to assess and how to assess it. Key to our approach is the development of a model of the knowledge and skills that multiple source comprehension comprises. The theoretical perspectives and assumptions described in Table 13.1 contributed to the development of that model.

EVIDENCE-CENTERED DESIGN
OF ASSESSMENT

We are using an evidence-centered approach to assessment design (ECD; Mislevy, Steinberg, & Almond, 2003) that offers a principled means of linking inferences about student knowledge to the evidence needed to support those inferences and the kinds of tasks that would elicit that evidence. ECD uses three types of models: the student model, the evidence model, and the task model.

The *student model* defines the knowledge, skills, and abilities (KSAs) that constitute the competencies of the domain and that are therefore important for an assessment to measure. *Domain* could refer to a specific content area (e.g., earth science), a process such as multiple-source comprehension, or the combination of the two (e.g., multiple-source comprehension in earth science). Regardless, the student model is based on a domain analysis that identifies the conceptual understandings, skills, and knowledge that define domain competence. The student model specifies the claims that one might want to make about what students know and are able to do in a specific area of knowledge. For example, a student who understands that anyone can post things on the Internet might look for information about the author or creator of Web pages they access as a means of judging the usefulness of the information.

The *evidence model* describes what would constitute evidence that a student had attained the KSAs outlined in the student model. Multiple-source comprehension relies on knowledge of generic reading strategies and skills, as well as knowledge and skills related to the epistemic practices of specific domains such as science and history. These practices include the role of multiple sources of information in the discipline (e.g., in "doing" science or history), as well as the ways in which members of a disciplinary community communicate with one another and establish new knowledge in the discipline.

The *task model* describes the situations and tasks that could be used to obtain the kinds of evidence specified in the evidence model.

TABLE 13.1. Theoretical Perspectives on Comprehension and Learning from Text and Other Information Sources

- Understanding and learning arise in the interaction of text and learner or learners.
  - Meaning is not in the text nor in the learner but is constructed.
  - Valid meaning construction is constrained by the contents of the text. That is, meaning is not relative, and the construction process is not an "anything goes" activity.
  - Meaning construction is situated in place, time, task, purpose, and goals, and these together affect what is important "in the text."
- Sources have structure and content.
- Learners have knowledge of structure, content, and strategies relevant to making meaning from information sources.
- Learners have interests, motivations, and emotional responses to information that affect their engagement with specific sources.
- Learning in the disciplines (subject-matter learning) includes learning the genres (forms) of the discipline.
  - These genres reflect rhetorical and substantive norms of argument and the accepted forms of communication among members of the discipline (cf. Goldman & Bisanz, 2002).
- Multimodal information sources are readily available and require new literacies for the 21st century.
  - A critical stance toward information sources has become more important because of the nonrefereed property of much of the information. It has not been vetted by the disciplinary community.
  - Increased availability of information sources makes it critical for learners to work across sources, as well as within, to create meaning and achieve deep comprehension.

Note. In this table, *text* and *information source* are used interchangeably.

Selected tasks will differ by the kinds of evidence that are required to support inferences of understanding. For example, a simple multiple-choice item could provide evidence of declarative content knowledge but might not provide evidence that students could gather data over time in multiple contexts or reason with data to construct a scientific argument. Similarly, a summarization task that required that students create a single summary of three or four documents would elicit different knowledge and skills than it would if the summary were of just one document.

Student Model for Multiple-Source Comprehension

The student model we have developed for multiple-source comprehension reflects contemporary research on single- and multiple-source comprehension in science and history content domains (e.g., Ashby, Lee, & Dickinson, 1997; Barton, 1996; Beck & McKeown, 1994; Britt & Aglinksas, 2002; Palincsar & Magnusson, 2001; Pressley, 2002; VanSledright, 2002a, 2002b; Wallace, Kupperman, Krajcik, & Soloway, 2000) and the limited research base on online and multiple-source comprehension skills (e.g., Britt, Perfetti, Sandak, & Rouet, 1999; Goldman, 2004; Goldman & Bloome, 2004; Greene, 1994; Rouet, Britt, Mason, & Perfetti, 1996; VanSledright, 2002a, 2002b; Wiley, Goldman, & Graesser, 2004; Wineburg, 1991, 1994, 1997). The major tenets of this research are consistent with the theoretical assumptions in Table 13.1. The constructs in the student model were also informed by a consideration of inquiry models being put forth by experts in the information sciences (Association of College and Research Libraries, 2002).

We postulated five major components for the student model and then "unpacked" the meaning of them. This unpacking process pushes the assessment designer, and it pushed us, to deeply consider what is meant by particular components or subcomponents. This iterative unpacking process is strikingly similar to the process Isabel employed in her efforts to break into the cognitive literature on reading. Our use of the iterative process led to the identification of subcomponents for each of the five components. Figure 13.1 provides an overview of the components and subcomponents.

1. *Interpreting the task* involves figuring out what is required and making a plan to accomplish it.
2. *Searching for resources* involves determining what to look for and where to find it.
3. *Sourcing* involves using information about the source to facilitate selecting appropriate materials for the task. Properties of the resource that are considered are the author, the publication venue, the recency or date of publication or posting to the Internet, the type (empirical report, review, fiction, primary, secondary), and the purpose or intent of the author (to inform, persuade, critique).
4. *Analyzing and synthesizing sources* involves what we traditionally think of as comprehension plus critical analysis of information within a source and across multiple sources. Even within a single source, synthesis and analysis take place. We have couched our synthesis processes in terms of the main elements of argument (claims and evidence) because of the inquiry frame

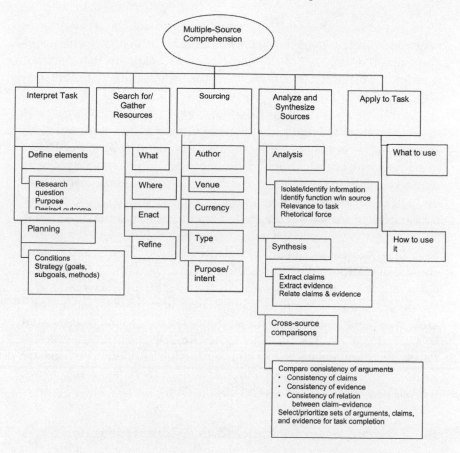

FIGURE 13.1. Student model for multiple-source comprehension.

we impose on multiple-source comprehension. Claim–evidence is a major rhetorical structure in history and in science. For sources that do not have a discernible claim–evidence structure, analysis involves identifying main ideas and details, and synthesis involves summarizing these within and across sources.

5. *Applying to task* involves deciding what information is most appropriate to use for the task and bringing it together to address the task. How the information is presented reflects the norms of communication appropriate in the task context.

Components and subcomponents express what constitutes competence for that component or subcomponent in the form of claim state-

ments about what students know and are able to do. The set of component and subcomponent claim statements constitute the student model
and express a "theory" of the knowledge and skills in that domain.
Examples of claim statements for the Sourcing subcomponents are provided in Table 13.2.

Although we have described these components linearly, we do not
mean to imply that the processes are executed one after another. On the
contrary, learners may be gathering, sourcing, and at least beginning
to analyze information sources at the same time. Attempts at synthesis
may reveal gaps in information and the need to seek additional sources
through another search process. Furthermore, evaluative processes are
operating at every level of the student model. For example, Search and
Sourcing both involve making evaluative judgments about the source,
including judgments about the trustworthiness of the author, the
amount of relevant information, and the currency and reliability of the
information. Evaluation is the process that leads to interactivity among
the various components and subcomponents of the student model,[2] and
thus it is a metacomponent of the student model (see similar discussion
in Azevedo, 2005; Quintana, Zhang, & Krajcik, 2005; Pressley, 2002).
Of the five components in the student model, our current efforts are
focused on the sourcing and the analysis–synthesis subcomponents,
with some attention to search and application.

Evidence Model for Multiple-Source Comprehension

The evidence model specifies what observations indicate the presence
of the knowledge and skills described by the student model. Each subcomponent and claim statement has an *evidence statement* associated
with it. These are stated in terms of the observables, or the characteristics of the work that an individual would have to produce to show his
or her level of proficiency with the KSAs identified in the claim statement with which the evidence statement is linked. The level of expected
competence is contained in scoring rubrics developed for specific work
products. The rubrics provide the means of examining developmental
trajectories for the specific observations or work products. The set of
evidence statements and their rubrics constitute the evidence model.

---

[2] Conversations with Dr. Emilio Sanchez while he was a visiting scholar at the University of
Illinois at Chicago were invaluable in moving our thinking in this direction.

TABLE 13.2. Claim and Evidence Statements for Sourcing Component

Subcomponent	Claim statement *Stem*: The student makes use of ...	Evidence statement *Stem*: The work includes information ...
Author	author information in the sourcing process.	about the credibility of the author or efforts to determine credibility of the author.
Venue	publishing location in the sourcing process.	about the credibility of the publication location or efforts to determine where something was published and its credibility.
Currency	publication relative to the content of the task in the sourcing process.[a]	indicating attention to date of publication in relation to task.
Type	differences among kinds of resources (e.g. primary vs. secondary; fiction vs. nonfiction; opinion piece/editorial vs. news story) relative to their utility for completing the task.	about differences among kinds of resources and their appropriateness for the task.
Purpose/intent	authorial intent and purpose in the sourcing process.	about possible goals of the author and implications of those for appropriateness for the task.

[a]In some cases, recency makes something a more valuable or reliable resource relative to the task (e.g., latest information on health value of taking vitamin C in the case of public health inquiry). In other cases, the older something is the more useful it is relative to the task (e.g., primary sources in the case of historical inquiry).

Table 13.2 illustrates evidence statements for the Sourcing subcomponent of the student model. Evidence statements are expressed in terms of features that are observable in the work or work product. The observables are indicators or behavioral expressions of the knowledge, skills, or strategies expressed in the claim statement. For example, a work product might be responses to the question "How useful would this source be for the task and why?" The response is the work product. We would infer that the student was making use of author information if the response contained statements about the author's reputation as a great historian. We are collecting data to inform the development of rubrics for the evidence statements.

Task Model

The task model is not an assessment activity per se but specifies the characteristics that an assessment activity needs to have so that the observable student work can provide evidence for its corresponding claim. For example, the evidence statement might specify that a student will select a particular source and provide four evaluative statements regarding the quality of that source in terms of author, currency, venue, and content. The task model would specify, among other things, how long the sources would be, how the evaluative statements should be presented, and whether the sources would be in science or history. The task model would also include a specification of the presentation materials and instructions that students use in creating their work products. Through this process, "item equivalence" of different task situations can be ascertained.

VALIDATING THE MULTIPLE-SOURCE COMPREHENSION STUDENT MODEL FOR MIDDLE SCHOOL STUDENTS

The theoretical and empirical basis of the student model described in the previous section reflects research on participants ranging from 10 years of age to college-level and beyond in cases of research on practicing scientists and historians. The purpose of our research was to develop an assessment prototype that would be relevant and appropriate for use with students between the age span of 10 and 15. To that end, we first conducted a series of descriptive microethnographic studies in fifth-grade classrooms to see what was actually happening with respect to teaching and learning about multiple-source comprehension skills. Second, we provided an inquiry task context that "walked" students through the five components of the student model. In the remainder of this chapter we provide elaborations on each of these classroom-based research efforts.

Opportunities for Multiple-Source Inquiry in Classrooms

A series of descriptive microethnographic studies were undertaken to document multiple-source activities that were occurring naturally in science and social studies classrooms. We focused on six to nine students in each of six fifth-grade classrooms (three science and three social studies). Focal students were selected across a range of reading proficiency (above average, average, and struggling readers) based on teacher ratings. In total, 39 one-hour observations were conducted (24 science, 15 social studies), during which 44 students were observed. We collected extended field notes and student artifacts as the main data sources. These field notes were transcribed, and student artifacts were digitized and linked to these transcriptions.

Data Coding and Reduction

Transcripts of the observations were coded to identify what classroom sources students typically interacted with and the functions they served with respect to learning. In this chapter we report only the findings regarding types of sources. Using methods of grounded theory and constant comparison, we identified 14 types of sources from which students could extract information that would assist them in accomplishing the tasks assigned in the classroom. Interrater reliability indicated 90% agreement on identification and assignment of sources to types. Differences between raters were resolved in conference. Table 13.3 contains the 14 types of sources and examples of them.

Results

There were several interesting trends in the data. First, in both science and social studies classrooms, teacher-led discussions were the dominant information sources available to the students. On average, these sources were observed approximately four to five times more frequently than any other type of source. Beyond the dominant sources, there were domain-related differences in the sources. Science classes featured a higher preponderance of demonstrations and tools than did social studies classes. In addition, students in science were provided with worksheets more than twice as often as students in social studies classrooms. In contrast, social studies classes featured a higher quantity of text sources and a greater variety of types of texts as compared with science classrooms.

When we mapped the presence of different resources against the components of the student model, we found that students in social studies had more opportunities to engage in multiple-source comprehension than students in science. This is consistent with the finding of more and a greater variety of text resources in social studies classrooms. There was some evidence of multiple-source comprehension within the components of interpretation, gathering, analysis–synthesis, and application in both social studies and science classrooms. Nevertheless, we

TABLE 13.3. Types of Sources Observed in Science and Social Studies Classrooms

	Type of source	Example
R1	INSTRUCTIONS Teacher directions and details for a given task or activity	Source: T tells students to make a T-chart on solar cookers, with one side labeled "interesting," and the other side labeled "questions." They are to brainstorm about the two (regarding solar cookers) in groups before any whole-class discussion. Category: INSTRUCTIONS
R2	TEXT (characterize) Textually oriented physical items that are used in relation to a task "Characterize" examples: • Textbook • Historical document • Worksheet • Whiteboard display • Magazine article • Overhead display • Oral reading	Example Source: Lab worksheet Category: TEXT/Worksheet/Target source
R3	T-LED DISCUSSION Teacher-led, whole-class discussions	Example Source: Discussion Category: T-LED DISCUSSION
R4	S-INITIATED DISCUSSION Whole-class discussion initiated by one or more students	Example Source: Students ask T questions about how light reflects off of the moon. (T merely mentioned this in passing, but students want to understand how this occurs.) Category: STUDENT-INITIATED DISCUSSION
R5	SMALL-GROUP DISCUSSION Small-group discussions occurring between two or more people, which can be characterized in the following ways, depending on how they were initiated: • Student–teacher • Teacher–student If no characterization is given, student–student interactions are assumed.	Example Source: T is circulating around the room. Students call him over for help because they are having difficulty trying to understand what is meant by "founding fathers." T assists students through discussion. Category: SMALL GROUP DISCUSSION/Student–teacher
R6	LECTURE Speech delivered to class by the teacher, with the purpose of helping them understand the subject matter at hand. Example of possible instances of a LECTURE: introduction to new material or intervention for misconceptions	Example Source: T introduces the "Gettysburg Address" to the class. Category: LECTURE

R7   VISUAL REPRESENTATION
Visual imagery or display of an item with the intention to aid in students' understanding of the task or subject matter

Example
Source: Image in the textbook of the formation of clouds over a lake. (T is pointing out elements on the page that students should pay attention to before they begin reading)
Category: VISUAL REPRESENTATION

R8   DEMONSTRATION
Teacher (or student) physically demonstrates (with or without props) how students should perform a particular task or how they ought to think of the subject matter (concretizing of concepts).

Example
Source: T uses his self-made solar cooker to model how students will position their thermometers and construction paper in their solar cookers.
Category: DEMONSTRATION

R9   ARTIFACT
Object passed around in class for student examination

Example
Source: Distributed objects, each representing different types of energy (calculator, candle, bell, wheel, penlight, wind-up toy); each group examines one object, then passes it on.
Category: ARTIFACT

R10   TOOL
Items of solely utilitarian nature used to complete tasks. Example: weights, tape measure.

Example
Source: Thermometer
Category: TOOL

R11   MULTIMEDIA
Presentation of information through applications and technologies that manipulate text, images, sound, and animation. Examples: videos and websites.

Example
Source: Interactive-style video on capturing solar energy
Category: MULTIMEDIA (video)

R12   PRIOR KNOWLEDGE REFERENCE
Teacher references to students' prior knowledge, with the intention to help them understand new material or assist them in their performance of a task. This category is modified by one of three subcategories:
• Mentioned
• Mentioned with relation to situation
• Mentioned with elaborated discussion

Example
Source: T asks for students to think about what they might already know about the topic in order to do the task; he evokes prior knowledge students might have about solar cookers, pointing out that they appeared in the video they saw last science class.
Category: PRIOR KNOWLEDGE REFERENCE/Mentioned with elaborated discussion

R13   WORK PRODUCT
Target source that has been completed by the student. May be used as a new source for a subsequent activity.

Example
Source: Completed energy chart worksheet; all 6 cells are filled out
Category: WORK PRODUCT

R14   QUESTION SET
Students are provided with questions to answer as a formal or informal check of their knowledge.

Example
Source: knowledge check questions about bird features
Category: QUESTION SET

found little evidence that students were asked to evaluate the quality of a source. Indeed, overall we observed very low incidence of instructional activities that involved simultaneous use of multiple sources in either social studies or science. Nor did we see any instruction on source evaluation nor discussion of the reasons it might be important. This was the case for both domains across source types and specific classroom instructional activities.

These findings, preliminary as they are, are consistent with previous research indicating that most students are simply not exposed to instructional situations that provide them with opportunities to develop the range of knowledge and skills captured in the student model of multiple-source comprehension (Goldman et al., 1999; Gomez & Gomez, 2007; Gomez, Herman, & Gomez, 2007; VanSledright, 2002a, 2002b; Wolfe & Goldman, 2005). The absence of opportunities to learn the knowledge and skills that define multiple-source comprehension clearly poses a dilemma for assessment design and administration. Without these opportunities, it would not be surprising to find only the most rudimentary knowledge and skills relative to multiple-source comprehension. However, students are learning analysis and synthesis for single sources, at least for text-based sources. In our second investigation, we gave students a multiple-source task for purposes of observing what they would do in such a situation.

A MULTIPLE-SOURCE INQUIRY
TASK IN HISTORY

We created a task using several sources and a "driving inquiry-oriented question" and structured the task so that students had opportunities to engage in all five components of the student model. We developed the inquiry questions in collaboration with the teachers of the classrooms in which we worked. Although we created tasks for both history and science, in this chapter we report only on the history task as conducted in one classroom, which we have since replicated in a second classroom. Our primary interest in this work was to gather information on how students used the sources in addressing the task and how information about the sources (e.g., author, year) and information in the sources was used in selecting what sources would be useful for the inquiry task and what sources were actually used when creating an essay to address the inquiry question.

The classroom in which we administered this task is located in a large urban school district. The school of which this classroom is a part averages standardized test scores in the third quartile for reading, with about 50% of the students in the school meeting grade-level reading standards. There were 30 students and one lead teacher in this self-contained classroom.

The inquiry task was oriented to the local context, and the question was introduced on the first day of the 4-day activity (45–60 minutes per day) by an anchor text (a secondary expository source): "Why did Chicago become a large city?" The anchor text and an accompanying video described present-day Chicago as the third largest city in the United States, even though in the early 1800s no one wanted to live there. There was a also a chart that provided population growth figures for each decade from 1830 to the present. Students brainstormed their initial ideas about how they would answer the question and the kinds of sources they thought would be helpful in answering the question. Note that, although the inquiry question was phrased as a *Why* question, it could just as easily have been worded *How was it that.* We used *why* to encourage students to provide explanations for the reasons they provided and because we wanted to be explicit about the need to provide *causal* or *because* statements in their responses. This is in contrast to recounting *that* Chicago grew or increased in population.

On the second day, we provided students with packets of information comprising five sources that contained text, charts, graphs, and tables. They were told that the information in the packet would help them address the inquiry question. Day 2 activities focused on source selection. Students read each source and individually wrote out responses to the question "Which two sources would you pick to answer the question about Chicago and why?" In small groups, students discussed their responses. A researcher facilitated the discussion and prompted students to elaborate on their answers, such as "How does that resource help you answer the question?" and "Why do you think these resources are the best?" On day 3, students individually wrote an essay addressing the inquiry question. They had the whole packet of sources available to them and were told that they could use any of the sources that they wished. After students had written their essays, researchers again led small-group discussions in which students shared their thinking about the reasons Chicago became a large city and the reasons that they selected the sources they used. The fourth day involved application of what they had learned about the reasons Chicago became a big city to predicting which of two imaginary cities had the best chance of growing into a big city based on the descriptions of these cities that we provided. Data from this task are not discussed in this chapter.

The Source Materials

The materials in the packet conveyed information about the late 19th century and early part of the 20th century during the period of immigration from Europe and the Great Migration from the southern states and the simultaneous boom in stockyard employment in Chicago. The sources reflected a range of primary sources (personal letters, newspaper ads, and editorials from the early 1900s) and secondary sources (a textbook selection on the railroad industry in Chicago, a website on immigration to Chicago and population growth). The sources were adapted from originals to be within the range of fifth-grade readers. The publication venue for each source was provided, as were the dates of publication.

All of the sources contained information relevant to addressing the inquiry question, but they differed in terms of how much relevant information they contained and the proportion of information that was relevant relative to the total information contained in the source. This variation was intentional: We wanted a complete explanation of the reasons that Chicago became a big city to involve extracting information across multiple sources within the set, with repetition of similar ideas occurring in different sources. The repetition provides an opportunity for students to engage in a developmentally appropriate form of what expert historians call *corroboration* (Wineburg 1991, 1994, 1997). In addition, previous research with college and high school students indicates that selection of sources and inclusion of information are often related to variables such as the frequency of occurrence of particular claims and evidence (Britt et al., 1999; Rouet et al., 1996). Table 13.4 shows the results of the content analysis for each of the sources in terms of the distribution of "big ideas" or major reasons that people wanted to leave where they were living (push forces) and immigrate to Chicago (pull forces). Table 13.4 shows that each source provided information relevant to three of the five big ideas but that the sources varied with respect to the proportion of information in a source that was relevant to the task. Furthermore, the big ideas were differentially elaborated,

TABLE 13.4. Content Analyses of the Sources with Respect to Five Major Forces Explaining Chicago's Growth

Big idea	Source 1 (17)	Source 2 (20)	Source 3 (12)	Source 4 (13)	Source 5 (28)
Economics	5	2	1	9	10
Politics	5	3	0	2	13
Location	0	0	6	0	0
Support population	6	8	0	0	4
Growth	0	0	2	6	0
% of sentences relevant to big ideas	64	65	67	92	89

Note: For each source, the number of sentences that conveyed information about each big idea (and total number of sentences in source). Some sentences in each source conveyed information about more than one big idea. *Source 1:* A primary source (a personal letter) from a woman in Georgia to a church in Chicago. *Source 2:* An editorial and newspaper advertisement dated 1915 that appeared in the *Chicago Defender,* a newspaper published by the Chicago African American community. *Source 3:* A textbook segment on the rise of Chicago as a railroad hub, along with a map showing the main rail lines between the North and the South. *Source 4:* An article from a website describing immigration to Chicago from 1830 to 1970 and providing information about where and why immigrants came, including a chart indicating the major immigrant groups in each decade from 1830 to 1970. *Source 5:* An op/ed page attributed to the *Chicago Tribune,* April 1925, that contained two opposing editorials about the stockyards, one authored by Michael Armour of the Armour meat-packing family and the other by Jane Addams, described as a person who helped immigrants.

with economic reasons the most heavily discussed in the sources and mentioned in each of the five sources. On the other hand, location was discussed in only one source.

The packet also contained task instructions and templates for documenting and reporting about their inquiry activity. A member of the research team and former fifth-grade teacher led the instruction of this inquiry task. All observations were video recorded, and audio recorders were placed on the desks of three small groups that were selected by the teacher as generally talkative and productive. We also collected photographs of student work artifacts produced during the task activity.

Data Analysis and Coding

Students' responses to the selection task were analyzed with respect to which sources they picked and the reasons they provided for selecting them. Reasons were classified with respect to whether they evaluated the source. Evaluative reasons, then, differentiated among different characteristics that were evaluated (e.g., quality or quantity of content, the venue from which the resource was drawn, author credibility or other sourcing information). The predominant nonevaluative response was to copy information from the text (e.g, "because it (the selected source) says [excerpt from selected source]). Other nonevaluative responses included prior knowledge associations not relevant to the task or other comments judged to be irrelevant. Reliability in applying the coding scheme was above 90%, and disagreements were resolved in discussion. Students' synthesis-essay responses were parsed into idea units. Idea units were then mapped to the content analysis of the big ideas that were reflected across the sources. Reliability in crediting student essays with big ideas was above 85%, and disagreements were resolved in discussion.

Results

Source Selection

Among the 20 students for whom we had source selection data, the source most frequently selected (65% of the students) was the website source about population growth and why people immigrated to Chicago. The second most likely source selected (50%) was the textbook selection about railroads (50%). The two newspaper sources each were selected by 35% of the students. The least frequently selected source was the personal letter (25%). Regardless of the source that was selected, the predominant responses for selecting a source were nonevaluative responses in which students listed relevant information from a source without providing any reasons why this information mattered. For example, 83% of the reasons provided for selecting the personal letter consisted of copied segments of text from the letter. When students did include evaluative statements, these statements tended to focus on the relationship of the information within the source to the task of determining the reasons that Chicago became a big city. Students very rarely looked beyond content to consider any characteristics of the source itself (e.g., who the author was, publication venue, date published, or intent).

We also looked at the co-occurrence of nonevaluative and evaluative responses within an individual student. For each source selection, we tabulated the number of students who provided only nonevaluative, only evaluative, or both kinds of reasons. The data indicate an interaction of the co-occurrence patterns with the type of source. That is, for the personal letter and the *Chicago Defender* sources, students tended to provide only information from the source itself rather than any evaluation of the source or information in it. However, for the textbook and Internet sources, students tended to give information from these sources *and* offer evaluations of them. Finally, the patterns indicated that providing only evaluative reasons for selecting any of the sources was infrequent (14–23% of the reasons). In other words, students infrequently just indicated something about the author, date, venue, where it was published, or purpose as the reason they selected it. These data indicate that students tend to focus on source content plus sourcing characteristics, but not solely on sourcing characteristics.

The findings for source selection are consistent with prior research that indicates that it is information quantity and accuracy that drive students' selections of sources (e.g., Goldman et al., 1999; VanSledright, 2002a, 2002b; Wolfe & Goldman, 2005). Based on the findings from our observations of classroom instructional practices of an absence of discussions about what is important in judging different sources, it is not surprising that students rely on information content and rarely mention the sourcing subcomponents that we have included in the student model (e.g., author, date).

Synthesis Essays

The content analysis of the essays responding to the inquiry question were mapped against the big ideas to determine what information from the sources students actually used as reasons or evidence in determining why Chicago became a big city. Across the 26 students who provided synthesis essays, the two most common reasons provided were general population growth (92%) and economy (85%). Political and social reasons were provided in 65% and 58% of the responses. Location (5%) was the big idea least frequently included in the essays. These data indicate that the big ideas about which there was the most information across the sources were the ones included most frequently in the essays. The more evidence overlapped across sources, the more likely students were to adopt it as being important to include in the essays.

Relationship between Source Selection and Use in Synthesis Essay

A final issue we address is the relationship between selection and synthesis components in the student model. We indicated in describing the model that the process of analyzing and synthesizing information across sources might result in a learner deciding that he or she had not selected sources that were sufficient to complete the inquiry task. The synthesis process might, for example, reveal that the sources actually contained information that conflicted. Or some information might stand out as needing further corroboration. In the context of the inquiry task we set up for students, we could examine a potential indicator of the role of the synthesis task on source selection, albeit an indirect measure: Although students had selected two sources as the best, when they did the synthesis essay, they actually had all five sources to work from and had had the benefit of an intervening discussion of the reasons particular sources had been selected by other students. We looked at the relationship between the percentage of students who selected each of the sources during source selection and the percentage of students who included ideas from each source.

The data, provided in Table 13.5, indicate that in general there is a shift between those sources selected during the initial source selection and those from which information was included in the synthesis essays. Although the immigration/population growth source remained the source from which information was most often selected, there was a shift away from the textbook source about railroads toward inclusion of information from the other sources. A related finding concerns source 5, the opposing editorials. As shown in the last two rows of Table 13.5, students appeared to be relatively adept at separating information supportive of the growth of Chicago from information that was not supportive of growth: 65% of the students included information from the supportive segment of source 5, whereas only 35% of the students included information from the nonsupportive segment. When they did include information from the nonsupportive editorial, it tended to be as a counterpoint to the other editorial (e.g., not everyone agreed that the stockyards were a good place to work).

The data on the relationship between source selection and use in the synthesis essay suggest that students' understanding of the sources may have changed as the demands of the task required them to consider one source in juxtaposition with other related sources. We have no direct evidence of this as yet, but it is consistent with our thinking about multiple-source comprehension tasks as useful for engaging students more deeply in meaning-making processes.

TABLE 13.5. Relationship between Sources Selected as Useful and Sources Actually Used in the Synthesis Essay

	Percent (#) students selecting each source	Percent (#) of student essays with information from each source	Mean elaboration units from each source included in synthesis essay
Source 1: Personal letter	25% (5)	65% (13)	1.00
Source 2: Chicago Defender ad	35% (7)	70% (14)	2.1
Source 3: Railroads (textbook)	50% (10)	45% (9)	0.9
Source 4: Population growth/ immigration (website)	65% (13)	95% (19)	3.75
Source 5: Op/ed page from newspaper	35% (7)	70% (14)	1.85
Source 5a: Pro work in stockyards (supportive)	n/a	65% (13)	1.45
Source 5b: Against work in stockyards (nonsupportive)	n/a	30% (6)	.4

Note. $n = 20$. Although 26 students provided synthesis essays, only 20 had also provided source selection data.

IMPLICATIONS FOR TEACHERS AND STUDENTS

Our observational data indicate that many sources of information are available in fifth-grade classrooms, although they are largely underutilized as intentional learning contexts. That is, information relevant to students' tasks is available through interactions with teachers and peers, in multimedia artifacts in their rooms, and through instructional texts. However, current practices direct students to these resources serially or sequentially (Goldman, 2004). Only rarely do teachers juxtapose multiple sources of information or do students make spontaneous connections among resources. As such, students effectively do not engage in intentional multiple-source comprehension; if it occurs at all, it is in a largely unguided and somewhat serendipitous fashion. Despite the absence of explicit multiple-source comprehension practice in the classrooms in which we worked, our data indicate that when students are presented with tasks that engage them in the processes involved in multiple-source comprehension, they have strong intuitions about how to select and make use of information. Although underdeveloped, these propensities provide a starting point for systematic instruction that could be guided by the student model for multiple-source comprehension. The student model provides teachers with a sense of the components and subcomponents involved in reading and learning from multiple sources. For example, the subcomponents of sourcing make explicit some of the characteristics of sources that ought to be considered in deciding on the usefulness of a source. The analysis–synthesis component defines various subcomponents involved in deciding whether different sources are making the same or different arguments and where those differences lie. Furthermore, the student model makes explicit the need to evaluate sources and the adequacy of the set of selected sources for addressing a specific inquiry task.

In undertaking the work of designing an assessment environment for multiple-source comprehension, we intended the output to be a diagnostic profile that could guide teachers' instructional decision making. We now see that the assessment environment may be equally if not more important as a tool for making practitioners aware of and knowledgeable about the knowledge, skills, and benefits of explicitly engaging in multiple-source comprehension.

By its design, the assessment environment, through the interrelationships of the student, evidence, and task models, will both characterize what students have learned and, through rubrics related to evidence statements, shed light on possible developmental pathways for future learning. This information can help students develop appropriate learning goals and self-assess their progress toward those goals. Thus we believe the assessment environment will enhance teachers' and students' knowledge and understanding of multiple-source comprehension; of what they do know and can do; and of where they need to go in further developing their multiple-source comprehension knowledge and skills.

FUTURE DIRECTIONS

Thus far we have made good progress in laying out the student model and the evidence model. We are now moving forward in our development of the *task model*, the third component in ECD. The empirical data collected to date is formative with respect to these efforts. It helps us understand the sorts of performances we can expect from students who have had relatively little in the way of systematic instruction in multiple-source comprehension. The work to date puts us in a better position to identify the variables that are important in an inquiry task that employs multiple sources, for example, the impact of the number of sources on integration skills and the transparency of information in charts, tables, and maps. We also have a better sense of the range of responses we can expect to tasks that ask students to explain their selections of sources and what makes a source useful. Similar to earlier findings (e.g., Goldman et al., 1999; VanSledright, 2000a, 2002b), students rely heavily on the sheer quantity of information when deciding what sources are useful and when they have enough sources. Thus, if we are interested in assessing students' judgments about the characteristics of sources (author, publication venue, data, etc.), we will need to specifically structure the task so that amount of information is taken out of the equation.

Although we are still in preliminary stages of analysis of how students respond to multiple-source instructional situations, there are clear directions for the design of the assessment environment and the empirical validation of it. As we develop and test our prototypes, we expect that we will further refine and sharpen our understanding of the knowledge and skills of multiple-source comprehension and of the benefits to understanding that accrue from the intentional construction of instructional activities that juxtapose a variety of information sources. Hopefully, by embodying this knowledge in a low-stakes assessment environment, the environment itself will be a valuable professional development tool for teachers and a learning tool for students.

ACKNOWLEDGMENTS

The assessment project described in the chapter is work funded, in part, by the Institute for Education Sciences, U.S. Department of Education (Grant No. R305G050091). Any opinions, findings, and conclusions or recommendations expressed in this material are those of the authors and do not necessarily reflect the views of the funding organization. We gratefully acknowledge the contributions to this work of our colleagues Meryl Bertenthal, Ken Fujimoto, Michael Manderino, and James W. Pellegrino. For further information about the work, contact *sgoldman@uic.edu, klawless@uic.edu*, or *kpg1321@gmail.com*.

REFERENCES

Ashby, R., Lee, P., & Dickinson, A. (1997). How children explain the why of history. *Social Education, 61*(1), 17–21.

Association of College and Research Libraries. (2002, January). *Information literacy compency standards*. Paper presented at the annual meeting of the American Library Association, San Antonio, TX.

Azevedo, R. (2005). Using hypermedia as a metacognitive tool for enhancing student learning? The role of self-regulated learning. *Educational Psychologist, 40*, 199–209.

Barton, K. (1996). Narrative simplifications in elementary students' historical thinking. In J. Brophy (Ed.), *Advances in research on teaching* (Vol. 6, pp. 51–84). Greenwich, CT: JAI Press.

Beck, I. L., & McKeown, M. G. (1994). Outcomes of history instruction: Paste-up accounts. In M. Carretero & J. F. Voss (Eds.), *Cognitive and instructional processes in history and the social sciences* (pp. 237–256). Hillsdale, NJ: Erlbaum.

Beck, I. L., McKeown, M. G., Sandora, C. A., Kucan, L., & Worthy, J. (1996). Questioning the Author: A year-long implementation to engage students with text. *Elementary School Journal, 96*, 385–414.

Britt, M. A., & Aglinksas, C. (2002). Improving students' ability to identify and use source information. *Cognition and Instruction, 20*, 485–522.

Britt, M. A., Perfetti, C. A., Sandak, R., & Rouet, J.-F. (1999). Content integration and source separation in learning from multiple texts. In S. R. Goldman, A. C. Graesser, & P. van den Broek (Eds.), *Narrative comprehension, causality, and coherence: Essays in honor of Tom Trabasso* (pp. 209–233). Mahwah, NJ: Erlbaum.

Coté, N., Goldman, S. R., & Saul, E. U. (1998). Students making sense of informational text: Relations between processing and representation. *Discourse Processes, 25*, 1–53.

Goldman, S. R. (1985). Inferential reasoning in and about narrative texts. In A. Graesser & J. Black (Eds.), *The psychology of questions* (pp. 247–276). Hillsdale, NJ: Erlbaum.

Goldman, S. R. (1997). Learning from text: Reflections on the past and suggestions for the future. *Discourse Processes, 23*, 357–398.

Goldman, S. R. (2004). Cognitive aspects of constructing meaning through and across multiple texts. In N. Shuart-Farris & D. M. Bloome (Eds.), *Uses of intertextuality in classroom and educational research* (pp. 313–347). Greenwich, CT: Information Age.

Goldman, S. R., & Bisanz, G. (2002). Toward a functional analysis of scientific genres: Implications for understanding and learning processes. In J. Otero, J. A. León, & A. C. Graesser (Eds.), *The psychology of science text comprehension.* (pp. 19–50). Mahwah, NJ: Erlbaum.

Goldman, S. R., & Bloome, D. M. (2004). Learning to construct and integrate. In A. F. Healy (Ed.), *Experimental cognitive psychology and its applications: Festshrift in honor of Lyle Bourne, Walter Kintsch, and Thomas Landauer* (pp. 169–182). Washington, DC: American Psychological Association.

Goldman, S. R., Hogaboam, T., Bell, L. C., & Perfetti, C. A. (1980). Short-term retention of discourse during reading. *Journal of Educational Psychology, 72,* 647–655.

Goldman, S. R., Meyerson, P., Wolfe, M. B. W., Mayfield, C., Coté, N. C., & Bloome, D. (1999, April). *"If it says so in the text book, it must be true": Multiple sources in the middle school social studies classroom.* Paper presented at the annual conference of the American Educational Research Association, Montreal, Canada.

Goldman, S. R., & Rakestraw, J. A., Jr. (2000). Structural aspects of constructing meaning from text. In M. L. Kamil, P. Mosenthal, P. D. Pearson, & R. Barr (Eds.), *Handbook of reading research* (Vol. 3, pp. 311–335). Mahwah, NJ: Erlbaum.

Gomez, L., & Gomez, K. (2007, January). *Preparing young learners for the 21st century: Reading and writing to learn in science.* Invited paper in the Occasional Paper Series of the Minority Student Achievement Network.

Gomez, L., Herman, P., & Gomez, K. (2007, February). Integrating text in content-area classes: Better supports for teachers and students. *Voices in Urban Education, 14.* Providence, RI: Annenberg Institute for School Reform.

Greene, S. (1994). The problems of learning to think like a historian: Writing history in the culture of the classroom. *Educational Psychologist, 29*(2), 89–96.

Loxterman, J. A., Beck, I. L., & McKeown, M. G. (1994). The effects of thinking aloud during reading on students' comprehension of more or less coherent text. *Reading Research Quarterly, 29,* 353–367.

McKeown, M. G., Beck, I. L., & Sandora, C. A. (1996). Questioning the author: An approach to developing meaningful classroom discourse. In M. G. Graves, B. M. Taylor, & P. van den Broek (Eds.), *The first R: Every child's right to read* (pp. 97–119). New York: Teachers College Press.

Mislevy, R. J., Steinberg, L. S., & Almond, R. G. (2003). On the structure of educational assessments. *Measurement: Interdisciplinary Research and Perspectives, 1,* 3–62.

New London Group. (1996). A pedagogy of multiliteracies: Designing social futures. *Harvard Educational Review, 66*(1), 60–92.

Palincsar, A. S., & Magnusson, S. J. (2001). The interplay of first-hand and second-hand investigations to model and support the development of scientific knowledge and reasoning. In S. M. Carver & D. Klahr (Eds.), *Cognition and instruction: Twenty-five years of progress* (pp. 151–193). Mahwah, NJ: Erlbaum.

Perfetti, C. A., & Goldman, S. R. (1976). Discourse memory and reading comprehension skill. *Journal of Verbal Learning and Verbal Behavior, 15,* 33–42.

Perfetti, C. A., Goldman, S. R., & Hogaboam, T. W. (1979). Reading skill and the identification of words in discourse context. *Memory and Cognition, 7,* 273–282.

Pressley, M. (2002). Metacognition and self-regulated comprehension. In A. E. Farstrup & S. Samuels (Eds.), *What research has to say about reading instruction* (pp. 291–309). Newark, DE: International Reading Association.

Quintana, C., Zhang, M., & Krajcik, J. (2005). A framework for supporting meta-cognitive aspects of online inquiry through software-based scaffolding. *Educational Psychologist, 40,* 235–244.

Rouet, J.-F., Britt, M. A., Mason, R. A., & Perfetti, C. A. (1996). Using multiple sources of evidence to reason about history. *Journal of Educational Psychology, 88,* 478–493.

VanSledright, B. (2002a). Confronting history's interpretive paradox while teaching fifth graders to investigate the past. *American Educational Research Journal, 39,* 1089–1115.

VanSledright, B. (2002b). *In search of America's past: Learning to read history in elementary school.* New York: Teachers College Press.

Wallace, R. M., Kupperman, J., Krajcik, J., & Soloway, E. (2000). Science on the Web: Students on-line in a sixth-grade classroom. *Journal of the Learning Sciences, 9,* 75–104.

Wiley, J., Goldman, S. R., & Graesser, A. (2004, January). *Taking a critical stance and learning from on-line scientific information: Evidence from eye-tracking and think-alouds.* Paper presented at the Conference on Text, Discourse and Cognition, Jackson Hole, WY.

Wineburg, S. S. (1991). Historical problem solving: A study of the cognitive processes used in the evaluation of documentary and pictorial evidence. *Journal of Educational Psychology, 83,* 73–87.

Wineburg, S. S. (1994). The cognitive representation of historical texts. In G. Leinhardt, I. L. Beck, & C. Stainton (Eds.), *Teaching and learning in history* (pp. 85–135). Hillsdale, NJ: Erlbaum.

Wineburg, S. S. (1997). Reading Abraham Lincoln: An expert/expert study in the interpretation of historical texts. *Cognitive Science, 22,* 319–346.

Wolfe, M. B., & Goldman, S. R. (2005). Relationships between adolescents' text processing and reasoning. *Cognition and Instruction, 23*(4), 467–502.

Zech, L., Gause-Vega, C., Bray, M. H., Secules, T., & Goldman, S. R. (2000). Content-based collaborative inquiry: Professional development for school reform. *Educational Psychologist, 35*(3), 207–217.

14

THE WORK OF CONSTRUCTING CONNECTIONS BETWEEN RESEARCH AND PRACTICE

What We Can Learn from Isabel L. Beck

Leona Schauble

In 1968, long before I (L.S.) met Isabel Beck, I completed undergraduate school and left my small liberal arts college in south central Maine to move to the big city—New York, that is. There I did some of the predictable things that you'd expect from a small-town girl escaping from New England: moved to East Harlem, enrolled briefly in graduate school (Columbia for philosophy), studied karate, inhaled, and, along with others in my generation, observed in amazement the assassination of Martin Luther King, the 1968 riots, and the Columbia University uprising. When she heard I was in New York, a college friend (a graduate of the Learning Research and Development Center [LRDC], by the way) phoned to persuade me to join a small group of education researchers and television producers who were working on a new television show called *Sesame Street*.

During my ensuing 20 years at the Children's Television Workshop, I developed a lasting fascination with trying to understand the varying ways that learning research can make productive contact with the design of learning environments. In my experience, people tend to assume either that the relationship between these two enterprises is straightforward and unproblematic (i.e., researchers figure out what people should do and then the practitioners go and do it—guess who thinks this?) or, alternatively, as fraught with conflict and oriented toward orthogonal goals (i.e., the goals and aesthetics of research and practice are so distinct that they proceed along nonintersecting paths; this is unfortunately but understandably the conclusion that teachers and other practitioners sometimes reach).

I tend to regard these two undertakings as being in a productive relationship when they are uncomfortably yoked. At the Children's Television Workshop our publicity staff liked to describe the partnership between (in our case) learning researchers, on the one hand, and television producers and writers, on the other, as an innovative, exciting "operational model." This is true, but it is equally true that from time to time we misunderstood each other, disagreed, and sometimes had out-and-out battles. Often these skirmishes were waged over competing values. The writers and producers worked within a culture that valued humor, creativity, originality, and whimsy. In contrast, the researchers worried about what, *in particular,* children were learning and were concerned as well about children's general welfare, including their emotions (do we really want the Wicked Witch of the West to threaten to turn Big Bird into a feather duster?), safety (if they are riding in a car, cast members must be wearing a seatbelt), health (should Cookie Monster constantly stuff himself with goodies while our children are enduring a crisis of childhood obesity?) and values (it isn't okay for Big Bird to pretend to choke to death as a way to get attention from adults).

The interactions between researchers and writers were positive overall, but there also was a good deal of tension, which was usually kept banked at a low level but sometimes lit up. When personalities and agendas were well managed, the tension was productive, because it fueled solutions that were informed by the best that both groups had to give. However, achieving these solutions demanded ongoing conversation, respect for each others' aesthetics and goals, and commitment to adopting both the perspective and the skills of those in the partner profession. Over time we learned that the most effective researchers were those who learned to think as writers think. It wasn't wise to tell a writer that we could be 95% confident that the segment he had lovingly written and shepherded through production would not teach viewers anything and, besides, bored children silly. We were much more likely to be heard if we could tactfully suggest a constructive repair: "What about shifting the timing of that joke so that it doesn't distract from the learning goal of the segment?" Similarly, the most effective writers were those who could put on a research "hat." Indeed, a few brave souls became so skilled at taking the alternative point of view that they switched altogether into the other role and adopted a new professional identity. Together and over time, the two communities forged an approach to television for children that would probably not have emerged in either community working solo. Forging and maintaining this approach, however, was enduring and effortful work, and it required time, space, institutional support, inventiveness, and intelligence. Not every researcher or writer could make it work, and both occupational worlds tended to exert a continual pull toward disciplinary isolation and specialization and away from the ambiguities and uncertainties of interdisciplinarity.

When I completed my PhD, I left New York and the Children's Television Workshop to move into academia. As I thought about my options, what intrigued me about LRDC was its history as being yet another kind of place where the relationships between research and practice were fostered and nurtured. We should probably advise all newcomers to the field of education research to think explicitly about the way they conceive of these relationships, because our assumptions about research and practice are highly influential in guiding us toward or away from particular kinds of research frameworks, questions, and methods. In my case, I was simply lucky. I had given a lot of thought to these issues in the context of educational television but had, as yet, devoted very little to the relationship between academic education research and the educational practice that takes place in classroom environments.

As is probably obvious, this introduction leads to my 20-year friendship with Isabel. Isabel was the first person on my meeting agenda when I arrived at LRDC one beautiful March day in 1987 to interview for a position as a postdoctoral fellow. From that first conversation, Isabel has been enormously influential in the way I think about these ideas of research and practice, not because she is in my academic specialty area (she isn't) but because both her thinking and activity around these ideas have always been models of depth, thoughtfulness, and personal integrity.

Isabel is a textbook example of a scholar who knows well that the study of learning and the world of education not only can but must find ways to learn from each other. A passionate commitment to constructing those connections both drives and informs her work. Yet she somehow has never fallen into the trap of assuming that forging these links is a rather straightforward matter of slogans and good intentions, the "translation" of research into the language of practice, or the delivery of curricula and recipes. In her teamwork with Moddy McKeown and other colleagues, Isabel has always taken the hard road, doing the difficult, if often invisible intellectual work of inventing, testing, and revising the "what comes next" that follows from her learning research. I suspect that Isabel does not think of this work as exploring the "implications" of her research. Rather, it is an integrated and logical part of her research, an activity as important for its contribution to deeper understanding as for its direct role in solving educational problems.

We academics tend to place a lot of value on knowing and understanding, but the distinctions we find interesting (some would say the hairs we like to split) are often poorly designed for guiding the decisions that teachers make. These decisions must often be made on the fly in the noisy environment of the classroom, and they require teachers to juggle imperfect information and competing goals. These conditions of use need to constrain both the content and form of any intervention that derives from research. Yet our field has not always taken teachers seriously as learners, so we have few empirically tested models of the development of teachers' thinking and decision making that are articulated for purposes of guiding instructional decisions. Most are not at the right level of detail; some are abstract and domain-general and do not sufficiently constrain the problem space that teachers work within; others are far too fine grained to be useful in classrooms (e.g., production models of thinking, which would overload anyone who tried to guide his or her practice according to those descriptions of learning). Although our field has a long tradition of concern with student knowledge, we tend not to think much about the long-term development of teachers' knowledge, and we sometimes behave as if knowing were the whole story, to a point at which we neglect to recall that, fundamentally, teaching also entails doing. For these reasons, decisions about teaching (including what to teach and how) rarely, if ever, follow directly and unproblematically from learning research. A second layer of intellectually demanding work is required to fill the gap between classroom practice and the results of learning research. Although it is not a central topic in her professional writing, Isabel understands this deeply.

Although Isabel certainly has an admirable and distinguished record of contributions to research, here I intend to draw attention to contributions that are a little more difficult for our field to observe directly but that are arguably at least as consequential in the larger world of education. Specifically, her work exemplifies an unusually thoughtful and principled stance about the relationships between learning research and practice. First, Isabel understands deeply something that many in our field tend to overlook or underestimate—namely, as I argued in the beginning of this chapter, that bridging the gap between research and practice takes extensive and thoughtful work by individuals who understand both of those worlds. As Isabel's colleagues know, she is adamant that the *details of implementation matter*; indeed, she treats them as an integral part of the theory of learning. Isabel embraces the work of crafting and testing these details as her own and does not regard it as having derivative or secondary value or as something to be handed off to others. Moreover, she has thought deeply about the nature of implementation, about what it takes for the outcomes of research to come alive in the practice of teachers.

First and obviously, making positive changes in the world of education entails *identifying the right problems*, those at the hub of known difficulties in teaching and learning. Here Isabel has an impeccable track record. The problems she has tackled include figuring out how to help children who do not automatically grasp the reading code, how to coax young readers to think like authors, and how to put into children's grasp words and ideas that otherwise would be out of reach. Her genius, then, is to forge and test interventions that have powerful leverage but also promise of becoming widespread. I have not discussed this directly with her, but I suspect that Isabel does not regard these interventions as outputs of her research. Instead, they are part of the research process—the goal is not simply to generate generalities or principles about knowledge but to understand the processes, contexts, and populations in which those principles are brought to life. Isabel's educational inventions are based on research-informed views about the development of disciplinary learning, rather than by notions of activity structures or motivation. They are within the grasp of typical teachers, although it is always clear that they require work and sustained effort to master. They are potentially scalable in that their adoption does not require dramatic changes to the institutions or structures of schooling.

Isabel intimately understands the people and contexts that she seeks to influence. Like the successful television researchers who learned to see through the eyes of a television writer, Isabel is masterful at stepping inside the mind of a teacher. Probably because she has *been* a successful teacher, she can imagine what they know, what they care about, what they need to know next, and how it can inform what they need to do.

For that reason, Isabel's instructional reforms are educative, even as they make contact with teachers' existing concerns and interpretations.

Isabel is acutely aware of the dangers of "lethal mutation." If teachers do not grasp the underlying principles that motivate prescribed changes in practice, they are likely simply to distort the new ideas by assimilating them into their existing practices. To be educative, a reform must be framed in a way that communicates its intent and discourages oversimplification and ritualization. Questioning the Author, a program whose title neatly encapsulates its raison d'etre, is a good example. The program (and even its title) provides a rich view of how a critical reader of literature approaches texts rather than detailing procedures or strategies that could readily freeze into brittle scripts. Questioning an author can be pursued in a wide variety of ways: We may wonder why the author wrote as she did, felt as he did, chose the phrasing and style that he did, emphasized or omitted what she did. The title of the program also suggests agency (*you*, the reader, have the right and responsibility to ask, and the author—often regarded as the authority—needs to justify him- or herself to *you*). Isabel and her colleagues spent many hours working with teachers to develop the sample questions, prompts, and contexts that would best initiate teachers into this kind of teaching while simultaneously minimizing the likelihood that they would interpret the program as a simple list of strategies or steps. Invention and intellect were devoted to finding out how understandings can be communicated to teachers in ways that affect what they do, not just what they think. The work focused on identifying a beginning repertoire for teachers that would achieve maximal leverage in terms of increasing the amount, depth, and variability of student response, which would, in turn, enhance teachers' continuing opportunities to learn.

The work of Isabel's that typically appears in research journals does not always spotlight the aspect of her work that I have been describing. For this reason, many researchers in the field may be less familiar with it and know less about it than we know about her talent for research. Given continuing concerns about the lack of impact that education research has on educational practice, it would be helpful for more of us to consider *how* Isabel has achieved so much success in this realm. I have argued that developing enduring links between research and practice requires enduring and effortful work, inventiveness, and intelligence. In Isabel's case, these are accompanied by flawless judgment, confidence, and personal persuasiveness. The field has a lot to learn from Isabel beyond her well-known research contributions. I find this an altogether happy thought, as I look forward to continuing to learn from Isabel for many years to come.

15

DECODING, VOCABULARY, AND COMPREHENSION

The Golden Triangle of Reading Skill

Charles Perfetti

The triangle has presented a strong symbol through the ages, representing ideas in religion, astrology, and sexual identity, as well as more specialized denotations. For example, in mathematics it is the symbol for a small difference, and on the dashboards of modern cars, the symbol for warning and emergency. Naturally, reading has its triangle as well: Triangle models of word identification represent the three constituents of written-word knowledge—graphic form (spelling), phonological form (pronunciation), and semantics (meaning). Triangle models generally denote the class of connectionist reading models (Seidenberg & McClelland, 1989) but, more specifically, versions of these models that exert a semantic influence on word identification (Harm & Seidenberg, 1999; Plaut, McClelland, Seidenberg, & Patterson, 1996).

THE DVC TRIANGLE

Given the prolific spread of triangle imagery—and despite the established status of the triangle as a representation of written word identification—I think proposing a new triangle is easily justified. The DVC triangle is the interconnected set of cognitive–linguistic components that make up general reading skill: decoding, vocabulary, and comprehension. Each of these is a complex constituent rather than an elementary unit, so each has its own constituents. For example, the decoding constituent consists of orthographic and phonological knowledge; comprehension includes a wide range of basic sentence, extended text, and general-knowledge-based inference procedures; vocabulary includes both a quantitative (number of words) component and a qualitative (specific word knowledge) component. The complexity of the triangle is a matter of grain size—relatively fine or relatively coarse. For general descriptive purposes, the coarse grain size shown in Figure 15.1 is about right. It expresses the interconnections among decoding, vocabulary knowledge, and comprehension that are central to skilled reading.[1]

The DVC model in Figure 15.1 is primarily a heuristic, suggesting a way to conceptualize reading skill (it is the triangle itself), while also illustrating causal relations among three critical constituents of reading skill (the sides of the triangle are directional arrows). Decoding leads to a word's meaning, but not to comprehension beyond the word directly. Comprehension affects vocabulary (word meanings are learned from context) but not decoding directly. And both the decoding–vocabulary and the vocabulary–comprehension relations are reciprocally causal.

Decoding–Vocabulary

Decoding affects vocabulary directly, because successful decoding events (1) retrieve meanings of familiar words, thus strengthening form–meaning connections, and (2) establish context-dependent links between unfamiliar words and meaning-bearing contexts. Vocabulary (knowledge of the meaning of a word) affects decoding because decoding a word whose meaning is known strengthens the connection between the word's orthographic form (its spelling) and its meaning. This process helps establish a word-specific representation, which is especially helpful for words with exceptional or irregular spelling–pronunciation mappings and theoretically helpful for all words, to some

---

[1] An important point in interpreting the triangle and in the discussion that follows is that a strict definition of decoding is the conversion of letter strings to phoneme strings. Word identification includes both decoding processes in this narrow sense and the retrieval of word-specific representations that uses knowledge about a word's spelling to identify it. In English, this word-specific process is needed for words whose spellings are exceptions to the dominant grapheme-to-phoneme mappings (Coltheart, Rastle, Perry, Langdon, & Ziegler, 2001) A finer grained triangle model would be needed to distinguish these two identification processes.

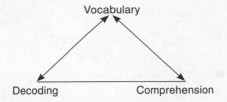

FIGURE 15.1. The DVC reading skill triangle. Abilities in decoding, vocabulary, and comprehension combine to produce general reading skill. Because the three constituents are interconnected, limitations in any one will affect at least one other constituent and will accordingly set a limit on overall skill. For some purposes decoding can be interpreted in its broad sense of word identification; for other purposes it is interpreted in its narrow sense of grapheme–phoneme conversion. (See Footnote 1.) These two would be differentiated in a finer grained triangle model.

extent. The importance of this meaning-to-form support is demonstrated by Nation and Snowling (1998), who found that word identification of comprehension-impaired readers was especially slow in identifying words that, theoretically, depend on frequent exposures (exception words). Simply put, as children decode words, they strengthen their vocabulary knowledge; and as children retrieve their knowledge of a word's meaning while decoding it, they strengthen the identifiability of that word.

Vocabulary–Comprehension

Comprehension is obviously dependent on knowing the meanings of words being read, and the DVC triangle represents this causal direction. At the moment a reader encounters a text, the ability to access the meaning of the word, as it applies in the context of this particular text, is critical. At the same time, achieving some comprehension from a segment of text that contains an unknown word also can cause the reader to learn something about the meaning of that word. Thus the causation runs both ways between word meaning and comprehension. That multiple causes can underlie the general correlation between vocabulary knowledge and comprehension has long been recognized (e.g., Anderson & Freebody, 1981; Beck, McKeown, & Omanson, 1987). Evidence for a reciprocal causation across measurement points, however, has come only recently from a longitudinal study by Wagner (2005).

Decoding–Comprehension?

The DVC triangle does not show causal arrows between decoding and comprehension in either direction. This is because the effects of decoding on comprehension are mediated by knowing the meaning of the decoded word. The effects of comprehension on decoding are mediated by achieving enough meaning from the text to verify the identity of a decoded word. Note that this assumption rests on the logic of cognitive event sequences in reading and not on correlations of skill assessments.

In practical terms, there is a strong causal relation between decoding and comprehension in that fluent or automatic decoding allows more processing resources to be available for comprehension (Perfetti, 1985). And comprehending a text aids word identification, especially for readers of low word reading skill (Perfetti, 1985; Stanovich, 1980). However, at closer distance, these causal effects depend on word meanings being produced by identification. Thus knowledge of word meanings (or vocabulary knowledge) has a pivotal position between word identification and comprehension (Perfetti, Landi, & Oakhill, 2005).

INDIVIDUAL DIFFERENCES
IN LEXICAL QUALITY

The DVC triangle identifies possible differences in reading skill at each point of the triangle and also at the four causal links (two for decoding–vocabulary and two for vocabulary–comprehension). These seven possible sources of reading skill variability obviously are not all independent, and all have causal links to knowledge sources outside the triangle. For example, knowledge of word meanings is affected by pre-literacy exposure to vocabulary, which is stunningly variable across demographic categories (Hart & Risley, 1995). But it is simple enough to summarize key relations in reading skill:

1. Skill in reading comprehension will be affected by skill in decoding and skill in vocabulary (which will not be independent, according to the model).
2. Skill in vocabulary will be affected by skill in comprehension and skill in decoding (which will be independent).
3. Skill in decoding (understood as word identification) will be predicted by vocabulary knowledge.

Decoding skill itself supports self-teaching of written-word representations, which allows children to move from a reading process entirely dependent on phonological coding of printed word forms to a process that accesses words quickly based on their orthography (Share, 1995, 1999).

To clarify the omission of decoding–comprehension effects, note that assessments of decoding do correlate with assessments of comprehension (Perfetti, 1985), but on the present assumption this correlation reflects a causal connection from decoding to comprehension that is mediated by knowledge of word meanings. The decoding–comprehension correlation may also partly reflect their shared influences from outside the triangle (e.g., phonological knowledge, other linguistic knowledge, and general intelligence).

Beyond the more obvious implications for individual differences, there is an interesting, less obvious one. Children with weak decoding skills may have to depend more on the vocabulary → decoding side of the triangle. Indeed, a semantics-to-decoding connection helps to compensate for weak decoding skills (Snowling, Hulme, & Goulandris, 1994).

The DVC triangle representation of individual differences approximates that captured by the lexical quality hypothesis (LQH—Perfetti, 2007; Perfetti & Hart, 2001). The LQH claims that knowledge about word forms (phonological, orthographic, and morphemic knowledge) affects reading comprehension in both obvious and less obvious ways. The particular DVC of Figure 15.1, by collapsing distinctions between orthographic and phonological knowledge and between word identification and decoding, misses some important details in lexical quality but captures the broad relations.

To convert the triangle into a processing scheme, Figure 15.2 shows a linear flow of knowledge of word form and meaning to the processes of word identification and comprehension, with feedback from comprehension back to the word knowledge level.

According to the DVC and the LQH, word meanings are central to comprehension and word identification. However, research on comprehension has often ignored vocabulary to focus on other comprehension issues (e.g., inference making, comprehension strategies). Nevertheless, knowledge of word meanings cannot be ignored in accounts of individual differences. Meanwhile, the search for cognitive mechanism differences, as opposed to knowledge differences, has had the effect

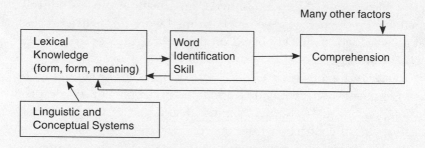

FIGURE 15.2. Simple schematic of the flow of information from knowledge about word form and meaning to comprehension through word identification. Lexical quality varies within the word-knowledge component and affects word identification and comprehension and is in turn modified by through both word identification (e.g., self-teaching) and comprehension (e.g., acquiring word meanings).

of suggesting that comprehension skill differences and knowledge differences (especially vocabulary) derive from differences in working memory resources (Daneman, 1988; Gathercole & Baddeley, 1989; Seigneuric, Ehrlich, Oakhill, & Yuill, 2000). Cognitive resource differences cannot, however, explain the massive differences observable in exposure to language that builds the vocabulary children are likely to encounter in written texts (Hart & Risley, 1995). Somehow, and this is central to understanding reading comprehension, children both before and after the beginnings of literacy differ greatly in the numbers of words they know in both the sense of familiarity and specific semantic knowledge. (See Reichle and Perfetti, 2003, for a framework that links this distinction to lexical quality in a memory-based approach to recognizing words.) Such word knowledge is not only instrumental to comprehension but also a signature for literacy.

Although here I focus on word meaning as pivotal, I need to emphasize that word-form knowledge is also critical in skilled reading. The development of word reading skill depends on the refinement of word representations by adding spelling knowledge to spoken-word representations. This refinement produces representations that increase in *precision*, knowledge of all the letters of a word, and *redundancy*, complete letter knowledge and complete phonemic knowledge with connections between the two. These characteristics allow word reading and meaning retrieval to be rapid and relatively automatic given a familiar printed word. Just as work on comprehension has sometimes ignored word meaning, research on word reading skill has tended to ignore spelling. We are learning, however, that even among "good readers," differences in knowledge of word spellings lead to differences in word reading processes (Andrews, 2008).

THE DVC TRIANGLE IN THE CONTEXT OF THE READING EDUCATION FIELD

It is useful to ground the DVC triangle in two contexts relevant to reading research. The first places the triangle idea in a personal historical context. My approach to reading has been fairly simple, grounded on the idea that reading is a process built on language. The distinctive part of reading, in this commonsense view, is written-word identification: The singular recurring cognitive activity in reading is the identification of words and the retrieval of their meanings. From this it follows that comprehension depends in part on successful word reading and that skill differences in comprehension can arise from skill differences in word reading. This was not an easy thing to acknowledge. I came to reading from training as a psycholinguist. Naturally, I became interested in reading comprehension as a language problem and, along with my graduate students, considered where "the action" was in reading comprehension skill. Syntactic abilities? Getting meaning from sentences and paragraphs? Higher level language knowledge? Despite the inherent interest of these possibilities to a psycholinguist, I thought the first step was to ask about word reading and the role it played in comprehension.

These observations on the role of word identification in reading were the core of a theory of comprehension skill that, over 25 years ago, I referred to as *verbal efficiency theory* (Perfetti, 1985): Word identification, the rapid retrieval of a word's phonology and meaning, was a limiting factor in comprehension. Verbal efficiency theory is the ancestor of the DVC triangle and the LQH and captures some of the same ideas.

I came to conclude, however, that verbal efficiency's emphasis on general *processes*—decoding, phonological processes, retrieval, memory, automaticity—did not quite capture the importance of knowledge. Verbal efficiency implied that skilled reading was about efficient processing mechanisms and that less-skilled reading was about these same mechanisms operating less efficiently. But where did differences in efficiency arise? Although differences in processing capacity provide a possible answer to this question, it did not seem plausible as the whole story. Skill differences were often specific to reading, and they were subject to practice effects. Instead, I concluded that the major source of reading ability is the knowledge a reader has about words, specific lexical representations. Knowledge plus practice that refines the knowledge and makes it more accessible leads to efficient processing. This perspective on the problem led eventually to the LQH (Perfetti, 2007; Perfetti & Hart, 2001). Although the lexical knowledge emphasis was an important refinement of the verbal efficiency hypothesis, this emphasis was already anticipated in *Reading Ability* (Perfetti, 1985), which has several observations that emphasized knowledge rather than process. For example, I argued in that volume that the retrieval of a lexical representation is high in quality "to the extent that it contains both semantic and phonetic information sufficient to recover its memory location. ... This quality must be retained long enough for subsequent processes to perform their work. Thus a 'name' without meaning and a meaning without a 'name' are both low quality" (Perfetti, 1985, p. 118).

The second context for the DVC is that it aligns well with the research of Isabel Beck. Indeed, it is remarkable that the whole of the triangle can be instantiated by the research career of Beck and her colleagues. Next, I consider each point of the triangle in turn.

Decoding

First, Beck's early work developing code-based reading instruction (Beck & McCaslin, 1978) sits at the decoding corner of the triangle. Her approach to decoding followed the foundational principles of alphabetic reading by directly teaching the correspondences between letters and phonemes. Its distinctive addition to this basic principle was a procedure to support blending, the integration of phonemes so that the child would learn to map letter sequences to phonological words (m-a-t → /mæt/) rather than only to isolated phonemes (m → /m/; a → /æ/; t → /t/). The basic good sense of this program, as well as its careful optimizing aspects, flew against the wind of the whole-language movement. Much later, with the return of good sense to the teaching of reading, Beck's *Making Sense of Phonics* (2006) reestablished the value of decoding instruction for a more receptive practice community.

Vocabulary

At the vocabulary corner of the triangle, the story is similar to the decoding story. Direct instruction in decoding was not in vogue at the time that Beck developed a direct instruction program, and neither was direct instruction in vocabulary, although for a different reason. Although no one argued against the value of direct instruction of vocabulary, little instruction actually occurred in schools (Scott, Jamieson, & Asselin, 2003). People generally assumed that such instruction was of marginal value, because most word learning occurs incidentally through reading and spoken-language experience. For example, Nagy and Herman (1987) estimated that vocabulary might grow by 2,000 to 3,000 words per year over grades 1–12. Thus, at best, direct instruction might help children learn a tiny percentage of the massive English vocabulary needed for academic success. I believe this observation is correct as far as it goes. But it does not take into account some important additional considerations. First are the massive individual differences that are present in vocabulary knowledge in school-age children, especially differences across different socioeconomic classes, that arise well before children enter school (Hart & Risley, 1995). If one could teach 100 words to a child who knows only 2,000 academically useful words (a possible estimate for a child entering first grade from a very low socioeconomic status [SES] background), the result would be a noticeable 5% gain. Even at 4,000 (2.5%) or 8,000 words (1.25%), it is not clear why one would want to dismiss the gains to vocabulary, except for issues of allotting instructional time. Second is the potential for vocabulary "spread." Words related to the meaning of a new word can be used in connection with the new word, and Beck and colleagues' robust vocabulary instruction (Beck, McKeown & Kucan, 2002) promotes high levels of verbal interaction around a taught word, inevitably strengthening the use of other words and the concepts underlying them. Third is the potential for enhancing a child's lexical awareness, that is, an increased attention to words, their meaning similarities, their differences, and perhaps even their forms. Part of this increased awareness depends on becoming interested in words and engaged in academic language production, as well as comprehension. Although it remains to be seen whether robust vocabulary instruction produces such gains, it is clear that this instruction, as developed by Isabel Beck and her colleagues, includes the kinds of meaningful engagement with language that could promote them.

Comprehension

"Comprehension" covers a lot of territory in reading, and the practical issues have tended to localize on a very broad part of it, the higher level comprehension ability to understand extended written tests, as indicated through answering questions, recalling, or summarizing stories. Beck and McKeown (2006) developed Questioning the Author as a way of guiding teachers to support what they saw as the critical component of comprehension: attention to the meaning of the text. As in Beck's other work, this idea is a blend of common sense with research and theory. Getting meaning from a text is about reading the words, encoding their meanings, using sentence structure to form their meanings into semantic content (e.g., propositions), and integrating these meanings with "prior" knowledge and across sentences (Kintsch, 1988; Perfetti, 1985). On this view, the central strategy for reading comprehension is to answer the question of, What does the text say? Other questions (including *why* questions) engage the reader with the content with the goal of supporting a text-based mental representation of the text. This content-based strategy may be more effective than strategies that aim at a general level (e.g., making inferences, monitoring for confusions) that only indirectly engage semantic content (McKeown, Beck, & Blake, in press).

THE COMPREHENSION–VOCABULARY LEG OF THE TRIANGLE

As I noted earlier, comprehension covers a large territory, and educational research in comprehension has attended more to the higher level part of this territory. But comprehension is also about understanding sentences through the meanings of the words they contain—local processes as opposed to global processes. I was able to join Beck, McKeown, and colleagues some years ago in studies that exemplify this level of comprehension and, more important, the link between word meanings and local comprehension. Beck, Perfetti, and McKeown (1982) instructed children in vocabulary and then inserted the newly learned words into sentences and measured the reading (sentence verification) times on the sentences. Children showed gains not only in word meaning measures but also on sentence verification when the sentences contained newly taught words. McKeown, Beck, Omanson, and Perfetti (1983) later found comprehension gains for passages following vocabulary training. Comprehension of texts allows readers to add new word meanings to their vocabularies, and learning new word meanings allows readers to comprehend texts that contain those words.

CONCLUSION

The DVC triangle reflects the interdependence of knowledge about word forms (decoding and word identification) and word meanings (vocabulary) and comprehension processes. The LQH formulates these dependencies in terms of the components of word knowledge and its consequences for comprehension. In this framework, once beginning reading—decoding—has been mastered, reading depends on a complex of acquired skills honed by effective reading experiences. Experiences that yield comprehension and also strengthen knowledge of word forms and meanings essentially provide practice for reading skill.

Research has contributed substantial knowledge that is of value for reading instruction. We know how to support instruction in decoding so that children can acquire the foundation point of the reading triangle. We are equally sure about the importance of vocabulary but less clear about how to ensure that it keeps up with demands of academic learning. Unlike decoding, which is the great equalizer for unequal opportunity, vocabulary is the reflection of unequal opportunity. Accordingly, it is an even bigger problem to tackle, although we do know how to help children learn word meanings. Comprehension would appear to be the biggest problem, but the research field has provided some useful guidance for comprehension instruction. Once we take into account the vocabulary–comprehension connection, the comprehension issue shrinks a bit. Being able to identify words and use their meanings is a large part of the issue, and with reading practice, especially effective text reading, to support knowledge of word forms and meanings, the comprehension issue becomes one of general language comprehension, certainly a big issue in itself.

Because the problems are specialized, researchers typically have pursued one or other corners of the triangle—justifiably so, because each corner represents complexity well beyond what I have implied here. For several reasons, I have found myself working on all the corners and legs of the triangle at one time or another and sometimes at the same time. Truly impressive, however, is what Isabel Beck has done in this triangle. Beyond experimental research, she and her colleagues have taken on the hard problems of instruction, at not one or two but all three points of the triangle. The result is three different projects of systematic, research-based interventions that help students to decode, to learn word meanings, and to comprehend.

REFERENCES

Anderson, R. C., & Freebody, P. (1981). Vocabulary knowledge. In J. T. Guthrie (Ed.), *Comprehension and teaching: Research reviews* (pp. 77–117). Newark, DE: International Reading Association.

Andrews, S. (2008). Lexical expertise and reading skill. *Psychology of Learning and Motivation, 49,* 249–281.

Beck, I. L. (2006). *Making sense of phonics: The hows and whys.* New York: Guilford Press.

Beck, I. L., & McCaslin, E. (1978). *An analysis of dimensions that affect the development of code-breaking ability in eight beginning reading programs.* Pittsburgh, PA: University of Pittsburgh, Learning Research and Development Center.

Beck, I. L., & McKeown, M. G. (2006). *Improving comprehension with Questioning the Author: A fresh and enhanced view of a proven approach.* New York: Scholastic.

Beck, I. L., McKeown, M. G., & Kucan, L. (2002). *Bringing words to life: Robust vocabulary instruction.* New York: Guilford Press.

Beck, I., McKeown, M., & Omanson, R. (1987). The effects and uses of diverse vocabulary instruction techniques. In M. McKeown & M. E. Curtis (Eds.), *The nature of vocabulary acquisition* (pp. 147–163). Hillsdale NJ: Erlbaum.

Beck, I. L., Perfetti, C. A., & McKeown, M. G. (1982). The effects of long-term vocabulary instruction on lexical access and reading comprehension. *Journal of Educational Psychology, 74,* 506–521.

Coltheart, M., Rastle, K., Perry, C., Langdon, R., & Ziegler, J. (2001). DRC: A dual route cascaded model of visual word recognition and reading aloud. *Psychological Review, 108*(1), 204–256.

Daneman, M. (1988). Word knowledge and reading skill. In M. Daneman, G. MacKinnon, & T. G. Waller (Eds.), *Reading research: Advances in theory and practice* (Vol. 6, pp. 145–175). San Diego, CA: Academic Press.

Gathercole, S. E., & Baddeley, A. D. (1989). Evaluation of the role of phonological STM in the development of vocabulary in children: A longitudinal study. *Journal of Memory and Language, 28,* 200–213.

Harm, M. W., & Seidenberg, M. S. (1999). Phonology, reading acquisition, and dyslexia: Insights from connectionist models. *Psychological Review, 106*(3), 491–528.

Hart, B., & Risley, T. (1995). *Meaningful differences in the everyday experience of young American children.* Baltimore: Brookes.

Kintsch, W. (1988). The role of knowledge in discourse processing: A construction–integration model. *Psychological Review, 95,* 163–182.

McKeown, M. G., Beck, I. L., & Blake, R. G. K. (2009). Rethinking reading comprehension instruction: A comparison of instruction for strategies and content approaches. *Reading Research Quarterly, 44*(3), 218–253.

McKeown, M. G., Beck, I. L., Omanson, R. C., & Perfetti, C. A. (1983). The effects of long-term vocabulary instruction on reading comprehension: A replication. *Journal of Reading Behavior, 15*(1), 3–18.

Nagy, W. E., & Herman, P. A. (1987). Breadth and depth of vocabulary knowledge: Implications for acquisition and instruction. In M. McKeown & M. E. Curtis (Eds.), *The nature of vocabulary acquisition* (pp. 19–36). Hillsdale, NJ: Erlbaum.

Nation, K., & Snowling, M. J. (1998). Semantic processing and the development of word recognition skills: Evidence from children with reading comprehension difficulties. *Journal of Memory and Language, 39*, 85–101.

Perfetti, C. A. (1985). *Reading ability.* New York: Oxford University Press.

Perfetti, C. A. (2007). Reading ability: Lexical quality to comprehension. *Scientific Studies of Reading, 11*(4), 357–383.

Perfetti, C. A., & Hart, L. (2001). The lexical bases of comprehension skill. In D. Gorfien (Ed.), *On the consequences of meaning selection* (pp. 67–86). Washington, DC: American Psychological Association.

Perfetti, C. A., Landi, N., & Oakhill, J. (2005). The acquisition of reading comprehension skill. In M. J. Snowling & C. Hulme (Eds.), *The science of reading: A handbook* (pp. 227–247). Oxford, UK: Blackwell.

Plaut, D. C., McClelland, J. L., Seidenberg, M. S., & Patterson, K. (1996). Understanding normal and impaired word reading: Computational principles in quasi-regular domains. *Psychological Review, 103*, 56–115.

Reichle, E. D., & Perfetti, C. A. (2003). Morphology in word identification: A word-experience model that accounts for morpheme frequency effects. *Scientific Studies of Reading, 7*(1), 219–238.

Scott, J. A., Jamieson, D., & Asselin, M. (2003). Casting a broad net to catch vocabulary instruction. *Elementary School Journal, 103*(3), 269–286.

Seidenberg, M. S., & McClelland, J. L. (1989). A distributed, developmental model of word recognition and naming. *Psychological Review, 96*, 523–568.

Seigneuric, A. S., Ehrlich, M. F., Oakhill, J. V., & Yuill, N. M. (2000). Working memory resources and children's reading comprehension. *Reading and Writing, 13*, 81–103.

Share, D. L. (1995). Phonological recoding and self-teaching: *Sine qua non* of reading acquisition. *Cognition, 55*, 151–218.

Share, D. L. (1999). Phonological recoding and orthographic learning: A direct test of the self-teaching hypothesis. *Journal of Experimental Child Psychology, 72*, 95–129.

Snowling, M., Hulme, C., & Goulandris, N. (1994). Word recognition and development: A connectionist interpretation. *Quarterly Journal of Experimental Psychology, 47A*, 895–916.

Stanovich, K. E. (1980). Toward an interactive–compensatory model of individual differences in the development of reading fluency. *Reading Research Quarterly, 16*, 32–71.

Wagner, R. (2005, April). *Causal relations between vocabulary development and reading comprehension.* Toronto, ON, Canada: American Educational Research Association.

16

ANOTHER SIDE OF ISABEL

Elizabeth Beck *and* Mark Beck

As the foregoing chapters reveal, Isabel Beck's relationships with her colleagues were not only professionally but also personally collegial and collaborative. The contributions to this volume demonstrate in a compelling way the mutual respect and friendships that developed over the years between Isabel and her peers and students.

But we felt that this book would not be complete without providing a glimpse of another side of Isabel—a side that only her children, Elizabeth and Mark, can reveal. Toward that end, we present the following excerpts from the remarks that they offered during the conference and dinner held in her honor. We think it quite fitting that they have the final word in this tribute to Isabel.

ELIZABETH BECK

Originally my brother, Mark, and I were supposed to do this together, but Mark is not here yet, and I will explain his absence in a minute.

My brother is extraordinary, and you will get a sense of that when he speaks at tonight's dinner. My brother became one of my heroes about 2 years ago, when he decided that life would be much better and he could make a larger contribution to the world by quitting law and going back to school to be an elementary school teacher. Mark graduated several weeks ago and is now working as a permanent substitute, so today he is with first-graders.

Mark is the child who, at the age of 5 (and let's be clear, this is the real story), told my mother that he had spelled a *bad* word, not using refrigerator magnets, as described in *Making Sense of Phonics*, but writing in the dirt on the car. In the book, Mom says that Mark wrote *t-i-i-p* to make *ship*, using the *ti* as in *portion*, but in reality Mark wrote *t-i-i-t*.

I, on the other hand, was the one described in the book as not caring so much about the words but more about the ideas behind them. As Mom said, I just did not "notice the patterns in written language." That is absolutely true, but again Mom cleaned up the story. My learning disabilities were such that written words did not make sense to me. For me, learning to read was excruciatingly painful and frustrating. I am sure my mom was extraordinary in her ability and patience, but my memory of it, even with the support my mother gave, was a very unhappy one.

As I think about my mom, I am confident that our experience narrowed her focus in two ways. First, she walked away from teaching me to read profoundly worried about children who had the issues that I had but who did not have someone to intervene. As someone deeply concerned about social justice, she could not abide this. Second, she must have known that there had to be a better way.

So, against that backdrop, Mom set out to address the twofold problem of ensuring adequate phonics-based instruction for all children who need it and doing it in a systematic and workable way so that teaching the process of decoding would not be a frustrating one for children and for teachers, too.

And at that point our lives changed. Mom threw herself into her job and education. My mother, as you all know, is very focused, and she is quick to point out that she is not very good at dual processing. Well, this meant that some of the things that "mothers do" just did not happen at our house. And, when one is busy, it is not uncommon for the things that she does not like to do to fall by the wayside. By her own admission, Mom "detests" cooking. Additionally, I think that, at some subconscious level, she ensured that she would be free of any expectation of cooking. There is debate about how many times the following sequence occurred—I say at least twice; Mom says only once. Here's what happened: Mom would come home from work and start the process of getting things ready for dinner, including turning on the knob to heat up the French fry oil, and then she would take a 20-minute nap while my dad kept us busy, often on the third floor of the house. Then the smoke would hit, my dad would run down to the kitchen, get us out of the house, and put the flames out. But once—or maybe twice—the curtains got involved, and the entire kitchen went up in flames. Even the firefighters agreed that Mom should not have to cook again.

Also, the world was progressing, and the idea of women and cooking was becoming disentangled. Isabel, always on the cutting edge of social justice, decided that cooking should be shared at our house. And she went a step further to include that we would all do our own shopping, because grocery shopping was not a lot better than cooking. Dad learned to make something called beer-battered shrimp, which was truly the most complicated thing ever made in our house. I made taco kits. Luckily, Mark went to camp, where he learned some skills, including cooking macaroni and beef on a campfire. At home, Mark cooked by standing on a stool to reach the stove. Even at 8 years old, he was expected to take his turn.

Mom and Dad were extraordinary, and with the help of Marva, who held us together, we were never the typical family. But we were the one that all of our friends wanted to hang with. My parents loved us, and they loved each other. Although the loss of my father was tragic, our lives were so much richer because of the love affair that my parents had.

When I was in graduate school, Mom worked with me on my writing, focusing on sentence structure, forming an argument, and organization, but it took tenacity on both our parts to overcome my disability. I guess she and I did a pretty good job because I recently had a book published by Oxford University Press.

I had planned to end by saying: Thanks so much for everything you do, Mom. Instead, I am going to end with a quote. And this quote is not from a book; rather, it is from an e-mail that my mom received last night: "Dear Ms. Beck, Thank you, thank you, thank you. Your book *Making Sense of Phonics* changed my daughter's life." The writer went on to explain that his daughter was struggling with spelling and reading and that her teachers were at a loss about what to do. The father did an Internet search and found Mom's phonics book. He ordered it, and after using the Syllasearch approach for 3 weeks, he reported that his daughter "decoded her first three-syllable word." The father wrote to Mom because he wanted her to know about the joy that she had brought to a child through her work. Finally, he asked for additional help in selecting new Syllasearch words. Hey, I'm no expert, but perhaps it's another retirement project.

MARK BECK

It is an honor for me to be here. I regret that I missed most of the conference, but, on the other hand, I was busy today at work as a substitute teacher implementing my mother's ideas in a hands-on way with kindergarten and first-grade students.

Part One

So, I understand that my sister, Elizabeth, may have touched upon the fact that, to put it bluntly, our mother starved us as we were growing up. The refrigerator was usually filled with Tab, orange juice, and Velveeta cheese, but not much else. My father, Carl, did much of the cooking. By the time I was about 9 years old, I was actually responsible for making dinner for the family on Wednesday nights. Elizabeth, I think you had Thursdays. Dad did most of the rest of the cooking. My sister went off to college, and my dad then passed away, when I was 15. My 84-year-old grandmother took over cooking on Monday nights.

But things didn't change much once Elizabeth and I grew into adulthood. My mother moved into a new house, with a much smaller kitchen—the cleanest kitchen in the world, by the way. Many of us probably remember the George Foreman Grill craze of approximately 10 years ago. Mom jumped on the bandwagon and purchased one. She really did and does want to be a good cook. Her big problem was where to keep it. First, she kept it inside her stove. It seemed like such a logical place, as she almost never turns on those knobs, but she managed to melt it. Then she decided to keep it directly on the burners.

One day, I was upstairs in her house, and as I came down, I smelled something indescribably terrible. I quickly ran to the kitchen. I noticed Mom hunched over the George Foreman Grill. The grill itself was engulfed in flames. Mom said matter-of-factly, "Well, it appears that we have a bit of a fire." And then she threw it into the sink.

Her calm demeanor in the presence of a flaming appliance is reflective of her overall attitude toward problem solving. Identifying the problem is the first step. "Well, it appears that we have a bit of a fire." There's no need to panic, just determine the next logical step. In this case, that was to submerge the item in the sink. Problem solved. It's time to move on. Her approach toward her work is fairly similar. Identify the problem: Children are not decoding in a systematic way.

Offer a practical solution: word building. Identify a problem: vocabulary instruction is superficial and given low priority by teachers. Offer a practical solution: robust vocabulary instruction. Identify a problem: discussion about text is superficial and unconnected. Offer a practical solution: Text Talk and Questioning the Author. My mother is a very pragmatic woman. Results are what matter to her more than abstract theoretical notions.

Part Two

Now, my experience has been that children don't really know what their parents do for a living. Of course they know the job title, the names of a few colleagues, and a very rough job description. But that's often about it. Along those lines, I recall a conversation I had with my sister about 10 years or so ago. My mother had just been chosen for the International Reading Association's Hall of Fame. Now, make no mistake about it. We realized that she was internationally recognized by her colleagues for groundbreaking research in the area of reading. We knew that her ideas and programs had been and were successfully being implemented in schools throughout the United States. We had known this since we were in high school. But, in terms of what she actually did when she arrived at the office every morning, we really didn't have a clue.

I can't remember which one of us initiated the conversation, but I do remember asking Elizabeth words to the effect of, "What exactly does she do that's so great?" Then there was a long, awkward pause as we both thought about the question, embarrassed that we didn't have much of an answer. Each of us muttered something. Elizabeth said something about "decoding." And I thought, "That does sound like it could be pretty important." And then Elizabeth mentioned word building. I think I said something along the lines of "Oh." And that's about as far as the conversation went.

Looking back, I think I can speak for Elizabeth and myself in saying we were a little embarrassed by that conversation. But the clincher occurred last night at the reception. My 3-year-old son Ethan listened to all of the speeches and then ran up to give his grandmother a big hug. He then quickly came back to me and said, "Can you tell me a little about the work she's done?" It's a good thing he didn't ask me 10 years ago. I don't know what I would have said.

Part Three

Well, today I'm in a pretty unique position. I actually have learned what my mother does. Three weeks ago, I graduated from the University of Pittsburgh School of Education and was certified to teach kindergarten through sixth grade in Pennsylvania. I, and my fellow graduate students, have studied, digested, and implemented Mom's ideas for more than a year. I am now one of those few adult children that actually knows a thing or two about what my mother does for a living.

About 2 years ago, as I began to consider a career change, I started enrolling in undergraduate education classes and volunteered in first-through third-grade classrooms to assist struggling readers. I knew very little about reading instruction at that point. I was feeling frustrated at not knowing what to do to help some of my students. One day, I was working with a first-grade student, and his teacher handed me a pretty neat little list of words that I had never seen before. Before I knew it, I was engaging with this student in an activity called "word building" (still not really knowing what that meant), and I saw his decoding skills improve markedly within a few weeks. It was only then that I looked on the bottom of the page and saw the words, "Reprinted with permission of Isabel Beck." I had no idea I was using my mother's material all that time. Of course, I was brand new to the field. I didn't understand why all these activities were working so well, but—make no mistake about it—they were.

Growing up, Mom always had very high expectations for Elizabeth and me. She always prodded and encouraged us to dig deeper, say more, draw connections, stay focused, and study and prepare more thoroughly. We were able to internalize those high expectations from a fairly early age. We knew not to take the easy way out. To me, Mom's approach toward raising us was the greatest compliment a parent could give us.

Mom's work at Pitt is broadly similar. She has extremely high expectations of her colleagues and of teachers and their students. Questioning the Author is a perfect example. When discussing text, teachers may want to take the easy way out. They may ask simple recall questions such as "What color shirt was he wearing?" Or "What did the father do once they arrived at the zoo?" Questioning the Author is much harder, much more rigorous. It's supposed to be. Questions are related to broader conceptual ideas. Students are challenged to think rather than simply recall. Ideas are discussed, not numbers and colors.

Most important, expectations are raised. It is the ultimate compliment to say to a student, "I know you can do better, dig deeper."

Now, I searched my brain to think of one appropriate adjective to describe Isabel Beck. The one I arrived at may shock you. Isabel Beck is, above all, humble. Yes, she is humble. Now, I know some of you may think that I am describing someone else. But I'll say it again. Isabel Beck is humble.

Mom has an unbelievable impact on how thousands and thousands of elementary school students learn to read. Her methods are research-based and practical, and they yield results. Believe me. I see it every single day. I carry around her book wherever I go. I gain an unbelievable sense of satisfaction when a student is able to "get it" because of my mother's research and activities. I am proud of the student, but even more proud of my mother.

Mom obviously knows about her awards and accolades, and she knows that she is in high demand as a speaker across the country. She knows she has accomplished much. But then again, at another level, she doesn't really know the impact she has had. Perhaps it is because she doesn't work directly with children all that much. You may not completely see it, Mom, but I do. I see the impact your work has on the students I work with on a day-to-day basis. I teach these children using your ideas. I know the gratification of watching a child's confidence build as she gradually learns to decode. I have witnessed over and over again the excitement of children completely engaged and excited about robust vocabulary instruction. I see what you've done for these children, Mom, and it's quite astounding.

INDEX

Page numbers followed by f indicate figure; n, note; and t, table.